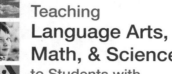

Teaching
**Language Arts,
Math, & Science**
to Students with
**Significant
Cognitive
Disabilities**

D0555307

Teaching
Language Arts, Math, & Science
to Students with
Significant Cognitive Disabilities

edited by

Diane M. Browder, Ph.D.

and

Fred Spooner, Ph.D.

Department of Special Education
and Child Development
College of Education
University of North Carolina at Charlotte

with invited contributors

·P·A·U·L·H·
BROOKES
PUBLISHING Co ®
OCM 63125799

Baltimore • London • Sydney

Paul H. Brookes Publishing Co.
Post Office Box 10624
Baltimore, Maryland 21285-0624

www.brookespublishing.com

Typeset by A.W. Bennett, Inc., Hartland, Vermont.
Manufactured in the United States of America
by Victor Graphics, Inc., Baltimore, Maryland.

The individuals described in this book are based on the authors' experiences and are composites or real people whose situations have been masked. Names and identifying details have been changed to protect confidentiality.

Second printing, December 2006.

Library of Congress Cataloging-in-Publication Data

Teaching language arts, math, and science to students with significant cognitive disabilities / edited by Diane M. Browder and Fred Spooner.
    p.   cm.
    Includes index.
    ISBN-13: 978-1-55766-798-4
    ISBN-10: 1-55766-798-5
    1. Children with mental disabilities—Education—United States. 2. Language arts—Study and teaching—United States. 3. Inclusive education—United States. 4. Academic achievement—United States. I. Browder, Diane M. II. Spooner, Fred.
    LC4616 .T43 2006
    371.92'8—dc22
                                         2006000231

British Library Cataloguing in Publication data are available from the British Library.

Contents

Part I	**Access to the General Curriculum**

Part II	**Language Arts**

Part III	**Math and Science**

About the Editors

Diane M. Browder, Ph.D., Snyder Distinguished Professor, Department of Special Education and Child Development, College of Education, University of North Carolina at Charlotte, 9201 University City Boulevard, Charlotte, NC 28223

Dr. Browder is Snyder Distinguished Professor and Doctoral Coordinator of Special Education at the University of North Carolina at Charlotte. Dr. Browder has more than 2 decades of experience with research and writing on assessment and instruction of students with severe disabilities. Recently, she has focused on alternate assessment and linking assessment and instruction to the general curriculum. She is Principal Investigator for an Institute of Education Sciences–funded center with a focus on teaching students with moderate and severe disabilities to read. She is a partner in the National Center on Alternate Assessment and Principal Investigator for Office of Special Education Programs–funded projects on access to the general curriculum.

Fred Spooner, Ph.D., Professor, Department of Special Education and Child Development, College of Education, University of North Carolina at Charlotte, 9201 University City Boulevard, Charlotte, NC 28223

Dr. Spooner is Professor of Special Education, Coordinator of the Adapted Curriculum (Severe Disabilities) Program, and Principal Investigator on a personnel preparation project involving distance delivery technologies at the University of North Carolina at Charlotte. Dr. Spooner has more than 2 decades of experience with research and writing instructional practices for students with severe disabilities. He is co-editor for *Teacher Education and Special Education* and serves as an associate editor for *Research and Practice for Persons with Severe Disabilities*. He was a co-editor for *TEACHING Exceptional Children* and an associate editor for *Teacher Education and Special Education*. Recently, he has focused on alternate assessment and linking assessment and instruction to the general curriculum and serves as a senior research associate for an Institute of Education Sciences–funded center with a focus on teaching students with moderate and severe disabilities to read.

About the Contributors

Martin Agran, Ph.D., Professor and Department Head, Department of Special Education, University of Wyoming, 1000 East University Avenue, Laramie, WY 82071

Dr. Agran is an associate editor of *Research and Practice for Persons with Severe Disabilities*. His research interests include the education of students with severe disabilities, self-determination/self-regulation, transition, and personnel preparation. Additionally, he is interested in international special education and has served as a Fulbright Scholar in the Czech Republic and a visiting professor in Russia. He has authored or coauthored 10 books and has published extensively in professional journals.

Lynn Ahlgrim-Delzell, M.S., Research Associate, University of North Carolina at Charlotte, 9201 University City Boulevard, Charlotte, NC 28223

Ms. Ahlgrim-Delzell has more than 25 years of experience working with individuals with disabilities in various capacities, including 12 years as a researcher. She is currently a research associate and part-time instructor at University of North Carolina at Charlotte. She has coauthored a number of articles and book chapters on issues pertinent to individuals with disabilities and is co-editor of a book on mental health in individuals with cognitive disabilities.

Stephanie Al Otaiba, Ph.D., Assistant Professor, Florida State University College of Special Education and Florida Center for Reading, 205 Stone Building, Tallahassee, FL 32306

Dr. Al Otaiba is an assistant professor in the College of Education at Florida State University and is also on the research faculty at the Florida Center for Reading. Prior to earning her doctorate at Vanderbilt University, she taught special education for 12 years. Her research focuses on early literacy interventions for diverse learners, response to intervention, and teacher preparation and professional development.

Michael D. Burdge, M.Sp.Ed., Technical Assistance Specialist, Inclusive Large Scale Standards and Assessment (ILSSA), Human Development Institute, University of Kentucky, 1 Quality Street, Suite 722, Lexington, KY 40507

After teaching students with severe disabilities for 24½ years, Mr. Burdge joined the ILSSA group and currently works with states in standards refinement and alternate assessment development and scoring, as well as in training teachers on best practices in instruction for students with significant cognitive disabilities. He has coauthored several articles and book chapters regarding alternate assessment and instruction for students with significant cognitive disabilities.

Jean Clayton, M.A., Technical Assistance Specialist, Inclusive Large Scale Standards and Assessment, Human Development Institute (ILSSA), University of Kentucky, 1 Quality Street, Suite 722, Lexington, KY 40507

Ms. Clayton is a consultant who assists states in designing, implementing, and scoring alternate assessments, training teachers, and developing assessment materials. Prior to joining ILSSA, she served as a special and general education teacher, inclusion facilitator, technology resource teacher, and served on school-level curriculum committees. She has presented at numerous national conferences and published in special education journals.

Belva C. Collins, Ed.D., Professor, University of Kentucky, 229 Taylor Education Building, Lexington, KY 40506

Dr. Collins is Professor in the Department of Special Education and Rehabilitation Counseling at University of Kentucky. She is the faculty coordinator of the program in moderate and severe disabilities. Dr. Collins has published extensively on functional skill instruction with response prompting strategies and is the author of a soon-to-be published text on foundations in moderate and severe disabilities.

Karena Cooper-Duffy, Ph.D., Associate Professor, Department of Human Services, Western Carolina University, 206 Killian Building, Cullowhee, NC 28723

Dr. Cooper-Duffy is an associate professor in the Special Education program at Western Carolina University. She specializes in severe and profound disabilities.

Ginevra Courtade-Little, M.S., Special Education Support Teacher, Charlotte-Mecklenburg Schools, 700 East Stonewall Street, Charlotte, NC 28202

Ms. Courtade-Little serves as a support teacher for which she conducts classroom consultations and training for participants in federal grants facilitating teaching academics to students with significant disabilities. She is currently pursuing her doctorate in special education at the University of North Carolina at Charlotte.

Anne P. Denham, Ed.S., M.A., Education Specialist in Assistive Technology, Inclusive Large Scale Standards and Assessment, Human Development Institute (HDI), University of Kentucky, 1 Quality Street, Suite 722, Lexington, KY 40507

Ms. Denham coordinated the Inclusive Education Initiative at the HDI to improve inclusive programming for students with significant cognitive disabilities and served as a team member on alternate assessment projects within several states. She is active on advisory boards in assistive technology and universal design for learning and served as a special education teacher, school technology coordinator, and assistive technology team leader prior to working for HDI. She has presented nationally and has published in the fields of special education and assistive technology.

Warren Di Biase, Ed.D., Associate Professor, University of North Carolina at Charlotte, 9201 University City Boulevard, Charlotte, NC 28223

Dr. Di Biase is currently the middle/secondary science educator at University of North Carolina at Charlotte. He has more than 20 years of experience as a high school teacher.

June E. Downing, Ph.D., Professor, California State University–Northridge, School of Education, 18111 Nordhoff Street, Northridge, CA 91330

Dr. Downing prepares teachers to meet the needs of students with moderate to severe and multiple disabilities. In this capacity, she teaches courses, advises students, and supervises teachers in their practicum experiences. She has provided in-service training to teachers, administrators, parents, and support staff around the United States and in other countries. Areas of research include investigating related topics such as educating all students together, enhancing the social-communicative skills of students with severe disabilities, adapting curricula for the unique needs of individual students, developing paraprofessional skills, and preparing teachers for inclusive education. She has published widely.

Claudia P. Flowers, Ph.D., Associate Professor, Department of Educational Leadership, University of North Carolina at Charlotte, 9201 University City Boulevard, Charlotte, NC 28223

Dr. Flowers is an associate professor in educational research and statistics at the University of North Carolina at Charlotte. Her research interests include educational measurement, research designs, and alternate assessments for students with significant cognitive disabilities.

Debby Houston, Ph.D., Associate in Research, Florida Center for Reading Research, Florida State University, 227 North Bronough Street, Suite 7250, Tallahassee, FL 32301

Dr. Houston is an experienced special education teacher, school district administrator, and state-level administrator. She currently designs training packages and materials for teachers to expand their skills in curriculum content, instruction, and application of research-based practices.

Bree A. Jimenez, M.Ed., B.S., Project Field Coordinating Teacher, Charlotte-Mecklenburg Schools, 100 East Stonewall Street, Charlotte, NC 28202

Ms. Jimenez is a Coordinating Teacher for Specialized Grants in the Charlotte-Mecklenburg school system. She is currently pursuing a doctoral degree in special education at the University of North Carolina at Charlotte. She has 6 years of teaching experience working with students with significant cognitive disabilities.

Jacqueline Kearns, Ed.D., Principal Investigator, Interdisciplinary Human Development Institute, University of Kentucky, 1 Quality Street, Suite 722, Lexington, KY 40506

Dr. Kearns is the principal investigator for the National Alternate Assessment Center at the University of Kentucky. She, along with Dr. Harold Kleinert, developed one of the first alternate assessments for the Kentucky Assessment and Accountability system in 1991. In addition to directing the National Alternate Assessment Center, she has directed three federally funded research projects and coauthored one of the first texts on alternate assessment.

Harold L. Kleinert, Ed.D., Executive Director, Interdisciplinary Human Development Institute, University of Kentucky, 113 Mineral Industries Building, Lexington, KY 40506

Dr. Kleinert has published widely in the area of alternate assessments for students with significant disabilities under IDEA, including research on the impact of inclusion of students with significant disabilities in large-scale assessment and accountability systems. He is the lead author of the text, coauthored with Jacqueline Kearns, *Alternate Assessment: Measuring Outcomes and Supports for Students with Disabilities* (Paul H. Brookes Publishing Co., 2001). He has extensive experience as a classroom teacher of students with significant cognitive disabilities.

Lou-Ann E. Land, M.Ed., Technical Assistance Specialist, Inclusive Large Scale Standards and Assessment (ILSSA), Human Development Institute, University of Kentucky, 1 Quality Street, Suite 722, Lexington, KY 40507

Ms. Land is a technical assistance specialist for ILSSA and the National Alternate Assessment Center at the Interdisciplinary Human Development Institute at the University of Kentucky (UK). Before beginning at UK, she taught students with moderate and severe disabilities for 19 years in both integrated and inclusive settings and was the Kentucky Special Education Teacher of the Year in 1991.

Daniel G. Perlmutter, Ph.D., Assistant Professor, Department of Biology, Western Carolina University, Cullowhee, NC 28723

Dr. Perlmutter established and directed an Upward Bound math and science educational program for 10 years. This educational outreach program provided high school students opportunities to work in research teams on original environmental and ecological investigations, publish their manuscripts, and present their findings at science symposia. He is a strong advocate for experiential learning in the sciences.

David K. Pugalee, Ph.D., M.Ed., Associate Professor, University of North Carolina at Charlotte, 9201 University City Boulevard, Charlotte, NC 28223

Dr. Pugalee has taught mathematics at the elementary, middle, and secondary levels before moving into higher education. He has published multiple research articles as well as practitioner-focused pieces in mathematics education, including books in the *Navigation* series by the National Council of Teachers of Mathematics. He recently published *Writing to Develop Mathematical Understanding* (Christopher-Gordon Publishers, 2005). His research interest is mathematical literacy: the relationship between language and mathematics learning.

Robert J. Rickelman, Ph.D., Professor and Chair, Department of Reading and Elementary Education, College of Education Building, University of North Carolina at Charlotte, 9201 University City Boulevard, Charlotte, NC 28223

Dr. Rickelman previously taught reading and English at the middle and high school levels. He is a past president of the College Reading Association and former co-editor of *Reading Research and Instruction*. He earned his doctorate in Reading Education from the University of Georgia. His current research interests are early literacy and the reading needs of older students.

Diane Lea Ryndak, Ph.D., Associate Professor, Department of Special Education, University of Florida, G305 Norman Hall, Gainesville, FL 32611

Dr. Ryndak completed her doctorate in the Department of Special Education at the University of Illinois at Urbana-Champaign. Since then, she has taught in teacher preparation programs, focusing on education teams meeting the needs of students with significant disabilities in inclusive general education contexts. She recently completed a Fulbright Research Award for which she worked with inclusive education technical assistance providers for the Polish Ministry of Education. She also conducts research and works with school districts that are striving for systemic change which results in the inclusion of students with significant disabilities in general education contexts.

Joseph K. Torgesen, Ph.D., W. Russell and Eugenia Morcom Chair of Psychology and Education, Florida State University (FSU), 227 North Bronough Street, Suite 7250, Tallahassee, FL 32301

Dr. Torgesen received his doctorate in developmental and clinical psychology from the University of Michigan and has been a member of the Psychology Department at FSU since 1976. Currently, he serves as the Director of the Florida Center for Reading Research and is a member of the National Board of Education Sciences. He has been conducting research about students with learning difficulties for more than 30 years.

Cheryl A. Van De Mark, Ed.D., Assistant Professor, School of Education, The Sage Colleges, 45 Ferry Street, Troy, NY 12180

Dr. Van De Mark taught grades 1–6 for more than 13 years before becoming the coordinator of Elementary Education at The Sage Colleges in Troy, New York. Her research interests focus on urban education, school leadership, and preparing teachers for standards-based curriculum and instruction.

Shawnee Wakeman, Ph.D., Research Associate, University of North Carolina at Charlotte, 9201 University City Boulevard, Charlotte, NC 28223

Dr. Wakeman has served as a special education teacher, a middle school assistant principal, and a research assistant on several U.S. Department of Education, Office of Special Education Program, grants. Her research interest includes the relationship of the principal to the education of students with disabilities. She is currently involved in several publications related to accessing the general curriculum for students with disabilities and alternate assessment.

Terri Ward, Ed.D., Assistant Professor of Special Education, The College of Saint Rose, 432 Western Avenue, Albany, NY 12203

Dr. Ward worked in public schools for 17 years as a special education teacher, inclusion facilitator, and technical assistance provider for systems change for inclusion in Florida and New York. Currently, she is an assistant professor of special education at the College of Saint Rose. Her research interests and work with schools focuses on preparing teachers for inclusive settings, the inclusion of learners with severe disabilities in standards-based general education settings, and the education of learners with cognitive disabilities in postsecondary settings.

Michael L. Wehmeyer, Ph.D., Professor of Special Education, University of Kansas, 1200 Sunnyside Avenue, Room 3136, Lawrence, KS 66045

Dr. Wehmeyer is Professor of Special Education; Executive Director, Kansas University Center on Developmental Disabilities; and Associate Director, Beach Center on Disability. He is also Editor-in-Chief for the journal *Remedial and Special Education* and an author of the American Association on Mental Retardation's *Supports Intensity Scale*. His areas of research include self-determination, access to the general curriculum for students with significant support needs, and technology use by people with cognitive and intellectual disabilities.

Foreword

In the mid-1990s, Steve, then a 24-year-old man with moderate mental retardation, told me and my university class how much he loved to read. Although I said nothing, I must admit I was disbelieving; I envisioned picture books, not real books, and being read to, but not reading independently. However, his mother followed Steve's comments with a report of her disappointment that he had not been taught to read during his years in special education classes. She proceeded to demonstrate the main steps of a reading program that she and her husband had devised for Steve. They began home tutoring in early elementary school when they first realized that Steve's teachers did not share their academic goals for him. The program was successful, and Steve, as an adult, used his reading skills daily both for enjoyment and in his mailroom job at the hospital.

Not surprisingly, our beliefs about curriculum for students with severe disabilities have undergone an evolution over the past 50 years. These beliefs have been greatly influenced both by research and by integration and inclusion. In the 1960s and early 1970s, before the Education for All Handicapped Children Act of 1975 (PL 94-142) and the Individuals with Disabilities Education Act (IDEA) of 1990 (PL 101-476), these students were considered fortunate if they attended school programs, most of which were private and situated in institutions, church basements, or Arc settings. Teachers, if they received training, were likely to follow Julia Molloy's (1963) practical curriculum; if teachers were untrained, the curriculum was oriented to activities "suited to their developmental levels" as well as the TLC ("tender loving care") approach.

After 1975, schooling for these students was required by the Education for All Handicapped Children Act of 1975 (PL 94-142), but this education was almost universally separate from children without disabilities. If lucky enough to be in a public school building, these students, regardless of their age and size, found themselves either stuck in elementary schools or marooned to the special wing or basement of whatever school they attended. During these times, TASH became a strong influence on educational programs for students with severe disabilities. The messages in the 1970s were to teach functional or meaningful skills and to respect the student's chronological age. Soon, thanks to leaders like Lou Brown of the University of Wisconsin, several additional themes emerged: 1) Use the community for instruction, 2) target and teach basic functional academic skills that have long-term use, and 3) promote social interactions between these students and their typical peers. It took years for these messages to become embedded in school programs across the country.

During the mid-1980s and early 1990s, the theme of integration was followed by that of inclusion. *Integration* meant mixing these students with their peers during less academic times (i.e., lunch, transportation, physical education, music). By contrast, *inclusion* refined the practice of integration by highlighting several characteristics: 1) All students were to attend their neighborhood school; 2) the number and types of students with disabilities in a school were to reflect the natural proportion, thereby eliminating "inclusion schools" and classrooms; and 3) students were to have membership status, not visitor status, in general education classrooms.

Each wave of this evolutionary process has led to both controversy and change. The most recent wave, initiated by the reauthorizations of IDEA in 1997 and 2004, concerned the provision of access to the general education curriculum for all students. The No Child Left Behind (NCLB) Act of 2001 (PL 107-110) clarified this obligation even further: States are required to design and implement academic content assessments of students in math, reading and language arts, social studies, and science. Students with severe disabilities, instead of being left out of this process, must master some alternate achievement standards for each grade level, rather than master all grade-level content. Ironically, some still debate whether "access to the general education curriculum" is best accomplished by being included. But researchers and many educators in the field of severe disabilities argue that "being there" *is* necessary but that it is not sufficient. To have access and also to learn, students need the individualized support of collaborative teams of general and special educators. These teams create adaptations that are "only as special as necessary" and that "facilitate both social and instructional participation in class activities" (Janney & Snell, 2004, pp. 40–41), while teams actively monitor student progress and make program improvements.

Even as these waves of evolutionary change roll by, most of us still hold stereotypes and assumptions about teaching meaningful academics to students with severe disabilities. These beliefs need to be examined and challenged or we will not be able to shape the outcomes made possible by NCLB. Such beliefs include the following:

- Students with moderate disabilities often can learn some functional academics such as sight words and addition, but these goals are not appropriate for students with severe and profound disabilities.

- If you take time to teach academics, students will not have time to learn the needed functional skills.

- If a student cannot walk, talk, or attend for longer than a few seconds, being in the general education classroom and having academic objectives just makes no sense.

This book lays a foundation of evidence that allows its readers to examine and adjust their views about academic curriculum access for students with severe disabilities and to broaden their grasp of effective teaching procedures.

Martha E. Snell, Ph.D.
The University of Virginia

REFERENCES

Education for All Handicapped Children Act of 1975, PL 94-142, 20 U.S.C. §§ 1400 *et seq.*

Individuals with Disabilities Education Act Amendments of 1997, PL 105-17, 20 U.S.C. §§ 1400 *et seq.*

Individuals with Disabilities Education Act of 1990, PL 101-476, 20 U.S.C. §§ 1400 *et seq.*

Individuals with Disabilities Education Improvement Act of 2004, PL 108-446, 20 U.S.C. §§ 1400 *et seq.*

Janney, R.E., & Snell, M.E. (2004). *Teachers' guides to inclusive practices: Modifying schoolwork* (2nd ed.). Baltimore: Paul H. Brookes Publishing Co.

Molloy, J.S. (1963). *Trainable children: Curriculum and procedures.* New York: John Day Co.

No Child Left Behind Act of 2001, PL 107-110, 115 Stat. 1425, 20 U.S.C. §§ 6301 *et seq.*

Preface

This volume has been written in an era of legislative advancement that requires that *all* children, including those with significant cognitive disabilities, not only have access to the general curriculum but also, through that access, show achievement of state academic content standards (i.e., reading, math, and science). We have no way of knowing how the current focus on accountability will evolve as politicians and educators debate how to improve America's schools, but we believe that the No Child Left Behind (NCLB) Act of 2001 (PL 107-110) has created a lasting expectation that all students can and must make progress in reading, math, and science. The purpose of this book is to find meaningful ways to help students with significant cognitive disabilities meet that expectation. We strongly believe that as parents and advocates of students with significant cognitive disabilities see students with significant disabilities making academic progress for perhaps the first time, educational teams will not likely retreat to an earlier time when there was little to no focus on academics for this population.

The focus on academics stems not only from NCLB but also from earlier legislation for students with disabilities. Access to the general curriculum was mandated by the reauthorization of the Individuals with Disabilities Education Act (IDEA) Amendments of 1997 (PL 105-17). IDEA 1997 is historically tied to the first piece of legislation in 1975 that addressed educating all children with disabilities (Education for All Handicapped Children Act of 1975; PL 94-142). Across the course of the last 30 years, each of the reauthorizations of IDEA (e.g., Individuals with Disabilities Education Improvement Act of 2004; PL 108-446), continues to make improvements to educational opportunities and services for children with disabilities at all levels of functioning. One of the historic requirements of this legislation is that students receive a *free appropriate public education* (FAPE) in the least restrictive environment. In the decades from the first passage of this federal law, educators have increasingly found ways to provide FAPE in inclusive schools and general education classrooms.

Some advocates for access to the general curriculum propose that access should always be provided in inclusive general education settings. What can become confused is access to the general curriculum as a place versus content. Although we are advocates of inclusion, it is important to note that access can take place wherever the student is located. Access to the general curriculum is mandated regardless of the environment. Even the latest reauthorization of IDEA, IDEA 2004, retains clauses about the *least restrictive environment* (LRE) and recommends that the LRE be evaluated on an individual basis. Although this book contains many ideas for teaching academics in general education settings, including chapters dedicated entirely to an inclusive approach, the book has also been written for creating access to general education content in whatever setting the student is served.

The person who provides this access to the general education content must be "highly qualified" to do so, as also mandated by IDEA 2004. That is, the teacher who will be providing instruction in reading, math, science, and other academic content needs background in these curricular areas. In addition to obtaining additional training, special educators are encouraged to engage in ongoing planning with general educators. Even teachers in a self-contained classroom can collaborate with general education teachers in their school to share materials, activities, and lesson plans to gain a better understanding of the general curriculum. In this spirit of collaboration, most of our chapters have been coauthored with general curriculum experts. These experts provide a deeper understanding of the constructs of the curriculum for which special educators then offer adaptations and applications.

In this volume we have consistently used the term *significant cognitive disabilities* instead of alternatives such as *severe disabilities* or *low-incidence disabilities*. The term *significant cognitive disabilities* was identified in IDEA 1997 when alternate assessments were required for students not able to participate in the general assessment with accommodations (National Center on Educational Outcomes, 2005). At one point, federal guidelines provided a definition for "significant cognitive disabilities." Section 200.1 of Notice of Proposed Rule Making of the *Federal Register* defined students with the most significant cognitive disabilities as

> Students with disabilities under the IDEA whose intellectual functioning and adaptive behavior were three or more standard deviations below the mean. The regulations removed this definition, thereby giving States greater flexibility in applying the provisions for including a limited number of proficient and advanced scores based on alternate achievement standards in calculating adequate yearly progress. (U.S. Department of Education, 2003, p. 68701)

For purposes of this book, we define a *student with a significant cognitive disability* as one who 1) requires substantial modifications, adaptations, or supports to meaningfully access the grade-level content; 2) requires intensive individualized instruction in order to acquire and generalize knowledge; and 3) is working toward alternate achievement standards for grade-level content. Typically, the term *student with significant cognitive disabilities* is a broader term than student with severe disabilities and can include some students with moderate disabilities. *Student with severe disabilities* may also include some students with autism and some with multiple disabilities (e.g., sensory, physical, and cognitive). The authors in the text sometimes use other terminology. We assume that when the term *significant cognitive disabilities* is used, it refers to the broader population we defined here.

Our goal for this book is to provide educational teams with new guidance for enriching access to the general curriculum for students with significant cognitive disabilities. We view this book as a starting point. We have focused on the three core content areas (reading, math, and science) targeted in current federal legislation and have invited contributors who are deeply immersed in planning for this content in their research and applications. Our hope is that this book will serve as a catalyst for other new resources as additional people contribute their knowledge. We hope it will also challenge educators to keep exploring the depth and breadth of the general curriculum to find ways to open this content to all students.

REFERENCES

Education for All Handicapped Children Act of 1975, PL 94-142, 20 U.S.C. §§ 1400 *et seq.*

Individuals with Disabilities Education Act Amendments of 1997, PL 105-17, 20 U.S.C. §§ 1400 *et seq.*

Individuals with Disabilities Education Improvement Act of 2004, PL 108-446, 20 U.S.C. §§ 1400 *et seq.*

National Center on Educational Outcomes. (2005). Special topic area: *Alternate assessments for students with disabilities.* Retrieved August 31, 2005, from http://education.umn.edu/nceo/TopicAreas/AlternateAssessments/alt_assess_FAQ.htm

No Child Left Behind Act of 2001, PL 107-110, 115 Stat. 1425, 20 U.S.C. §§ 6301 *et seq.*

U.S. Department of Education. Title 1: Improving the Academic Achievement of the Disadvantaged; Final Rule, 68 Fed. Reg. 236 (Dec. 9, 2003).

Chapter 1

Why Teach the General Curriculum?

Fred Spooner and Diane M. Browder

Something radically different is happening in educational services for students with severe disabilities. Students are not only present in typical classrooms, they also are expected to make progress on state academic content standards. Even students who are in a self-contained, specialized school must be assessed in reading, math, and science per the requirements of the No Child Left Behind (NCLB) Act of 2001 (PL 107-110). Access to the general curriculum was required in earlier federal legislation (Individuals with Disabilities Education Act [IDEA '97] Amendments of 1997, PL 105-17), but now the requirements are specific. Access means more than being exposed to content such as reading and mathematics—access means academic progress. Although it does not necessarily mean mastering all of the grade-level content, it does mean mastering some alternate achievement standards for each grade level.

How did we reach this current era of expecting students with severe disabilities to make academic progress, and does it make sense? In this first chapter, we provide a description of the general curriculum and the historical events that led up to NCLB, and we address the concerns that arise in teaching academic content to students with severe disabilities. *Something* has changed. Educators need to understand the context and rationale for this change before beginning the creative work needed to develop meaningful academic instruction for students who may not have received exposure to this content in prior years.

GENERAL CURRICULUM

To understand how to access the general curriculum, it is important to be knowledgeable about the general curriculum. This is not an easy task for two reasons. First, the United States is the only major world power without a national curriculum (English & Steffy, 2001). Instead, each state determines priorities for student learning. Second, there are a surprising number of meanings assigned to the term *curriculum* (Cuban, 1992). Curriculum may refer to the overall educational program, the textbooks used in the classroom, or the full range of experiences students have in school. In this book, curriculum will be used to refer primarily to the content of instruction; that is, what students are taught.

Following this definition, the general curriculum is what typical students are taught in public schools at each grade level. The general curriculum can also be difficult to pinpoint. As Cuban (1992) suggests, the *taught* curriculum is not always the *intended* curriculum. Is the general curriculum what occurs in Mr. Williams' eighth-grade social studies classroom or what the school board approved for social studies content?

Since the mid-1980s, professional organizations and states have defined *standards*. Standards are general statements of what students should know or be able to do when they complete each grade level or by the end of their overall school program. The general curriculum can be easier to grasp by reviewing a state's standards. These standards are nearly always available on the web site for each state's education agency. An important starting point for understanding access to the general curriculum is to obtain a copy of these state standards. There may be more than one set of standards. One set may be the academic content standards that specify what students should know. Another may specify the achievement standards, or how students demonstrate mastery of the content. Because there is no national curriculum, these standards will differ for each state. There may also be differentiation of the standards by grade level. For students with severe disabilities, there may be guidelines for how to access these standards (e.g., curriculum frameworks) and alternate standards for achievement at each grade level.

One of the characteristics of curriculum is that it has domains. Functional curriculum for students with severe disabilities has focused on domains of daily living such as home, the community, and work. Most general curriculum standards focus on traditional academic domains such as reading, mathematics, science, and social studies. A sequence of skills is usually developed within and across grade levels and contained in textbooks adopted by the school system. Some states have standards related to life skills domains that are applicable to all students.

All states now have large-scale assessments to determine whether students have made progress on state standards. NCLB requires assessing students annually in grades 3–8 in reading, math, and science. Many state assessments are traditional multiple-choice tests, but some also use performance tasks and portfolios. All states have also developed alternate assessments for students with disabilities who cannot take these large-scale assessments with accommodations.

Alignment is another important concept to consider in understanding the general curriculum. Alignment refers to the extent of content match. Ideally, a match exists between the state standards, the focus of the state's assessment, and the instruction students receive. *Teaching to the test* occurs when the focus of instruction is only the content of the assessment. In contrast, when there is little to no alignment between the assessment and instruction, students may be evaluated unfairly. Access to the general curriculum for students with severe disabilities occurs when their instruction and assessment aligns with state standards. Access to the general curriculum does not mean that all educational goals link to academic content standards. It does mean that some goals are academic and have sufficient alignment to state standards to prepare students for the assessments required by NCLB.

To synthesize these concepts, the general curriculum can be understood as the state's academic content standards and what is taught to typical students. Ideally, there will be a match between instruction, state standards, and the assessment. In contrast, *deep curriculum alignment* will occur when students not only receive instruction on the standards addressed by the assessment, but teaching is not limited to the test (English & Steffy, 2001, p. 110). For students with severe disabilities, the goal is also deep curriculum alignment. This deep alignment will be characterized by instruction that is rich in academic content that matches the general education class for the student's grade level, but is not limited to this content.

CONTEXT FOR THE CHANGE
TO ASSESSING ACADEMIC CONTENT STANDARDS

Since the early 1980s, the American educational system has been involved in a curriculum revolution. As special educators focused on how to serve students in inclusive settings, it was inevitable that they would be drawn into this revolution. As Pugach and Warger (1996) noted, "With the advent of inclusion, special education, willingly or not, has been thrust into the midst of the setting in which curriculum reform is being played out, namely the general education classroom" (p. 2).

The current curriculum revolution began in the early 1980s with a series of school reform reports. The most influential of these was *A Nation at Risk* (National Commission on Excellence in Education, 1983). The primary message of these reports was an attack on American schools for failing to prepare students for the 21st century and the emerging global economy. Subject-area organizations began to respond to the pressure for reform through developing subject-area standards. For example, the National Council of Teachers of Mathematics (NCTM) developed standards that were adopted by many states as state curriculum frameworks (O'Neil, 1993). Promoting school reform by defining standards gained further momentum with the passage of Goals 2000: Educate America Act of 1994 (PL 103-227). This legislation encouraged states to set standards based on those identified at the national level. State and federal policymakers also began to push for school *accountability*. Accountability could be demonstrated through the use of large-scale assessments of state standards.

At first, this reform movement seemed to bypass students with disabilities who were often exempted from these large-scale assessments. By the mid-1990s, special educators began to express concern about omitting students with disabilities from the growing focus on school accountability. The National Center on Educational Outcomes (NCEO) noted that large numbers of students with disabilities were excluded from state assessment and accountability systems (Erickson, Thurlow, & Thor, 1995). One of the consequences of allowing students with disabilities to be exempted from state assessments was the increase in rates of referrals to special education (Allington & McGill-Franzen, 1992).

The 1997 amendments to IDEA required that states include students with disabilities in state and local assessments with accommodations as needed. Students not able to participate with accommodations must be given an alternate assessment. Earlier, the Improving America's Schools Act of 1994 (PL 103-382), an amendment to the Elementary and Secondary Education Act, required that students with disabilities have access to the general curriculum and be included in state and local assessments.

At first, educators did not realize that the inclusion of all students with disabilities in state assessment systems had curricular implications for students with severe disabilities. Since the 1980s, the use of a separate functional curriculum model had been predominant for students with severe disabilities. Early in the development of alternate assessments, Thompson and Thurlow (2001) found that many states used functional skills to develop their alternate assessments with no link to state academic standards. As awareness grew about the purpose of the alternate assessments, states began to shift their focus to academic content (i.e., reading, math, and science) to assess progress on state standards.

The need for this shift in thinking can be illustrated by the following quote from a mid-1990s book on curriculum reform in special education: "For students with severe disabilities, curriculum reform is not nearly so central a goal as reform that enables students to be accepted as full members of the classroom community; separate, distinguishable curriculum goals will always be needed for this population" (Pugach & Warger, 1996, p. 3). What educators now realize is that while students with severe disabilities continue to need some separate, distinguishable goals (e.g., therapy goals, life skills), they also need goals that are aligned with the same academic content as their typical peers.

Expecting students with severe disabilities to make progress on academic content standards set by the state for all students became policy with the passage of NCLB. NCLB requires statewide accountability systems based on challenging standards in reading, science, and mathematics; annual testing in grades 3–8; and annual statewide progress objectives ensuring that all groups meet proficiency within 12 years. The Title I Regulation on Alternate Achievement Standards (2003) made it possible for school systems to count up to 1% of students with significant cognitive disabilities as proficient in computing adequate yearly progress through the use of alternate achievement standards. These alternate achievement standards can be assessed through alternate assessment, but these assessments must be aligned with a state's academic content standard, promote access to the general curriculum, and reflect professional judgment of the highest achievement standards possible.

This provision of alternate achievement standards for NCLB made December 9, 2003 a historic day for students with significant cognitive disabilities. For the first time, federal policy set the expectation that students with significant cognitive disabilities should be expected to show progress on state standards in reading, math, and science. Depending on how states and local school systems respond to this provision, December 9, 2003 could someday be viewed as the date when students with severe disabilities gained access to the curriculum revolution of the current school reform movement in the United States.

Given that federal policy has created the expectation for students with severe disabilities to have access to the general curriculum, some educators may wonder about the appropriateness and feasibility of this new direction. Ford, Davern, and Schnorr (2001) noted that in the rush to assess all students on state standards, the temptation has been to define anything, no matter how trivial, as an access goal. Subsequent research by Browder, Flowers, et al. (2004) provided evidence that some of the skills targeted for alternate assessments may not have been either academic or functional. Curriculum experts found that some states' alternate assessment performance indicators had weak links to reading and math content. In a further analysis of these performance indicators, Browder et al. (2003) found that some required no effort on the part of the student or were so vague that anything might pass as progress. This poor alignment was not surprising, given the small body of research on teaching academics to students with severe disabilities (Browder et al., 2003).

In contrast, some states have developed alternate assessments with strong links to academic standards (Browder, Flowers, et al., 2004), and the most frequently assessed items in alternate assessments are academics (Browder, Alhgrim-Delzell, et al., 2005). There also 30 studies demonstrating that students with significant disabilities can learn reading skills such as picture identification, sight words, comprehension, and fluency (Browder, Wakeman, Spooner, Ahlgrim-Delzell, & Algozzine, 2005).

To consider the rationale for teaching general curriculum to students with severe disabilities, it is important to consider four questions related to 1) equal access, 2) functional curriculum, 3) inclusion, 4) self-determination and individualization, and 5) evidence-based practice. Each of these considerations will now be described.

QUESTIONS ABOUT TEACHING ACADEMIC CONTENT TO STUDENTS WITH SEVERE DISABILITIES

Why Teach Academic Content?

The primary reason to teach academic content to students with severe disabilities is to promote equal access to the educational content all students receive. In the past, educators have sometimes assumed that students with severe disabilities needed a totally separate functional curriculum based on the nature and severity of the disability. Sometimes this decision has been made as early as entry into school. Because of the lack of opportunity to receive instruction in content such as reading and math, many students' potential to learn these skills is unknown.

Although not all students with severe disabilities will learn to read or do math, all may benefit from learning selected content within each grade level of their school career. Baumgart et al. (1982) and Ferguson and Baumgart (1991) have described strategies for students to have meaningful, partial participation in activities typical of their same-age peers. Similarly, students with severe disabilities may benefit from looking at a book and hearing the story, even if unable to read most of the text. Students may gain useful skills in graphing, even if unable to perform all different types of data analysis.

Some students may go far beyond these basics to acquire a measure of literacy. For example, Ryndak, Morrison, and Sommerstein (1999) provide a case-study description of reading progress made by a student with severe disabilities in an inclusive setting. Students who have physical and sensory challenges or challenging behavior may be especially susceptible to being underestimated for their academic potential. Once educators discover ways to create access to the academic content, students may produce surprising results.

What About Functional Curriculum?

One concern about the movement toward a more academic curriculum for students with severe disabilities is that the progress students have made to date using a functional curriculum approach could be compromised. Most states' alternate assessments focused frequently, if not entirely, on academic domains (Browder, Ahlgrim-Delzell, et al., 2005). If a new academic focus is to be forged, and functional skills instruction not compromised, it is important to understand the origins and purpose of functional curriculum.

The creation of the functional curriculum can be largely credited to the work of Lou Brown and his students (e.g., Nietupski, Hamre-Nietupski, Baumgart, Pumpian) at the University of Wisconsin–Madison. Prior to this focus on functional curriculum, experts proposed use of a developmental curriculum model (Browder et al., 2003). Borrowing from early childhood, the developmental model was, probably, the first curricular approach used in teaching students with severe disabilities and was adopted in the absence of any other approach to impart skills to students with severe disabilities in the mid-1970s. The developmental model was based on the assumption that the educational needs of persons with severe disabilities could be met best by focusing on their mental age as derived from a developmental assessment and using preexisting infant and early childhood developmental curricula, in some cases, emphasizing Piagetian cognitive stages (Bricker & Iacino, 1977; Robinson & Robinson, 1983; Stephens, 1977). Teaching academics is not a return to the developmental model. In contrast, educators have sometimes used a readiness approach to teaching academics to students with severe disabilities, which assumed that a student was not ready to learn academics until more fundamental life skills (e.g., toileting, grooming) were mastered. In contrast, students not classified as disabled were rarely required to master all life skills (e.g., keeping their rooms clean, washing their hands without reminders) before receiving the opportunity to learn to read.

Subsequent to the passage of the Education for All Handicapped Children Act of 1975 (PL 94-142), in the mid-1970s Brown and colleagues (Brown, Nietupski, & Hamre-Nietupski, 1976) challenged the field to reject the developmental model in favor of an approach they called *the criterion of ultimate functioning*, which would, in part, use the community to create a curriculum based on current and future environments. They introduced the term *functional* to refer to a new curriculum model that promoted community access by targeting skills needed to function in daily life, and they described four domains of functional skills to consider: community, vocational, domestic, and recreational. They emphasized the importance of teaching *chronologically* age-appropriate skills (i.e., not mental-age-matched skills). The functional curriculum model was *transformational* as experts emphasized, discontinuing instruction on skills that were not useful in current and future real-life environments (Donnellan, 1984). Students with severe disabilities were no longer viewed as needing to "get ready" with a series of developmental skills, but instead to learn skills that they needed now. An unintended consequence of the focus on teaching skills needed for home and community is that some educators began to develop highly specialized learning environments and curricula that were totally separate from the typical school experience.

In our view, there is a continued and ongoing importance in teaching functional skills to students with severe disabilities and having students apply those skills in community environments. Extending the curriculum for students with severe disabilities to include academic tasks is not like the transformation that occurred when educators began to forgo skills that were not age appropriate to focus on functional ones. Instead, using an additive approach, it is possible to focus on both academics and functional skill needs. Students with severe disabilities continue to need instruction that prepares them for life after high school, including such tasks as grocery shopping, preparing a meal, cleaning a house or apartment, negotiating forms of public transportation (e.g., bus, subway, taxi), getting along with co-workers, and paying bills. Preparation for transition to work also is critically important for the continued success of students with severe disabilities.

These real-life activities can also provide a meaningful context for academic learning. The acquisition of sight words will be more meaningful when paired with functional activities such as learning to recognize warnings on product labels (Collins & Stinson, 1995), shop for groceries (Lalli & Browder, 1993), or keep track of a job list (Browder & Minarovic, 2000). Counting and discriminating between types of money will be more useful when paired with learning to make purchases (Westling, Floyd, & Carr, 1990) or buy a snack (Gardill & Browder, 1995; McDonnell, 1987).

Does Inclusion Achieve Access to the General Curriculum?

Awareness of the importance of social inclusion for students with severe disabilities emerged in the mid-1980s through the 1990s. Most educators did not reject the need for students to acquire real-life skills in community contexts, but they also valued inclusion in general education for the relationships that could be fostered with peers. Educators noted the importance of social skills to quality of life and that participation in social activities is a critical way in which individuals develop and learn (Staub, Peck, Gallucci, & Schwartz, 2000). To achieve social inclusion, educators focused less on the deficits of a student and more on the ways in which the environment could be enhanced to promote a student's group membership (e.g., as a member of a typical school). Haring (1991) described the rich and diverse approaches to building social relationships through the use of contextual variables including contextual enhancement (e.g., Gaylord-Ross & Haring, 1987), behavioral conceptualizations (e.g., Horner, 1980; Wahler & Fox, 1981), ethnographic research (e.g., Barker, 1968), classroom grouping in instructional designs (e.g., Peck & Cooke, 1983), social climate (e.g., Peck, 1986), and social responsiveness (e.g., Kaiser, Alpert, & Warren, 1987).

Education in inclusive settings that foster social relationships between students with disabilities and peers who are nondisabled continues to be an important priority for quality of life. In contrast, inclusive placement may help facilitate students with severe disabilities being present and part of regular school environments, but will not likely, by itself, facilitate the necessary instruction in academic content that is now required by NCLB. Social inclusion can provide a meaningful context for academic learning. Promoting social inclusion and academic learning can be compatible goals.

Given the importance of social inclusion, educators need to be clear that access to the general curriculum is not synonymous with inclusion. Just because students with severe disabilities are attending regular schools and are present in classrooms with their typically developing peers does not necessarily mean that they are receiving instruction in academic content areas (e.g., literacy, math, science). Placement in separate settings also does not mean that they are *not* receiving access. Whereas access to general curriculum may be easier to achieve in the general education settings where it is taught, inclusion is not a prerequisite to general curriculum access. Students in all types of educational settings must be assessed on their states' academic content standards. To achieve this, students in self-contained settings also need access to the general curriculum.

Will the Focus on State Standards
Compromise Individualization and Self-Determination?

Curriculum planning for students with severe disabilities requires individualization (Knowlton, 1998). For example, curriculum resources such as *The Syracuse Curriculum* (Ford et al., 1989), *Choosing Outcomes and Accommodations for Children* (COACH; Giangreco, Cloninger, & Iverson, 1993), and the Activities Catalog (Wilcox & Bellamy, 1987) provide guidelines for selecting individual, priority skills for the student. Many planning teams have used a functional curriculum guide like a catalog. The team studies the guide for options and selects those that best meet the needs of the individual. In contrast, state standards specify outcomes to be achieved by all students. Even alternate achievement standards provide outcomes to apply to all students with significant cognitive disabilities. The concern that arises is whether teaching and assessing these standards compromises the individualization that has been a foundation of curriculum planning for this population.

The weakness of the catalog approach typical of functional curriculum guides is that it does not ensure that a sequence of skills will be taught. A student may have a goal such as washing hands or tying shoes in first or in tenth grade. Or, a student may work on making a purchase in third grade using a streamlined dollar counting strategy and then go back to counting coins in ninth grade. The communication symbols learned in elementary school may be unknown to the middle-school teacher, if not documented in the individualized education program. Although this lack of sequential instruction can be overcome through longitudinal planning and careful documentation of progress, the general curriculum is typically sequential.

For example, following academic content standards for the students' same-age peers, the student will receive different reading instruction in eighth grade versus first grade. Whereas in first grade the student may have worked on phonemic awareness and the reading of children's stories, in eighth grade the student will more likely be participating in reading poetry and classic literature.

Individualization within this sequence is possible. One student may learn to follow the first-grade reading instruction on word analysis in close parallel to typical peers, but use an augmentative communication device to provide nonverbal responses. Another may focus more on phonemic awareness of words using a sound or eye gaze to indicate recognition when the teacher alters the word in a repeated story line. In eighth grade, one student may use sight words and pictures to follow a story summary for *Romeo and Juliet*. Another may listen as peers read the full script and then use an augmentative communication device to ask or answer questions. The best alternate assessments will also allow students to demonstrate achievement of state standards at each grade level using a variety of response modes.

Along with individualization, the concern arises about whether the attention being given to the achievement of state academic content standards will compromise goals for self-determination. Browder et al. (2003) found that almost no alternate assessment performance indicators reflected a self-determination focus. That is, few incorporated skills such as problem solving, goal setting, choice, and self-awareness. Test et al. (2004), Wehmeyer, Field, Boren, Jones, and Mason (2004), and Palmer, Wehmeyer, Gipson, and Agran (2004) all have noted that the current emphasis on helping students show progress in academic content makes it difficult for teachers to find time to teach self-determination curriculum.

Wehmeyer, Lattin, and Agran (2001) proposed that self-determination can be a curriculum augmentation strategy. One way in which teachers may be able to create access to the general curriculum is through the use of self-determination skills. For example, graphing may have little meaning to a student with severe disabilities when initially presented, unless it is combined with goal setting and self-evaluation. After this personal application, it may become clearer to the student how graphing can be used to evaluate others' goals. Similarly, self-awareness can be promoted through writing instruction. Students may develop a picture/word journal about their likes and dislikes in an English class. Or, they may develop a thinking map showing the contrast between the main character in a story and their own life (e.g., *Oliver Twist had no parents; I live with my mother and aunt*).

Is Teaching Academic Content Standards an Evidence-Based Practice?

In addition to making statements about schools being held accountable for annual yearly progress, in an effort to close the achievement gap for disadvantaged, disabled, and minority students, NCLB also requires schools to use educational practice that is based on scientific research. In an effort to assist in the process, The National Research Council (2002) of the National Academy of Sciences developed a set of six guiding principles. The application of these six principles has been controversial within the special education community, including experts in severe disabilities (Spooner, 2003; Spooner & Browder, 2003). One of the controversies has been whether the single-subject research often used with students with low-incidence disabilities meets the criteria for scientifically based research. Increasingly, educational leaders have acknowledged the importance of including single-subject research in considerations of evidence-based practice (Whitehurst, 2004).

Horner et al. (2005) provided guidelines for reviewing single-subject research to glean evidence-based practices. They suggested that for a practice to be evidence based it should adhere to the following criteria:

1. Practice is operationally defined

2. Context in which the practice is used is defined

3. Practice is implemented with fidelity

4. Results from the single-subject research document the practice to be functionally related to change in the dependent measures

5. Experimental effects are replicated across a sufficient number of studies, researchers, and participants to allow confidence in the findings

The standard proposed by Horner et al. is a minimum of five single-subject studies, conducted by at least three different researchers in three different geographic locations, with those five studies including a total of at least 20 participants.

In our work, we have begun to apply the Horner et al. (2005) standards to examine the degree to which the practices used to teach reading to students with severe disabilities (i.e., moderate, severe or profound mental retardation, autism or developmental disabilities) are evidence based. To date, we have found 128 experiments that were published in 119 journal articles between the years 1975 and 2003. Across that 28-year time span, investigators in 88 of the experiments used single-subject designs.

Given that there are at least 30 experiments in which one or more participants labeled with severe mental retardation acquired reading skills, this is adequate overall evidence for teaching reading content to this population (Browder, Wakeman, et al., 2005). We also applied the Horner et al. (2005) criteria to see whether these experiments were of sufficient quality and number to identify specific evidence-based practices. In general, we found strong support for using massed trial instruction with systematic fading to teach specific skills such as sight words. In contrast, fewer studies focused on the other components proposed by the National Reading Panel (2000), such as phonics/decoding and phonemic awareness. These findings will be described in more detail in Chapter 4.

Overall, there is evidence that students with significant disabilities can learn to read. In contrast, educators do not yet have sufficient research to use as guidance for teaching the broad spectrum of states' academic content standards. We do not yet know enough about how to teach students to read using phonics and comprehension strategies. We do not yet know how to teach students with significant disabilities to solve math problems or understand concepts of geometry. The purpose of this book is to summarize what research exists on teaching academics to this population and to identify innovations in research and practice about how to go beyond teaching only functional academics such as sight words for daily living and money for purchasing.

In each chapter in this book, the authors begin by reviewing the major concepts for the academic content area from a general education perspective. Next, they review the existing research on teaching this content to students with significant cognitive disabilities. Then, the authors provide practical guidelines for teaching academic content based on their experiences with teachers. NCLB requires assessing, and thus teaching, academic content standards while the research evidence is being collected. We have invited authors who are collecting this evidence from both research and practice to provide guidance for the future.

SUMMARY

Access to the general curriculum means having the opportunity to learn the same academic content as typical peers for a student's grade level. Because of the strong focus on functional curriculum in the last two decades, educators need resources to know how to teach this content. NCLB requires that all students be assessed in reading, math, and science. For students to show progress on state standards in these assessments, they will probably need an alternate assessment. States may also apply alternate achievement standards for a small percentage of students with significant disabilities, but these standards will also focus on reading, math, and science content. Promoting access to the general curriculum does not mean abandoning functional skills instruction, but it may mean adding new academic goals. Access may also mean finding ways to include academics in real-life activities so that academic learning is meaningful. Access is not the same as inclusion in general education, but creating opportunities for students to receive instruction in academic content from general educators with support may be more efficient than trying to re-create this instruction in separate settings. Social inclusion also continues to be an important goal for quality of life and as a context for learning. Access to the general curriculum does not mean abandoning a student's need for individualization, but it does mean following a sequence of skills that progress across grade levels. Self-determination strategies also can be taught concurrently with academic learning or used as way to gain skills through self-directed learning. Evidence does exist that students with significant disabilities can learn academic skills. Much more research is needed to address the broad spectrum of academic content typical of general education and to offer guidance for how to teach these skills. Given the urgent need for this guidance, this book will provide a summary of both evidence-based practices and the authors' innovations from their work with teachers and students with significant disabilities. We have no way of knowing how much students will learn, but we expect we will be amazed by the abilities of students with significant disabilities as our opportunities and methods for teaching academic content evolve.

REFERENCES

Allington, R., & McGill-Franzen, A. (1992). Unintended effects of educational reform in New York. *Educational Policy*, *6*, 397–414.

Barker, R.G. (1968). *Ecological psychology: Concepts and methods for studying the environment of human behavior*. Stanford, CA: Stanford University Press.

Baumgart, D., Brown L., Pumpian, I., Nisbet, J., Ford, A., Sweet, M., et al. (1982). Principle of partial participation and individualized adaptation in educational programs for severely handicapped students. *The Journal of The Association for Persons with Severe Handicaps*, *7*, 17–27.

Bricker, D.D., & Iacino, R. (1977). Early intervention with severely/profoundly handicapped children. In E. Sontag, J. Smith, & N. Certo (Eds.), *Educational programming for the severely and profoundly handicapped* (pp. 166–176). Reston, VA: Division on Mental Retardation, Council for Exceptional Children.

Browder, D.M., Ahlgrim-Delzell, L., Flowers, C., Karvonen, M., Spooner, F., & Algozzine, R. (2005). How states define alternate assessments for students with disabilities and recommendations for national policy. *Journal of Disability Policy Studies*, *15*, 209–220.

Browder, D.M., Flowers, C., Ahlgrim-Delzell, L., Karvonen, M., Spooner, F., & Algozzine, R. (2004). The alignment of alternate assessment content to academic and functional curricula. *Journal of Special Education*, *37*, 211–224.

Browder, D.M., & Minarovic, T. (2000). Utilizing sight words in self-instruction training for employees with moderate mental retardation in competitive jobs. *Education and Training in Mental Retardation and Developmental Disabilities*, *35*, 78–89.

Browder, D.M., Spooner, F., Ahlgrim-Delzell, L., Flowers, C., & Algozzine, B. (2004, May). A comprehensive literature review of data-based studies investigating access to the general curriculum: 1975–2003. In F. Spooner (Chair), *Accessing the general curriculum for students with significant disabilities*. Symposium presented at the annual meeting of the Association for Behavior Analysis, Boston.

Browder, D.M., Spooner, F., Ahlgrim-Delzell, L., Flowers, C., Karvonen, M., & Algozzine, R. (2003). A content analysis of the curricular philosophies reflected in states' alternate assessments. *Research and Practice for Persons with Severe Disabilities*, *28*, 165–181.

Brown, L., Nietupski, J., & Hamre-Nietupski, S. (1976). Criterion of ultimate functioning. In M.A. Thomas (Ed.), *Hey, don't forget about me! Education's investment in the severely, profoundly, and multiply handicapped* (pp. 2–15). Reston, VA: Council for Exceptional Children.

Collins, B.C., & Stinson, D.M. (1995). Teaching generalized reading of product warning labels to adolescents with mental disabilities through the use of key words. *Exceptionality*, *5*, 163–181.

Cuban, L. (1992). Curriculum stability and change. In P.W. Jackson (Ed.), *The handbook of research and curriculum*. New York: Macmillan.

Donnellan, A.M. (1984). The criterion of the least dangerous assumption. *Behavior Disorders, 9*, 141–150.

Education for All Handicapped Children Act of 1975, PL 94-142, 20 U.S.C. §§ 1400 *et seq.*

English, F.W., & Steffy, B.E. (2001). *Deep curriculum alignment: Creating a level playing field for all children on high-stakes tests of educational accountability*. Lanham, MD: The Scarecrow Press.

Erickson, R.N., Thurlow, M.L., & Thor, K. (1995). *State special education outcomes, 1994*. Minneapolis: University of Minnesota, National Center on Educational Outcomes. (ERIC Document Reproduction Service No. ED404 799)

Ford, A., Davern, L., Meyer, L., Schnorr, R., Black, J., & Dempsey, P. (Eds.). (1989). *The Syracuse community-referenced curriculum guide for students with moderate and severe disabilities*. Baltimore: Paul H. Brookes Publishing Co.

Ford, A., Davern, L., & Schnorr, R. (2001). Learners with significant disabilities: Curricular relevance in an era of standards-based reform. *Remedial and Special Education, 22*, 214–222.

Ferguson, D.L., & Baumgart, D. (1991). Partial participation revisited. *The Journal of The Association for Persons with Severe Handicaps, 16*, 218–227.

Gardill, M.C., & Browder, D.M. (1995). Teaching stimulus classes to encourage independent purchasing by students with severe behavior disorders. *Education and Training in Mental Retardation and Developmental Disabilities, 30*, 254–264.

Gaylord-Ross, R., & Haring, T. (1987). Social interaction research for adolescents with severe handicaps. *Behavior Disorders, 12*, 264–275.

Giangreco, M.F., Cloninger, C.J., & Iverson, V.S. (1993). *Choosing Outcomes and Accommodations for Children (COACH): A guide to planning inclusive education*. Baltimore: Paul H. Brookes Publishing Co.

Goals 2000: Educate America Act of 1994, PL 103-227, 20 U.S.C. §§ 5801 *et seq.*

Haring, T.G. (1991). Social relationships. In L.H. Meyer, C.A. Peck, & L. Brown. (Eds.), *Critical issues in the lives of people with severe disabilities* (pp. 195–218). Baltimore: Paul H. Brookes Publishing Co.

Horner, R.D. (1980). The effects of an environmental "enriched" program on the behavior of institutionalized profoundly retarded children. *Journal of Applied Behavior Analysis, 13*, 473–493.

Horner, R.H., Carr, E.G., Halle, J., McGee, G., Odom, S., & Wolery, M. (2005). The use of single subject research to identify evidence-based practice in special education. *Exceptional Children, 71*, 165–179.

Individuals with Disabilities Education Act Amendments of 1997, PL 105-17, 20 U.S.C. §§ 1400 *et seq.*

Kaiser, A.P., Alpert, C.C., & Warren, S.F. (1987). Teaching functional language: Strategies for language intervention. In M.E. Snell (Ed.), *Systematic instruction of persons with severe handicaps* (3rd ed., pp. 247–272). Columbus, OH: Charles E. Merrill.

Knowlton, E. (1998). Considerations in the design of personalized curricular support for students with developmental disabilities. *Education and Training in Mental Retardation and Developmental Disabilities, 33*, 95–107.

Lalli, J.S., & Browder, D.M. (1993). Comparison of sight word training procedures with validation of the most practical procedure in teaching reading for daily living. *Research in Developmental Disabilities, 14*, 107–127.

McDonnell, J. (1987). The effects of time delay and increasing prompt hierarchy strategies on the acquisition of purchasing skills by students with severe handicaps. *The Journal of The Association for Persons with Severe Handicaps, 12*, 227–236.

National Commission on Excellence in Education. (1983). *A nation at risk: The imperative for educational reform*. Washington, DC: U.S. Government Printing Office.

National Reading Panel. (2000). *Teaching children to read: An evidence-based assessment of the scientific research literature on reading and its implications for reading instruction*. Washington, DC: U.S. Department of Health and Human Services.

National Research Council. (2002). *Scientific research in education*. R.J. Shavelson & L. Towne (Eds.), Center for Education, Division of Behavioral and Social Sciences and

Education, Committee on Scientific Principles for Education Research. Washington, DC: National Academy Press.

No Child Left Behind Act of 2001, PL 107-110, 115 Stat. 1425, 20 U.S.C. §§ 6301 *et seq.*

O'Neil, J. (1993). Can national standards make a difference? *Educational Leadership, 50*(5), 4–8.

Palmer, S.B., Wehmeyer, M.L., Gipson, K., & Agran, M. (2004). Promoting access to the general curriculum by teaching self-determination skills. *Exceptional Children, 70,* 427–440.

Peck, C.A. (1986). Increasing opportunities for social control by children with autism and severe handicaps: Effects on student behavior and perceived classroom climate. *The Journal of The Association for Persons with Severe Handicaps, 10,* 183–193.

Peck, C.A., & Cooke, T.P. (1983). Benefits of mainstreaming at the early childhood level: How much can we expect? *Analysis and Intervention in Developmental Disabilities, 3,* 9–22.

Pugach, M.C., & Warger, C.L. (1996). Treating curriculum as a target of reform: Can special and general education learn from each other? In M.C. Pugach & C.L. Warger (Eds.), *Curriculum trends, special education and reform: Refocusing the conversation* (pp. 1–22). New York: Teachers College Press.

Robinson, C.C., & Robinson, J.H. (1983). Sensorimotor functions and cognitive development. In M.E. Snell (Ed.), *Systematic instruction of the moderately and severely handicapped* (2nd ed., pp. 226–266). Columbus, OH: Charles E. Merrill.

Ryndak, D.L., Morrison, A.P., & Sommerstein, L. (1999). Literacy before and after inclusion in general education settings: A case study. *The Journal of The Association for Persons with Severe Handicaps, 24,* 5–22.

Spooner, F. (Ed.). (2003). Special exchange series: Perspectives on defining scientifically based research [Special series]. *Research and Practice for Persons with Severe Disabilities, 28*(3).

Spooner, F., & Browder, D.M. (2003). Scientifically based research in education and students with low incidence disabilities. *Research and Practice for Persons with Severe Disabilities, 28,* 117–125.

Staub, D., Peck, C.A., Gallucci, C., & Schwartz, I. (2000). Peer relationships. In M.E. Snell & F. Brown (Eds.), *Instruction of students with severe disabilities* (5th ed., pp. 381– 408). Upper Saddle River, NJ: Prentice Hall.

Stephens, B. (1977). Piagetian approach to curriculum development. In E. Sontag, J. Smith, & N. Certo (Eds.), *Educational programming for the severely and profoundly handicapped* (pp. 237–249). Reston, VA: Division on Mental Retardation, Council for Exceptional Children.

Test, D.W., Mason, C., Hughes, C., Konrad, M., Neal, M., & Wood, W.M. (2004). Student involvement in individualized education program meetings. *Exceptional Children, 70,* 391–412.

Thompson, S.J., & Thurlow, M.L. (2001). *2001 State special education outcomes: A report on state activities at the beginning of a new decade.* Minneapolis, MN: University of Minnesota, National Center on Educational Outcomes.

Title I Regulation on Alternate Achievement Standards Summary of Key Provisions, 68 Fed. Reg. 236 (Dec. 9, 2003) (to be codified at 34 C.F.R. pt. 200).

Wahler, R.G., & Fox, J.J. (1981). Setting events in applied behavior analysis: Toward a conceptual and methodological expansion. *Journal of Applied Behavior Analysis, 14,* 327–339.

Wehmeyer, M.L., Field, S., Doren, B., Jones, B., & Mason, C. (2004). Self-determination and student involvement in standards-based reform. *Exceptional Children, 70,* 413–426.

Wehmeyer, M.L., Lattin, D., & Agran, M. (2001). Achieving access to the general curriculum for students with mental retardation. *Education and Training in Mental Retardation and Developmental Disabilities, 36,* 327–342.

Westling, D.L., Floyd, J., & Carr, D. (1990). Effects of single setting versus multiple setting training on learning to shop in a department store. *American Journal on Mental Retardation, 94,* 616–624.

Whitehurst, G.J. (2004, July). *Closing plenary session: Comments from IES.* Paper presented at the 2004 OSEP Research Project Directors' Conference. Washington, DC.

Wilcox, B.L., & Bellamy, G.T. (1987). *The Activities Catalog: An alternative curriculum for youth and adults with severe disabilities.* Baltimore: Paul H. Brookes Publishing Co.

Chapter 2

Promoting Access to the General Curriculum for Students with Significant Cognitive Disabilities

Michael L. Wehmeyer and Martin Agran

In Chapter 1, you read about legislation that is the impetus for a focus on the general curriculum and state standards, and learned how the Individuals with Disabilities Education Act (IDEA) Amendments of 1997 (PL 105-17) defines the general curriculum. Subsequent chapters provide strategies to promote the progress of students with significant cognitive disabilities in core content areas. This chapter provides an overview of how to ensure student access to the general curriculum, whether that is content in math, science, literacy, social studies or any other content area, through the description of a multilevel approach to promote such access. We begin with an overview of what we know about access to the general curriculum for students with significant cognitive disabilities.

ACCESS TO THE GENERAL CURRICULUM AND STUDENTS WITH SIGNIFICANT COGNITIVE DISABILITIES

One purpose of the IDEA '97 access mandates was to raise expectations for all students with disabilities. Necessarily, what teachers believe about access and standards for students with severe disabilities is the first step to understanding the degree to which students with significant cognitive disabilities have such access. Agran, Alper, and Wehmeyer (2002) conducted a statewide survey of teachers working with students with severe disabilities about their perception of the access requirements and their students. A high proportion (81%) indicated that their students were included in general education classrooms at least a portion of the school day. Encouragingly, when asked whether ensuring students' access to the general curriculum would help *increase educational expectations* for students with severe disabilities, 75% of teachers agreed to some degree. However, 63% indicated that they believed access to the general education curriculum was *more* important for students with mild disabilities. Table 2.1 provides information on ways the respondents developed curriculum for students with severe disabilities, and how, if at all, this included the general curriculum. Although between 11% and 23% of respondents indicated that they used several different ways to ensure some level of access, the largest proportion (37%) indicated that students were receiving an educational program developed outside the context of the general curriculum (see Table 2.1). Information about support, assessment, and plan-

Table 2.1.   Most common approaches for curriculum development (responses [*N* = 84])

Students with disabilities in my class participate in the same general education curriculum objectives and the same activities as students without disabilities.	11%
Students with disabilities participate in modified general education curriculum objectives.	13%
Students with disabilities participate in modified standards for performance on general education objectives.	17%
Students with disabilities demonstrate mastery of general education curriculum objectives in modified or alternative ways.	23%
Students with disabilities have functional academic rather than general education curriculum objectives.	37%

Source: Agran et al., 2000.

Table 2.2.   Support, assessment, and planning (responses [*N* = 84])

Type or level of support	
Teacher associate (para-educator)	57%
Peer-mediated support	7%
Adapted materials	36%
Students in general education classrooms are evaluated by	
Standard grading	5%
Alternative grading of progress	10%
Based on social appropriateness	6%
Based on degree of participation	5%
As stipulated in an individualized education program (IEP)	74%
Extent involved in curriculum planning meetings with general educators	
Frequently	35%
My input is sometimes requested	18%
Rarely	20%
Never	27%

Source: Agran et al., 2000.

ning can be found in Table 2.2. A little over one third of teachers indicated that they were frequently involved in curriculum planning meetings with general educators. Most teachers identified a paraprofessional as the primary means of supporting students in the general curriculum, with one-third indicating that materials were adapted. Nearly three quarters of respondents indicated that students with disabilities were evaluated exclusively by criteria stipulated in the individualized education program (IEP) (see Table 2.2).

The majority (85%) of teachers indicated that students with severe disabilities should not be held to the same benchmarks or standards as students without disabilities, and more than half (53%) reported their school district had no clear plan for ensuring access to the general education curriculum for students with severe disabilities. Teachers ranked resistance from general educators and students' challenging behaviors as the most significant barriers to access, followed by resistance from administrators. Thus, the message from teachers from this survey was mixed with regard to access and students with severe disabilities. Teachers agreed that a focus on the general curriculum would raise expectations for their students, and some teachers engaged in curriculum planning with regular educators and modified the curriculum. However, the prevailing opinion was that students with disabilities should not be held to the same standards as other students, and that access was more important for students with mild disabilities.

Two observational studies we have conducted provide more information about issues of access for this population and, in some ways, mirror the teacher survey findings. Wehmeyer, Lattin, Lapp-Rincker, and Agran (2003) conducted an observational study of 33 students with mental retardation to examine the degree to which they were involved in tasks related to the general curriculum, using the codes listed in Table 2.3. Students were observed in naturally occurring classroom contexts from 120 to 240 minutes, at an average of 202 minutes. Overall, almost 110 hours of observations were coded (see Table 2.3).

There were encouraging results with regard to the percentage of time students with mental retardation were engaged in a task related to a school district standard, either working on the same task as peers or on a task related to a different standard or benchmark (70% of intervals). This varied considerably by student level of disability, however, with students with limited support needs (mild disabilities) engaged in a task linked to a standard on 87% of intervals, and students with significant cognitive disabilities doing so 55% of the time. Students served in the general education classroom were observed working on tasks linked to a standard 90% of intervals, whereas students served primarily in self-contained settings engaged in tasks related to a standard in only 50% of the observation intervals.

Table 2.3.   Observation codes for access study

All students in class (including target student) are working on a task associated with a standard.

Student is involved in or is expected to be involved in the same activity/task as the other students.

Student is working on or is expected to work on an activity that is driven by a different standard/benchmark than that of the other students.

Target student is working on a standard identified for grade level other than the student's current grade.

No students in the class (including target student) are working on a task associated with district standard or benchmark.

Target student is working on a task linked to an individualized education program (IEP) goal or objective.

Target student is receiving accommodation (any support that helps the student accomplish the task, but does not change or modify the curriculum itself; e.g., using a peer to take notes, using a calculator, and so forth).

Target student is working on adapted task or activity (coded when student was involved in a similar activity or task as the rest of the class, but activity was adapted/changed in a way that made the content different from that of the other students).

Target student is working on a task or activity that augments the curriculum (i.e., involved in any activity that was teaching students strategies or skills to more effectively learn the content in the curriculum; e.g., including learning strategies like memorization or mnemonics, content enhancement strategies, self-directed learning strategies, and so forth).

Source: Wehmeyer et al., 2003.

Overall, students were working on a task linked to an IEP for 22% of the intervals, were provided accommodations to work on a task linked to a standard 5% of the time, were working on an adapted task 3% of the time, and were being taught strategies to improve their capacity to engage with the general curriculum only 0.15% of the time. Moreover, there were significant differences by setting (inclusive or self-contained) in a number of areas. Students served in inclusive settings were significantly more likely to be working on a task linked to a standard in general, and to be working on an adapted task. Students educated primarily in self-contained settings were significantly more likely to be working on a task linked to a standard below grade level or on a task not linked to a standard, and to be working on a task linked to an IEP objective.

In a second study using a computer-based data collection system, Soukup, Wehmeyer, Bashinski, and Bovaird (2004) examined the degree to which 19 late elementary-age students with mental retardation had access to activities that could be linked to district standards in social studies and science, and the degree to which such access was influenced by inclusion in general education, accommodations, and curriculum modifications. In 61% of intervals ($n = 3,420$, 20-second intervals), students' activities could be linked to a grade-level standard, and in an additional 20% of intervals could be linked to an off-grade-level standard. However, when examined based on how much time the student spent in the general education classroom, 83% of intervals for students in a high-inclusion group and 93% of intervals for students in a moderate-inclusion group could be linked to grade-level standards, whereas none of the intervals for students in the low-inclusion group (e.g., self-contained classroom) were linked to grade-level standards (groups did not differ by level of impairment). In only 18% of the intervals was a curriculum adaptation in place to support a student, and there was no instance in which students were being taught learning-to-learn strategies and other strategies to enable them to interact with content.

IMPLICATIONS

There is much to learn about the degree to which students with significant cognitive disabilities have access to the general curriculum, but these studies provide preliminary evidence of the state of the field. First, it was evident that the place in which students with severe disabilities had access to the general curriculum was in the general education classroom. Students were overwhelmingly more likely to be involved in grade-normed tasks linked to the general curriculum in the general education class setting. Second, it appeared that IEP goals were not well integrated with the general curriculum and largely described tasks outside the general curriculum. Third, there were very few curriculum modifications being used to support students to succeed in general curriculum-related tasks, with only limited accommodations available, and almost no efforts to teach students with mental retardation the learning-to-learn, cognitive, or self-regulation strategies that could improve their performance in the general curriculum.

Although the 1997 IDEA Amendments stipulated that all students with disabilities need to be involved with and progress in the general curriculum, the findings reported to date suggest that the educational programs of a majority of students with severe disabilities remain largely outside of the general curriculum. Their IEP goals are generally not aligned with the general curriculum, and students' involvement with and participation in the general curriculum (and, in turn, in the general education classroom) have not been realized to the extent possible as envisioned by the access to the general education mandates.

The following sections of the chapter describe practices investigated to enhance access and yield positive, meaningful, and challenging learning experiences for students with significant disabilities. In particular, the value of self-regulation and student-directed learning strategies is advanced.

DISTRICT-LEVEL ACTIONS TO PROMOTE ACCESS

School reform efforts in the era of the No Child Left Behind (NCLB) Act of 2001 (PL 107-110) begin with and are centered on the establishment of standards. The process of setting standards to facilitate change in the educational system involves the establishment of content or performance outcomes that serve as exemplars of high-quality outcomes of the educational process. Not only are these standards the basis for accountability assessment procedures, but they also form the basis for establishing the general curriculum and, thus, directing instruction for all students. NCLB requires that states establish "challenging academic content and student academic achievement standards that will be used by the State, its local education agencies (LEAs), and its schools" (§ 200.1[a]). Amendments to NCLB allow states to set alternate achievement standards that differ in complexity from the established grade-level achievement standard, but requires that these alternate achievement standards must be aligned with the state's academic achievement standards; that is, the same academic achievement standards exist for all students.

Two aspects of the standards-setting process seem particularly important to promote access. First, standards should be set across a broad array of content areas if the general curriculum is to be appropriate for all students. Currently, NCLB requires standards only for a limited set of academic content areas, and many content areas important to students with significant cognitive disabilities, including functional or life skills content or transition content, are not well integrated into the standards or, consequently, into the curriculum.

Second, if students with widely varying skills, backgrounds, knowledge, and customs are to progress in the general curriculum, the standards on which the curriculum is based, as well as the curriculum itself, must embody the principles of universal design (discussed subsequently) and be written to be open-ended and inclusive, not close-ended and exclusive. The terms *open-ended* and *close-ended* refer to "the amount of specificity and direction provided by curriculum standards, benchmarks, goals, or objectives at both the building and classroom levels" (Wehmeyer, Sands, Knowlton, & Kozleski, 2002, p. 126). Close-ended standards are specific and require narrowly defined outcomes or performance indicators, such as "writing a five-page paper on the cause of the Civil War." Open-ended standards do not restrict the ways in which students exhibit knowledge or skills and focus more on the expectations that students will interact with the content, ask questions, manipulate materials, make observations, and then communicate their knowledge in a variety of ways (e.g., orally, through videotape, writing and directing a play). Open-ended designs allow for greater flexibility as to what, when, and how topics will be addressed in the classroom (Stainback, Stainback, Stefanich, & Alper, 1996) and are more consistent with universally designed curriculum, ensuring that more students, including students with mental retardation, can show progress in the curriculum (Wehmeyer, Sands, et al., 2002).

CAMPUS- AND BUILDING-LEVEL ACTIONS TO PROMOTE ACCESS
Establishing a Vision and a Mission that Includes All Students

A mission statement is a statement of the overall purpose of an organization. Values statements identify the priorities for an organization, and vision statements detail where the organization wants to be in the future. At the campus level, administrators and faculty need to have the latitude to decide how they will implement instruction so as to achieve the standards. This often begins with a process that 1) determines a shared mission and vision for all students in the school; 2) sets goals that involve all students; 3) ensures a fit among vision, goals, and standards/curriculum; 4) identifies targeted outcomes; 5) sets standards for professional practice and identifies needed in-service and training; and 6) identifies how the organizational structure of campus facilitates or hinders goal achievement and implementation of the plan. Students with significant disabilities need to be reflected in these actions. Such efforts communicate the commitment of the school's leadership that diversity is valued, and that whatever is necessary will be done to ensure that children with diverse backgrounds and abilities are successful. This is a necessary, but not sufficient, step in ensuring access for students with severe disabilities. There are many schools in which the mission and vision statements declare their intention to educate all children, but that mission and vision is not followed up with action to achieve that goal or guarantee that best practices will be used to achieve the outcomes articulated in the mission.

Curriculum Mapping

Many schools use a curriculum mapping process to carry out their mission or vision statement. This process involves the collection of information about each teacher's curriculum, including descriptions of the content to be taught during the year, processes and skills emphasized, and student assessments given, using the school calendar as an organizer. Through a variety of review steps involving all school personnel, a curriculum map is developed for the school. Through this process, schools can find gaps or repetition in the curriculum content. Schools can then be sure they are teaching all parts of the curriculum framework, performance objectives, and other standards at the appropriate grade/course (Jacobs, 1997). This can be used to identify where in the curriculum students with severe disabilities can receive instruction on content from the general curriculum that is based on the student's unique learning needs.

Inclusion and Access to the General Curriculum

The place where students with significant intellectual disabilities have access to the general curriculum is the general education classroom. This point was made previously, but it bears repeating. If students with significant cognitive disabilities are to achieve access to the general curriculum, it will be in the context of the general education classroom with students receiving the supplementary aids and supports, high-quality instruction, and curriculum modifications they need to succeed. In fact, Turnbull, Turnbull, and Wehmeyer (2006) have suggested that the access to the general curriculum initiative constitutes a third generation of inclusive practices. The first generation focused on changing prevailing educational settings for students with disabilities from separate, self-contained settings to the regular education classroom. First-generation inclusion was additive in nature. That is, resources and students were "added" to the general education classroom. The second generation of inclusive practices was more generative in nature, in that instead of focusing on moving students from separate settings to regular classroom settings, second-generation practices focused on improving practice in the general education classroom. Research and practice during this phase emphasized aspects of instructional practices that promoted inclusion, such as collaborative teaming and team teaching, differentiated instruction, developing family/school/community partnerships, and so forth.

The most salient characteristic of the third generation of inclusion is that the focal point for such efforts switches from advocacy and supports with regard primarily to *where* a student receives his or her educational program, which Turnbull et al. (2006) suggest was the focus of the first two generations of inclusive practices, to a focus on *what* the student is taught. The third generation of inclusion presumes a student's presence in the general education classroom, and instead of a focus on integration into the classroom, the emphasis is on the quality of the educational program in that setting. Nothing about the first or second generations of inclusion is either obsolete or unimportant. In fact, both remain critical to ensure high-quality educational programs for students with disabilities. The need to consider issues pertaining to third-generation inclusive practices is, in fact, an outcome of the success of these first two generations' efforts. That is, as more students with disabilities are educated and successfully supported in the general education classroom, the expectations for students has become higher and higher, such that we have reached a point in the evolution of inclusive practices at which we need to consider how we maximize participation in the general classroom and progress in the general curriculum.

WHOLE-SCHOOL INTERVENTIONS

Whole-school interventions are, quite simply, those that are implemented throughout the school campus. Such interventions have the effect of minimizing the need for more individualized interventions. For example, if all students in a school receive instruction using universally designed materials (discussed subsequently), there will not be a need to make individualized adaptations for students with disabilities, and all students will benefit from using the materials. The same is true for implementing empirically validated, high-quality instructional strategies. When this happens, all students benefit.

Schoolwide Positive Behavior Supports

One area of schoolwide emphasis to promote access is the implementation of positive behavior supports (PBS). Positive behavior supports focus on two primary modes of intervention: altering the environment before a problem behavior occurs, and teaching appropriate behaviors as a strategy for eliminating the need for problem behaviors to be exhibited (Carr et al., 2000). Significantly for educators, positive behavior supports have focused considerable attention on addressing problem behaviors in school settings and in addressing school violence (Horner, Albin, Sprague, & Todd, 2000; Sugai & Horner, 1994; Turnbull & Turnbull, 2001) by providing interventions at an individual, classroom, or whole-school level. Positive behavior support has been demonstrated to reduce office referrals in schools, create classroom environments that are more conducive to learning, and assist students with behavior problems to improve their behavior. Positive behavior support involves application of behaviorally based approaches to enhance the capacity of schools, families, and communities to design environments that improve the fit or link between students and the environments in which teaching and learning occur. Attention is focused on creating and sustaining school environments that improve lifestyle results (e.g., personal, health, social, family, work, recreation) for all children and youth by making problem behavior less effective, efficient, and relevant, and desired behavior more functional. Additionally, we would suggest, such schoolwide efforts create a learning climate in which all children have the opportunity to learn.

Universal Design for Learning

A second whole-school intervention to promote access involves schoolwide adoption of universally designed materials and, in general, of the principles of universal design for learning. Orkwis and McLane (1998) defined *universal design for learning* as "the design of instructional materials and activities that allows the learning goals to be achievable by individuals with wide differences in their abilities to see, hear, speak, move, read, write, understand English, attend, organize, engage, and remember" (p. 9). The onus is on curriculum planners and designers to employ principles of universal design to ensure that students with a wide range of capacities can access, advance, and succeed in the curriculum.

Researchers at the Center for Applied Special Technology (CAST, 1998–1999) suggested three essential *qualities* of universal design for learning. These qualities are that the curriculum is designed to 1) provide *multiple representations* of content, 2) provide *multiple options for expression* and control, and 3) provide *multiple options for engagement* and motivation. These are described below.

Curriculum provides multiple means of representation. Researchers at CAST suggested that "universally designed materials accommodate diversity through alternative representations of key information. Students with different preferences and needs can either select the representational medium most suitable for them, or gather information from a variety of representational media simultaneously." Web pages designed to be accessible present an example of using multiple means of representation. One of the benefits of the Internet is the capacity to use graphic images in a variety of ways, from icons to hyperlinked pictures and streamed video. However, for a person who is blind or visually impaired and is using a text-reader to access the web site, graphic depictions may make the site and the information contained therein inaccessible. As an alternative, accessible web sites include text descriptions of images and pictures. Similarly, the design of curricular materials should include multiple representations of important topics, features, or points. Such representations include a variety of methods of presentation of the material based on learner needs and characteristics. Students with significant cognitive disabilities, for example, need print information to be presented with graphic depictions, free from unnecessary clutter, and with key information repeated or highlighted.

Curriculum provides multiple means of expression. CAST researchers noted that the dominant means of expression used in schools has been written. However, there are a variety of ways of student responding that could indicate progress, including "artwork, photography, drama, music, animation, and video" (CAST, 1998–1999) that would enable students to express their ideas and their knowledge.

Curriculum provides multiple means of engagement. Student engagement in learning has long been an indicator of motivation in the classroom. By the utilization of multiple representation and presentation modes, particularly those that involve digital representation of knowledge which are graphically based and incorporate video, audio, and other multimedia components, student engagement, and as such student motivation, can be enhanced. Universally designed curriculum takes into account individual student interests and preferences and individualizes representation, presentation, and response aspects of the curriculum delivery accordingly. Current technologies allow that level of individualization and, thus, provide greater flexibility in ways for the student to engage in learning (CAST, 1998–1999).

Principles of Universal Design   The Trace Center identified seven principles of Universal Design to consider when designing assistive technology (see http://www.tracecenter.org/). Applying these principles to the design, development, and presentation of curricular materials can ensure that students with significant cognitive disabilities have access to content information. As noted, most content, particularly in core academic areas, is presented through print-based mediums (textbooks, worksheets) and lectures. Students who cannot read well or who have difficulty with memory or attention, including students with intellectual disabilities, do not have access to the content presented through these mechanisms and, thus, will not have the opportunity to learn the content. Applying principles of Universal Design to curriculum development can address this barrier by providing curriculum adaptations (e.g., modifications to how the content is represented, how it is presented, or how students engage with the content).

Bowe (2000) noted that Universal Design should be distinguished from simply using assistive technology to provide access to the general curriculum for students. The use of assistive technology comes *after* curriculum materials have been developed and, in most cases, after teachers have planned instruction. The advantage to Universal Design for Learning is that it takes place before materials are made and teachers decide how to teach. That is, access is built in from the beginning, thus eliminating the need for many adaptations.

Most people think of Universal Design only as captioning videos, offering digital documents so students can change the font face, size, or color, or providing texts on computer disks so that students can listen to them through screen reading software. Providing flexible materials is certainly an important part of Universal Design for Learning. However, for students with significant cognitive disabilities to access the general curriculum, educators must apply the principles of Universal Design to other aspects of the learning experience as well. Bowe (2000) looked at the application of Universal Design principles to education, which include

1. *Equitable use.* Materials can be used by students who speak various languages, address a variety of levels in cognitive taxonomies, providing alternatives that appear equivalent and, thus, do not stigmatize students.

2. *Flexible use.* Materials provide multiple means of representation, presentation, and student expression.

3. *Simple and intuitive use.* Materials are easy to use and avoid unnecessary complexity, directions are clear and concise, and examples are provided.

4. *Perceptible information.* Materials communicate needed information to the user independent of ambient conditions or the user's sensory abilities, essential information is highlighted, and redundancy is included.

5. *Tolerance for error.* Students have ample time to respond, are provided feedback, can undo previous responses, can monitor progress, and are provided adequate practice time.

6. *Low physical and cognitive effort.* Materials present information in "chunks" that can be completed in a reasonable time frame.

Designing educational materials and technology used in instruction with principles of Universal Design in mind is critically important for students with intellectual disabilities and presents an obvious role for technology in promoting access.

INSTRUCTIONAL METHODS TO PROMOTE INCLUSION AND ACCESS

The implementation of high-quality, empirically validated instructional methods and strategies schoolwide is a critical feature of ensuring access for students with significant intellectual disabilities. Indeed, many of these instructional methods and strategies emerged from previous research on strategies to promote inclusive practices. Moreover, as with all whole-school interventions, all students benefit from the implementation of such strategies. Instructional strategies that nurture the development of problem solving and critical thinking skills, for example, are important for all students, not just students with disabilities.

There is not sufficient space in this chapter to discuss such strategies in any detail (see Browder, 2001; Kennedy & Horn, 2004; Orelove, Sobsey, & Silberman, 2004; Ryndak & Alper, 2003; Snell & Brown, 2001; Wehmeyer, Sands, et al., 2002, for recent treatments of these strategies). In general, whole-school implementation of high-quality instruction will include a wide array of interventions, including instructional strategies and classroom ecological interventions (Avramidis, Bayliss, & Burden, 2002). For example, during the course of a school day, a teacher will utilize a variety of instructional groupings or arrangements (e.g., whole-class instruction, teacher-directed small-group instruction, cooperative learning groups, peer-directed instructional activities, independent seat work) through which to present lesson content. For students with significant intellectual disabilities (indeed, students with disabilities in general), "whole-class and independent seat work arrangements often pose the most problems" (Udvari-Solner, 1993, p. 4). Large-group instruction and independent seat work require all students to maintain attention over extended periods of time, to interact only passively with the information to be learned, and to self-reliantly receive and process information that is presented in the same manner. To increase the likelihood that students who have significant cognitive disabilities will have access to the general curriculum, teachers should diversify their selection of instructional arrangements and not rely solely on these grouping strategies.

A critical schoolwide strategy to ensure opportunities for all students to be actively involved in work tasks to the greatest extent possible is *differentiated instruction*. Differentiated instruction involves a teacher implementing a wider range of learning methodologies, increasing students' access to instructional materials in a variety of formats, expanding test-taking parameters, and varying the complexity and nature of content presented during the course of a unit of study (Tomlinson, 1999, 2001, 2003). Research has demonstrated that teachers can effectively differentiate curricular content, the instructional process, product requirements, and/or assessment practices to facilitate students' access to, and success within, the general curriculum (Kronberg, 1999). Examples of curricular content differentiation include reducing the number of math problems assigned to certain students or giving students the option of taking a weekly spelling pretest to opt out of spelling for that week.

Differentiating the instructional process can be accomplished through myriad techniques that should be implemented schoolwide to the benefit of all students, including providing visual or graphic organizers to accompany oral presentations; incorporating the use of models, demonstrations, or role play; utilizing teacher presentation cues (e.g., gestural, visual, or verbal) to emphasize key points; scaffolding key concepts to be learned; and getting students more actively involved in the learning process through the implementation of every pupil response techniques (e.g., lecture response cards, thumbs up/thumbs down) or the incorporation of manipulatives for student use (Janney & Snell, 2004).

In addition to the efficacy of these schoolwide instructional strategies, research has empirically validated several ecological or environmental modifications to the physical conditions in which learning is to take place that should be implemented schoolwide. It is commonly accepted that the environmental context of the school and classroom affects students' abilities to acquire information and demonstrate what they have learned. Adaptation of environmental conditions for students with significant intellectual disabilities enables them to better attend to and cope with the multiple demands that typify classroom instruction (Ault, Guy, Guess, Bashinski, & Roberts, 1995; Siegel-Causey & Bashinski, 1997). The most obvious ecological modifications are those made for students who have sensory impairments and which alter the sensory characteristics of a learning environment (e.g., lighting, glare, noise level, movement requirements).

This certainly does not constitute a comprehensive treatment of high-quality instructional methods and strategies; we have not discussed a number of critical methods and strategies, such as collaborative teaming, strategies to promote social inclusion, communication strategies, and peer support, to name a few. Indeed, many of the following chapters will identify high-quality instructional strategies for use to promote progress in core content areas. In general, however, the more that high-quality instructional strategies can be implemented that support all students on a campus, the more likely that students with significant cognitive disabilities will be able to have access to the general curriculum.

CURRICULUM PLANNING AND
EDUCATIONAL DECISION MAKING TO PROMOTE ACCESS

The education of students with disabilities has always emphasized the importance of individualized planning, a value that should not be abandoned when focusing on the general curriculum. Indeed, the IDEA '97 regulations discussing the access mandates noted that they were intended ". . . to maximize the students' interaction with the general curriculum" (Wehmeyer, Lattin, & Agran, 2001, p. 41), not to require that a student's educational program be derived exclusively from the general curriculum. Conversely, though, these mandates make it clear that the IEP is not, in and of itself, a curriculum. The IEP should be a plan to identify goals and objectives needed to enhance, not replace, the general curriculum (Nolet & McLaughlin, 2000).

The access mandates require that the IEPs of students receiving special education services identify specific accommodations and curriculum modifications to ensure student involvement with and progress in the general curriculum. These accommodations and modifications should be designed to increase the likelihood that students with disabilities, including students with intellectual and developmental disabilities, benefit from instruction in the general curriculum.

This process, as well as the process of individualization and the design of an "appropriate" education program for students with significant cognitive disabilities, occurs in the context of an IEP team meeting. It is critical, then, that the IEP team works to develop an educational program that is based on the general curriculum, as well as a student's unique learning needs. Figure 2.1 (modified from Wehmeyer et al., 2001) presents a decision-making process to achieve this outcome. Before describing the steps to this process, it is worth noting that such decision making and planning needs to be collaborative, involving key stakeholders such as the student and his or her parents, and be person centered and family focused (see Figure 2.1).

In this process, the decision-making process *begins* with the general curriculum, taking into account individual student needs. Traditionally, most curriculum decision-making processes for students with severe disabilities begin not with the general curriculum but, instead, with individually determined content needs. In some cases efforts are made to overlay or map these individually determined needs onto the general curriculum, or, more frequently, fitting individually determined needs into the routine of the typical instructional day. The result from this is often an alternate curriculum, one that is outside of the general curriculum.

Even when state, district, and campus level efforts have ensured that standards are open-ended, and that schools have a mission and vision that includes all students and have implemented high-quality educational strategies and supports on a schoolwide basis, the general curriculum will still need to be modified for most, if not all, students with significant cognitive disabilities. That process begins with the consideration of supplementary aids and supports to ensure access and progress. IDEA '97 defined supplementary aids and services as "aids, services, and other supports that are provided in general education classes or other education-related settings to enable children with disabilities to be educated with nondisabled children to the maximum extent appropriate" [§ 602(29)]. Such supplementary aids and supports include modifications to the curriculum

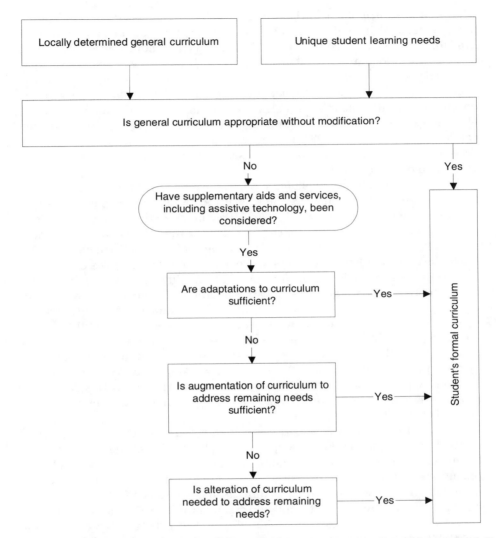

Figure 2.1.   Model for designing curriculum to provide access to general curriculum. (From Wehmeyer, M.L. [with Sands, D.J., Knowlton, H.E., & Kozleski, E.B.]. [2002]. *Teaching students with mental retardation: Providing access to the general curriculum* [p. 55]. Baltimore: Paul H. Brookes Publishing Co. Reprinted by permission.)

(discussed subsequently) or the classroom (room or seating arrangement), extended time to complete tasks, extended school year services, assistive technology devices, a paraprofessional or note-taker, and other accommodations to promote regular classroom participation.

This will include the consideration of the special factors required in IDEA '97, including consideration of behavioral strategies and supports if the child's behavior impedes his or her learning or that of others; the child's language needs if the child has limited English proficiency; providing for instruction in braille if a child is blind or visually impaired; the communication needs of the child if a child is deaf or hard of hearing; and whether the child requires assistive devices and services. Obviously, if districts and schools have implemented PBS schoolwide or utilize curricular materials that are universally designed, there will be less need to create highly individualized modifications. For example, if a textbook is available in a digital talking book (DTB) format (essentially an electronic file using XML markup language, similar to the HTML used for web pages), specially designed software programs can read this file and convert it to multiple formats, similar to the way a web browser reads HTML and formats the product accordingly. Outputs available through such conversions include electronic braille, electronic large print, virtual sign language, foreign language, and video/audio captioning. Moreover, the DTB format itself allows for a wide array of modifications to assist students with cognitive disabilities, including the capacity to provide audio output of written text.

Once supplementary aids and services have been identified for a student, the next step involves consideration of ways to modify the curriculum itself to ensure content. We (Wehmeyer, Lance, & Bashinski, 2002; Wehmeyer, Sands, et al., 2002) have suggested two such levels, adapting the curriculum and augmenting the curriculum. The first level of modification involves curriculum adaptations. Curriculum adaptation refers to the application of principles of Universal Design for Learning (discussed previously) to modify the way the curriculum looks (representation), is presented (presentation), or the ways in which students respond or engage with the curriculum. Adaptations to the way curricular content is *represented* refer to the way in which the information in the curriculum is depicted or portrayed, specifically how curricular materials are used to depict information. As noted, the dominant representation mode in education involves print materials, usually through texts, workbooks, and worksheets. Curriculum adaptations modify that representation so a wider array of students can progress, ranging from changing font size to using graphics to using technology and electronic text.

There are a number of traditional teaching strategies that are, in essence, curriculum adaptations. For example, research has shown that students with learning disabilities can better acquire information in a written text if advance organizers are used. Peleg and Moore (1982) defined an advance organizer as "an introduction presented to learners before the material to be taught containing an overview of the structure of the unit and creating a connection between the new material to be learned and information already learned" (p. 621). Bulgren and Lenz (1996) noted that advance organizers can promote learning with low-achieving students, although there are issues that teachers should be aware of with students with cognitive disabilities, who benefit primarily when the organizers are explicit and students are prompted to actively use them (Bulgren, Schumaker, & Deshler, 1988; Lenz, Alley, & Schumaker, 1987).

There are only a limited number of research studies on the efficacy of the use of advance organizers with students with intellectual disabilities. Reis (1986) found that advance organizers in the form of knowledge statements (defines certain concepts in the content in advance), and purposive statements (provides students with a description of what he or she was supposed to listen for in particular), improved comprehension performance of students with and without mental retardation (group), with all students performing better in the knowledge plus purpose statements condition than in all other conditions (knowledge statement only, purpose statement only, no advance organizer). Similarly, Chang (1986) found that the use of an advance organizer prior to viewing a film facilitated comprehension for students with and without mental retardation, with no differential effect based on disability (e.g., students with mental retardation benefited as much from the advance organizers as students without). Although traditional, text-based advance organizers may have limited benefit to students with significant cognitive disabilities, the advent of the use of electronic text and digital media provides a new opportunity to examine the potential utility of such curriculum adaptation strategies. Universally designed advance organizers combined with features found in digital formats, such as the DTB format, may prove to be ways to enhance the performance of students with severe disabilities.

Adaptations in curriculum *presentation* modify the way teachers convey or impart information in the content in curriculum. Such presentation has, historically, been through written formats (chalkboards or overheads) or verbally (lectures). These primary means of presentation have drawbacks for many students who read ineffectively (or do not read at all) or who have difficulty attending to or understanding lecture formats. There are a variety of ways of changing the presentation mode, from using video sources, to reading (or playing an audiotape of) written materials to web-based information.

Curriculum adaptations that modify the student's *engagement* with the curriculum have an impact on the ways in which students respond to the curriculum. Again, the typical means of student engagement within the curriculum involves written responses or, perhaps less frequently, oral responses or reports. There are, however, a variety of ways in which students can respond to content beyond a written report, from multimedia presentations such as PowerPoint or through video, to performance-based expressions and artistic products.

The second level of curricular modification to achieve access involves curriculum *augmentation* (Knowlton, 1998; Wehmeyer et al., 2001). With curriculum augmentation the standard curriculum is enhanced with "meta-cognitive or executive processing strategies for acquiring and generalizing the standard curriculum" (Knowlton, 1998, p. 100). Such augmentations do not change the curriculum, but add to or augment the curriculum with strategies for students to succeed within the curriculum. The most frequently identified curriculum augmentations instruct students in cognitive strategies or learning-to-learn strategies that enable them to perform more effectively with content in the general curriculum, including reading, writing, note-taking, memory, and test-taking strategies. Although primarily developed with students for learning disabilities (Deshler, Ellis, & Lenz, 1996), these strategies can be used with other students. Table 2.4 lists popular curriculum augmentations that may be of use for students with intellectual disabilities. Additionally, Wehmeyer, Field, Doren, Jones, and Mason (2004) noted that strategies to teach students with disabilities, including students with more severe disabilities, to become more self-determined are examples of curriculum augmentation strategies appropriate for this population. Such strategies allow students to manage, direct, and regulate their own learning, and permit students to plan, execute, and evaluate actions based on problem solving and self-directed decision making (Agran, King-Sears, Wehmeyer, & Copeland, 2003). Promoting self-determination encourages active student involvement and is strongly associated with enhanced motivation and positive learning outcomes (Mithaug, Mithaug, Agran, Martin, & Wehmeyer, 2003). Promoting self-determination involves efforts to address multiple components using multiple strategies (see Table 2.5), and it is beyond the purview of this chapter to discuss all of these. Suffice it to say, these strategies allow students the means to self-direct their own curricular adaptations and, by doing so, promote their involvement in the general curriculum (Agran et al., 2003).

One instructional model to promote self-determination that has been empirically validated to promote student involvement in the general curriculum is the Self-Determined Learning Model of Instruction (SDLMI; Agran, Blanchard, & Wehmeyer, 2000; Mithaug, Wehmeyer, Agran, Martin, & Palmer, 1998; Palmer, Wehmeyer, Gipson, & Agran, 2004; Wehmeyer, Palmer, Agran, Mithaug, & Martin, 2000). The SDLMI incorporates principles of self-determination and student-directed learning to form an instructional model (Agran et al., 2003). It involves a three-phase problem-solving process in which students identify and set a goal, develop and execute an action plan to achieve the goal, and evaluate progress in achieving the goal, modifying either the goal or action plan as needed. Application of this model of teaching enables students to identify problems (desired goals), solutions to the problem, barriers to goal attainment, and consequences or outcomes of executed solutions. The model provides students with a skills set that allows them to respond effectively to the demands of the general curriculum. Palmer et al. (2004) found that teachers implementing the model could enable students with significant cognitive impairments to achieve goals linked to grade-level district science and social studies standards.

Table 2.4. Cognitive or learning strategies appropriate for students with mental retardation

Strategy domain	Specific strategy	Definition
Rehearsal strategies	Shadowing	Teaching students to repeatedly read aloud a written section, vocalize thinking (think aloud), or repeat information presented orally verbatim
	Verbatim notes	Teaching students to copy sections of text to rehearse information
Encoding and retrieval strategies	Organization and elaboration	Teaching students to organize information to facilitate learning or form additional links with information
	Graphic organizers	Teaching students to use visual representations of concepts or topics
	Semantic mapping	Teaching students to "brainstorm" about words related to specific vocabulary words
	Question–answer relationships	Teaching students how to ask questions in order to better understand a specific text
	Mnemonics	Teaching students to form associations between content areas
	Key-word method	Teaching students to associate specific images with particular words or constructs
	Rhymes	Teaching students to create rhymes to enhance memorization

From Wehmeyer, M.L. (with Sands, D.J., Knowlton, H.E., & Kozleski, E.B.). (2002). *Teaching students with mental retardation: Providing access to the general curriculum* (p. 63). Baltimore: Paul H. Brookes Publishing Co.

Table 2.5. Self-determination strategies

Goal setting

Antecedent and picture cue regulation

Self-instruction

Problem solving

Self-monitoring

Self-evaluation

Self-reinforcement

It is only at the final step in the decision-making process that alternative curricular content is considered. Prior to this, the IEP team has examined ways in which student accommodations and modifications to the general curriculum can be implemented to meet the student's educational needs. The IEP team must then consider the student's other educational needs, those that are not represented in the general curriculum. As students with significant cognitive disabilities get older, it is the case that the gap between age and grade-normed achievement standards and the student's capacity and instructional needs grows. Through the establishment of open-ended standards across multiple areas, the disconnect between the needs of students with more severe disabilities and the general curriculum at middle school and secondary levels could be minimized. Nevertheless, even in such circumstances, there are likely areas of instructional need pertaining to self-care and grooming, social skills development, preparation for employment and independent living, and other functional life skills areas that will remain a need for some students with significant cognitive disabilities and necessitate the inclusion of goals pertaining to these instructional areas on the IEP. If, however, the IEP team has followed a process similar to that identified in Figure 2.1, it is likely they will have fulfilled the IDEA '97 mandate to maximize a student's participation in the general curriculum.

CLASSROOM-LEVEL ACTIONS TO ENSURE ACCESS

Classroom-level actions to ensure access to the general curriculum for students with significant cognitive disabilities are, obviously, not orthogonal to previous actions, particularly to the IEP decision-making process. For example, it will be teachers who have expertise in curriculum adaptations and augmentations and who can inform IEP teams on the types of modifications that might be appropriate and useful for a given student. Indeed, it is inappropriate for IEP teams to go much beyond identifying the types of such modifications that could be implemented for a given student. It is at the classroom level that such practices are fleshed out and implemented. There are a number of classroom-based practices that both precede the implementation of curriculum adaptations and augmentations and that further support student access.

Creating Learning Communities

Just as one of the first steps in promoting access was to implement positive behavior supports on a schoolwide basis to facilitate a positive climate for learning, so too is it important to create a positive learning community in one's classroom to ensure access for all students. Wehmeyer, Sands, et al. (2002) discussed the importance of creating such learning communities, in which students understand their roles and responsibilities, have a voice in the establishment of classroom rules and activities, and respect and value one another, in the education of students with intellectual disabilities. Learning communities support diversity across all ages, as well as providing the foundation for active involvement of students in their own educational planning and decision making. Learning communities are intentionally created environments in which students learn to respect individual differences, work in a self-directed manner, apply problem-solving and decision-making strategies to educational problems, and participate in setting classroom rules. Teachers who create learning communities do so by gaining knowledge about the abilities of all their students; developing systematic ways to collect information on student progress that is meaningful and can be used to plan future lessons; using collaborative teaching, grouping, and differentiated instruction to individualize student educational experiences; and taking on the roles of coach and facilitator as well as instructor.

Assessment

When creating a positive learning community and when designing unit and lesson plans, assessment is inseparable from instruction. Teachers need to assess first for the purposes of knowing their students. What do they know? What do they want to know? What is important for them to know? How do they learn best? What are their strengths and needs in the cognitive, affective, communicative, and physical domains? What are the cultural expectations and values that this group of students and their families bring to the classroom? What are their strengths and preferences? Data regarding students with significant intellectual disabilities can be derived from classroom observation, structured task analyses, student-report measures, and other means of assessing student strengths. Synthesizing this data provides a "class map" of students' strengths, preferences, and needs and will be invaluable to making instructional decisions such as how to differentiate instruction, what particular instructional strategy to use, or what adaptations to the curriculum would be beneficial (Wehmeyer, Sands, et al., 2002).

Designing Units of Study

Units of study are the "maps" that teachers create to organize and plan for how they are going to support students to learn and demonstrate their understanding of the content, skills, processes, and knowledge required to achieve grade-level and broader school outcomes. Broadly, unit planning models tend to be organized by subject area, discipline structure, integrated designs, learner-centered designs, experience-centered designs, problem-centered designs, and life-situations designs (Wehmeyer, Sands, et al., 2002). Such units of study identify what needs to be accomplished by the end of the school year, district standards and benchmarks, and student knowledge and instructional needs. Once teachers understand the big picture for the school year, they must "backward map" to determine what students will need to know and do by the middle of the year, and then plan for more manageable instructional units. When a teacher has an overall idea of what needs to be accomplished by the end of the school year and has "chunked" that content, skills, and knowledge into midyear and quarterly components, he or she is ready to plan units of instruction (Wehmeyer, Sands, et al., 2002).

Lesson Planning

Once learning targets have been identified, information needed to plan day-to-day activities that will support students to achieve unit outcomes is available. Generally, this planning leads to lesson plans, which serve as a tool for breaking large units of study into smaller, manageable increments. The amount of time needed for a particular lesson will vary according to the complexity of the learning targets and the number of tasks needed to scaffold students' readiness levels to meet those targets. Generally, lesson plans set forth the topic or theme of the lesson, clear expectations as to the purpose of the lesson (rationale), how the lesson will be conducted (activities), what students are expected to accomplish (objective), and how those accomplishments will be measured and accounted (evaluation).

Important to the success of students with significant cognitive disabilities, the lesson plan should also describe the cognitive, affective, and communicative and physical/health demands required of each learning target, and identify at which point various students will enter the learning sequence and what each student will need to succeed. Three lesson planning tools, *task analysis*, *cognitive taxonomies*, and *learning taxonomies*, are important to ensure the success of students with severe disabilities.

Task Analysis   The use of task analysis enables teachers to break down the component parts of skills or knowledge sets to understand the demands to be made of students, and to match those demands with the *class map*. Task analysis is a process that can be applied to help make decisions about the requisite skills that need to be taught as well as in some cases, the order in which skills or knowledge should be taught. The steps in task analysis include defining instructional objectives, breaking the desired outcomes into component parts, and sequencing steps for teaching purposes.

Cognitive Taxonomies   Cognitive taxonomies are used to classify the cognitive demands of learning targets (Biehler & Snowman, 1993). Perhaps the most familiar cognitive taxonomy is the one developed by Bloom and associates (1956). Bloom's taxonomy is a means of categorizing the cognitive skills students use when achieving learning targets. As one ascends Bloom's taxonomy, the cognitive demands from students are more complex.

As cognitive taxonomies are applied in lesson planning activities, teachers track whether they are introducing students to increasingly complex skills and content. When learning objectives are set, students are expected to demonstrate their competence across levels of higher-ordered thinking skills and content types. Teachers should not automatically assume that students with significant cognitive disabilities can perform only at lower levels of cognitive taxonomies. Instead, they should apply what they understand about a student's cognitive abilities and create materials and supports that allow students to achieve at multiple levels.

Learning Taxonomies   Once a learning target has been specified, curriculum decision makers also must consider the previous experiences of the learner with a skill or topic. Haring, Liberty, and White (1980) categorized learning into five phases: 1) acquisition, 2) fluency, 3) generalization, 4) adaptation, and 5) maintenance. This hierarchy helps teachers to distinguish between those curriculum activities they might use if learners had no prior experience with a task or skill to be learned versus those that might be used to make sure that students continue to maintain their accuracy with a well-learned skill, and provides the basis for further differentiation.

Using information derived from unit and lesson planning, teachers can begin to match learning targets with the learning needs of students and can make decisions about materials and instructional strategies they will incorporate into instruction, incorporating the supplementary aids and services and curriculum modifications discussed in the IEP meeting. Finally, when this level of detail has been applied to unit and lesson plans, teachers will be able to identify those students who may not benefit from planned instruction and who may require additional adaptations, augmentations, or alternative curricular activities.

Curriculum Overlap

A final classroom-level action that will be important to ensure access for students with significant cognitive disabilities involves *curriculum overlap*. Curriculum overlap occurs when teachers and students address more than one content area in a given activity or series of lessons (Villa et al., 1995). For example, in a high school biology course, cooperative groups were assigned to conduct experiments on wind flow and weather patterns. A student with significant cognitive disabilities might be involved with this activity, and, in addition to contributing to his group's report, have instruction and assessment focused on an IEP objective pertaining to improving collaboration skills.

SUMMARY

The IDEA '97 access to the general curriculum mandates are intended to improve educational outcomes for all students with disability by aligning special educational practices with school reform initiatives. Such desired outcomes involve increased participation and progress in the general curriculum. Unfortunately, however, there appears to be a presumption that students with severe disabilities cannot, or perhaps should not, be involved in such efforts. We would suggest, however, that this is not the case. Through efforts that focus on all levels of the educational enterprise, beginning with standards setting and curriculum design, and involving the district-, school-, and classroom-level actions detailed in this chapter, students with significant cognitive disabilities can receive an educational program that is based on the general curriculum as well as the student's unique learning needs. In particular, we suggest that self-determination and student-directed learning strategies hold great promise for student success because they have been shown to greatly enhance student motivation, ownership, and involvement in the learning process, and, by doing so, heighten student engagement and processing of content in the general curriculum.

REFERENCES

Agran, M., Alper, S., & Wehmeyer, M.L. (2002). Access to the general curriculum for students with significant disabilities: What it means to teachers. *Education and Training in Mental Retardation and Developmental Disabilities, 37*, 123–133.

Agran, M., Blanchard, C., & Wehmeyer, M.L. (2000). Promoting transition goals and self-determination through student-directed learning: The self-determined learning model of instruction. *Education and Training in Mental Retardation and Developmental Disabilities, 35,* 351–364.

Agran, M., King-Sears, M.E., Wehmeyer, M.L., & Copeland, S.R. (2003). *Student-directed learning.* Baltimore: Paul H. Brookes Publishing Co.

Ault, M.M., Guy, B., Guess, D., Bashinski, S., & Roberts, S. (1995). Analyzing behavior state and learning environments: Application in instructional settings. *Mental Retardation, 33,* 304–316.

Avramidis, E., Bayliss, P., & Burden, R. (2002). Inclusion in action: An in-depth case study of an effective inclusive secondary school in the south-west of England. *International Journal of Inclusive Education, 6*(2), 143–163.

Biehler, R.F., & Snowman, J. (1993). *Psychology applied to teaching* (7th ed.). Boston: Houghton Mifflin.

Bloom, B.S., Englehart, M.B., Furst, E.J., Hill, W.H., & Krathwohl, D.R. (Eds.). (1956). *Taxonomy of educational objectives. The classification of educational goals. Handbook I: Cognitive domain.* New York: McKay.

Bowe, F. (2000). *Universal design in education: Teaching nontraditional students.* Westport, CT: Greenwood Publishing Group.

Browder, D. (2001). *Curriculum and assessment for students with moderate and severe disabilities.* New York: Guilford Press.

Bulgren, J., & Lenz, K. (1996). Strategic instruction in the content areas. In D. Deshler, E. Ellis, & K. Lenz (Eds.), *Teaching adolescents with learning disabilities* (2nd ed., pp. 409–473). Denver: Love Publishing.

Bulgren, J.A., Schumaker, J.B., & Deshler, D.D. (1988). Effectiveness of a concept teaching routine in enhancing the performance of LD students in secondary-level mainstream classes. *Learning Disability Quarterly, 11,* 3–17.

Carr, E.G., Horner, R.H., Turnbull, A.P., Marquis, J.G., McLaughlin, D.M., McAtee, M.L., et al. (2000). *Positive behavior support for people with developmental disabilities: A research synthesis.* Washington, DC: American Association on Mental Retardation.

Center for Applied Special Technology. (1998–1999). The national center on accessing the general curriculum. Retrieved January 13, 2005, from http://www.cast.org/ncac/

Chang, M.K. (1986). *Advance organizer strategy for educable mentally retarded and regular children.* (ERIC Document Reproduction Service No. ED268718)

Deshler, D.D., Ellis, E.S., & Lenz, B.K. (1996). *Teaching adolescents with learning disabilities: Strategies and methods* (2nd ed.). Denver, CO: Love Publishing.

Haring, N.G., Liberty, K.A., & White, O.R. (1980). Rules for data-based strategy decisions in instructional programs: Current research and instructional implications. In W. Sailor, B. Wilcox, & L. Brown (Eds.), *Methods of instruction for severely handicapped students* (pp. 159–192). Baltimore: Paul H. Brookes Publishing Co.

Horner, R.H., Albin, R.W., Sprague, J.R., & Todd, A.W. (2000). Positive behavior support. In M.E. Snell & F. Brown (Eds.), *Instruction of students with severe disabilities* (5th ed., pp. 207–244). Upper Saddle River, NJ: Prentice Hall.

Individuals with Disabilities Education Act Amendments of 1997, PL 105-17, 20 U.S.C. §§ 1400 *et seq.*

Jacobs, H.H. (1997). *Mapping the big picture: Integrating curriculum and assessment K–12.* Washington, DC: Association for Supervision and Curriculum Development.

Janney, R., & Snell, M.E. (2004). *Teachers' guides to inclusive practices: Modifying schoolwork* (2nd ed.). Baltimore: Paul H. Brookes Publishing Co.

Kennedy, C.H., & Horn, E.M. (2004). *Including students with severe disabilities.* Boston: Allyn & Bacon.

Knowlton, E. (1998). Considerations in the design of personalized curricular supports for students with developmental disabilities. *Education and Training in Mental Retardation and Developmental Disabilities, 33,* 95–107.

Kronberg, R. (1999, March). *Creating and nurturing inclusive school communities.* Paper presented at the 5th Mid-West Regional Conference on Inclusive Education, Omaha, NE.

Lenz, B.K., Alley, G.R., & Schumaker, J.B. (1987). Activating the inactive learner: Advance organizers in the secondary content classroom. *Learning Disability Quarterly, 10*(1), 53–67.

Mithaug, D.E., Mithaug, D.A., Agran, M., Martin, J.E., & Wehmeyer, M.L. (2003). *Self-determined learning theory: Construction, verification, and evaluation.* Mahwah, NJ: Lawrence Erlbaum Associates.

Mithaug, D., Wehmeyer, M.L., Agran, M., Martin, J., & Palmer, S. (1998). The self-determined learning model of instruction: Engaging students to solve their learning problems. In M.L. Wehmeyer & D.J. Sands (Eds.), *Making it happen: Student involvement in educational planning, decision making, and instruction* (pp. 299–328). Baltimore: Paul H. Brookes Publishing Co.

No Child Left Behind Act of 2001, PL 107-110, 115 Stat. 1425, 20 U.S.C. §§ 6301 *et seq.*

Nolet, V., & McLaughlin, M. (2000). *Accessing the general curriculum.* Thousand Oaks, CA: Corwin Press.

Orelove, F.P., Sobsey, D., & Silberman, R.K. (2004). *Educating children with multiple disabilities: A collaborative approach* (4th ed.). Baltimore: Paul H. Brookes Publishing Co.

Orkwis, R., & McLane, K. (1998, Fall). A curriculum every student can use: Design principles for student access. ERIC/OSEP Topical Brief. Reston, VA: Council for Exceptional Children.

Palmer, S., Wehmeyer, M.L., Gipson, K., & Agran, M. (2004). Promoting access to the general curriculum by teaching self-determination skills. *Exceptional Children, 70,* 427–439.

Peleg, Z.R., & Moore, R.F. (1982). Effects of the advance organizer with oral and written presentation on recall and inference of EMR adolescents. *American Journal of Mental Deficiency, 86,* 621–626.

Reis, E.M. (1986). Advance organizers and listening comprehension in retarded and nonretarded individuals. *Education and Training of the Mentally Retarded, 21,* 245–251.

Ryndak, D.L., & Alper, S. (2003). *Curriculum and instruction for students with significant disabilities in inclusive settings* (2nd ed.). Boston: Allyn & Bacon.

Siegel-Causey, E., & Bashinski, S.M. (1997). Enhancing initial communication and responsiveness of learners with multiple disabilities: A tri-focus framework for partners. *Focus on Autism and Other Developmental Disabilities, 12,* 105–120.

Snell, M.E., & Brown, F. (2001). *Instruction of students with severe disabilities* (5th ed.). Upper Saddle River, NJ: Prentice Hall.

Soukup, J., Wehmeyer, M.L., Bashinski, S., & Bovaird, J. (2004). *Access to the general curriculum of students with intellectual and developmental disabilities and impact of classroom ecological and setting variables.* Manuscript submitted for publication.

Stainback, W., Stainback, S., Stefanich, G., & Alper, S. (1996). Learning in inclusive classrooms: What about the curriculum? In S. Stainback & W. Stainback (Eds.), *Inclusion: A guide for educators* (pp. 209–219). Baltimore: Paul H. Brookes Publishing Co.

Sugai, G., & Horner, R.H. (1994). Including students with severe behavior problems in general education settings: Assumptions, challenges, and solutions. In J. Marr, G. Sugai, & G. Tindal (Eds.), *The Oregon Conference Monograph, 6* (pp. 102–120). Eugene, OR: University of Oregon.

Tomlinson, C.A. (1999). *The differentiated classroom: Responding to the needs of all learners.* Alexandria, VA: Association for Supervision and Curriculum Development.

Tomlinson, C.A. (2001). *How to differentiate instruction in mixed abilities classrooms* (2nd ed.). Alexandria, VA: Association for Supervision and Curriculum Development.

Tomlinson, C.A. (2003). *Fulfilling the promise of differentiated classrooms: Strategies and tools for responsive teaching.* Alexandria, VA: Association for Supervision and Curriculum Development.

Turnbull, A.P., & Turnbull, H.R. (2001). Extending a school-wide approach of positive behavior interventions and support to families and the community. *Families, professionals, and exceptionality: Collaborating for empowerment* (4th ed.). Upper Saddle River, NJ: Prentice Hall.

Turnbull, H.R., Turnbull, A.P., & Wehmeyer, M.L. (2006). *Exceptional lives* (5th ed.). Columbus, OH: Merrill/Prentice Hall.

Udvari-Solner, A. (1993). *Curricular adaptations: Accommodating the instructional needs of diverse learners in the context of general education.* Topeka, KS: Kansas State Board of Education.

Villa, R.A., Van der Klift, E., Udis, J., Thousand, J.S., Nevin, A.I., Kunc, N., et al. (1995). Questions, concerns, beliefs, and practical advice about inclusive education. In R.A. Villa &

J.S. Thousand (Eds.), *Creating an inclusive school* (pp. 136–161). Alexandria, VA: Association for Supervision and Curriculum Development.

Wehmeyer, M.L., Field, S., Doren, B., Jones, B., & Mason, C. (2004). Self-determination and student involvement in standards-based reform. *Exceptional Children, 70*, 413–425.

Wehmeyer, M.L., Lance, G.D., & Bashinski, S. (2002). Promoting access to the general curriculum for students with mental retardation: A multi-level model. *Education and Training in Mental Retardation and Developmental Disabilities, 37*, 223–234.

Wehmeyer, M.L., Lattin, D., & Agran, M. (2001). Promoting access to the general curriculum for students with mental retardation: A decision-making model. *Education and Training in Mental Retardation and Developmental Disabilities, 36*, 329–344.

Wehmeyer, M.L., Lattin, D., Lapp-Rincker, G., & Agran, M. (2003). Access to the general curriculum of middle-school students with mental retardation: An observational study. *Remedial and Special Education, 24*, 262–272.

Wehmeyer, M.L., Palmer, S.B., Agran, M., Mithaug, D., & Martin, J. (2000). Promoting causal agency: The self-determined learning model of instruction. *Exceptional Children, 66*, 439–453.

Wehmeyer, M.L. (with Sands, D.J., Knowlton, H.E., & Kozleski, E.B.). (2002). *Teaching students with mental retardation: Providing access to the general curriculum.* Baltimore: Paul H. Brookes Publishing Co.

Chapter 3

Building Literacy for Students at the Presymbolic and Early Symbolic Levels

June E. Downing

"Reading!? He can't read! He can't even talk!"

Combating this sentiment requires some courage, a clear understanding of others' perceptions, and knowledge of what is possible. Clearly, judging certain students as being incapable of engaging in literacy activities based on some preconceived notions of ability level does not have merit. Too many individuals who have been told that they can't do something have gone on to prove the teller wrong. A more positive approach is to regard all students as capable of learning and then ensure that the appropriate supports and strategies are provided to make this a reality.

The act of reading can either be narrowly defined as decoding and comprehending written text, which automatically excludes those unable to access print, or more broadly to include listening, and communication, and therefore includes everyone. Writing skills also can be defined in equally narrow terms to be inclusive of only those able to successfully manipulate the alphabetic code. For the purpose of this chapter, literacy will be considered in quite broad terms so as to be inclusive of all students (and older individuals), regardless of labels or ability level. Literacy will be conceptualized as ways of learning about and sharing information with others. The varied means by which this can occur allows for the involvement and active participation of everyone.

Furthermore, the value of teaching literacy skills to those with the most complex disabilities should not be in question. Although some might tout the need for the teaching of "functional life skills" for these students, in this author's mind, that's exactly what reading is—a very functional life skill. Reading and writing provide lifelong opportunities for learning, for sharing what we know with others, and for enjoyment. Literacy skills allow us to learn about our world, and as such, they are critical skills that must be provided to all students.

LITERACY INSTRUCTION FOR STUDENTS WITHOUT DISABILITIES

Considerable attention has been paid to improving literacy instruction for all children. Several federal initiatives have been implemented, such as the Goals 2000: Educate America Act of 1994 (PL 103-227) and the No Child Left Behind (NCLB) Act of 2001 (PL 107-110), which specifically address the literacy skills of all students. Given that the development of effective literacy skills is considered a critical foundation for later success at school and into adult life (Gurry & Larkin, 1999; Kliewer & Landis, 1999), such federal initiatives sought to ensure that all Americans become literate citizens. Accessing information in any subject area depends on solid literacy skills of listening, comprehending, reading, and writing.

Experts in literacy recommend a balanced approach to literacy instruction (Cunningham, 1999; Gambrell & Mazzoni, 1999; Honig, 1996). Students are exposed to elements of guided reading, specific word study (e.g., sight words and decoding), writing, and self-selected and independent reading. The teacher's responsibility is to interest students in high-quality and meaningful literacy experiences, while also ensuring that students acquire essential fundamental skills as needed.

LITERACY FOR STUDENTS WITH SIGNIFICANT COGNITIVE DISABILITIES

Students targeted within this chapter typically have severe and multiple impairments that have made learning many basic skills particularly challenging. These students may be beginning communicators who have not yet acquired a truly symbolic means of understanding and making their needs known. As described by Arthur (2003), these students may have sensory, physical, and severe cognitive disabilities and have limited communication skills. In addition, these students also may have limited life experiences due to their multiple and severe disabilities, as well as serious health issues. The focus of their early years may have been on gaining and maintaining their health and acquiring basic physical skills, instead of exploring and gaining greater understanding of their world. For example, instead of taking a child with severe and complex needs to a library, a grocery store, or the beach, the child might have been left at home to remain in a safer and more familiar environment. Even when these children are included in typical activities with their families, they may struggle to receive adequate information either visually or auditorially and may have a very difficult time trying to integrate this information. As a result of limited exposure to environments and activities, the ability to acquire awareness and meaning of the world is diminished (Blischak, 1995; Lewis & Tolla, 2003). Literacy builds on this meaning and understanding of representative symbols that describe life activities and events. Due to their significant challenges, these students usually find it quite difficult to master literacy following a pure phonics or whole-language approach. They need an approach that allows for the expression of literacy skills in different modalities and by different means.

Certainly, elements of the recommended balanced and more comprehensive approach apply quite well to students with significant disabilities. For instance, context-based literacy experiences are essential, as well as literacy that has meaning for the child. Experts in the field affirm that students with significant disabilities do not necessarily learn literacy differently from students without disabilities (Katims, 2001; Koppenhaver, 2000). However, they need different ways to express what they know. Teachers need to learn how to adapt the core curriculum so that students with the most complex disabilities can have true access. Students with significant disabilities who do not engage in literacy activities in a conventional manner require highly qualified teachers who know how to interpret literacy standards for all students and make these standards meaningful and relevant for them. Unfortunately, in a national survey to special education directors, Heller, Fredrick, Dykes, Best, and Cohen (1999) found that not one respondent felt that teachers were well-prepared to teach literacy skills to students who were nonverbal. Because a high-quality teacher is considered the single most important factor in students' learning (Mainger, Deshler, Coleman, Kozleski, & Rodriguez-Walling, 2003), such a finding is troublesome.

Perhaps most essential is for those providing opportunities for and instruction in literacy to broaden their beliefs regarding literacy to include emergent skills regardless of the age or ability level of the student. For example, skills such as learning to recognize the meaning of a picture or object, making marks on paper, and requesting more of a story by tapping on the page must all be considered literacy skills. Students should be recognized for their ability to demonstrate such skills, which serve as a foundation for more advanced skills.

GENERAL GUIDELINES FOR LITERACY INSTRUCTION

This chapter will discuss recommended approaches in general when introducing literacy activities to students with significant disabilities who may just be beginning to learn about the use of symbols. These approaches include recognizing the link between communication and literacy, maintaining high expectations for these students to acquire literacy, making literacy materials and activities accessible, following the interests of the child, and engaging in direct and systematic instruction. Each of these recommended approaches will be discussed in the following sections, with several examples provided to highlight points being made.

Life Experiences as a Basis for Literacy

Emergent literacy begins at home as parents and other caregivers interact with their children, read to them, and encourage use of writing tools (e.g., crayons, markers). Considerable attention has been focused on the importance of early literacy at home for the development of future literacy skills (Adams, 1990; Neuman, 1999; Sulzby & Teale, 1991). The more young children engage in early literacy at home, the more children appear to be ready for more structured literacy in school (DeTemple, 2001). Children need to be provided with different literacy materials (books, paper, writing tools) and encouraged to make use of these items. They also need to observe others engaged in speaking, listening, reading, and writing to further develop their skills.

Reading and rereading familiar and favorite stories helps the student sequence events and anticipate what might occur next. Unfortunately, children with severe disabilities often spend less time reading with their family members. In a comparison of preschoolers with severe disabilities who use augmentative communication devices with their peers without disabilities, Light and Kelford Smith (1993) found that the preschoolers with disabilities were read to less often, had less access to writing and drawing materials, and had very limited access to technology. Children with a very critical risk for failing to develop literacy skills may not be receiving the amount of time in basic literacy activities that provide foundational skills. They may not have easy access to needed materials.

In addition, early life experiences and the communication that occurs around them serve as a basic foundation for future reading and writing about these experiences. Children acquire language as they engage in familiar activities and hear their family members label and describe what is happening. Children can be shown photographs of these events and then be encouraged to draw their interpretation of what they experienced. Unfortunately, children with severe and multiple disabilities may not be expected to participate like other children and therefore may miss both the actual experiences as well as the encouragement and opportunity to describe their impressions through modified and augmented means. Family members may not know how to engage their child in such literacy experiences, especially if the child does not have a formal symbol system and is physically disabled, sensory impaired, and dealing with severe cognitive challenges.

Families and teaching staff may need to encourage students with significant disabilities to participate in a wide array of life experiences and then engage the students in understanding, talking about, and reading about these experiences. Taking photographs and collecting memorabilia of these experiences (whether daily experiences such as bathing or eating with the family, or more infrequent experiences such as a trip to the museum) will help to provide necessary materials needed to assist the student to recall the experience, acquire labels for the experience, and respond to questions regarding the experience. For example, one family enjoys going skiing and surfing. A seventh grader in this family is fully included in these outings despite the fact that he is totally blind, is nonverbal, and has extremely limited movement of his body. He also uses a wheelchair. Adaptations and accommodations are provided, such as extensive physical support while surfing (held by another on the surfboard). By participating in such activities, this student can then be helped to recall the experience by feeling representative materials, such as some material similar to a wet suit, sand, and a fiberglass piece for the surfboard that have been affixed to pages with a storyline written around them. Both visual and tactile materials can be used for reading and writing about a variety of life experiences. Their use is explained in further detail in the section on augmented communication.

The Link Between Communication and Literacy

A strong relationship exists between basic literacy skills and communication (Mirenda & Erickson, 2000). Every time a message is sent and understood by the receiver, communication has occurred. The message can be done in a nonsymbolic manner (e.g., a facial expression, a gesture, a sound) or it can be done symbolically with speech, signs, pictures, or print (Beukelman & Mirenda, 2005). Documenting the message in some manner highlights the relationship between literacy and communication. The message is displayed and must be "read" to select it. In selecting the message to convey it to another, the message is then "written." Understanding that people, places, items, and actions all have names that can be used to refer to them represents a foundational step for both literacy and communication. As such, literacy learning, like communication, starts in the home as children first learn about the world. Perhaps the relationship between communication and literacy is most clear when the use of augmentative and alternative communication (AAC) devices is considered.

Augmentative Communication Systems

When speech is not a reliable system for communication, alternative means must be found to support the individual's communicative efforts. Several alternative systems are available and can be used by the individual based on physical, sensory and cognitive capabilities, preferences, and the demands and expectations of the social environment (Beukelman & Mirenda, 2005). These systems can be either unaided (nothing added to the individual, such as the use of facial expressions or sign) or aided (something added to the individual, such as an electronic device or simple photo album). Typically, students with significant disabilities will use both forms of communication together, depending on what is most effective and efficient given the situation.

With aided communication systems, whole messages and elements of messages are presented visually or tactilely as static symbol systems. As a result, when a student makes use of the system and selects a message, he or she has necessarily engaged in listening to the communicative partner, comprehension, reading, and writing. An example of an aided communication system showing one request symbol for a student having significant and multiple impairments is depicted in Figure 3.1.

All symbols or messages on a device are labeled in print (and if needed, braille) to clarify the message for others. These labels also serve to provide the reader with the concept that something important is on the page. Regular use of the device along with systematic instruction also provides the opportunity to gain sight-word recognition. When print is not provided, this learning opportunity is denied.

For students just beginning to understand that their actions affect others (e.g., they cry and someone comes to them), aided communication devices should be easy to use both physically and cognitively. Typically, one movement will produce an entire message (e.g., student hits a leaf switch that activates a voice output device that says, "I want out of this wheelchair!"). The student does not have to sequence several different symbols to arrive at the message. To make the connection with more conventional literacy, students must see the message in pictorial/written format or feel the message with representative items as they learn to use the device to communicate their intent. For example, given the communicative intent to get out of the wheelchair, the student should see a representative photograph (maybe of being lifted out of the chair) with the message written below it. Using a voice output communication device, the student would also hear the message. For the student who needs tactile representation, a similar seatbelt buckle might be used for the message.

Student preference and understanding as well as the cultural and familial values of the family must be considered when developing symbols for a student to use (Huer, 2000). Symbols used to represent specific messages may be interpreted differently depending on cultural values and experiences. Huer (2000) compared the ability of adults from four ethnic groups (European American, African American, Chinese, and Mexican) to identify 41 graphic symbols (Picture Communication Symbols [PCS], DynaSyms, and Blissymbols). The findings from this initial study suggested that participants did perceive the symbols differently given their ethnic and cultural backgrounds. Therefore, such personal variables must be considered when developing symbol systems for a student to use. A team approach with the family at the core is recommended to facilitate the development of the

Figure 3.1.   Sample whole-object symbol that is part of a student's augmentative and alternative communication system.

most appropriate system for the student. The role that this system will play in the development of literacy skills also should be considered.

High Expectations for Literacy

   Attitudes   A tremendous barrier to literacy access and instruction to students with significant disabilities is the expectation that they will not benefit. Teachers may view students as having too significant cognitive and physical (and sensory) impairments to engage in literacy experiences (Fossett, Smith, & Mirenda, 2003; Katims, 2001; Kliewer, 1998). In a study by Zascavage and Keefe (2004), a distinct barrier to literacy instruction to students with severe speech and physical impairments was related to reported negative attitudes, by teachers and administrators alike, that such students would not be able to benefit from instruction.

   Family members also may share these low expectations and place more value on other issues such as health concerns, physical development, and beginning communication (Light & Kelford Smith, 1993; Marvin, 1994). Family members may not receive sufficient responses from their children during literacy experiences to value such times. Children with significant and multiple impairments may struggle to engage in joint attention of an activity with their parents (e.g., attend to the same page of a book; Cress, 2002). When students with significant disabilities are considered to be unable to benefit from literacy instruction due to any real or perceived limitations, they are consequently denied access and opportunity to learn.

   The alternative is to expect all students, no matter the severity of the impairment(s), to benefit from literacy activities and direct instruction and, therefore, to spend quality time involved in such activities. Students with significant disabilities can and do benefit from literacy instruction (Kliewer & Biklen, 2001; Ryndak, Morrison, & Sommerstein, 1999). Certainly they can't benefit if they are never provided access. Knowing that students can benefit from involvement in literacy activities should greatly increase the amount of time that these students spend in literacy activities. Broadening the view of what constitutes literacy for these students and providing them with unique ways to partially participate should serve to raise expectations.

Students will be affected by our expectations of them, whether high expectations or low. For example, if we do not expect students to read a schedule, we do not make a schedule for these students or we don't add words to a pictorial/tactile schedule. If, in fact, we expect students to read or learn to read (at whatever level), we will make sure they have and use their schedule and that words will be on these schedules regardless of their ability to decode. If we do not expect a student to understand a spelling worksheet, the student will not receive one. If we do expect this student to participate in the spelling activity, we will adapt it as needed using words with pictures and/or items and teach the student how to complete it. Wehmeyer (2003) warns against lowering our expectations of students having intellectual impairments and instead stresses the right of all students to have access to the core curriculum. Such access can help to ensure higher expectations. Expectations for the student with significant disabilities to engage in literacy activities will serve as the catalyst to create the necessary adapted materials to make this happen.

When students with significant disabilities are educated as full-time members of their age-appropriate classrooms, they should be expected to engage in all literacy activities that would naturally occur within this setting. In fact the general education classroom environment itself is considered to offer considerable support for literacy learning for students with severe disabilities (Koppenhaver, 2000; Ryndak et al., 1999). Zascavage and Keefe (2004) found that the policy of segregating students with severe speech and physical impairments represented an opportunity barrier to literacy acquisition because students were denied access to instruction that other students would typically receive. Although they may not be able to access literacy in exactly the same manner as their peers without disabilities, the expectation for active and meaningful participation should occur. Teachers, when passing out books and other literacy materials, should hand one to these students, even though adapted material also will be used. Classmates may read to their peers with significant disabilities, highlight pictorial or tactile information in books, and label idiosyncratic drawings for reading purposes. Students with significant disabilities can read a passage to the class if it has been previously recorded by a peer or sibling and is interfaced with a switch. Students with significant disabilities can be asked to help turn pages in a book being read, identify a pictured item for the class to spell, or help paint a group project based on a poem that was read. Countless ways exist for teachers to recognize what students can do regarding literacy and then support such involvement.

State Standards in Literacy and Students with Significant Disabilities   Regardless of educational placement, however, expectations for literacy involvement always should be evident. Literacy is part of the core curriculum for all students and, therefore, the expectation for learning to occur with regard to literacy skills should be clearly apparent regardless of disability labels or ability levels. In support of high expectations for students with significant disabilities is the need to refer to state standards in literacy for all students (Browder, Fallin, Davis, & Karvonen, 2003; Wehmeyer, 2003).

Teachers will need skills to assist them in interpreting content standards and performance standards in literacy to meet the needs of students who lack conventional literacy skills. Unfortunately, only a few states have been able to clearly align alternate assessments to state standards in literacy and other areas (Browder, Spooner, et al., 2003). Although weak links exist in some states, the lack of clear standards for students with the most severe disabilities in literacy creates an additional challenge for teachers. When interpreting standards in literacy for students with very significant intellectual disabilities, every effort should be made to ensure that the link to literacy is clear. General educators should be able to identify the interpreted performance standard as clearly falling under the area of literacy. For example, for the broad literacy standard of reading for multiple purposes, an interpretation for a student with significant disabilities could include learning to read a tactile schedule to determine next activities. The connection to reading is clear. However, if the student's goal is to pass out books to other students, the relationship to conventional literacy skills is not evident. Expectations for literacy learning are absent.

Make Literacy Accessible and Provide Opportunities

Students with significant disabilities often have severe cognitive, physical, and/or sensory impairments that can make access to literacy materials a challenge. Print alone is not an adequate mode for these students. They may not have the hearing or auditory comprehension to benefit from material being read to them. Some of these students will not be able to physically manipulate writing tools. Therefore, these students are often automatically excluded from most (if not all) typical literacy experiences in schools. These students will need to access alternative symbols, such as pictures, photographs, objects, and parts of objects, along with print (and braille as needed). Such a need requires advance planning by educational team members to become familiar with curricular topics so that accommodations that may be extensive can be made in a timely manner for individual students as needed.

Adapting Materials   Students with significant disabilities will need adapted materials to be actively involved in literacy activities. Students who are functionally blind and those with significant cognitive disabilities will need to have materials with objects and parts of objects (Downing & Chen, 2003; Lewis & Tolla, 2003). These objects will have a close tactile resemblance to what they represent for a student who is blind (not a visual one). For example, a story about a girl on a swim team may be represented by a swimsuit (or piece of swimsuit), racing swim cap, and a piece of towel all of which are affixed to individual thick cardboard pages in a book format. A greatly simplified text accompanies each page. Figure 3.2 depicts two pages of an adapted social studies text for a fifth grader during a lesson on Native Americans. Creating books of this nature (versus just having items available) helps develop the concept of books and reading. Students can learn to handle books, orient them correctly, and turn pages as they follow

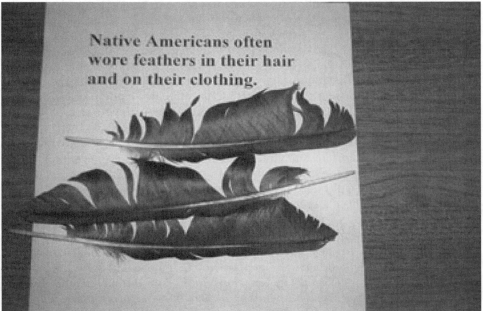

Figure 3.2. Two pages of an adapted fifth-grade social studies lesson on Native Americans.

the progression of the story. See Downing (2005) for specific examples across ages kindergarten through twelfth grade (see Figure 3.2).

When subject matter to be learned deals with highly abstract information, especially in the upper grades, the need to adapt for cognitive accessibility becomes particularly important. Information will need to be simplified and basic concepts clarified. For example, a seventh-grade social studies class is studying Africa as a core curriculum content area. A student in this social studies class, David, has severe cognitive disabilities, physical disabilities, and no speech or vision. David needs specifically adapted materials to help him gain an understanding of this content. A tactile book has been made for him of some products of Africa. The pages are sturdy cardboard and contain the following items: A swath of some African cloth, cotton balls, a bag with specific oils, beads used for barter, and wheat chaffs. There is accompanying text on each page for a peer or teacher to read to him. Although this adaptation does not address all the information that other students will have, it does provide him with some accessible information that coincides with and supports what he is hearing. In general, big ideas will have to be ascertained from grade-level material and made so that some if not all of the information is accessible to a student with significant cognitive disabilities. Adapted material should make the information as clear and easy to access as possible.

A student who is just learning symbolic representation may benefit from using the most concrete representation (e.g., objects, parts of objects; Cress, 2002; Rowland & Schweigert, 2000). For a student who is able to make use of visual information, photographs of objects can be paired with the items they represent. Then, as the student begins to understand the symbol, greater focus can be placed on the photographic representation and less on the actual object. When pictorial information is used, care should be taken to enlarge it as needed, reduce background clutter, and make use of color for additional cues. Initially the pictorial information should resemble the actual items(s) as closely as possible.

Materials will need to be adapted for ease in physical manipulation as well as cognitive understanding. Students with severe physical as well as cognitive disabilities may not be able to easily handle either reading or writing materials. Accommodations to ease physical accessibility might include the use of slant boards to hold materials, adapted page turners, adapted grippers to hold writing implements, page fluffers to separate pages, adapted keyboards for computer access, and taped reading material with a switch interface to a cassette recorder or CD/DVD player. Different switches can make use of the student's most controlled movements and allow the student to turn on and off recorded material. The purpose of such physical accommodations is to increase the active participation of the student in literacy activities.

Teachers in the area of severe and multiple disabilities will need specific strategies and guidelines to help them understand how best to adapt strategies and materials used for the majority of students. Fortunately, the field of assistive technology offers a wide array of supportive equipment and software for students unable to access literacy materials in a more conventional manner. Teachers need to be knowledgeable regarding availability of appropriate technology, where to obtain equipment, how to program them, and how to make effective use of them within meaningful daily activities. Such information is needed if they are to effectively support students' efforts at every level of literacy. Unfortunately, financial issues facing most schools and school districts and the lack of training received by teachers to make the most effective use of such technology represent substantial barriers to ensuring literacy access (Zascavage & Keefe, 2004). Such barriers need to be acknowledged and strategies to overcome them (e.g., obtaining donated equipment/software, requiring the necessary training) actively pursued.

Follow Interests of Students and Ensure Meaning   In general, students with and without disabilities demonstrate greater interest in literacy instruction when they can see the purpose and when they have some control over the topics (Fisher & Kennedy, 2001; Swartz & Hendricks, 2000). Following a student's interests has considerable merit for students with significant disabilities who may not always see the rationale behind instruction. For example, Kliewer (1995) studied an inclusive preschool and determined that literacy had to be useful and have a clear purpose for children to engage in it. Even for very young children, Dunst, Hamby, Trivette, Raab, and Bruder (2000) found that children are more likely to engage in activities in which they are interested.

Teachers can be creative in taking what interests the child and making that the focus for literacy learning. For instance, if a student shows a strong appreciation for the color yellow, that preference can be used to support her communication with others, reading, and writing. Stories with lots of yellow items may hold her interest, or stories can be specifically designed for her that deal with yellow items, such as balloons, cars, clothes, or flowers. She can be encouraged to write (mark, scribble, draw) on yellow paper or with a yellow crayon or marker. The idea is to follow her lead and introduce literacy activities around this interest.

Following a student's preference, that student can be encouraged to engage in specific activities on a regular and frequent basis. Representative symbols need to be shown (and used) during such activities to help the student form a clear association between the symbol and activity (Cress, 2002; Rowland & Schweigert, 2000). Then, using these symbols, story lines can be developed around them and these personally created stories read and reread with the student. Again, by using the student's unique interests, greater repetition of familiar stories and increased time engaging with that story (and its representative symbols) may be possible.

Offer Choices   Whenever possible, offering students choices involved with their literacy experiences is recommended. Choices could include topic of material to read, place to read or write, length of time, writing implement (e.g., glitter pen, markers, chalk, colored pencil), and writing material (e.g., cards, magic slate, dry-erase board, colored paper, magnetic board). The rationale behind this recommendation is that giving students as much control over literacy activities as possible is apt to increase their interest and time they are willing to spend in literacy instruction (Lohrmann-O'Rourke & Browder, 1998; Swartz & Hendricks, 2000). The focus is more on the actual literacy and less on the means (e.g., not everyone will be interested in writing with a pen or pencil on lined paper). Research on the impact of following the preferences of individuals with significant disabilities has demonstrated that these individuals will remain engaged for longer periods of time with preferred versus nonpreferred materials or activities (Moes, 1998). Giving students as many choices as possible regarding literacy activities is definitely preferable to forcing students into one way with the end result of making literacy a negative experience.

Identify Preferences   When student preference is hard to discern, family members can be quite helpful in sharing this information. Working closely with family members is essential because these individuals know the student the best and can provide very useful information with which to guide the educational program. These individuals know what the student enjoys at home and can bring photographs and representative items that can be used when designing literacy materials.

When student preference regarding topic cannot be respected (i.e., when a specific content is being taught), the literacy experience should still remain as meaningful as possible. Emphasizing the relevance of the activity and/or materials to the student's life should help motivate the student to remain engaged and learning. Of course, meaningfulness has importance for all learners, not just those with significant disabilities. For example, an eighth-grade class is studying the solar system. Although this subject is of minimal interest to Rayna, who has severe and multiple disabilities, she does like bright colors. By creating planetary bodies of iridescent colors and glitter, Rayna is willing to handle these items and learn about the colors. Despite abstract core curriculum, adapted materials can be used to highlight certain aspects and motivate the student to actively participate.

Natural Opportunities for Literacy Instruction

Considerable support exists for teaching a variety of skills within naturally occurring opportunities (Dunst et al., 2000; Kaderavek & Justice, 2002). Students seem to acquire skills more quickly or easily when skills occur as part of a natural routine. Therefore, recognizing such learning opportunities and supporting students during these opportunities should become a priority for all team members.

Those supporting the student's literacy development should perform an analysis of the school environment to determine where and when literacy opportunities naturally occur (Downing, 2005). Once identified, a determination can be made as to how to best make use of these opportunities. Some opportunities are quite obvious and require little accommodation, such as reading bathroom signs on doors and deciding which one to enter. Reading one's name on a cubby to place personal items represents another natural reading opportunity for a young child. Likewise, adding one's name to a center before engaging in the activity there by affixing a sticky-backed self-photograph represents another way to write. Putting materials away into labeled (and pictured) cabinets or shelves could serve as a reading opportunity at any age.

Students with significant cognitive and multiple disabilities may not be accessing conventional print or engaging in conventional writing; however, they can still benefit from typical literacy activities if some accommodations have been made. For example, when a fifth-grade class is instructed to spend 20 minutes reading a book of their choice, the student with significant cognitive disabilities in this class also has the option of selecting reading material and then either listening to a teacher or paraprofessional read it or use a switch to activate a cassette recorder and hear a taped version. The student is offered age-appropriate magazines, comics, or picture books, or specifically created photograph books from home. Table 3.1 represents opportunities that naturally arise throughout the school day for a middle school student having severe and multiple disabilities.

When taking advantage of literacy opportunities that exist naturally throughout each day, emphasis should be placed on the interactive nature of these opportunities. Instead of just passively reading to students, showing them pictures or having them watch others engaged in literacy activities, students need to be actively engaged in the process. Greater meaning will be attributed to literacy experiences when students can play a more active and involved role. Koppenhaver, Erickson, and Skotko (2001) studied the impact of interactive strategies used by mothers of four young girls (ages 3–7 years) with Rett syndrome during storybook reading. These four children were given augmentative communication

Table 3.1. Natural literacy learning opportunities for a middle school student

Read lunch pictorial menu

Read restroom signs (universal icons)

Read highlighted name on papers

Read posters in classrooms

Read pictures in all texts

Read slide shows and videos shown in class

Sign name with a signature stamp

Read computer screen

Interact socially with the aid of photo albums with messages

aids and were supported by their mothers through specific questions, comments, and wait time to use their augmentative aids. Greater involvement was reported when mothers responded to their children's attempt and expected them to interact. These same strategies should be used by school personnel and classmates in efforts to make literacy less passive and more meaningful and interesting.

Creating Meaningful Literacy Opportunities

Multiple ways exist to create meaningful literacy experiences for students with significant disabilities across the school day (see Downing, 2005). The need to create meaningful literacy experiences for students exists when insufficient opportunities appear naturally. Developing unique materials and adding them to activities increase the number of opportunities for literacy learning to occur.

The use of a daily planner or schedule for each student offers one such opportunity. Such schedules can be used several times each day and, depending on how they are developed, can engage the student in reading, writing, and math skills (see Downing, 2005). Downing and Peckham-Hardin (2001) described several different types of schedules for students with significant disabilities and the many skills that can be taught through consistent use. Not only does a personal schedule help the student transition from activity to activity, but knowing the day's activities provides support for reading and deciphering the symbols in the schedule. Schedules can be constructed with pictures, photographs, small objects, and parts of objects depending on the needs of individual students. These symbols *always* should be labeled with print (and braille where indicated) to allow for the development of more advanced literacy skills. See Figure 3.3 for an example of a daily schedule designed for a student who is learning to read tactile symbols. Students can read pictorial or tactile information and then learn to read single letters or words in print, or even short phrases as their skills develop. Schedules should grow with the student and should not remain static. They can be constructed quite simply for students just beginning to understand concrete symbols and become more complex and challenging as the student acquires greater symbolic understanding (see Figure 3.3).

Students with significant and multiple disabilities who are just beginning to understand symbols often have a hard time understanding and retaining directions. People without disabilities can write down directions and refer to them to

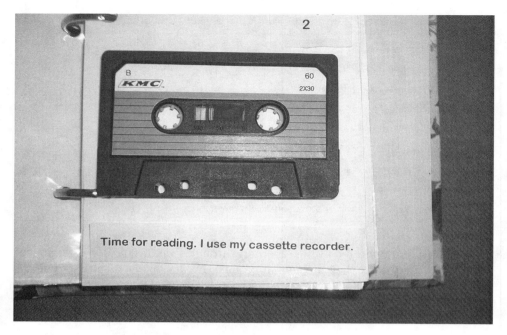

Figure 3.3. Sample daily schedule or planner for a student who is learning to read tactile symbols.

aid memory retention. However, reading such directions would be well beyond the ability level of those students targeted in this chapter.

To help students understand expectations and to provide an opportunity to engage in reading, directions or steps to tasks can be created using simple pictures, photographs, or objects and parts of objects. Students can read the information to help them understand and participate in different activities. Following completion of each step in the activity, they can engage in writing by checking off, covering up, or removing the step. For example, a high school student who is just beginning to learn the meaning of some pictures follows the pictorial/written steps to develop his film during his photography class. A photograph has been taken of an item that best represents each main step.

The resemblance between the photograph and the item is very clear, making it easier for the student to recognize. Photographs are placed in a column with directions, and clear contact paper covers all steps. As the student is assisted to perform each step, he is taught to make a mark over the photograph with a black marker. In this way he is reading—learning to comprehend and to understand the importance of writing (e.g., checking it off).

For a student who cannot yet understand pictorial information (or for students unable to perceive visual information) objects and parts of objects can be used. For example, a fifth grader with severe and multiple disabilities uses an object direction board to guide him through an art activity. The first step is represented by a number one, a raised dot for one, and by a part of the art medium being used (e.g., clay or fabric or wire). The directions might be written, *Get the clay* or *Get clay*. The step of obtaining a work apron to protect clothing is represented by the end of an apron tie, which is placed next to the numeral two and two raised dots. Even though the student cannot see (or is unable to decode text), print directions always are added. Print clarifies for others supporting this student and may be recognized as a sight word eventually by those students able to perceive print. The ultimate goal of such literacy learning is to support increased independence and involvement by the student in meaningful and valued activities (Agran, King-Sears, Wehmeyer, & Copeland, 2003). Many different activities or portions of activities can be represented symbolically to provide the student with literacy access to a familiar routine that occurs frequently. Utilization of these familiar routines provides a practical means of supporting literacy learning for students learning about symbolic representation.

Another way to create literacy opportunities for a student with very complex and multiple disabilities is to retell activities that the student has participated in using photographs, drawings, and/or parts of objects used in these activities. Language experience stories are not new to the field (Neuman, 1999; Wood, Lasker, Siegel-Causey, Beukelman, & Ball, 1998). The extreme relevance to the individual student is obvious. The student can access these documented experiences during social times such as lunch or recess and also during any time of the day when students have free time or make-up work time. Because the student has participated in the activity, the photographs, drawings, and representative items should serve to help the student recall the sequence of events. The student then is encouraged to read and reread these experiences with support from more capable readers. Students can be supported to write (by sequencing) using such materials as well.

Systematic Instruction

Teachers in the area of severe and multiple disabilities may need to learn specific strategies to provide literacy instruction for their students. These students do not need to be taught literacy in a qualitatively different way than their peers without disabilities (Erickson, Koppenhaver, Yoder, & Nance, 1997). Instead, quality literacy instruction has application for all students, with attention given to the unique needs of students who have severe disabilities, such as the need for adapted materials and the adapted manner in which the student conveys understanding.

Typically, students with significant disabilities require direct and systematic instruction to learn most skills (Justice & Pullen, 2003; Rowland & Schweigert, 2000). Literacy skills involving communication, listening and understanding, reading, and writing all require carefully planned instruction for the student to be successful. Whatever literacy skills the student has need to be recognized and systematic instruction should be used to build on these skills. Such instruction involves the following components: identify and define the desired behavior, determine the shaping procedure, fade prompts, and measure the effectiveness of the intervention. Furthermore, such instruction requires a team approach. Building on the student's current strengths and the demands of the given task, the team needs to work together to determine the most effective means of helping the student acquire the desired skill(s).

Identify and Define the Desired Behavior   Before instruction can occur, the exact behavior(s) must be clearly identified and behaviorally defined so that all team members know the desired outcome. Is the student to scan three different pictorial/written messages on an augmentative communication device and make a selection? Is the student to identify her name (which is in red) from three name stamps in order to sign her name to papers? Is the student to answer a comprehension question related to a story by feeling two objects and choosing the correct one? Is the student to listen to a spelling word and look at the correct pictorial option from a field of three? The specific behaviors identified should reflect the desired goals of family and student and be related to state standards as well. Defining the target behavior operationally will help all team members to facilitate the behavior whenever it might occur throughout the day (e.g., recognizing the bathroom sign for boys by using the correct door, recognizing one's name by pointing to it). The operational definition also aids in the collection of data to measure accurate progress.

Determine the Shaping Procedure   Once the target behavior has been carefully identified and described, the team's next responsibility is to develop a plan of how to shape the behavior so that it will be demonstrated by the student when it is needed. This plan should be developed so that all team members will feel comfortable with the procedure and will be able to implement it in a very similar manner.

The shaping procedure will contain the prompts and sequence of prompts used to help the student acquire the target behavior. A recommended practice in the field is to avoid overprompting or manipulation of a student (Billingsley, 2003; Billingsley & Kelley, 1994). Prompts are only used as needed with the intent to draw the student's attention to the naturally occurring stimuli (e.g., literacy materials). Drawing attention to the natural stimulus will involve the first set of prompts. For example, a high school student who is blind and nonverbal is being asked to check her daily schedule to see what is next. The target behavior for this student involves placing at least one of her hands on the open page before her, feeling the object that represents the current activity, turning the page, and feeling the object that represents the next activity. The first part of that target behavior involves getting her to place at least one hand on top of her schedule book that is opened to the correct position when she hears the question, "Where do we go now?" If she does not do this movement within 5 seconds of the question (verbal prompt), she will be told that the current class is over (represented by the object on the page in front of her) and that we need to find out what comes next. Another wait time of 5 seconds will be given and then the schedule page will be tapped and the instructor will ask, "Where's your schedule?" If her hand does not go to her schedule, the page will be tapped again while she is given a forward motion at the elbow and asked again to find her schedule. If this does not produce the desired response, the book will be brought to her and she will be guided under her forearm until she places her hand on the representative item. This type of prompting sequence will be carefully spelled out for all team members so that consistency is ensured and the student is not overmanipulated to perform. See Figure 3.4 for an example of an instructional procedure used to teach a student to engage in pictorial writing.

Fade Prompts

Once a prompting strategy has been used successfully and the student is beginning to demonstrate some progress in skill acquisition, a systematic fading procedure should be implemented (Billingsley, 2003). With increased fading of supportive prompts, the student can demonstrate increased mastery of certain

Student: Cassie
Grade: 4
Activity: Journal writing
Support: Occupational therapist (OT)
Scenario: The fourth-grade teacher has asked her students to spend 15 minutes writing in their daily journals. Students are to work independently but can help one another with spelling, grammar, and punctuation.

The OT is working with Cassie in the classroom. Some of Cassie's objectives include handling items, recognizing pictorial information, modified pointing to indicate decisions using pictures, and responding to questions.

Because Cassie does not use speech and is just beginning to understand some pictures, Cassie's mother has written a note to school describing their weekend. Cassie is writing about the weekend activities.

Instructional prompting sequence for the OT

- Presents her with two pictures (only one is correct and relevant)
- Asks her which one she did on the weekend
- Waits to the count of 5
- Repeats the question while pointing to each picture and stating what it is
- Waits to the count of 5
- Moves each picture closer to Cassie and asks if she did one or the other as she moves each picture
- Waits to the count of 5
- Guides Cassie at her forearm toward the correct answer and tells her what she did ("You went swimming!")
- Supports at Cassie's wrist while Cassie works to pick up the correct picture
- Points to outlined shape on the journal page
- Waits to the count of 5
- Taps the outlined shape where the picture goes and tells her where the picture goes
- Writes the sentence, "I went swimming" under the picture and reads it back to Cassie

Figure 3.4.   Instructional procedure for teaching a student to write with pictures.

skills, and so a fading procedure needs to be determined at the onset of instruction and then modified accordingly.

Fading procedures could involve providing less physical support to perform a skill (e.g., touching a picture), increasing the wait time before a desired response, increasing the number of options provided, or reducing the number of verbal cues. Any of these procedures could reflect improved skill acquisition and the need for less support. For example, a fourth-grade student with severe and multiple disabilities is being taught to first select and then make use of different colored markers to create colorful designs on paper that reflect his interpretation of a particular story read in class. He does this while his classmates without disabilities write a reflective short paper. Initially, this student needs to be physically supported at the wrist and elbow to make marks (write) on his paper. The fading procedure involves gradually removing the support at his wrist to the forearm, then to the elbow, and then fading that support to just a tap on his elbow once the chosen marker has been positioned in his hand. Eventually, the markers and the blank paper may serve as a sufficient and natural stimulus to produce the desired response.

Care must be taken regarding fading procedures to ensure that the student is receiving the necessary support while acquiring the skill, but not too much support so that the student is not challenged. Fading too quickly could result in the student never reaching desired fluency. Fading too slowly could result in the student becoming overly dependent on others to perform the desired skill. Careful observation of the student while he or she is engaged in targeted literacy activities should assist in the determination of an effective fading procedure.

Measure the Effectiveness of the Intervention

Schools and teachers are accountable for student learning. NCLB states that a goal for all children is to be reading on grade level. Whether or not all students reach this goal, all students have the right to be taught as many literacy skills as possible. Regardless of the severity of their disabilities, students with significant disabilities should be expected to learn and to demonstrate progress toward meaningful goals (Ford, Davern, & Schnorr, 2001).

Ensuring that students experience literacy is a beginning step, but this is insufficient to ensure that students are learning and making progress toward desired goals. Specific skills that indicate student progress must be identified for each student. Individualized education program (IEP) goals and objectives related to literacy need to be clearly stated so that the target skill is measurable. Vague IEP objectives that do not clearly relate to state standards in literacy should be avoided. Furthermore, active engagement by the student is the overall goal, and IEP goals and objectives should reflect this. Passive goals, such as, "Leighton will be read to twice each day for at least 20 minutes each time," do not state what the student is to learn. In addition, it is questionable if the student even needs to be awake for mastery to occur. A more active objective might read, "When read to by a peer or teacher who pauses after reading each page, Leighton will make a noise or movement within 5 seconds of the page being read to indicate the need to have the next page read. She will do this a minimum of 4 times per class period reading for 10 class periods." When the target behavior is described, the conditions are stated for the behavior to occur, and the criteria are provided for mastery of the objective, data can be collected and progress measured.

Data Collection

Routine and systematic collection of data is critical if progress toward literacy goals is to be evaluated. This does not mean that data will be collected for every trial that the student is given, but that regular probes are conducted routinely so that information pertaining to the student's progress can be attained. Data collection should not be difficult or time consuming for team members.

The target literacy behavior needs to be clearly described as well as the conditions under which it will occur. Criterion for mastery should make sense given the target behavior and make it possible to objectively determine whether mastery has occurred. Data sheets can be kept with the materials that the student will use, and the sheets should be somewhere easily accessible for all staff to use. In addition to ready access to data collection sheets, the actual process of using the form should be clear and should not interfere with instruction. Figure 3.5 provides an example of a data sheet for the objective stated earlier for Leighton. Information is collected on the actual target behavior (e.g., indicating that a page should be turned) as well as contextual data (e.g., the story being read). Such contextual information can provide insight into student interest and motivation (see Figure 3.5).

Objective: When read to by a peer or teacher who pauses after reading each page, Leighton will make a noise or movement within 5 seconds of the page being read to indicate the need to have the next page read. She will do this a minimum of 4 times per class period reading for 10 class periods.

Key: M = movement, V = vocalization/sound, — = no response within 5 seconds (tally the number of opportunities as the denominator)

Date	10/5	10/7	10/8	10/9	
Story: *The Boy from the Cay* Read by: Susan (peer)	MM ——— 111111 (opportunities)	MV ——— 11111	V ——— 1111	VVM ——— 111111	

Figure 3.5.   Sample data collection form for an eighth-grade student in language arts.

Team Approach

Perhaps of greatest importance is the need to work as a collaborative team in support of enhanced literacy learning. Skills involved in working as an effective collaborative team need to be taught and practiced by all team members in order to avoid disjointed service delivery. Typically, educational teams are composed of team members who have received different training and have accumulated different experiences. Each person comes to the team with different cultural values and beliefs regarding the education of students in general, and students with severe disabilities in particular. Learning how to work together to keep the best interests of the student in the forefront requires considerable attention (Cloninger, 2004; Hunt, Soto, Maier, Muller, & Goetz, 2002). As noted by professionals and paraprofessionals at a fully inclusive elementary school, learning to collaborate and developing the process of teaming took considerable effort despite having the full support of the principal and other team members (Downing, Spencer, & Cavallaro, 2004).

Educational teams supporting students with severe and multiple disabilities usually are composed of a relatively large number of individuals representing many diverse disciplines (e.g., occupational therapy, speech and language services, physical therapy, vision services). Learning how to work with so many different professionals as well as family members requires specific skills and training that will probably need to be ongoing. Research is needed to determine how each of these team members can best contribute to a student's IEP, especially pertaining to the acquisition of literacy skills.

SUMMARY

If we are truly to leave no child behind, then literacy instruction must be provided to all children, regardless of labels and negative connotations pertaining to those labels. This chapter has attempted to clarify what literacy instruction can mean to those students who often bear the most challenging types of disabilities and who are often perceived by others as being unable to engage in any kind of academic instruction. General strategies and considerations have been presented to serve as guidelines for school personnel and family members to support the literacy learning of their children. These guidelines include raising expectations for all students and maintaining the belief that literacy is truly for everyone, modifying and making literacy materials accessible for the unique abilities and needs of students, following the interests of students, and engaging in systematic and direct instruction of literacy skills for students who struggle to acquire them incidentally.

A critical aspect of this chapter is the integral relationship that exists between communicative interactions and literacy learning. As students with severe and complex needs begin to recognize and acquire basic symbols to use during communication exchanges, these same symbols can then be used for literacy instruction. Consequently, increased interactions and experiences are needed to support the development of enhanced literacy skills for these students.

Although some of the suggestions provided to increase literacy learning for students with the most complex disabilities have been substantiated by research in the field, others still require this validation. For instance, research is needed that will examine the best manner of addressing unique literacy needs without removing the student from typical literacy environments and engaging in isolated and developmentally sequenced skills. Certainly, adapting the core curriculum becomes somewhat more challenging as the student progresses through the school system. Teachers of students in secondary schools will need research on the most effective adaptations of highly abstract subject matter to address literacy skills in order to make the material applicable and meaningful for students with severe intellectual and multiple impairments. As Zascavage and Keefe (2004) conclude from their study, personnel preparation programs will need to accept the challenge of instructing teachers in the most effective ways to address the literacy needs of those students who have traditionally been overlooked.

Research also is needed to determine what family members and teachers consider to be literacy experiences for students. How are these individuals interpreting different experiences that hold potential for literacy learning? Given the answers to this question, further investigation is needed to explore how these care providers and educators are making literacy activities accessible to students with different significant needs and how they are facilitating the development of literacy skills on a daily basis.

The suggestions presented in this chapter concerning literacy opportunities and experiences can serve as a catalyst for educators to be more inclusive with regard to their understanding of what literacy means for students who may just be beginning to learn about symbolic representation. These students need the most creative and individualized support to recognize and make sense of the world around them. They may not talk, or walk, or move their bodies well, or understand abstract symbols, but they can be included in our literacy goals for all students if we maintain high expectations, a commitment to learning, and an inclusive attitude.

REFERENCES

Adams, M.J. (1990). *Beginning to read.* Cambridge, MA: Harvard University Press.

Agran, M., King-Sears, M.E., Wehmeyer, M.L., & Copeland, S.R. (2003). *Teachers' guides to inclusive practices: Student-directed learning.* Baltimore: Paul H. Brookes Publishing Co.

Arthur, M. (2003). Socio-communicative variables and behavior states in students with profound and multiple disabilities: Descriptive data from school settings. *Education and Training in Developmental Disabilities, 38,* 200–219.

Beukelman, D.R., & Mirenda, P. (2005). *Augmentative and alternative communication: Supporting children and adults with complex communication needs* (3rd ed.). Baltimore: Paul H. Brookes Publishing Co.

Billingsley, F. (2003). Principle and practices for instructing students with significant needs in inclusive settings. In D.L. Ryndak & S. Alper (Eds.), *Curriculum and instruction for students with significant disabilities in inclusive settings* (2nd ed., pp. 362–381). Boston: Allyn & Bacon.

Billingsley, F.F., & Kelley, B. (1994). An examination of the acceptability of instructional practices for students with severe disabilities in general education settings. *Journal of the Association for Persons with Severe Handicaps, 19,* 75–83.

Blischak, D.M. (1995). Thomas the writer: Case study of a child with severe physical, speech, and visual impairments. *Language, Speech, and Hearing Services in Schools, 26,* 11–20.

Browder, D.M., Fallin, K., Davis, S., & Karvonen, M. (2003). Consideration of what may influence student outcomes on alternate assessment. *Education and Training in Developmental Disabilities, 38,* 255–270.

Browder, D.M., Spooner, F., Algozzine, R., Ahlgrim-Delzell, L., Flowers, C., & Karvonen, M. (2003). What we know and need to know about alternate assessment. *Exceptional Children, 70,* 45–61.

Cloninger, C.J. (2004). Designing collaborative educational services. In F.P. Orelove, D. Sobsey, & R.K. Silberman (Eds.), *Educating children with multiple disabilities: A collaborative approach* (4th ed., pp. 1–30). Baltimore: Paul H. Brookes Publishing Co.

Cress, C.J. (2002). Expanding children's early augmented behaviors to support symbolic development. In J. Reichle, D.R. Beukelman, & J.C. Light (Eds.), *Exemplary practices for beginning communicators: Implications for AAC* (pp. 219–272). Baltimore: Paul H. Brookes Publishing Co.

Cunningham, J.W. (1999). How we can achieve best practices in literacy instruction. In L.B. Gambrell, L.M. Morrow, S.B. Neuman, & M. Pressley (Eds.), *Best practices in literacy instruction* (pp. 34–48). New York: Guilford Press.

DeTemple, J.M. (2001). Parents and children reading books together. In D.K. Dickinson & P.O. Tabors (Eds.), *Beginning literacy with language: Young children learning at home and school* (pp. 31–52). Baltimore: Paul H. Brookes Publishing Co.

Downing, J.E. (2005). *Teaching literacy to students with significant disabilities: Strategies for the K-12 inclusive classroom.* Thousand Oaks, CA: Corwin Press.

Downing, J.E., & Chen, D. (2003). Using tactile strategies with students who are blind and have severe disabilities. *Teaching Exceptional Children, 36*(2), 56–60.

Downing, J.E., & Peckham-Hardin, K. (2001). Daily schedules: A helpful learning tool. *Teaching Exceptional Children, 33*(3), 62–68.

Downing, J.E., Spencer, S., & Cavallaro, C. (2004). The development of an inclusive charter elementary school: Lessons learned. *Research and Practice for Persons with Severe Disabilities, 29,* 11–24.

Dunst, C.J., Hamby, D., Trivette, C.M., Raab, M., & Bruder, M.B. (2000). Everyday family and community life and children's naturally occurring learning opportunities. *Journal of Early Intervention, 23,* 151–164.

Erickson, K.A., Koppenhaver, D.A., Yoder, D.E., & Nance, J. (1997). Integrated communication and literacy instruction for a child with multiple disabilities. *Focus on Autism and Other Developmental Disabilities, 12,* 142–150.

Fisher, D., & Kennedy, C.H. (2001). Differentiated instruction for diverse middle school students. In C.H. Kennedy & D. Fisher (Eds.), *Inclusive middle schools* (pp. 61–72). Baltimore: Paul H. Brookes Publishing Co.

Ford, A., Davern, L., & Schnorr, R. (2001). Learners with significant disabilities: Curriculum relevance in an era of standards-based reform. *Remedial and Special Education, 22,* 214–222.

Fossett, B., Smith, V., & Mirenda, P. (2003). Facilitating oral language and literacy development during general education activities. In D.L. Ryndak & S. Alper (Eds.), *Curriculum and instruction for students with significant disabilities in inclusive settings* (pp. 173–205). Boston: Allyn & Bacon.

Gambrell, L.B., & Mazzoni, S.A. (1999). Principles of best practice: Finding the common ground. In L.B. Gambrell, L.M. Morrow, S.B. Neuman, & M. Pressley (Eds.), *Best practices in literacy instruction* (pp. 11–21). New York: Guilford Press.

Goals 2000: Educate America Act of 1994, PL 103-227, 20 U.S.C. §§ 5801 *et seq.*

Gurry, S.E., & Larkin, A.S. (1999). Literacy learning abilities of children with developmental disabilities: What do we know? *Currents in Literacy.* Retrieved June 17, 2003, from Lesley University, Hood Children's Literacy Project, http://www.lesley.edu/academic_centers/hood/currents/v2n1/gurry_larkin.html

Heller, K.W., Fredrick, L., Dykes, M.K., Best, S., & Cohen, E. (1999). A national perspective of competencies for teachers of individuals with physical and health disabilities. *Exceptional Children, 65,* 219–234.

Huer, M.B. (2000). Examining perceptions of graphic symbols across cultures: Preliminary study of the impact of culture/ethnicity. *Augmentative and Alternative Communication, 16,* 180–185.

Hunt, P., Soto, G., Maier, J., Muller, E., & Goetz, L. (2002). Collaborative teaming to support students with augmentative and alternative communication needs in general education classrooms. *Augmentative and Alternative Communication, 18,* 20–35.

Justice, L.M., & Pullen, P.C. (2003). Promising interventions for promoting emergent literacy skills: Three evidence-based approaches. *Topics in Early Childhood Special Education, 23,* 99–113.

Kaderavek, J., & Justice, L.M. (2002). Shared storybook reading as an intervention context: Practices and potential pitfalls. *American Journal of Speech-Language Pathology, 11,* 395–406.

Katims, D.S. (2001). Literacy assessment of students with mental retardation: An exploratory investigation. *Education and Training in Mental Retardation and Developmental Disabilities, 36,* 363–372.

Kliewer, C. (1995). Young children's communication and literacy: A qualitative study of language in the inclusive preschool. *Mental Retardation, 33,* 143–152.

Kliewer, C. (1998). Citizenship in the literate community: An ethnography of children with Down syndrome and the written word. *Exceptional Children, 64,* 167–180.

Kliewer, C., & Biklen, D. (2001). "School's not really a place for reading": A research synthesis of the literate lives of students with severe disabilities. *Journal of the Association for Persons with Severe Handicaps, 26,* 1–12.

Kliewer, C., & Landis, D. (1999). Individualizing literacy instruction for young children with moderate to severe disabilities. *Exceptional Children, 66,* 85–100.

Koppenhaver, D.A. (2000). Literacy in AAC: What should be written on the envelope we push? *Augmentative and Alternative Communication, 16,* 270–279.

Koppenhaver, D.A., Erickson, K.A., & Skotko, B.G. (2001). Supporting communication of girls with Rett syndrome and their mothers in storybook reading. *International Journal of Disability, Development, and Education, 48,* 395–410.

Lewis, S., & Tolla, J. (2003). Creating and using tactile experience books for young children with visual impairments. *Teaching Exceptional Children, 35*(3), 22–28.

Light, J., & Kelford Smith, A. (1993). The home literacy experiences of preschoolers who use augmentative communication systems and their nondisabled peers. *Augmentative and Alternative Communication, 9,* 10–25.

Lohrmann-O'Rourke, S., & Browder, D.M. (1998). Empirically based methods to assess the preferences of individuals with severe disabilities. *American Journal of Mental Retardation, 103,* 146–161.

Mainger, R.W., Deshler, D., Coleman, M.R., Kozleski, E., & Rodriguez-Walling, M. (2003). To ensure the learning of every child with a disability. *Focus on Exceptional Children, 35*(5), 1–12.

Marvin, C. (1994). Home literacy experiences of preschool children with single and multiple disorder. *Topics in Early Childhood Special Education, 14,* 436–454.

Mirenda, P., & Erickson, K.A. (2000). Augmentative communication and literacy. In A.M. Wetherby & B.M. Prizant (Eds.), *Autism spectrum disorders: A transactional developmental perspective* (pp. 333–367). Baltimore: Paul H. Brookes Publishing Co.

Moes, D.R. (1998). Integrating choice-making opportunities within teacher-assigned academic tasks to facilitate the performance of children with autism. *Journal of the Association for Persons with Severe Handicaps, 23,* 319–328.

Neuman, S.B. (1999). Creating continuity in early literacy: Linking home and school with a culturally responsive approach. In L.B. Gambrell, L.M. Morrow, S.B. Neuman, & M. Pressley (Eds.), *Best practices in literacy instruction* (pp. 258–270). New York: Guilford Press.

No Child Left Behind Act of 2001, PL 107-110, 115 Stat. 1425, 20 U.S.C. §§ 6301 *et seq.*

Rowland, C., & Schweigert, P. (2000). Tangible symbols, tangible outcomes. *Augmentative and Alternative Communication, 16,* 61–78, 205.

Ryndak, D.L., Morrison, A.P., & Sommerstein, L. (1999). Literacy before and after inclusion in general education settings: A case study. *Journal of the Association for Persons with Severe Handicaps, 24,* 5–22.

Sulzby, E., & Teale, W.H. (1991). Emergent literacy. In R. Barr, M.L. Kamil, P. Mosenthal, & P.D. Pearson (Eds.), *Handbook of reading research* (Vol. 2, pp. 727–757). White Plains, NY: Longman.

Swartz, M.K., & Hendricks, C.G. (2000). Factors that influence the book selection process of students with special needs. *Journal of Adolescent and Adult Literacy, 43,* 608–618.

Wehmeyer, M.L. (2003). Defining mental retardation and ensuring access to the general curriculum. *Education and Training in Developmental Disabilities, 38,* 271–282.

Wood, L.A., Lasker, J., Siegel-Causey, E., Beukelman, D.R., & Ball, L. (1998). Input framework for augmentative and alternative communication. *Augmentative and Alternative Communication, 14,* 261–267.

Zascavage, V.T., & Keefe, C.H. (2004). Students with severe speech and physical impairments: Opportunity barriers to literacy. *Focus on Autism and Other Developmental Disabilities, 19,* 223–234.

Chapter 4

From Sight Words to Emerging Literacy

Diane M. Browder, Ginevra Courtade-Little,
Shawnee Wakeman, and Robert J. Rickelman

When Karla began first grade, she had no academic individualized education program (IEP) objectives. Instead, her previous IEP team had focused on her need to acquire a system of communication (she was nonverbal), to become consistent in toilet training, to learn to feed herself, and several other important life skill goals. Her teacher, Ms. Ramirez, was convinced that all students should have the opportunity to gain literacy skills. She began with Karla's interest in Disney movies. She found a book of stories based on these movies and began to read it with Karla. Karla showed keen interest in the stories by laughing, clapping, and pointing to the pictures. Ms. Ramirez then developed a picture communication board for the main characters of the story (e.g., Woody, Buzz Lightyear, Seth, Andy). As she read the story, she had Karla point to the picture on her communication board as well as on the page in the book. Next, she decided to ask Karla comprehension questions after reading the story. "Who was Andy's first favorite toy?" Karla pointed to *Woody*. She then asked, "When did Buzz Lightyear arrive?" Excitedly, Karla began to blow on the picture of the birthday cake as if blowing out the candles. "Yes!" Ms. Ramirez replied. "Buzz Lightyear was Andy's birthday present." In just a few months, Karla had begun to use picture/word symbols to show her understanding of a story. Her mother was delighted when the IEP team met again to discuss how to teach Karla to read.[1]

Often when students such as Karla, who is nonverbal and has many life skill needs, begin to show the ability to learn symbols, the instructional approach is to teach sight words that relate to activities of daily living. These sight words can be an important tool for students, allowing them to become more independent in their home, job, and community environments. Unfortunately, sight-word instruction is sometimes the only reading instruction students with significant cognitive disabilities receive. Like all first graders, Karla needs the opportunity to gain broad literacy skills and to have the opportunity to experience the joy of reading. Older students also can benefit from being exposed to the literature that enriches our culture, such as poetry, plays, short stories, and nonfiction. This chapter provides guidelines for teaching sight words that are useful to daily living, but also

---

[1] We express our appreciation to Ms. Bree Jimenez, teacher, Charlotte-Mecklenburg Schools, Charlotte, NC; and doctoral student, Special Education Program, UNC Charlotte, for sharing this reading exercise that was used in her class.

provides a broader approach to literacy that can be used to help students participate in diverse reading activities.

THE GOAL OF LITERACY FOR ALL CHILDREN

Before describing the specific guidelines for promoting literacy for students such as Karla, it is important to consider what educators know about how children learn to read. The National Reading Panel (NRP, 2000), in response to a charge from Congress to assess the status of research-based knowledge in teaching children to read, identified five components of reading: phonemic awareness, phonics, vocabulary, fluency, and comprehension. Although the NRP's findings were the source of some debate (Allington, 2002; Shanahan, 2003), most experts would agree that these focal areas are all important elements in learning to read.

How these elements are best taught and learned also has been the source of many debates. Multiple learning models have been outlined to explain how children learn to read (Ruddell, Ruddell, & Singer, 1994). Pearson and Stephens (1994) presented a history of more than 30 years of research in literacy, discussing the shifting focal points and beliefs about how best to teach and learn reading. They define reading as ". . . a complex, orchestrated, constructive process through which individuals make meaning" (p. 35). Amid this complexity, there are linguistic, cognitive, social, and political elements that come into play, causing much debate about how children learn to read.

In this sometimes confusing environment, epitomized by the "great debate"—pitting teaching phonics against meaning-based methodology—practitioners struggle to make decisions about best practices. There is, however, some general agreement about models of learning to read that have been consistently supported by research over the years. For instance, Adams (1990) summarized consistent research documenting that phonics instruction can be integrated easily into more holistic methodologies to foster skilled reading. A more detailed model of the stages of learning to read was proposed by Chall (1996). This model, which outlines developmental reading stages for preschool through adult readers, provides a good background for a general understanding of how reading ability might be developed. Basically, Chall states that there are six stages along a developmental continuum (Heilman, Blair, & Rupley, 2002). According to Chall, stages can overlap and are not fixed by grade level (e.g., a student could be at Phase 0 yet be in high school), although they can be seen as representative of abilities typically manifested within a particular age-level range. Therefore, the age guidelines presented in Table 4.1 are typical indicators rather than strict levels of the development of reading.

Emergent literacy, then, can be defined in broadest terms as the process of becoming literate, beginning at birth and developing throughout a lifetime. How this ability develops and how quickly each reader progresses through each developmental stage can vary considerably. However, because these broad phases are not very helpful in terms of how to best foster this skill in learners, a more focused definition is still needed.

Sulzby and Barnhart (1992) developed a more functional definition of emergent literacy. They stated that emergent literacy involves the reading and writing behaviors of children that precede and then develop into conventional literacy. They agree with Chall that this process is developmental and can be applied to all children. However, the success of development for any one child is greatly

Table 4.1.   Chall's stages of reading development

Stage 0 (Pre-reading, birth to age 6): The learner "pretends" to read, following adult role models. They tend to rely heavily on pictures for understanding the story context. They can name most/all letters of the alphabet, along with some words/signs from environmental print. Being able to identify their name is a typical first step. They can retell a story with some accuracy after listening to it being read.

Stage 1 (Initial reading/decoding, ages 6–7): The learner develops letter–sound relationships and is able to read high-frequency words by sight. They can sound out one-syllable, phonetically regular words. The focus at this stage is on decoding rather than meaning.

Stage 2 (Confirmation and fluency, ages 7–8): The focus shifts from identifying words individually and moves to becoming a more fluid, fluent reader. The reader recognizes word patterns (common prefixes, suffixes, and roots) and reads by combining elements of decoding and sight words within a context of making meaning.

Stage 3 (Reading to learn the new, ages 8–14): There is a major shift from learning to read to reading to learn. Reading is a now used as a tool to acquire new knowledge and to experience new feelings and attitudes. The focus for the reader is generally on a single viewpoint (self-centered).

Stage 4 (Multiple viewpoints, ages 14–18): There is another major shift from single to multiple points of view. The reader can analyze his or her reading and think critically about ideas presented in text.

Stage 5 (Construction and reconstruction, ages 18 and older): The reader can make value judgments about written material at high levels of abstraction. The reader can critically synthesize the works of other writers and form his or her own opinion based on facts, at times inventing new points of view that are different from those read.

Source: Chall, 1996.

influenced by literacy events in their lives. For instance, some children come to school already knowing how to read. They have experienced rich literacy activities before entering school, provided by parents and other adults who have served as appropriate role models of literate adults. These children are actively involved in reading signs and symbols in grocery stores, on streets, and in the surrounding community. They are actively engaged in art and play activities where they use early forms of writing to label drawings and pictures. They have "read" many books with others, often mimicking adult models, and know the conventions of print—how to hold a book, how to differentiate words from pictures, what terms such as *page* and *word* mean. Other children, however, come from settings where there are few such experiences, and they generally experience more difficulties and delays in learning to read. In fact, a national panel of experts serving on a presidential commission to study reading research in the 1980s (Anderson, Hiebert, Scott, & Wilkinson, 1985) determined that one of the biggest influences on whether a child will become a successful reader was whether they had been consistently read to before entering school.

Koppenhaver (1993) noted that students with disabilities often have had fewer opportunities to engage in literacy activities. Sometimes children with physical, cognitive, and sensory challenges have not had these early literacy experiences because of both the challenge of making materials accessible and prior low expectations about students with significant cognitive disabilities learning to read. Sometimes they have had these experiences in early childhood programs but are then shifted into a nonacademic setting for their school program. Although students may not learn to read per se, they may benefit from acquiring emergent literacy skills. For example, students who are able to interpret meaning from pictures and key words can enjoy and gain information from magazines. Students who can use pictures to retell a familiar story may gain important communication skills.

EMERGENT LITERACY AND FUNCTIONAL READING: COMPATIBLE GOALS?

Whereas the goals of emergent literacy are to promote experiences with book and print that provide a foundation for learning to reading, functional reading involves being able to recognize specific sight words and use them in daily routines. Browder (2001) defined the characteristics of functional reading as 1) the acquisition of specific sight words that have immediate functional use, 2) an alternative way to learn reading skills when literacy is not being achieved, and 3) a way to gain quick success in reading that may encourage the future pursuit of literacy. Numerous studies demonstrate that students with moderate and significant mental retardation can learn sight words (Browder & Xin, 1998). Intervention studies have illustrated how students can use sight words to perform daily living skills such as cooking (Collins, Branson, & Hall, 1995) and to read product warning labels (Collins & Griffen, 1996). Individuals with mental retardation have also used sight words for self-instruction on the job (Browder & Minarovic, 2000).

In contrast, a sight-word-only approach has several important limitations. First, students can learn to name sight words with little to no comprehension of the functional use of this skill. Browder and Xin (1998) noted that most studies on sight words have not measured comprehension or functional use. Both Conners (1992) and Katims (2000) also noted that reading instruction in general education focuses on gaining meaning from print versus simply identifying individual words. Thus, a second limitation of a sight-word-only approach is that it does not teach words in a larger language context. Joseph and Seery (2004) noted that a functional reading approach uses a whole-word approach without phonetic analysis. In contrast, Groff, Lapp, and Flood (1998) noted the need for explicit phonics instruction for students who struggle with literacy. In a review of the literature, Joseph and Seery (2004) found that students with mental retardation have the potential to learn phonics skills, but research studies have rarely focused on this critical component of learning to read.

Given these limitations, should functional reading no longer be an appropriate goal? It would be unfortunate to disregard the success students have had in learning sight words and their usefulness to tasks of daily living. The authors take the perspective that it is possible to embed sight-word instruction within a broader approach to literacy. There are three possible options for synthesizing sight words with literacy instruction. The first is to provide two concurrent forms of reading instruction—one that focuses on promoting literacy and the other on the systematic instruction of sight words in the context of daily living as a "safeguard" for having some functional reading if the student does not learn to read. A second option is to provide extensive literacy instruction in the elementary grades and transition to a functional reading approach if progress is not made by late middle school or high school. A third option is to make sight-word instruction part of the literacy program.

Sight-word instruction can be integrated with an emergent literacy program if used to promote the *concept of word*. The concept of word is an important early phonemic awareness skill for beginning readers that involves recognizing words as distinct elements within a text. Specifically, it is the ability to match spoken sounds with words in text (Bear & Barone, 1989). For example, Morris (1993) had students read a sentence until they had it memorized. Then students were asked to read the sentence and point to each word as it was read, to assess how well they were matching their verbal utterances to the printed symbols. Students can also demonstrate the concept of word by filling in a word in a repeated story line or "writing" what they hear through lines and spaces to indicate the number of words. Gately (2004) recommended several strategies for teaching the concept of word that could be used concurrently with sight-word instruction. One is to teach picture–word matching and then to embed these pictures into a written text. For example, the student might learn to match words such as *cookies*, *pizza*, and *popcorn* to pictures and then learn to read sentences such as, "I like cookies" and "I like pizza." In a study on sight-word instruction, Browder and Shear (1996) taught students weather-related sight words using a massed-trial format with known words interspersed. Students then learned to read the words in "story starters" such as, "It is cold," and "It is windy." Although they did not use pictures, their research illustrates that students can generalize from flash cards to embedding the words in text.

Gately (2004) also described the use of symbol-reading books that teachers can generate with software such as Writing with Symbols 2000 (http://www.widgit.com) or Boardmaker (http://www.mayer-johnson.com). Teachers might use a sight-word instruction strategy to help students master a set of high-frequency symbols concurrent with providing instruction in reading symbol sentences. A third option is language experience stories in which students compose a story with the teacher based on a shared experience. These stories can often highlight target sight words. For example, a story about going to the symphony might contain the following underlined sight words: *We went to the symphony. We rode a bus. Both the girls and boys went. We had to enter quietly. The music was excellent.*

As these examples illustrate, it is not necessary to choose between a functional reading and a literacy-based approach to reading. Students can benefit from having sight-word instruction that is blended with literacy activities. It is also important to promote broader emergent literacy concepts, as shown in Table 4.2.

RESEARCH ON TEACHING READING TO STUDENTS WITH SIGNIFICANT DISABILITIES

Incorporating sight words with emergent literacy instruction builds on the strong foundation of research showing that students with moderate and significant disabilities can master sight-word reading. In contrast, minimal research has been focused on teaching this population other reading skills. In a comprehensive review of research with students with moderate and significant disabilities, Browder, Wakeman, Spooner, Ahlgrim-Delzell, and Algozzine (in press) found 128 studies in literacy between 1975 and 2003. In organizing these studies by the NRP's "Big Ideas" for reading, they found that most studies focused on the teach-

Table 4.2.   Emergent literacy concepts

Concept	Elementary age application	Middle/high school application
Concept of print		
Knows that a book is for reading	Chooses book for peer to read	Identifies class novel using picture symbols or book titles
Identifies front, back, bottom, top of book	Orients book and shows peer where to begin reading	Turns pages and points out each picture to share word/photo book of school activity with peer
Turns pages properly	Turns pages as they read	
Knows that pictures and words are related	Points to pictures and key words	Follows symbol/word sentences that summarize class discussion by using laser pointer
Recognizes the difference between words and pictures	Finds page in book that has a favorite story	
Knows where to begin reading a page	Locates book to read together when told title	Uses words with environmental cues to communicate preferences (e.g., logo for stores, restaurants, brands)
Knows what a title is		
Identifies page numbers		
Knows print is read from left to right		
Knows that print is oral language written down		
Reads environmental print and logos		
Concepts of words		
Knows what a word is	Uses assistive technology to participate in story reading by communicating repeated story line or filling in word	Finds and highlights key word in text (e.g., name of main character)
Can point to words on a page		
Finger points readings of memorized texts		Points to each word of language experience story as read by peer
Demonstrates one-to-one correspondence	"Reads" books adapted with symbol writing	
Reads own name	Finds personal belongings labeled with name	"Reads" memorized job instructions pointing to each word
Recognizes names in various formats		
Concept of letter		
Discriminates letters from symbols and from each other	"Spells" letters in name	Sorts mail by first letter of last name
Writes letter-like and letter forms	Identifies first letter of the story character's name by pointing	Initials form with letters of first and last name
Begins to name letters	Uses assistive technology to communicate letter that comes next in alphabet	Identifies school teams in upcoming game by discriminating between first letter of names
Sings and says alphabet		

Concepts in first column from Gately, S.E. (2004). Developing concept of word: The work of emergent readers. *TEACHING Exceptional Children, 36*(6), 16–22.

ing of sight-word vocabulary (80). Some (36) also measured words read per minute or the number of errors made (fluency). Fewer than half of these studies measured comprehension (31). Only a few studies focused on phonemic awareness (5) or phonics (13).

Research on Teaching Sight Words

Of the 80 studies that investigated sight words, most researched individuals with moderate mental disabilities as participants (72). For instance, Collins and Griffen (1996) examined the correct identification of key words and motor responses to potentially dangerous products by students with moderate mental retardation using a constant time-delay method. In a constant time-delay procedure, the teacher showed each sight word and immediately modeled the correct response (no delay). The student then repeated the word. After a predetermined number of trials at no delay, the teacher then paused between showing the word and modeling the response (e.g., 4-second delay of prompt). If students are taught to wait for the prompt when not certain of their response, word acquisition can occur with few to no errors. Using a constant time-delay procedure, students in Collins and Griffen's (1996) study were successful in identifying the key words and generalizing the skill to other products. Gast, Wolery, Morris, Doyle, and Meyer (1990) evaluated the effectiveness of the use of a constant time-delay procedure in a small-group arrangement when teaching sight words to students with moderate disabilities. Most participants learned all of their targeted words and at least some of the words that were taught to other group members.

Progressive time delay is a variation of this prompt-fading strategy that has also been successful in teaching sight words. For example, Rehfeldt, Latimore, and Stromer (2003) taught adults with moderate mental retardation to match pictures with sight words through a progressive time-delay format. All individuals made positive gains in naming pictures, reading sight words, and matching pictures to words. Progressive time delay can be used across days (e.g., Monday at zero delay, Tuesday at 2 seconds delay) or across trials within a day as illustrated by Browder and Minarovic (2000).

A third variation of this systematic prompting technique is to only implement the zero delay (teacher-modeled trials) with noninstructional probes to check for word mastery. Schuster, Griffen, and Wolery (1992) compared student performance when taught using a constant time-delay procedure and a simultaneous prompting procedure.

Although fewer in number, there has been some research on teaching sight words or picture symbols to students with significant disabilities. Some of these have used unique prompting strategies. For example, Sheehy (2002) examined the effects of cue integration to teach word recognition to students with significant disabilities. Participants received sight-word instruction in three conditions: 1) the word alone, 2) integrated picture cuing (Rebus symbols embedded within target words), and 3) a handle technique. The handle technique is a cue that is elicited from the student's personal vocabulary. The student's understanding or meaning for the word is incorporated into a mnemonic cue or handle, which can be an abstract shape or line within the written word. The students had higher word recognition scores in the handle technique over the other two conditions. Other studies with students with significant disabilities have incorporated computerized instruction. Mechling and Langone (2000) evaluated the effectiveness of a computer video program on increasing the number of correct photographs of everyday events or items selected by individuals with significant disabilities. Parents of the individuals identified nine items in the community that they felt were important for the individuals to learn. Outcomes indicated that correct selection of the prompted photograph increased for participants and some participants were able to generalize the photos in the community. Finally, time-delay instruction using flash cards has also been effective with students with significant disabilities (Gast, Doyle, Wolery, Ault, & Farmer, 1991).

When considering all of the studies on teaching reading to this population, the strongest support (23 studies) can be found for conducting massed trial instruction of sight words using systematic prompt fading such as time delay. An alternative to time delay, which relies on teacher modeling of the response, is to embed the cues within the materials (within stimulus prompts). Two applications of this procedure include *stimulus shaping* and *stimulus fading*. In stimulus shaping, the target word is presented with distractors in an easy discrimination

Table 4.3.   Methods of prompting used in teaching sight words

Method	Reading format	Prompt used	Example	Research
Response prompting				
1. Post-response prompting: interspersal method	Expressive reading: student reads flash cards rapidly without interruption until error.	Intersperse high ratio of known words to reduce errors. Use expanded error correction.	Expanded error correction: 1. Repeat word 2. Spell it 3. Trace it 4. Repeat it	Browder and Shear (1996)
2. Post-response prompting: feedback only	Can be expressive (say word) or receptive (point to word).	Simple correction of any word missed	"No, the word is *coffee.*"	Lalli and Browder (1993)
3. Simultaneous prompting	Usually expressive	Teacher models answer on every trial; probe independent reading.	"Read *hamburger.*"	Schuster, Griffen, and Wolery (1992)
4. Time delay: constant time delay (CTD)	Usually expressive; can be receptive	Usually teacher models correct answer. First trials at no delay; remainder trials at delay interval of 4–5 seconds	On first day, teacher shows each word and models it. "Read *gym.*" On rest of days, teacher waits for student to read word 4–5 seconds before prompting.	Gast, Doyle, Wolery, Ault, and Baklarz (1991)

5. Time delay: progressive time delay (PTD)	Usually expressive; can be receptive	Same as CTD, but delay intervals change across sessions.	First day is 0 delay; then 2 seconds; 4 seconds; 6 seconds.	Browder, Hines, McCarthy, and Fees (1984); Collins and Stinson (1995)
6. Least intrusive prompts	Expressive or receptive	Give several levels of assistance until student says word.	Gesture toward word; point to correct word; guide hand to point to correct word.	Gast, Ault, Wolery, Doyle, and Belanger (1988); Karsh and Repp (1992)
Stimulus prompts				
1. Stimulus fading	Can be expressive or receptive	Correct word is highlighted with color or picture cue which is faded across trials.	Correct word is highlighted with red; over trials becomes darker until all letters are black	Lalli and Browder (1993)
2. Stimulus shaping	Always receptive	Uses an easy to hard discrimination with distracter symbols and words.	– exit – sun exit tooth exit x-ray ten eat x-ray exit	McGee, Krantz, and McClannahan (1986)
3. Task demonstration model	Always receptive	Same as stimulus shaping, but also vary irrelevant stimuli.	In above example, exit would also be presented in varied typeset, color, size.	Karsh and Repp (1992); Karsh, Repp, and Lenz (1990)

From Browder, D.M. (2001). *Curriculum and assessment for students with moderate and significant disabilities.* New York: Guilford Press. Reprinted by permission.

(e.g., – *exit* –). Over teaching trials, the discrimination is made more complex by making the distractors more similar to the target word (e.g., *x-ray, exit, eat*). Stimulus shaping is a component of the commercially available Edmark Reading Program (http://www.edmark.com). In stimulus fading, some recognizable stimulus (e.g., a picture) is embedded with the word and reduced in salience over time (e.g., the picture is made fainter over teaching trials while the word stays constant). A summary of the methods of prompting and fading supported by research on sight-word instruction is shown in Table 4.3.

Research on Teaching Other Reading Skills

Much less research is available on how to teach the other components of reading to students with significant disabilities. For example, Browder et al. (in press) found only four studies on phonics instruction that included students with significant disabilities (Basil & Reyes, 2003; Bjorgum & Hudler, 1977; Hoogeveen &

Smeets; 1988; Hoogeveen, Smeets, & van der Houven, 1987). Although these studies offer some support for teaching phonics to students with significant disabilities, because all four used different strategies, no specific evidence-based practice for phonics instruction can be discerned.

Browder and Xin (1998) noted that sight-word research has primarily focused on word identification, with fewer studies measuring either academic or functional tasks that reflect comprehension. Browder et al. (in press) found four studies that used academic tasks to measure comprehension with students with significant disabilities (Basil & Reyes, 2003; House, Hanley, & Magid, 1980; Romski, Sevcik, Robinson, Mervis, & Bertrand, 1996; Wheldall & Mittler, 1977). For example, Wheldall and Mittler (1977) measured the number of pictures identified correctly from each stimulus sentence with students with significant disabilities. More frequently, researchers used a daily living task such as using the sight words to prepare recipes (Browder, Hines, McCarthy, & Fees, 1984) or demonstrate safety responses (Collins & Griffen, 1996).

Whereas most research has focused on the number of words read, a few have incorporated a second task for comprehension. Rarely have measures included fluency, however. Some researchers have compared two reading procedures using the number of errors or miscues as well as words acquired. For example, Karsh, Repp, and Lenz (1990) studied the effectiveness and efficiency of a stimulus shaping procedure called the *task demonstration model* (see Table 4.3) and a least intrusive prompting hierarchy to teach sight words to students with moderate and significant disabilities. Students acquired a higher percentage of words and made fewer errors in the task demonstration model over the standard prompting hierarchy. Timed reading probes have only been used in a few studies (Singh & Singh, 1984, 1985, 1988), and none of these was with students with significant disabilities. For example, Singh and Singh (1985) used 100-word passages read in 5 minutes or less to measure error correction procedures with students with moderate mental disabilities.

Innovations for Teaching Reading to Students with Significant Cognitive Disabilities

Although the research on using systematic prompting to teach sight words provides a strong evidence base for teaching reading to students with significant disabilities, some newer procedures are emerging through case study descriptions of practice that reflect a broader approach to literacy. The first method is to embed the students' reading instruction in the ongoing literacy program of general education. Ryndak, Morrison, and Sommerstein (1999) described a case study of a student with moderate to significant disabilities who was provided with typical reading instruction. The student's use of expressive and written language increased dramatically over a 7-year inclusion period during which instruction was based on both the student's functional needs as well as the general education curriculum. Similarly, Kliewer and Biklen (2001) described case studies of several students with significant disabilities included in typical reading programs. They discussed the importance of a meaningful social context for promoting literacy concepts.

A second emerging approach to promote broader literacy skills is to use assistive technology to create greater access to reading materials. Erickson and Koppenhaver (1995, 1997, 1998) described an embedded literacy program for students with significant physical and cognitive disabilities that used technology to support student communicative and literacy efforts. Phonics, comprehension activities, and writing were stressed throughout the students' daily schedules. Computer programs and switches were used to allow students opportunities to interact with literacy materials. Students became active participants in their learning.

From Research to Practice

Research provides consistent evidence that students will acquire sight words and picture vocabulary through systematic, massed trial instruction. Students can become fluent in their identification and use of words. The NRP (2000) stated that repeated exposure to vocabulary items is important for gains in learning and that vocabulary learning generally leads to gains in comprehension. Explicit or systematic instruction in comprehension strategies then leads to understanding and independent use.

Some emerging evidence also suggests that students may benefit from phonetic instruction when it is provided in a systematic manner (Joseph & Seery, 2004). However, there seems to be a gap in the research in determining the effectiveness in phonemic awareness instruction with students with significant disabilities and specific methods for phonics instruction. Recent innovations focus on increasing expectations for literacy through exposure to typical reading programs with peer or technology support. The recommendations to follow incorporate the strong research on sight-word acquisition, but also build on recent innovations to teach this and other specific skills in the context of a comprehensive literacy program.

DEVELOPING COMPREHENSIVE LITERACY PROGRAMS
Adapting Units and Lesson Plans of the General Education Teacher

The first step in developing a comprehensive literacy program is to identify the reading curriculum to be introduced. Building on the innovations of Ryndak et al. (1999) and Kliewer and Biklin (2001), we recommend that a good source for a curriculum is the reading program at the student's grade level. Specific skills such as sight-word acquisition can be developed while also exposing students to the literature experienced by typical peers. Although the most efficient approach to creating access to the typical language arts program is to have students receive instruction in general education classes with support, students in all settings need the opportunity to learn literacy skills. This requires building a close partnership with language arts teachers. Through this partnership, the special educator can begin to align what is being taught in special education programs with what is being taught in general education by requesting access to the materials and lesson plans being used by the language arts teacher. In exchange, many language arts teachers are eager for ideas for creative adaptations of their plans for slow learners.

The typical language arts program will often follow a unit approach. A unit involves teaching a concept or theme and integrating many subjects into that theme. For example, one of the units in the third-grade Open Court Reading Series is storytelling. In this unit, students learn about storytelling and different kinds of stories. Students study folktales, the use of visual aids (i.e., totem poles) to tell stories, discuss story telling techniques, and discuss the way family traditions are passed down through stories. Ideas for integrating other curriculum areas are given. For example, students learn how history is passed down through story-telling (social studies). Students also create collages (art) that tell a story (Open Court Reading, 2000). Although research does not yet exist on teaching units to students with significant disabilities, students with mild disabilities have shown improved performance with a unit approach (Englert, Raphael, & Mariage, 1994; Mastropieri & Scruggs, 1994). According to Onosko and Jorgensen (1998), there are eight essential elements of an inclusive unit design: 1) a central unit issue or problem, 2) an opening grabber or motivator, 3) lessons that are linked to the central issue or problem, 4) richly detailed source material, 5) culminating projects, 6) varied lesson formats, 7) multiple assessments, and 8) varied modes of student expression.

Choosing and Introducing the Theme   The central issue/problem or theme is the backbone of the unit. By focusing on themes chosen by the language arts teacher, the special educator can align instruction with the inclusive context. This alignment may facilitate sharing materials, participating in special events (e.g., field trip or guest speaker), and helping to facilitate planning for participation in general class instruction. In order to get students excited about a unit, teachers typically begin with an opening grabber or motivator such as a short story, film clip, or field trip.

Linking a Series of Lessons and Activities   Lessons that follow the opening grabber must be linked to the central issue or theme of the unit. One way the general education teacher may do this is to identify key ideas that relate to the problem or identify additional questions that need to be answered as part of the problem. Graphic organizers, such as sequence charts and Venn diagrams, may be used to link the lessons together. Lessons will typically follow varied structures to keep the students interested, including library days, cooperative group work, student-to-student conferences, and visitor days.

Synthesis and Assessment   To end the unit, students are typically given the opportunity to synthesize what they have learned with a culminating activity. Examples of culminating activities include speeches, skits, poster displays, and small-group presentations. Throughout the unit, the teacher monitors ongoing student progress. Assessments may vary in format and include class discussion, oral question and answer quizzes, take-home assignments, and in-class activities.

Adaptations and Support   In order to be sure that a unit is accessible to all students with disabilities, supports and accommodations will need to be provided. Onosko and Jorgensen (1998) recommend the use of the following five supports: 1) people support from classmates or adults, 2) modified materials or provisions or technology, 3) individualization of performance standards and expectations, 4) personalized instruction, and 5) uniquely designed evaluation and grading plans. Table 4.4 gives an example of a unit and the adaptations made for Michelle, a sixth grader with significant disabilities. Michelle communicates using a communication board with eight picture arrays. She also is learning to use an IntelliKeys (http://www.intellitools.com) keyboard to answer questions (see Table 4.4).

Components of a Lesson Plan

Once broad decisions are made about using a comprehensive language arts program, the planning should shift to more specific decisions. As mentioned previously, the first decision is for the planning team to select a reading curriculum, preferably the same one used in general education. Next, the special and general education teachers must plan how the lesson units can be adapted for increased access for students with significant disabilities. Finally, the teacher team should plan out the daily language arts lessons. Although these lessons may vary, it can be helpful to follow a template that includes 1) the source of the lesson, 2) at least one objective statement, 3) an attention-getter to introduce the lesson, 4) a

Table 4.4. Example of a middle school unit with planned support for students with significant disabilities

1. Central unit issue or problem
   The Depression and the book *Bud, Not Buddy* by Christopher Paul Curtis

2. An opening grabber or motivator
   A movie clip showing children and their families during the Depression

3. Lessons that are linked to the central issue or problem
   Lesson 1—Introduction of the story and pre-reading activities; vocabulary lists from the first three chapters
   Lesson 2—Reading of chapters 1–3; vocabulary activity: context clues; make "helping people" pamphlets; quiz on first section: new vocabulary
   Lesson 3—Reading of chapters 4–8; vocabulary activity: substitutions; class discussion: compare and contrast the 1930s with today; quiz: new vocabulary
   Lesson 4—Reading of chapters 9–11; vocabulary activity: descriptions using adjectives; create stained art scenery; quiz: new vocabulary
   Lesson 5—Reading of chapters 12–14; vocabulary activity: write a story with new vocabulary; hold a class debate on labor unions; quiz: new vocabulary
   Lesson 6—Reading of chapters 15–19; vocabulary activity: find vocabulary in magazines or newspapers to post on a bulletin board; map the places the band went; quiz

4. Richly detailed source material
   Use of newspaper clippings from the Depression era, visits from people who lived through that time, video clips of people speaking about their experiences

5. Culminating projects
   Students will choose from one of the following activities:
   • Create a map showing where Bud's story takes place
   • Create an imaginary interview with one of the characters from the book
   • Give an oral presentation about the book
   • Write a review of *Bud, Not Buddy*
   • Write a letter to a friend explaining *Bud, Not Buddy*
   • Create a video of your favorite part of the story
   • Illustrate 10 scenes in the story

6. Varied lesson formats
   Class discussions, quizzes, whole-class activities, individual activities

7. Multiple assessments
   Quizzes, oral questions and answers, culminating activity to show comprehension

8. Varied modes of student expression
   Written activities, kinesthetic activities

(continued)

Table 4.4. *(continued)*

Supports for Michelle

Support	Example
People support	A peer of Michelle's will audiotape a modified version of the book. An unabridged version of the book will also be available on tape.
Modified materials or provisions of technology	Michelle's teacher will create a modified book that coincides with the sections of chapters her classmates are reading. The book will contain picture symbols and pictures of concepts in the text. Michelle will learn a shortened picture symbol vocabulary list instead of the same vocabulary. One of her communication board overlays will contain these pictures for use in the lessons.
Individualize performance standards and expectations	Michelle will point to pictures to identify her new vocabulary list (5 words). Michelle will answer questions about each section of the story.
	Michelle will use an IntelliKeys keyboard and talking word processing software to give a short presentation of the book.
Personalized instruction	Michelle will be asked yes/no questions and use pictures to answer questions about the book.
Uniquely designed evaluation and grading plans	Michelle will be graded on her shortened quizzes and her ability to manipulate the keyboard to make her presentation.

Source: Clark, 2001.

plan for encouraging participation in story reading, 5) a review of the story to increase comprehension, 6) a follow-up group skill drill, and 7) the opportunity for independent practice. Students will more likely benefit from having this reading lesson in a small-group (four or fewer students). A format for planning the lesson is shown in Figure 4.1.

Source of the Lesson and Objectives   The source of the lesson will be the specific unit, reading lesson, or other curriculum to be used for the lesson. Commercial reading materials often provide a teacher's guide that specifies the daily lesson. Usually, this plan will need to be modified to optimize participation and skill building for the student with special needs. The first step in this modification is to determine the specific objective for this student in this lesson. For example, the lesson plan may focus on having students make and justify predictions when reading a mystery. Typical students may do this through verbal debate or written responses. The objective for the student with significant disabilities may be to select pictures used to illustrate three characters and then choose the one for the person they predict committed the crime.

Sometimes the student may get to select the story to be read. Students who are physically unable to select a book from a shelf might have the option of choosing among books that are presented or through picture arrays. Book

Student's name:
Teacher:
Date of lesson:
Location of lesson:
Who will teach lesson/read story:

Curriculum: What curriculum is being used to develop this lesson?

Literature: What book or story will form the basis for this lesson?

Objectives: What grade-level standards are addressed in this lesson? What priority skills do you want this student to demonstrate in this lesson?

Anticipatory set: How will you start the lesson?

Lesson input: How will this student participate in the reading of the story?

Assessment: What responses will be used to check for this student's comprehension as the story is read again or reviewed?

Guided group practice: What specific decoding skills are targeted and how will students demonstrate these (phonemic awareness, phonics, sight words, picture symbols)? Lesson may only target one or two "big ideas" of reading.

"Big idea" of reading target	Typical student activity	Response for this student
Comprehension		
Fluency		
Phonemic awareness		
Phonics (letter-sound association)		
Vocabulary		

(continued)

Figure 4.1.   Language arts lesson plan form.

Figure 4.1.   *(continued)*

Individual practice: What specific skills will be taught for ongoing progress in learning to read? Will this be 1:1 instruction or self-directed?

	Target skills/activity for this student
Comprehension	
Fluency	
Phonemic awareness	
Phonics (letter-sound association)	
Vocabulary: Sight words or other symbols	
Writing	

choices can also be made accessible by photographing the book covers for a communication board overlay. If digital photographs are used, the student may be able to choose books to be read by touching choices on a screen or touching a switch that scans over choices.

Introducing the Story   To introduce the story, language arts teachers often use a discussion format. Students with significant disabilities may need materials that use one or more of the five senses to focus attention and introduce the story (e.g., taste an apple for a book on Johnny Appleseed; feel the wind from a fan in a story about wind). To promote print awareness, the teacher may also have the student physically orient the book, point to the title and author of the book while the teacher reads these, and preview pictures. The following are some ideas for attention-getters for four books that could be used with students at various age levels:

- To introduce *My Crayons Talk* (Hubbard, 1999), Mr. Moore brings out a box of crayons and asks the first-grade students what they think the crayons would say if they could speak. Reading level: ages 4–8 (publisher), school library journal (preschool to Grade 1)

- To introduce *Polar Bear, Polar Bear, What Do You Hear?* (Martin & Carle, 1991), Ms. Simmons plays an audio recording of animal sounds and asks the kindergarten students what animals are making the sounds. Ages infant to preschool, Preschool to Grade 1 (school library journal)

- To introduce *The Wild Whale Watch* (A Magic School Bus Chapter Book; Moore, 2000), Mr. Everly shows his third-grade students a short video about whales and begins a discussion about different types of whales his students have seen. Reading level: ages 4–8 (7–9, publisher) third-grade accelerated reader

- To introduce *Black Diamond: The Story of Negro Baseball Leagues* (McKissack & McKissack, 1998), Mrs. Walters shows photographs of baseball teams before and after racial integration in the leagues and asks her sixth-grade students to compare and contrast what they see. Ages 9–12 (12 and up, publisher)

Participation in the Reading of the Story   Next, planning is needed for how the student will participate in the reading of the story. Students with significant disabilities may not attend to books read by teachers or peers without being allowed opportunities for interaction in the reading. One option is to modify the book itself by using laminated symbols or photocopies that correspond to the book being read. The symbols or pictures can be affixed to each page so the student can pull off or put on pictures as the words are read.

> Mrs. Smith is reading *Leo the Late Bloomer* (Kraus, 1994) to her class. To ensure that Cassie, a 6-year-old with limited verbal skills and significant developmental delays, is able to participate, she has made some accommodations for her. Mrs. Smith photocopied pictures from the text (pictures of Leo, of a book, and of writing), laminated them, and then affixed them to the book with Velcro. As Mrs. Smith reads, "Leo was a late bloomer," Cassie puts the picture of Leo on the page. When Mrs. Smith reads, "He couldn't read," Cassie puts the picture of a book on the page.

Another way to get students to participate in story reading is to have the student be the group's "reader" by playing a book on tape or a CD. The recorded book may be connected to a PowerLink (http://www.ablenetinc.com) and a switch to make it easier to operate the tape/CD player. Students also can be the reader for part of the story by using a Step-by-Step (http://www.ablenetinc.com) preprogrammed to "read" a segment of the story. The teacher must record each page of a short story in the device. A BookWorm (http://www.ablenetinc.com) can also be used to record stories page by page. Some technology does not require prerecording the story. Reading pens enable the student to scan the words to produce oral reading of the text. A LeapPad (http://www.leapfrog.com) has prerecorded stories that students can read using a reading pen. Students who are beginning to attend more to the printed words may participate using a strategy to focus on the words being read. The WYNN software (http://www.freedomscientific.com) can be used to transform printed pages into electronic text. The computer can then be used to read the text aloud. Each word is highlighted as the text is read.

Books used in typical classes also may not be accessible for some students because of the lack of pictures, text that is beyond the students' language comprehension, or being made of materials that are difficult for the student to see or manipulate. The student may have visual or sensory challenges that might require adaptations. For books with few to no pictures, visual graphics may be used to supplement the text (e.g., Writing with Symbols 2000, http://www.widgit.com; Boardmaker symbols, http://www.mayer-johnson.com). These may be attached to the page with text or form a supplemental book for the students' use.

Difficult text may be simplified either through using high-interest–low-vocabulary versions of the book, such as the Weiser Educational Classic Literature series (http://www.weiser-ed.com) or through teacher-developed versions of the story. Books can be made easier to manipulate by taking the pages apart, attaching them to cardboard, laminating them, and reassembling the book using three-ring binder clips. The book also may be scanned and put on the computer for ease of manipulation.

Assess and Teach Comprehension   One way to discover whether students with limited language and reading skills are comprehending what is being read is to involve the students in reading the book using *repeated story line responding*. Using any book that has a repeated line throughout and a BIGmack (http://www.ablenetinc.com), the students can indicate that they are following the story as it is read.

> Ms. Hrubik read *What's in My Pocket* (Williams, 1994) to her first-grade class. The repeated line in the story is *Pocket, pocket, what's in my pocket?* The teacher used a BIGmack to record this repeated line and placed a picture symbol of a pocket with the words *Pocket, pocket, what's in my pocket?* underneath on the BIGmack. As Ms. Hrubik read the story, she prompted Taylor to fill in the line at the appropriate point in time. As she progressed through the story, she waited longer for Taylor to initiate the repeated story line by hitting the BIGmack switch. By using this same book at other times with Taylor, he began to anticipate when to read his line.

Interactive language charts also can be used to target early literacy development. Teachers can use sentence strips and picture symbols or written words to develop a chart. Sentences can be written with blanks for the students to give the appropriate answer. The teacher can then determine whether the students comprehend the story by the answers that they give.

> Mr. Green reads *Dear Zoo* (Campbell, 1986) to his students. He develops an interactive language chart with the sentence, *I wrote to the zoo to send me a pet. They sent me a _____ , I sent him back!* Mr. Green then rereads the first page of the story. In the story the first pet sent is a camel. After the page is read, he then asks, "What animal did the zoo send?" The students are then asked to find the picture symbol of the correct animal from a choice of three and add it to the sentence. Mr. Green and the student then read the sentences together.

Thinking Maps (http://www.thinkingmaps.com) are graphic organizers that can be used to help students with comprehension of what they have read. A thinking map can used to show relationships between characters, concepts, and events in a story. Thinking maps are visual and therefore may be beneficial to students with significant disabilities. Thinking maps are typically used with written words but can be adapted with picture symbols, photographs, or objects. The following are examples for using different thinking maps.

Bubble map. A bubble map is used to describe characteristics. Students can identify the main character, whose picture can be placed in the center bubble. Pictures of attributes that describe the character and pictures that do not describe the character can then be shown to students to give them a choice. The students can then place the correct picture on the map.

Flow map. A flow map is used to show sequencing. Teachers could use photocopied pictures from the story and have the students sequence the order of the events in the story on the map.

Double bubble map. A double bubble is used to compare and contrast concepts. Teachers can choose two concepts, events, or characters and place pictures of the chosen items in the center of the map, then have students place pictures or words that are common to both objects in the middle. Pictures/words that are only a characteristic of one event, concept, or character are then placed on the outside of the corresponding picture.

Multi-flow map. A multi-flow map is used to show cause and effect. Students can place pictures of actions or events that caused the main event in the story, followed by pictures of what happened after the main event.

Another option is to check for comprehension through use of a *functional activity* that may be used at the end of the lesson. These activities may include using the words in a schedule or activity guide, following directions to prepare food or other products, planning an activity such as shopping or dining, or playing a game.

> Ms. Sloan had read a book on the importance of recycling during a unit on the environment. After reading the book and using a language chart to check for comprehension, she gave the students printed instructions for recycling discarded items at school. Hwang's instructions were developed using Writing with Symbols 2000 (http://www.Mayer-Johnson.com). The teacher prompted Hwang to point to each symbol and then perform the action. For example, Hwang found the can and placed it in the bin for cans.[2]

Guided Group Practice   Skill building will include practice with vocabulary that the students are learning. Students may practice with symbols and pictures, participate in a phonemic awareness activity (sounds, words, letters), or practice sight-word identification. Several studies have demonstrated benefits for students learning new skills such as sight words in a small-group instruction format (Hoogeveen, Smeets, & Lancioni, 1989; Rehfeldt et al., 2003; Worrall & Singh, 1983). If students are prompted to attend to the student taking a turn, they may also learn the response through observation. An example of how to conduct sight-word training in a small-group format is found in Gickling, Hargis, and Alexander (1981). Training sessions of four words with three to five students followed a five-step format with an optional sixth step. Each subject took turns 1) looking closely at the printed word when the instructor pronounced the word, 2) verbally repeating the word, 3) listening while the instructor used the word in a sentence, 4) repeating the word and using it in his or her own sentence, and 5) looking at the word again and naming the word. The optional sixth step was

---

[2] The authors thank the teacher Susan Flynn for sharing this lesson idea and letting us observe her instruction. The student's name has been changed to protect confidentiality.

either to shuffle the cards and have students take turns naming the words again, or to place all the cards in front of the students and point to each word and have students name it.

Independent Practice   Self-directed activities are also important for promoting literacy skills. These may include looking at a book, producing an art project related to the story, matching pictures and words, or other tasks that can be performed with little to no teacher assistance. Teachers can encourage *interaction with books* by having an extensive book collection that is accessible to all students. Younger students may like to read big books (mainly picture books that are larger than ordinary). Older students may also enjoy picture books that have age-appropriate themes. Picture books such as *Mufaro's Beautiful Daughters: An African Tale* (Steptoe, 2003) and *Why Mosquitoes Buzz in People's Ears: A West African Tale* (Aardema, 1978) tell folk stories through the use of limited text and pictures. Other picture books address current issues (e.g., homelessness), such as *We Are All in the Dumps with Jack and Guy* (Sendak, 1993), or historical events (Japanese internment camps), such as *Baseball Saved Us* (Mochizuki, 1993).

Students may browse the hard copy of the book, listen to it on tape, or view it using computer software. Living Books (http://www.broderbund.com) and the UKanDu reading series (http://www.donjohnston.com) are interactive stories on CD that students can read. The pages can be turned automatically, with the click of a mouse or with a switch. Touch screens can allow students who do not understand the cause and effect of a mouse to control what they are reading. Start-to-Finish books (http://www.donjohnston.com) are classics and nonfiction books that are available at a second/third-grade or fourth/fifth-grade reading level. These books can also be read aloud.

Assistive technology can also be used for helping students with *decoding* and *comprehension*. Teachers can use the software with a group of students or work one-on-one with individual students. Most software includes a scanning ability, meaning a switch can be used. For students who can work independently, there are programs that have the ability to stop the student after a certain numbers of errors are made, so that the teacher can check on the student (e.g., Edmark Reading Program, http://www.riverdeep.net). Table 4.5 gives some examples of software and the concepts that can be taught with each.

In light of the strong evidence that individual, massed trial instruction promotes the acquisition of picture and word reading (Browder et al., in press), it is also important to provide *systematic instruction of sight words or symbols*. The teacher can select a set of words, pictures, or symbols for instruction. These may include functional words useful in daily living (Browder, 2001) or high-frequency words (e.g., Dolch, 1950). It may also include Boardmaker symbols or other words with visual graphics that can be used to build sentences (e.g., Boardmaker symbol = for *is*). These words or symbols are then put on flash cards. In massed trial instruction, the teacher can display each word and ask the student to read it. If the student is nonverbal, a three-word array can be displayed and the student asked to point to the word. If using time delay, the teacher can immediately model by saying or selecting the word as it is displayed. If the student is correct, the teacher can offer praise. If incorrect, the teacher can give the correct answer and have the student repeat it. Figure 4.2 illustrates a time-delay procedure for

Table 4.5. Examples of education reading software

Software	Skills/concepts taught
Bailey's Book House (Riverdeep; http://www.riverdeep.net)	Letters, words, rhyming, prepositions, adjectives, sentence building
Edmark Words Around Me (Riverdeep; http://www.riverdeep.net)	Word identification, plurals, categorization, sameness, difference
Simon Sounds it Out (Don Johnston, Inc.; http://www.donjohnston .com)	Letter sounds, word families, onsets, rimes
Edmark Reading Program (Riverdeep; http://www.riverdeep.net)	Comprehension of sight words through story reading, picture matching
IntelliTools Reading: Balanced Literacy (IntelliTools; http://www.intellitools.com	Phonics, guided reading, comprehension
Start-to-Finish books (Don Johnston, Inc.; http://www.donjohnston .com)	Reading comprehension through end-of-story quizzes

teaching sight words or symbols. This method was used by Browder and Minarovic (2000). The specific word comprehension activity differs from the original research, and it has also been modified to use a receptive reading format for nonverbal students.

Putting It All Together   Figure 4.3 shows an example of a lesson plan that incorporates all of the components described. Jorge Gonzales is a second-grade student who is nonverbal and classified as having autism. He uses picture/word symbols to communicate what he selects from a word bank in a notebook or a communication wallet (for frequently used words). Jorge can identify 20 sight words, but he does not demonstrate comprehension of them. Because he learns best with visual cues, his teacher has decided to combine phonemic awareness of initial consonant sounds with the visual referent of the letter. Jorge has good motor skills and is able to turn pages in a book, but he often seems to do so for the sensory feedback it provides rather than to attend to the pictures or story. This lesson also targets social awareness and creates the opportunity for Jorge to practice his IEP skill to use objects or pictures to initiate interactions with peers (see Figure 4.3).

Writing Skills

Students with significant disabilities often lack the fine motor control or cognitive skills to write like their typical peers. However, the ability to create written language is important for all students, because it opens another important avenue for communication. Students who learn to write their names and other personal information, take notes, compose letters, complete job applications, and create journals develop skills with lifelong utility.

There are several options for teaching skills students can use to achieve these tasks. The best choice is to teach students who can acquire manuscript writing and spelling to do so because it provides the most flexibility for written communication.

When teaching manuscript writing, there is no correct letter to start with. Some letters will be more functional for students, such as the first letter of their

---

Target words

the, is, first, second, third, reading, math, lunch, teacher, Ms. Jones, we have, class

Materials

Each word is printed on a 3 × 4-inch index card; strips are also prepared for sentence completion (e.g., *First we have____. Lunch is _____. The math teacher is _____*). Make pictures that correspond with the sentence strips.

Probe

Before beginning instruction, assess the student's recognition of each word. Put three words in front of the student. Say, "Point to the word *teacher*." Wait about 5 seconds for a response. Score the response on your data sheet as correct (+) or incorrect (-). Repeat for all words on the list. Give no feedback except to praise the student for working with you on the probe.

Instruction

1. Put three cards in front of student.
2. Say, "Point to the word *lunch*."
3. While saying "lunch," model pointing to the correct word immediately (no delay).
4. If the student is correct, provide praise: "Good, the word is *lunch*."
   If the student is incorrect, provide correction: "No, this is the word *lunch*." Because errors should not occur with the immediate model of the correct answer, you may need to stop and practice imitating pointing where the teacher points or use a different prompt like physical guidance.
5. Repeat steps 1–4 for all words in the set at no delay. Be careful to place the correct answer in different locations in the array (e.g., not always in the middle).
6. Now repeat the trials, but wait 2 seconds before modeling the answer like this:
   - "Point to the word *the*."
   - Wait 2 seconds (counting silently *one thousand one, one thousand two*)
   - If the student *anticipates* the correct answer *before* the prompt, praise with enthusiasm: "Wow! 'the'! You found it before I could show you!"
   - If the student *waits* for help, praise, "Good, you showed me *the*."
   - If the student *makes an error before the prompt,* correct and remind to wait. "No, this is *the*. If you don't know, WAIT and I will help you." Go back to the zero-delay round when an error occurs.
   - If the student *makes an error after the prompt*, correct and remind to follow your lead. Go back to the zero-delay round when an error occurs. Consider again if you need to stop the sight-word instruction to establish following your prompt, because there should be no errors after the prompt is given.
7. After you get through all words at 2 seconds with or without prompts, but without any errors, go to 4 seconds. Then do a round at 6 seconds and 8 seconds. If you get an error at any point, go back to zero and build up again. You may stop before getting to 8 seconds if you have had to return to zero a few times.

Comprehension

1. Display three sight words including the correct answer and a sentence strip (e.g., "We have _____ first" with words *math, lunch, reading*.
2. Begin with no delay to show the student the correct answer in the same way you did sight-word instruction, only now you put the word in the sentence after the student selects it.
3. The student then chooses between three pictures that go with the sentence. Again, use no delay to prompt the correct response.

Begin with about three sentences and repeat them, delaying the prompt by 2 seconds each round. As the student begins to anticipate the correct answer, add new sentences using the same time-delay sequence.

Figure 4.2.   Illustration of using progressive time delay to teach sight words.

names. Letters can also be taught in groups by shape. Teachers can assist students by using a graduated guidance technique (starting with full physical assistance, then partial assistance, then a light touch only). Students can also be provided with letters to trace or directional arrows to help them make correct strokes. Some students may need light tech adaptations such as a pencil grip, a slanted writing surface, or a stencil.

Other students may make more progress learning to write through typing on a computer keyboard. If the keys are too small for the student to isolate, an adapted keyboard with larger keys can be used. IntelliKeys (http://www.intellitools.com)

is an alternative keyboard that plugs into any computer and has multiple overlays that can be used to facilitate keyboarding. The keyboard has a QWERTY overlay that is larger than a typical keyboard. Overlays can also be customized to facilitate writing about certain topics using words or pictures. Typing does require the acquisition of spelling skills. However, computer software that anticipates words can simplify the demands of learning to spell. Students can select the correct word using sight-word recognition. Write:Outloud (http://www.donjohnston.com/) is a talking word processor. As students type, the words can be read aloud. Students can also use Write:Outloud to recheck sentences or paragraphs they have written by having the entire text read back. As the text is read, it is also highlighted. Co:Writer 4000 (http://www.donjohnston.com) is word prediction software that can be added to Write:Outloud or any other word processor or email program. As students type words, the software anticipates word options it thinks will be typed in next. The software includes topic dictionaries that can be used for specific students or assignments. The basic dictionaries contain only the words the student knows. Teachers can also customize dictionaries to contain new vocabulary students are learning.

For other students, writing may be achieved by using picture, phrase, and sight-word selection from a software program for assisted writing. Clicker 5 (http://www.cricksoft.com) is software that contains a talking word processor and grids that students can choose pictures or words from to create text. Students can type in words from a keyboard or use pre-made or customized grids to create sentences. The sentences are then read back to them.

> Janet has recently been job sampling to find work she would like to do next year. Her teacher would like her to produce a journal that she can take home and to other service providers to help her explain which occupations she does and does not like. Janet's teacher has created an overlay for her IntelliKeys keyboard. The overlay includes pictures of the jobs she has sampled and sentence starters such as, *I would like to work at* ____; *I also liked* ____; and *I would not like to work at* ____. Using the keyboard, Janet can choose a sentence starter and then choose a picture to complete her sentence. The sentences appear in a word processing program and can be printed out for Janet to add to her job journal.

Students who rely on computers for composing text may still want to learn to sign their name on business forms and personal correspondence. Any distinctive mark can be shaped toward a signature. Some students may also want to pair this mark with a rubberized name stamp.

> Robbie is a 12-year-old with significant cognitive delays and limited movement of his hands. Robbie's teachers and therapists attempted to teach Robbie to write his name with a pencil. They tried different size pencils and grips, different types of writing surfaces, and helped him with exercises to increase his coordination. Still, Robbie was unable to grip the pencil with enough strength to write. Robbie's teacher then decided to give Robbie a stamp to use. The first stamp had a large handle that Robbie could grip. Robbie practiced stamping in boxes and lines on paper to improve his accuracy. Robbie's teacher then ordered him a smaller, personalized stamp with his name on it. Robbie learned to use the stamp and then make a distinctive, sweeping underline as his signature.

Student's name: *Jorge Gonzales*
Teacher: *Ms. Anderson in partnership with Mr. Hendricks, second-grade language arts*
Date of lesson: *September 15 and 16*
Location of lesson: *Practice lesson with Ms. Anderson, then with peers in second grade*
Who will teach lesson/read story: *Ms. Anderson*

Curriculum: What curriculum is being used to develop this lesson?

Supplemental children's literature recommended for second-grade series; Mr. Hendrick's literacy lesson using this story planned for Tuesday, September 16th

Literature: What book or story will form the basis for this lesson?

The Giving Tree by Shel Silverstein

Objectives: What grade-level standards are addressed in this lesson? What priority skills do you want this student to demonstrate in this lesson?

Mr. Hendrick wants students to identify characteristics of altruism.

For Jorge:
- *Identify picture/word for give*
- *Answer 2 wh questions about a story*
- *Identify initial g sound*
- *Give peer a picture card Jorge prepares in advance*

Anticipatory set: How will you start the lesson?

Fill a paper bag with things that come from trees. Brainstorm with the class and make a list of things that come from trees. Jorge will choose items that do and do not come from trees. Discuss trees and how they help people with all the things they give us. Predict what the tree will give in this story by pre-viewing 1–2 pictures. Have Jorge point to picture in the book and choose a peer to make a prediction.

Lesson input: How will this student participate in the reading of the story?

Every time the word give is read, Jorge will find the word/symbol for give.
Students, including Jorge, take turns pointing to people or the tree giving in the story

Assessment: What responses will be used to check for this student's comprehension as the story is read again or reviewed?

Ask wh questions to Jorge about the book. Jorge will indicate by pointing to word/symbols.
1. What did the tree give the boy?
2. Why did the tree give the boy his branches?

Guided group practice: What specific decoding skills are targeted and how will students demonstrate these (phonemic awareness, phonics, sight words, picture symbols)? Lesson may only target one or two "big ideas" of reading.

"Big idea" of reading target	Typical student activity	Response for this student
Comprehension	*Students describe how they might give*	*Show the symbol for give and have Jorge give a peer his card (at the end of the lesson)*
Fluency		
Phonemic awareness		
Phonics (letter-sound association)	*Two sounds of g in give and generosity*	*Select g when asked sound that give begins with*
Vocabulary	*Read and define generosity*	*Find word/symbol for give*

Figure 4.3. Example of an elementary lesson for a student with significant disabilities.

Individual practice: What specific skills will be taught for ongoing progress in learning to read? Will this be 1:1 instruction or self-directed?

	Target skills/activity for this student
Comprehension	*Independently: Review The Giving Tree by turning each page in a computerized version* *Put sight words in sentence starters and match to pictures*
Fluency	
Phonemic awareness	
Phonics (letter-sound association)	*1:1 practice drill on selecting pictures for initial consonant sounds including g*
Vocabulary: Sight words or other symbols	*Massed trial on identifying word/symbol for give, along with 10 review words*
Writing	*Independently: Select a picture to make a card for peer; stamp his name on a card*

Teaching Language Arts, Math, and Science to Students with Significant Cognitive Disabilities by D.M. Browder and F. Spooner. Copyright © 2006 Paul H. Brookes Publishing Co., Inc. All rights reserved.

SUMMARY

This chapter focused on teaching reading to students with significant disabilities who may be nonverbal and have few reading skills aside from some sight words or picture use. Research demonstrates that students with significant disabilities can learn to identify sight words and pictures or other symbols using a massed trial format with systematic prompting and fading such as time delay. Some research illustrates how to assess and teach comprehension using an academic task such as matching the word to pictures or an application to a functional activity such as cooking. Although a small number of studies illustrate that students with significant disabilities can learn phonics, the variation in methods used in these few studies does not point to a specific method for instruction.

The shortcoming of a sight-word-only approach is that students are limited to the vocabulary that is introduced. Many sight-word studies have not incorporated comprehension. Fewer still have linked the words to passage reading. Some recent innovations suggest that students with significant disabilities can gain broader literacy skills when these are aligned with general education reading and incorporate the use of technology. Sight-word instruction can be compatible with this broader literacy approach if used to promote the concept of word within text as well as to perform functional activities.

In this chapter, guidelines are given for adapting both units of instruction and daily lesson plans. To adapt units of instruction, specific supports can be targeted to help the student participate in varied activities and achieve individualized objectives. For the daily lesson plan, this chapter offers a template for planning a language arts lesson with the oral reading of a story as the primary activity. Although this is not the only format for language arts lessons, it is one frequently used in general education and one that introduces students to the literature of their chronological age group. Using this template, teachers can identify ways for the student to participate in the reading of the story, demonstrate comprehension, and build specific reading skills within a small group. After the group lesson, the student can independently interact with a book and receive systematic instruction in vocabulary, comprehension, and other reading skills.

Writing is a companion skill to reading in the acquisition of literacy. Current technology makes it possible for students to compose text using picture or sight-word icons. Students may also want to develop a distinctive signature.

This chapter has offered guidance for a comprehensive reading program for students who begin at an emergent literacy stage. The hope and expectation is that they will gain prereading skills and then move on to higher stages of literacy. Through interaction with books and participation in stories, sight-word drill, and some phonemic awareness, the guidelines offered here promote early reading skills. The next chapter provides guidance for teaching students who have gained these early reading skills to learn to read. Although beginning reading instruction early is beneficial, we recommend not giving up on reading at any age. The strategies suggested in this chapter can be adapted for high school students who participate in typical English classes by using age-appropriate materials. For example, students may participate in learning classic novels through the use of teacher summaries of the chapters that use visual graphics. Because many of these students never had intensive reading instruction, providing this opportunity to gain early reading skills provides an opportunity to move toward literacy.

REFERENCES

Adams, M.J. (1990). *Beginning to read: Thinking and learning about print.* Cambridge, MA: The MIT Press.

Allington, R.L. (2002). *Big brother and the national reading curriculum: How ideology trumped evidence.* Portsmouth, NH: Heinemann.

Anderson, R.C., Hiebert, E.F., Scott, J.A., & Wilkinson, I.A.G. (1985). *Becoming a nation of readers: The report of the commission on reading.* Washington, DC: The National Institute of Education.

Aardema, V. (1978). *Why mosquitoes buzz in people's ears: A west African tale.* New York: Puffin Books.

Basil, C., & Reyes, S. (2003). Acquisition of literacy skills by children with severe disability. *Child Language Teaching & Therapy, 19*(1), 27–48.

Bear, D.R., & Barone, D. (1989). Using children's spelling to group for word study and directed reading in the primary classroom. *Reading Psychology, 10,* 275–292.

Bjorgum, L., & Hudler, M.N. (1977). Teaching adult retarded persons reading through mental effectiveness training. *Mental Retardation, 15,* 18–20.

Browder, D.M. (2001). *Curriculum and assessment for students with moderate and severe disabilities.* New York: Guilford Press.

Browder, D.M., Hines, C., McCarthy, L.J., & Fees, J. (1984). A treatment package for increasing sight word recognition for use in daily living skills. *Education and Training of the Mentally Retarded, 19,* 191–200.

Browder, D.M., & Minarovic, T.J. (2000). Utilizing sight words in self-instruction training for employees with moderate mental retardation in competitive jobs. *Education and Training in Mental Retardation and Developmental Disabilities, 35,* 78–89.

Browder, D.M., & Shear, S.M. (1996). Interspersal of known items in a treatment package to teach sight words to students with behavior disorders. *Journal of Special Education, 29,* 400–413.

Browder, D.M., Wakeman, S.Y., Spooner, F., Ahlgrim-Delzell, L., & Algozzine, B. (in press). Research on reading for individuals with significant cognitive disabilities. *Exceptional Children.*

Browder, D.M., & Xin, P.Y. (1998). A meta-analysis and review of sight word research and its implications for teaching functional reading to individuals with moderate and severe disabilities. *Journal of Special Education, 32,* 130–153.

Campbell, R. (1986). *Dear zoo.* New York: Little Simon.

Chall, J.S. (1996). *Stages of reading development* (2nd ed.). New York: Harcourt Brace.

Clark, S.K. (2001). *A guide for using* Bud, not Buddy *in the classroom.* Westminster, CA: Teacher Created Materials.

Collins, B.C., Branson, T.A., & Hall, M. (1995). Teaching generalized reading of cooking product labels to adolescents with mental disabilities through the use of key words taught by peer tutors. *Education and Training in Mental Retardation and Developmental Disabilities, 30,* 65–75.

Collins, B.C., & Griffen, A.K. (1996). Teaching students with moderate disabilities to make safe responses to product warning labels. *Education and Treatment of Children, 19,* 30–45.

Collins, B.C., & Stinson, D.M. (1995). Teaching generalized reading of product warning labels to adolescents with mental disabilities through the use of key words. *Exceptionality, 5,* 163–181.

Conners, F.A. (1992). Reading instruction for students with moderate mental retardation: Review and analysis of research. *American Journal on Mental Retardation, 96,* 577–597.

Dolch, E.W. (1950). *Teaching primary reading* (2nd ed.). Champaign, IL: Garrard Press.

Edmark Reading Program. (2002). Redmon, WA: Riverdeep. Retrieved January 14, 2005, from http://www.riverdeep.net

Englert, C.A., Raphael, T.E., & Mariage, T.V. (1994). Developing a school-based discourse for literacy learning: A principled search for understanding. *Learning Disability Quarterly, 17,* 2–32.

Erickson, K.A., & Koppenhaver, D.A. (1995). Developing a literacy program for children with severe disabilities. *The Reading Teacher, 48,* 676–684.

Erickson, K.A., & Koppenhaver, D.A. (1997). Integrated communication and literacy instruction for a child with multiple disabilities. *Focus on Autism and Other Developmental Disabilities, 12,* 142–151.

Erickson, K.A., & Koppenhaver, D.A. (1998). Using the "Write Talk-nology" with Patrik. *TEACHING Exceptional Children, 31*(1), 58–64.

Gast, D.L., Ault, M.J., Wolery, M., Doyle, P.M., & Belanger, S. (1988). Comparison of constant time delay and the system of least prompts in teaching sight word reading to students with moderate retardation. *Education and Training in Mental Retardation, 23,* 117–128.

Gast, D.L., Doyle, P.M., Wolery, M., Ault, M.J., & Baklarz, J.L. (1991). Acquisition of incidental information during small group instruction. *Education and Treatment of Children, 14,* 1–18.

Gast, D.J., Doyle, P.M., Wolery, M., Ault, M.J., & Farmer, J.A. (1991). Assessing the acquisition of incidental information by secondary-age students with mental retardation: Comparison of response prompting strategies. *American Journal of Mental Deficiency, 96,* 63–80.

Gast, D.L., Wolery, M., Morris, L.L., Doyle, P.M., & Meyer, S. (1990). Teaching sight word reading in a group instructional arrangement using constant time delay. *Exceptionality, 1,* 81–96.

Gately, S.E. (2004). Developing concept of word: The work of emergent readers. *TEACHING Exceptional Children, 36*(6), 16–22.

Gickling, E.E., Hargis, C.H., & Alexander, D.R. (1981). The function of imagery in sight word recognition among retarded and nonretarded children. *Education and Training of the Mentally Retarded, 16,* 259–263.

Groff, P., Lapp, D., & Flood, J. (1998). Where is the phonics? Making a case for its direct and systematic instruction. *The Reading Teacher, 52,* 138–141.

Heilman, A.W., Blair, T.R., & Rupley, W.H. (2002). *Principles and practices of teaching reading* (10th ed.). Upper Saddle River, NJ: Prentice Hall.

Hoogeveen, F.R., & Smeets, P.M. (1988). Establishing phoneme blending in trainable mentally retarded children. *Remedial and Special Education, 9*(2), 45–53.

Hoogeveen, F.R., Smeets, P.M., & Lancioni, G.E. (1989). Teaching moderately mentally retarded children basic reading skills. *Research in Developmental Disabilities, 10,* 1–18.

Hoogeveen, F.R., Smeets, P.M., & van der Houven, J.E., (1987). Establishing letter-sound correspondences in children classified as trainable mentally retarded. *Education and Training in Mental Retardation, 22,* 77–84.

House, B.J., Hanley, M.J., & Magid, D.F. (1980). Logographic reading by TMR adults. *American Journal of Mental Deficiency, 85,* 161–170.

Hubbard, P. (1999). *My crayons talk.* Minneapolis, MN: Sagebrush Education Resources.

Joseph, L.M., & Seery, M.E. (2004). Where is the phonics? *Remedial and Special Education, 25,* 88–94.

Karsh, K.G., & Repp, A.C. (1992). The task demonstration model: A concurrent model for teaching groups of students with severe disabilities. *Exceptional Children, 59,* 54–67.

Karsh, K.G., Repp, A.C., & Lentz, M.W. (1990). A comparison of the task demonstration model and the standard prompting hierarchy in teaching word identification to persons with moderate retardation. *Research in Developmental Disabilities, 11,* 395–410.

Katims, D.S. (2000). Literacy instruction for people with mental retardation: Historical highlights and contemporary analysis. *Education and Training in Mental Retardation and Developmental Disabilities, 35,* 3–15.

Kliewer, C., & Biklen, D. (2001). "School's not really a place for reading": A research synthesis of the literature lives of students with severe disabilities. *Journal of The Association for Persons with Severe Handicaps, 26,* 1–12.

Koppenhaver, D.A. (1993). Classroom literacy instruction for children with severe speech and physical impairment (SSPI): What is and what might be. *Topics in Language Disorders, 13*(2), 1–15.

Kraus, R. (1994). *Leo the late bloomer.* Minneapolis, MN: Sagebrush Education Resources.

Lalli, J.S., & Browder, D.M. (1993). Comparison of sight word training procedures with validation of the most practical procedure in teaching reading for daily living. *Research in Developmental Disabilities, 14,* 107–127.

Martin, B., & Carle, E. (1991). *Polar bear, polar bear, what do you hear?* New York: Henry Holt & Company.

Mastropieri, M.A., & Scruggs, T.E. (1994). Text versus hands-on science curriculum: Implications for students with disabilities. *Remedial and Special Education, 15,* 72–84.

McKissack, P.C., & McKissack, F.L. (1998). *Black diamond: The story of Negro baseball leagues.* New York: Scholastic.

Mechling, L., & Langone, J. (2000). The effects of a computer-based instructional program with video anchors on the use of photographs for prompting augmentative communication. *Education and Training in Mental Retardation and Developmental Disabilities, 35,* 90–105.

McGee, G.G., Krantz, P.J., & McClannahan, L.E. (1986). An extension of incidental teaching procedures to reading instruction for autistic children. *Journal of Applied Behavior Analysis, 19,* 147–157.

Mochizuki, K. (1993). *Baseball saved us.* New York: Lee & Low Books.

Moore, E. (2000). *The wild whale watch* (A Magic School Bus Chapter Book). New York: Scholastic.

Morris, D. (1993). The relationship between children's concept of word in text and phoneme awareness in learning to read: A longitudinal study. *Research in the Teaching of Reading, 27,* 133–153.

National Reading Panel. (2000). *Teaching children to read: An evidence-based assessment of the scientific research literature on reading and its implications for reading instruction* (NIH Pub. No. 00-4754). Washington, DC: U.S. Department of Health and Human Services.

Onosko, J.J., & Jorgensen, C.M. (1998). Unit and lesson planning in the inclusive classroom: Maximizing learning opportunities for all students. In C.M. Jorgensen (Ed.), *Restructuring high schools for all students* (pp. 71–106). Baltimore: Paul H. Brookes Publishing Co.

Open Court Reading. (2000). *Level 3, book 2.* Columbus, OH: SRA/McGraw-Hill.

Pearson, P.D., & Stephens, D. (1994). Learning about literacy: A 30-year journey. In R.B. Ruddell, M.R. Ruddell, & H. Singer (Eds.), *Theoretical models and processes of reading* (4th ed., pp. 22–42). Newark, DE: International Reading Association.

Rehfeldt, R.A., Latimore, D., & Stromer, R. (2003). Observational learning and the formation of classes of reading skills by individuals with autism and other developmental disabilities. *Research in Developmental Disabilities, 24,* 333–358.

Romski, M.A., Sevcik, R.A., Robinson, B.F., Mervis, C.G., & Bertrand J. (1996). Mapping the meanings of novel visual symbols by youth with moderate or severe mental retardation. *American Journal on Mental Retardation, 100,* 391–402.

Ruddell, R.B., Ruddell, M.R., & Singer, H. (Eds.). (1994). *Theoretical models and processes of reading* (4th ed.). Newark, DE: International Reading Association.

Ryndak, D.L., Morrison, A.P., & Sommerstein, L. (1999). Literacy before and after inclusion in general education settings: A case study. *Journal of The Association for Persons with Severe Handicaps, 24,* 5–22.

Schuster, J.W., Griffen, A.K., & Wolery, M. (1992). Comparisons of simultaneous prompting and constant time delay procedures in teaching: Sight words to elementary students with moderate mental retardation. *Journal of Behavioral Education, 2,* 305–325.

Sendak, M. (1993). *We are all in the dumps with Jack and Guy: Two nursery rhymes with pictures.* New York: HarperCollins.

Shanahan, T. (2003). Research-based reading instruction: Myths about the National Reading Panel report. *The Reading Teacher, 56,* 646–655.

Sheehy, K. (2002). The effective use of symbols in teaching word recognition to children with severe learning difficulties: A comparison of word alone, integrated picture cueing and the handle technique. *International Journal of Disability, Development, and Education, 49,* 47–59.

Singh, N.N., & Singh, J. (1984). Antecedent control of oral reading errors and self-corrections by mentally retarded children. *Journal of Applied Behavior Analysis, 17,* 111–119.

Singh, J., & Singh, N.N. (1985). Comparison of word-supply and word-analysis error-correction procedures on oral reading by mentally retarded children. *American Journal of Mental Deficiency, 90,* 64–70.

Singh, N.N., & Singh, J. (1988). Increasing oral reading proficiency through overcorrection and phonic analysis. *American Journal on Mental Retardation, 93,* 312–319.

Steptoe, J. (2003). *Mufaro's beautiful daughters: An African tale.* Pine Plains, NY: Live Oak Media.

Sulzby, E., & Barnhart, J. (1992). The development of academic competence: All our children emerge as writers and readers. In J.W. Irwin & M.A. Doyle (Eds.), *Reading and writing connections: Learning from research* (pp. 120–144). Newark, DE: International Reading Association.

Wheldall, K., & Mittler, P. (1977). On presenting pictures and sentences: The effect of presentation order on sentence comprehension in normal and mentally handicapped children. *British Journal of Educational Psychology, 47,* 322–326.

Williams, R.L. (1994). *What's in my pocket?* (Emergent Reader Science Series, Level 2). Huntington Beach, CA: Creative Teaching Press.

Worrall, N., & Singh, Y. (1983). Teaching TMR children to read using integrated picture cueing. *American Journal of Mental Deficiency, 87,* 422–429.

Chapter 5

Learning to Read: Phonics and Fluency

Debby Houston,
Stephanie Al Otaiba, and Joseph K. Torgesen

Charlie is a fun-loving 7-year-old boy with a missing front tooth and a crooked smile. He loves to run fast and play with his dog. But, sometimes when he doesn't get his way or when something is hard for him, he shuts down, pouts, and refuses to look at his teacher. This year Charlie attends a first-grade classroom in his neighborhood school. He is the only child with a cognitive disability and he has Down syndrome. At the beginning of the school year, Charlie's mom took digital pictures of his sister, his dog and cat, and his parents and grandparents for Charlie to bring to school. These names were some of the first words Charlie read.

THE SCIENTIFIC KNOWLEDGE BASE ABOUT READING AND READING INSTRUCTION

Knowledge derived from the scientific study of reading, reading development, and reading instruction over the past 20 years provides a very rich context for current efforts to develop effective instructional procedures for all children. In fact, the new "science of reading" is one of the major reasons for current optimism that, as a nation, we can do better than we have ever done before in teaching all children to read (Snow, Burns, & Griffin, 1998). Scientific studies of reading have produced two strands of knowledge that may both contribute to current efforts to develop more effective ways to teach reading skills to students with various levels of developmental disabilities.

The first kind of knowledge about reading has contributed to a new level of understanding of reading processes in skilled readers, the processes involved in learning to read, and what makes reading difficult for many children. Cognitive psychologists and neuropsychologists have done much of this work. The second strand of knowledge involves instructional methods. This knowledge has been generated by systematic research to determine methods of instruction that are most effective for teaching critical reading skills at various levels of development. Our current knowledge is strongest for instruction at the beginning stages of learning to read.

Much of the new knowledge about reading and reading instruction has been summarized and evaluated in three significant documents. The first document was a book commissioned by the U.S. Department of Education and written by Marilyn Adams, a cognitive psychologist, called *Beginning to Read: Thinking and Learning About Print* (Adams, 1990). In 1995, the U.S. Department of Education and the National Institutes of Health jointly commissioned the National Academy of Sciences to assemble a group of scientists and educators to carefully consider the voluminous research on reading available at that time and produce a consensus report. The 2-year deliberations of this commission produced a volume titled *Preventing Reading Difficulties in Young Children* (Snow et al., 1998), which included very specific recommendations for instruction derived from research. These first volumes summarized research on reading processes and reading instruction, and they both concluded that research converged on the same conclusions about what children needed to learn to become good readers. Finally, in 1997, the Congress asked the U.S. Department of Education and the National Institute of Child Health and Human Development (NICHD) to jointly supervise the work of a committee to analyze the most rigorous experimental research on reading instruction with a view to forming conclusions about "what works" in reading instruction (NICHD, 2000). The major conclusions from this work have been summarized in a nontechnical way in a small volume titled *Put Reading First: The Research Building Blocks for Teaching Children to Read,* which is available free of charge from the National Institute for Literacy.

As we shall see in later sections of this chapter, there is limited research on teaching reading to students with moderate disabilities, like Charlie, who was described at the beginning of the chapter. However, there are a number of important conclusions about reading and reading instruction from the broader research on reading and reading disabilities that should be very valuable for educators in their efforts to provide effective reading programs for these students.

In the first section of the chapter, we begin by describing the scientific knowledge base about reading instruction. The "simple view" of reading provides a useful framework for discussing skills and knowledge required for proficient reading. This framework may be particularly helpful in identifying factors that are likely to affect the ultimate level of reading skill achieved by students with moderate disabilities. Next, it is helpful to consider what is known about the major stages typically developing children go through in learning to read and effective instructional strategies for the major reading components that are used in general education settings.

In the second section of the chapter, we shift our focus to what is known about effective reading instruction for students with moderate disabilities. We will use the *learning to read* and *reading to learn* developmental stages as a way of organizing the existing research. Although this research was conducted with students with moderate mental retardation, autism spectrum disorder, or significant language delays, we make a case for and demonstrate how this research can extend to students with significant cognitive disabilities as defined by No Child Left Behind (NCLB) Act of 2001 (PL 107-110). Because the scientific knowledge base about reading instruction for struggling students has only been applied in a limited fashion to students with moderate or significant cognitive disabilities, we highlight some ongoing issues that may have an impact on interpretation of the research.

In the third section of the chapter, we will describe suggested reading instruction for each of the five components of reading (i.e., vocabulary, phonemic awareness, phonics, fluency, and comprehension) for students with significant cognitive disabilities. In this later section, we will focus on providing examples and practical references for commercially available materials for teaching students at the learning to read and reading to learn stages of development. We also provide guidelines for taking a problem-solving approach to using assessment to inform instruction, which is required under NCLB. This assessment section provides helpful references for using screening, progress monitoring, and diagnostic assessments. Finally, we summarize and describe implications for practice and directions for future research.

THE SIMPLE VIEW OF READING

The best measure of a student's success in learning to read is the ability to comprehend, or understand, what he or she reads (Snow, 2002). The "simple view" of reading (Gough, 1996) is that reading comprehension depends on two broad sets of skills and knowledge. The first group of skills are those required to accurately and fluently identify the words in text, and the second set of skills are those required for comprehending language whether in oral or written form. Comprehending the meaning of written language is heavily dependent on the same set of verbal or language comprehension skills that contribute to the understanding of oral language. The main difference is that in reading, the student must also be able to accurately identify words in printed form.

If a student cannot accurately identify, or decode, most of the words in a passage of text, it will be very difficult to comprehend the meaning of the passage. Likewise, if a student can read the text accurately but does not know the meaning of many of the words, or cannot comprehend the concepts expressed, then reading comprehension will suffer. In short, the simple view of reading states that students use word recognition skills to identify written words while simultaneously using their general verbal knowledge and language comprehension abilities to construct the meaning of what they are reading.

Of course, comprehending written material is not exactly like comprehending oral language. For one thing, in oral language comprehension, the listener cannot easily skip back to previous material to correct a misunderstanding. For another, the reader can adjust the pace of reading to allow for more difficult material, whereas that is not always possible when one is listening to oral language. So, there are a number of strategies that readers can use to improve their comprehension that are not available to listeners (Snow, 2002). However, the fact remains that most of the language skills that contribute to reading comprehension are also required when comprehending oral language. Therefore, the simple view of reading is that successful reading is based on the ability to decode or read words as well as the ability to comprehend language.

STAGES IN LEARNING TO READ

The ability to read generally develops in a predictable way for most individuals. Our discussion is organized around three stages that represent the common path toward proficient reading ability: prereading, learning to read, and reading to learn. The overview draws on models of reading development by Jeanne Chall (1983), Linnea Ehri (1998, 2002), and Louise Spear-Swerling and Robert J. Sternberg (1996).

In the prereading stage, children are developing the fundamental language skills that are necessary for learning to read, and they are also acquiring beginning levels of print awareness. The learning to read stage focuses on building skills to read words; in the reading to learn stage, students expand their reading vocabulary and comprehension skills and learn more about using reading as a learning tool. The stages represent phases of progression through the reading development process, but they are not meant to suggest that instruction should focus on only one set of skills during each stage. For example, language development to build vocabulary and general knowledge is important throughout each phase. In addition, even after students enter the reading to learn phase, they continue to acquire knowledge about words that help them become more accurate and fluent readers. Furthermore, comprehension is the goal of reading at all levels, even though the learning to read stage emphasizes developing decoding skills.

Prereading Stage

Language development is the primary focus for children in this stage (Whitehurst & Lonigan, 1998). As students develop expressive language that allows them to communicate their thoughts, and receptive language that allows them to understand what they hear, they are acquiring the vocabulary and verbal thinking skills that are essential for reading comprehension. During this period, they also begin to be aware that print represents spoken words, and they may begin to acquire some initial familiarity with letters. Students often learn to recite the alphabet during this phase. Given the right learning opportunities, students in the prereading phase may also begin to acquire some initial awareness of the phonological structure of words (i.e., that words can be divided into parts or that they can have the same beginning or ending sounds) (Lonigan, Burgess, & Anthony, 2000).

They may also learn to recognize some very familiar words by sight. For example, children learn to recognize their own names, names of playmates, or family members. Additionally, familiar signs and words are recognized (i.e., the word *stop* as it occurs in stop signs, the word *McDonald's* associated with the golden arches, the word *look* because it has two "eyes" in the middle) by their distinctive visual appearance and the context in which they typically occur (Ehri, 1998). Students use memorization as the method to learn to recognize these words, and they are not yet actively using the regular relationships between letters and sounds in their reading. This is an important point, because it would be extremely difficult for anyone to learn enough words through memorization to become a fluent reader at even the third-grade level. Students in the prereading stage also begin to pretend to read and develop basic concepts about print (holding the book upright, pointing to words as they tell the story, left-to-right orientation).

The Learning to Read Stage

At the beginning of this stage, students shift from using arbitrary distinctive visual features to recognizing words (i.e., a word's shape, or its length, or the "tail" on the last letter in the word *dog*) to using the relationships between letters and sounds in words as their main clue to a word's identity. It is during this stage that students master the alphabetic principle so that they can reliably use the correspondences between letters and sounds in words as an aid to accurately guessing the identity of words they have never seen before in print (Rayner, Foorman, Perfetti, Pesetsky, & Seidenberg, 2001).

At the beginning of this stage, students may only sound out a few of the letters in a word before they try to guess what it is, and they will often make mistakes. As students become more skilled at using "phonics" to decode new words, they accurately sound out more of the phonemes in words (particularly the vowels), and they become more accurate readers. At the same time they are learning to use letter–sound cues to help them read novel words, students are also learning that another important clue to the identity of new words comes from the meaning of what they are reading. Their task in learning to read new words is to use as much information as they can from their knowledge of letter–sound relationships and then combine that with their sense of the meaning of the passage, to find a word that matches the sounds they have decoded and also makes sense in the context of what they are reading. In fact, scientists who study the reading process have suggested that teachers should encourage students to first sound out words as much as they can, and then think of a word that has those sounds in it that also fits the meaning of what they are reading (Snow et al., 1998). Once students learn to do this consistently, they are on their way to becoming accurate and fluent readers.

As students practice using their phonics and contextual skills to identify the unknown words they encounter in text, they gradually learn to recognize more and more words by sight (Share & Stanovich, 1995). Students form memory representations for words after they have identified them correctly in print several times (Rietsma, 1983). These representations are created quickly in most students because they are able to use their awareness of the sounds in words to help them remember their spellings (Ehri, 2002). Students who have not developed good phonics skills will have more difficulty learning to recognize words at a single glance. As this phase continues, students also become familiar with common letter sequences such as *ing*, *at*, or *un* that help them decode words in larger chunks.

The real key to the successful conclusion of the learning to read phase is to acquire powerful phonemic decoding skills while building a large vocabulary of words that can be recognized by sight. In fact, it is the latter accomplishment that is the key to fluent reading (Torgesen, Rashotte, & Alexander, 2001). As students learn to recognize more and more words at a single glance, they become more and more fluent readers.

It is important to note that, if our goal is to have students read accurately and fluently above a first- or second-grade developmental level, it will be very difficult to directly teach them to recognize instantly all the words they will need to know. There are simply too many different words to learn. That is why it is important for students to develop skill and confidence in being able to "attack" words they have never seen before in print using a combination of phonemic analysis and contextual skills. If they rely on context alone to identify new words, they will make too many mistakes and will not be able to build the memory representations for words that are the basis for fluent reading. If they do not learn to use phonemic analysis as they encounter new words, they also will not be able to use their awareness of the sounds in words to help them remember word spellings, and their memories for words will be weak. Thus, the key to becoming a fluent and accurate reader at the third- or fourth-grade level is to acquire good alphabetic reading skills (phonics), and then practice using those skills with lots of reading. As students acquire a larger and larger vocabulary of words they can recognize by sight, this paves the way for students' attention to shift from laboring to identify words to getting information from what they read.

The Reading to Learn Stage

Throughout the learning to read phase, teachers need to help students expand their vocabulary and language comprehension skills. During this phase, students continue to expand their background knowledge and vocabulary while they increase the capacity to quickly identify words. They begin to read to gain new information from a wide variety of reading materials and topics. Students spend time thinking about what they read while they are reading. They are just beginning to develop reading comprehension strategies. These strategies allow them to identify facts, descriptions of concepts, or different viewpoints in what they are reading.

In the middle of this stage, students link information and use strategies that apply their own vocabulary and prior knowledge to analyzing text and reading critically. Students begin to apply their strategies to gain meaning from multiple viewpoints and analyze more complex texts to identify layers of facts and concepts. Strategies expand to build toward proficiency in analyzing text and critical reading (Snow, 2002).

The reading to learn stage actually never ends, because the student's vocabulary and background knowledge become continually more sophisticated. They are able to use what they read to formulate their own ideas and construct their own judgments about how the information applies to their own ideas. Students are able to decide if what they read provides adequate information for their purpose and to identify when they need to locate additional sources of information. Just as students were developing comprehension skills as they were learning to read, students continue to use decoding skills from the previous stage when the situation requires it (i.e., decoding technical words or foreign language terms).

CONCLUSIONS ABOUT EFFECTIVE INSTRUCTIONAL PRACTICES

In summarizing research on reading instruction, it is useful to address conclusions in two main areas. The first area involves the content, knowledge, and skills to be taught, and the second area involves methods of effective instruction. The Report of the National Reading Panel (NICHD, 2000) identified five critical areas of reading instruction and growth that should be part of any comprehensive effort to build proficient reading skills. These areas are 1) phonemic awareness, 2) phonics, 3) fluency, 4) vocabulary, and 5) comprehension strategies. They will each be addressed briefly in turn.

Phonemic Awareness

Phonemic awareness is the ability to recognize and manipulate individual sounds, or phonemes, in spoken words (Wagner & Torgesen, 1987). This ability is critical to helping students make the connections between phonemes in words and the letters that represent the sounds in written words. Students who do not have this ability will struggle with learning to read and spell. The good news is that students can be taught to develop their phonemic awareness skills through systematic, explicit instruction (Ehri et al., 2001). Phonemic awareness is most closely associated with the prereading stage of reading development, although for many children, particularly those at risk for reading difficulties, it can extend into the learning to read stage. At a beginning stage of development in phonemic awareness, students can learn to judge whether two words rhyme. Later, they will be able to tell which of several words begin with the same sound as a target word. More complete development of phonemic awareness is shown when students can pronounce all the separate sounds in a word like *cat* (c-a-t) or *first* (f-ir-s-t).

Phonics

Phonics instruction refers to understanding and learning the regular relationships between spoken sounds and letters in words. It builds the bridge between letters in written language and the individual sounds in spoken language. Once students are aware of sounds in spoken language, they can use phonics to decipher and write new words. After reviewing recent research on reading from a number of disciplinary perspectives, Rayner et al. (2001) concluded that "mastering the alphabetic principal" was essential to becoming a good reader. Phonics knowledge gives students a tool to decode words that they have not learned to read by sight. Just as with phonemic awareness, phonics instruction should be systematic and explicit. Phonics instruction is specifically taught to students in the learning to read stage. Students will use phonics knowledge throughout the reading process as they encounter words that are not automatically recognized.

Fluency

Fluency instruction and practice helps students develop skills to read text accurately and quickly. Although being able to recognize most words at a single glance is very important for fluency, fluency goes beyond just recognizing individual words. Students are fluent when they are able to read text smoothly, accurately, and with expression (Meyer & Felton, 1999). In order to read with expression, students must comprehend the meaning of what they are reading. Thus, when we say that a student is a fluent reader, we mean that he or she can read text at the appropriate grade level at the proper rate and with good comprehension. Once students have acquired the skills to read accurately, fluency develops most directly through extended reading practice. The development of fluency is a skill that is emphasized at the learning to read stage, but fluency with increasingly difficult material continues to develop long after entering the reading to learn stage.

Vocabulary

Vocabulary instruction focuses on building knowledge of what words mean. Students use this knowledge to make sense of the words they hear in language or read in text. When students are confronted with written words that are not part of their oral vocabulary, they must learn the meaning of the words before the text will make sense to them. Students learn most of their vocabulary indirectly through their daily experiences. Some vocabulary should be taught directly, such as meaning for specific words and strategies to learn new words. Vocabulary instruction should be a part of reading instruction from the very beginning, and this is likely to be particularly true for students with moderate disabilities. In fact, for students with limited oral language skills, a lack of understanding of the meaning of words is likely to be one of the major factors that will limit their ability to comprehend written material. Remember, students will be able to comprehend written material at no higher level than they can comprehend oral language. Thus, enhancement of language skills is an important part of reading instruction for all students. Recent research has developed ways to teach vocabulary that are more likely to aid reading comprehension than many of the methods used in the past (Beck, McKeown, & Kucan, 2002).

Text Comprehension

Instruction in text comprehension strategies gives students skills that allow them to make sense of what they read. Good readers have a reason for reading: they want information, pleasure, or to meet a personal goal. They also think about what they are reading as they read. While reading, they may adjust reading speed if the text is unfamiliar, they may think about their previous knowledge and try to link it to the new information, or they may check facts that are not clear as they read. Once students are able to gain meaning from recognized words, they begin to build comprehension skills. Reading comprehension can be improved through explicitly teaching students strategies and how to use the strategies (NICHD, 2000). As with vocabulary, comprehension instruction should occur from the beginning of reading instruction. For students who have not yet learned to read words accurately, comprehension skills can be taught through oral language activities. Once students have mastered basic comprehension, and word reading skills, then attention shifts during the reading to learn stage to even more complex comprehension and text study strategies.

METHODS OF EFFECTIVE READING INSTRUCTION

Perhaps the most important conclusion to draw from recent research on instruction for students with disabilities is that it should focus on the same major dimensions of knowledge and skill that are taught in the regular classroom, but it must be more *explicit* and *intensive* than classroom instruction in order to help children with mild to moderate disabilities acquire useful reading skills.

Explicit instruction is instruction that does not leave anything to chance, and it does not make assumptions about skills and knowledge that children will acquire on their own. For example, explicit instruction requires teachers to make direct connections between the letters in print and the sounds in words, and it requires that these relationships be taught in a comprehensive fashion. It also requires that the meanings of words be taught directly and practiced explicitly so that they are accessible when children are reading text (Beck et al., 2002). Finally, it requires not only direct practice to build fluency (Mercer, Campbell, Miller, Mercer, & Lane, 2000), but also careful, sequential instruction and practice in the use of comprehension strategies to help construct meaning (Mastropieri & Scruggs, 1997).

There is now substantial evidence that, in addition to being more explicit, reading instruction for students with disabilities must be considerably more intensive than that provided for most children (Vaughn & Linan-Thompson, 2003). Teaching children individually or in very small groups typically achieves greater intensity of instruction, which will almost certainly be required to teach critical skills to students with moderate disabilities.

WHAT DO WE KNOW REGARDING HOW STUDENTS WITH MODERATE DISABILITIES LEARN TO READ?

Individuals typically develop reading by proceeding through the broad stages of prereading, learning to read, and reading to learn described in the previous section. However, we do not know if students with moderate or significant cognitive disabilities progress through the stages in the same fashion as typical peers (Mirenda & Erickson, 2000). Because Chapters 3 and 4 addressed research and instructional issues and strategies for the prereading stage, the next section of this chapter focuses primarily on the learning to read and reading to learn stages.

Learning to Read: What Is Possible for Students with Moderate Disabilities?

Case studies and anecdotal accounts document that it is possible for persons with moderate disabilities to learn to recognize words and comprehend text. These individuals have developed sufficient general language and word recognition skills to gain meaning from text, albeit generally at a slower pace than their same-age peers (Bos & Tierney, 1984; Bracey, Maggs, & Morath, 1975; Gersten et al., 1998; Kay-Raining Bird et al., 2000).

Specifically, an emerging and encouraging body of research indicates that students with moderate disabilities have been able to learn to use phonics to decode words (Kay-Raining Bird et al., 2000; Nietupski, Williams, & York, 1979; O'Connor, Notari-Syverson, & Vadasy, 1996; Singh & Singh, 1988). This could mean that our expectations for reading potential may have been too limited for these students. These studies begin to show that students with moderate disabilities may respond to reading skills instruction. However, we wish to emphasize that this body of research is still in an exploratory stage; thus, we do not understand how much instruction and practice is required for students with moderate disabilities to learn phonics skills and to be able to generalize the skills to new words.

Reading to Learn: What Is Possible for Students with Moderate Disabilities?

Even less is known about how likely it is for students with moderate disabilities to be able to read to learn. To enter this phase, students will need to have acquired fluent decoding skills and a large vocabulary of words that can be recognized by sight in order to gain understanding from text. Very little research exists to describe the potential for students with moderate disabilities to achieve reading comprehension above a basic level. There are documented cases, more in popular rather than scientific press, describing students with moderate disabilities who have been able to learn to read and understand text, albeit at a lower level of sophistication than their typically developing peers (see, however, Bochner, Outhred, & Pieterse, 2001). There is also preliminary research which indicates that students with moderate disabilities have demonstrated the ability to retell facts, and determine the main idea (Luftig & Johnson, 1982). They have also been able to make inferences from narrative text (Bos & Tierney, 1984).

Issues that May Affect How Students with Significant Cognitive Disabilities Develop Reading Skills

Relationship Between Language and Reading Acquisition   According-ing to Rayner et al. (2001), typically developing students acquire reading based on cognitive, linguistic, and social skills that develop from the earliest age. Consequently, the relationship between language development and the reading process presents a critical issue for students with significant cognitive disabilities. It is common for students with significant cognitive disabilities to experience delays in developing general language skills, including both expressive and receptive skills. Most students also need extended time and practice to master many skills, including those associated with general language development. They may require assistive technology or augmentative communication devices to support their learning and communication. General language comprehension is key to developing phonemic awareness skills that help students to recognize and manipulate sounds in words. In addition, listening comprehension that develops as part of general language ability is the foundation for reading vocabulary and understanding.

Limited Access to Literacy Activities and Instruction   A second issue for students with significant cognitive disabilities at all reading stages is access to home literacy activities and to classroom instruction and intervention designed to build reading ability. A survey of parents of children with disabilities and parents of typically developing children compared the amount of time spent reading to children and the parents' expectations for literacy (Fitzgerald, Roberts, Pierce, & Schuele, 1995). Parents of students with moderate disabilities indicated they spent much less time reading to the children and had lower expectations for reading and literacy than parents of typically developing children. The impact of this finding is that most students with moderate disabilities may enter school with much less exposure to print than typically developing students.

This access to literacy issue is compounded when these students enter school. Researchers have conducted studies (Kliewer & Landis, 1999; Marvin & Mirenda, 1994) to explore the amount of instructional time teachers of students with moderate disabilities devoted to reading instruction compared to teachers of typically developing students. The results indicate that only small amounts of reading instruction time are provided to students with disabilities compared with typically developing students. When coupled with the smaller amount of time to which they are exposed to print outside of school, the limited reading instruction time can significantly impact the possibility of learning to read for students with moderate disabilities.

Not only has instructional time been limited, but also for most students with significant cognitive disabilities, reading instruction has primarily focused on teaching students to recognize functional sight words frequently encountered and necessary in our everyday life (e.g., *exit* and *stop*). These functional words are usually taught as whole words that can be recognized by sight. See, for example, reviews by Conners (1992) and Browder and Xin (1998). The words are often presented in lists with no instructional effort made to help children generalize to word reading within passages, stories, and other connected text. Consequently, the student's reading is limited to recall of this limited pool of sight words. It is important to note that this instructional strategy requires the student to utilize a significant amount of the finite amount of memory available for remembering whole chunks of information. The consequence is that it will be difficult to memorize enough words to become a fluent reader beyond a very basic set of words (Wren, 2000).

We do not disagree that a functional sight vocabulary is important for students with significant cognitive disabilities to be able to make meaningful choices and participate in their communities. However, the absence of instruction that teaches them how to use letter–sound relationships to decipher new words will limit their reading potential. Additionally, the student must be directly taught any new words that are added to their reading vocabulary. Consequently, many students with significant cognitive disabilities have a very limited reading vocabulary and have no strategies for learning new words they encounter.

Unclear Expectations About How Much Growth to Expect The third issue of concern is anticipating the reading level a student with significant cognitive disabilities can be expected to achieve. We have little information about predictors of future reading success, yet we know that there are large individual differences in children's responsiveness to reading instruction (Al Otaiba & Fuchs, 2002). In addition, we do not have a complete picture of the rate at which students with significant cognitive disabilities can be expected to master phonic and other reading skills. There are also gaps in knowledge related to the optimal amount of practice required to master skills and how these translate to support a student reaching his or her optimal reading level.

Consider, for example, the reading to learn stage. Typically, a student must be able to decode one- or two-syllable words and read basic words fluently at a rate of about 100 words per minute to reach this stage (Hasbrouck & Tindal, 1992). This generally equates to about a third-grade reading level. Case studies and anecdotal reports document instances in which individuals with moderate disabilities are able to read newspapers, young adult novels, and other reading materials at about the fourth- or fifth-grade reading level (Bochner et al., 2001; Carr, 1988). However, the research literature is not clear about *which* students with moderate disabilities can be expected to read above a third-grade level.

In summary, the research base for instructional techniques that are most effective (with the best result) and efficient (with the least effort) to provide optimal benefit to the student is in the early stages. For any reader, comprehension is the ultimate goal of reading. Because reading comprehension is heavily dependent on general language comprehension (Stanovich, 1985), general language ability takes on even greater importance for students with significant cognitive disabilities. Students may be able to recognize or decode words, but they must also have the language capacity to understand the meaning of the words they read. For most students, the nature of their disability requires additional instruction and practice to develop language skills. Therefore, using the most effective interventions and instruction to expand language knowledge at this stage is important to both communication and the future ability to learn to read. Clearly, there is not instructional time to waste.

SUGGESTED READING INSTRUCTION
FOR STUDENTS WITH SIGNIFICANT COGNITIVE DISABILITIES

As described earlier, there is a clear understanding of how typical students develop reading skills. In addition, there is a strong research base to indicate the components required to provide effective reading instruction for struggling readers. Each of the five components (phonemic awareness, phonics, fluency, vocabulary, and text comprehension) plays an integral part in reading development, although the emphasis will vary depending on the skill of the learner and his or her stage of reading. For instance, phonemic awareness is an early skill that provides the foundation for learning and using phonics rules. Similarly, emphasis is placed on decoding and fluency in the beginning reading stages. Vocabulary and comprehension are important at every level.

The following section presents a discussion of the five components of reading instruction for students with significant cognitive disabilities. The information in this section reflects the current research literature for students with *moderate* disabilities and practical knowledge from using the components of reading instruction for typical students. Although sufficient research does not yet exist on the applicability of these methods for students with more severe cognitive disabilities, we recommend that teachers try these procedures if the goal is for the student to become a competent reader. It is important to remember that many questions remain about how students with significant disabilities progress through the stages of reading development. We recognize that the three stages are not as discrete as described and that individual students may need instruction in skills across overlapping stages. Due to the overarching importance of vocabulary in general language ability for students with moderate disabilities, we have chosen to address it first.

Building and Sustaining a Language for Reading: Vocabulary Instruction

In Chapters 3 and 4, numerous guidelines were provided for building communication skills for students who are nonverbal and may be beginning to learn to use symbolic communication as a foundation to promote literacy. Some students with significant cognitive disabilities use verbal skills or have expanded use of augmentative communication systems. Building on these skills is an important starting point for teaching students to learn to read. Students who have well-developed general language skills are better prepared to achieve a higher level of reading comprehension (Wren, 2000). Therefore, opportunities to use language and develop vocabulary are critical in all student environments. This can be done through general conversations between adults and children and by using targeted activities.

With a young child, parents and teachers can use dialogic reading, a method that includes structured comments to build language and to expose children to reading (Whitehurst & Lonigan, 2001). Dialogic reading, also called shared-storybook reading or guided reading, differs from typical read-alouds by explicitly and systematically encouraging children to be active participants in the reading process (e.g., Bus & Van IJzendoorn, 1999; Pellegrini, Galda, Flor, Bartini, & Charak, 1997; Whitehurst & Lonigan, 1998). Over the past 25 years, a body of research has shown that adult–child shared storybook reading can be an effective strategy for enhancing language and literacy development for young children who are typically developing (Elley, 1989; Hockenberger, Goldstein, & Hass, 1999) as well as for young children with disabilities (e.g., Crain-Thoreson & Dale, 1999; Dale, Crain-Thoreson, Notari-Syverson, & Cole, 1996; Saint-Laurent, Giasson, & Couture, 1998). Specifically, researchers have reported that shared storybook reading improved vocabulary development (Arnold, Lonigan, Whitehurst, & Epstein, 1994; Robbins & Ehri, 1994), enhanced narrative skills (Purcell-Gates, 1996; Snow, 1993), and developed literate language or the ability to talk about the content of books (Pellegrini et al., 1997). There is also growing evidence that several additional important precursor skills related to successful literacy may be supported by storybook reading, including concepts about print (Whitehurst & Lonigan, 1998), phonological awareness (McFadden, 1998), and alphabetic awareness (Bus & van IJzendoorn, 1999; Crain-Thoreson & Dale, 1999). Shared storybook reading can also foster dialogues about social and emotional development (see, e.g., Van Kleek & Vander Woude, 2003).

The structured interactions that occur during dialogic reading vary by ability level. Students may be asked to name objects found in story pictures. Students with more language experience may be asked to talk about experiences that are similar to those that occur in a story. Table 5.1 presents a sample of a dialogic reading interaction (adapted from Zevenbergen & Whitehurst, 2003).

Table 5.1.   Example of a dialogic reading interaction

Teacher:	Here is a new story called, *I Knew You Could.* What is that?
Charlie:	Choo-choo.
Teacher:	Yes, it says *choo-choo* and it's a train. Can you say *train*?
Charlie:	Train.
Teacher:	Good. "I knew you could! And you knew it too—That you'd come out on top after all you've been through." You were trying hard to build something this morning. What were you building?
Charlie:	Tower.
Teacher:	Yes, you were building a tall tower. It kept falling down, but you stayed on track and kept working hard. "First of all, you must find your own track." Which track do you think the train is going to take?
Charlie:	This one.
Teacher:	That's right, does the train look happy to be on its own track?
Charlie:	Points to smile, "Yeah."
Teacher:	"On your new trip, you'll make plenty of stops . . . Some will surprise you and some will be planned. And you'll roll through each one saying, 'I think I can!'" I think the train feels happy. Your turn, how does the train feel now? (Teacher points to the picture of the train running in the dark toward a light, with a fearful expression.)
Charlie:	Scared.
Teacher:	I think you are right. Let me read some more. ". . . You might even get scared or a little bit sad, wondering if maybe your track has gone bad." Where is the train going now?
Charlie:	To the light.
Teacher:	You see he is going toward the light. "Before you know it, some light will be showing. And then you'll be out, heading to a new place. You'll be ready for the next tunnel you face." (Call Charlie's attention to an event during the day.) I remember you went down the slide today, and then you went through the tunnel. It was dark in the tunnel and light outside. Tell me about this picture.

(continued)

Table 5.1.   *(continued)*

Charlie:	Train out!
Teacher:	Yes, the train is out of the tunnel. We saw a picture like this before. What is the train doing on these pages?
Charlie:	Going fast!
Teacher:	Yes, and here it says you can ask a friend for help. Do you ever need help?
Charlie:	Swing.
Teacher:	Yes, you need help to go on the swing.
Charlie:	Look!
Teacher:	Yes, here it says that "the world is so wide, full of all kinds of people with their own trains to ride." Oh-oh, that is a big hill. What would you do if you were the train?
Charlie:	Go up fast!
Teacher:	Wow, I know you could. The train is working hard to go up the hill. This says, "Just trust in yourself, and you'll climb every hill. Say 'I think I can' and you know what? You will!" You know what? I bet you will try hard to work later today during centers.

Source: Zevenbergen and Whitehurst, 2003.

Note: Teacher is reading aloud *I Knew You Could* (2003) by Craig Dorfman. This story is loosely based on the classic tale, *The Little Engine That Could,* by Watty Piper, published for the first time in 1930.

Two commercially available general education curricula that focus explicitly on language development are SRA Language for Learning (Engelmann & Osborn, 1999) and Elements of Reading Vocabulary (Beck & McKeown, 2004). Following is an example of supporting language development based on a kindergarten lesson from Elements of Reading Vocabulary.

> Ms. Whalon prepares to read *We're Going on a Bear Hunt* from her Read-Aloud Anthology adapted from Michael Rosen and Helen Oxenbury's classic tale that describes a hunt through the grass, a river, mud, and a snow storm. Ms. Whalon selects four words from the story to pre-teach: *wavy, alert, squishy,* and *tiptoe.* She starts her lesson by explaining to the children that bears live in the forest so the children will have to go "a long, long way" to find the bear. She briefly explains, draws, and acts out the words she had chosen to pre-teach. For example, she shows the children how to squish their hands together to simulate the sound of the squishy mud. She invites a student to stand on tiptoe with her and pretend to tiptoe quietly around the classroom. Next, Ms. Whalon reads the story. Meanwhile, she models simple movements for each action in the story and invites the children to join in. After the story, Ms. Whalon invites children to a storyboard with characters to retell the story. She praises them for being *Word Watchers* and sends home a "Word Watchers Certificate" to show their parents they learned *squishy* and *tiptoe.* This lets the parents know to encourage students to use these words at home.

Even as students master beginning reading skills and enter the reading to learn stage, they continue to expand the breadth of their language ability through a wide range of experiences and opportunities to build their listening vocabulary and interact with new ideas. They need activities structured to deepen language knowledge from simple descriptions and responses to using language to understand details and make connections to new concepts. It is therefore important to teach content-specific vocabulary prior to text reading. This will likely be very important for students with significant cognitive disabilities, whose language skills often develop more slowly. When students are able to use their general language knowledge to determine what is more or less important, to decipher the general topic of conversation, or to retell facts or the sequence of events, these verbal skills can be applied to a story they read. In addition, students will need to continue to build general vocabulary knowledge as they build skills for work, independent living, and leisure activities. These can become rich opportunities to expand reading vocabulary as well.

Building a Sound Foundation for Learning to Read: Phonemic Awareness

Beginning to recognize and work with individual sounds in spoken words is another important component of reading instruction for all students. Activities can be used to train students to recognize sounds and put sounds together to make words (e.g., /m/ /a/ /n/ "man"). For typical students, phonemic awareness develops gradually during the preschool and kindergarten years. It develops hierarchically, in a steplike fashion that builds on itself: rhyme and first sound awareness, or alliteration, are easier than blending and segmenting, which are easier than manipulation and deletion. Table 5.2 illustrates this hierarchical progression of typical phonological development.

This awareness of sounds in speech progresses from an awareness of individual words in sentences, to syllables, and on to individual sounds in words (Snider, 1995; Torgesen & Mathes, 1998). The following examples demonstrate that it is easier to hear larger units (e.g., words and syllables) than individual phonemes (i.e., phonemic awareness).

Table 5.2. Phonemic and phonological awareness skills

Skill	Words	Chunks of words	Phonemic level
Rhyme	Cat, bat, which picture rhymes with *cat* and *bat*?		
First sound awareness	What word starts with /c/? *car* or *butterfly*?		
Blending		See if you can guess my word. /pan/ /cake/ See if you can guess my word. /b/ /oy/	I'm thinking of an animal. Can you guess my word? /c/ /a/ /t/
Segmenting		I can clap the sounds in Batman. /bat/ /man/	Can you say each sound in *stop*?
Deletion		Say *pancake*. Say it again without the *pan*.	Say *fast*. Say it again without the /s/.

- The sentence *I can play* has 3 words.

- The word *batman* can be broken into 2 big units or syllables /bat/ + /man/.

- The word *man* can be broken into 2 small units, the first sound or *onset*, /m/ and the rest of the word or *rime*, /an/.

- *Man* can also be broken into its smallest units, called *phonemes*, /m/ + /a/ + /n/.

For students with significant cognitive disabilities, these skills may develop more slowly. Research (Al Otaiba & Hosp, 2004; Fuchs et al., 2001; O'Connor, Jenkins, & Slocum, 1995) shows that students can be taught phonemic awareness using the same instructional strategies that are used with typical students, such as clapping words in sentences or the syllables in words. Rhyming games are useful to help children attend to phonemes in words, starting with indicating whether two words rhyme and progressing to generating rhyming words on their own. Teachers should frequently assess knowledge and progress to guide instruction in this critical reading area.

Although phonemic awareness is typically associated with the earliest reading stage, progression through the skill levels is often uneven and can extend into other stages. Students will need continued review of basic skills. They will also need opportunities to learn more complex skills such as recognizing blends, manipulating sounds in words, and putting two words together. This additional practice and review will support students as they develop stronger skills that will build toward learning decoding skills. Evidence suggests that some children with moderate disabilities can learn to read despite their lack of higher level phonemic awareness skills, such as counting and deleting phonemes within words (Cossu, Rossini, & Marshall, 1993). Table 5.3 provides a list of references to published curricula for teaching these skills.

Building an Understanding of the Code: Phonics Instruction

Phonics is the third important component of reading instruction and incorporates both decoding and sight-word approaches. It is premature to claim that methods for teaching letter–sound relationships are just as effective for students with disabilities as they are for typically developing students. However, students with moderate disabilities benefit from direct instruction methods that include a systematic, structured instructional sequence with individualized practice and feedback leading to mastery. Initial information suggests that these students benefit from phonics instruction that uses a direct instruction approach (Adams & Engelmann, 1996). Using this method will allow teachers to provide complete skill coverage and monitor student performance to ensure that students have sufficient practice to lead to mastery and automatic use of the skills.

Research is just emerging on the best sequence and progression to use when developing decoding skills. However, most teacher guides that accompany general education core reading curricula provide a recommended scope and sequence that progresses from letter sounds, to simple decodable words (e.g., *cat*, *fish*, *cake*), to words with more complex phonics patterns (*meat* or *clean*), and then to multiple syllable words (e.g., *exit* or *hamburger*).

Although most researchers agree it is important for students to learn to decode words phonemically, or sound-by-sound, some students may benefit from

Table 5.3. Phonological awareness supplemental programs

Program	Suggested instructional grouping strategy	Approximate time
Kindergarten Peer-Assisted Literacy Strategies (Fuchs et al., 2001; Mathes, Clancy-Menchetti, et al., 2000)	Peer tutoring	20 minutes 3 days per week
First Grade Peer-Assisted Learning Strategies (Mathes, Torgesen, et al., 2000)		
Ladders to Literacy (O'Connor et al., 1998)	Whole, small, individual	Varies by activity
Phonemic Awareness in Young Children (Adams et al., 1998)	Whole, small, individual	15–20 minutes per day
Phonological Awareness: Assessment and Instruction (Lane & Pullen, 2004)	Whole, small, individual	Varies by activity
Road to the Code (Blachman et al., 1998)	Small, individual	15–20 minutes 4 days per week

initial word-family instruction. For example, Bourassa and Levy (2001) worked with students with mild retardation to compare onset-rime (e.g., /b/ /est/ and /n/ /est/) with whole-word instruction to build reading vocabulary. The results indicated that the students were able to learn to recognize words more rapidly using onset-rime instruction and were able to generalize the skill to new words in the same family. Given that students did respond to the use of rimes in instruction, it may be useful for teachers to focus first on the most frequently occurring rimes when teaching decoding. By doing so, students would be more likely to encounter and read a larger number of words that contain frequently occurring rimes.

Several research studies reveal promising instructional strategies for teaching phonemic decoding skills to students with moderate disabilities. One study used step-by-step procedures (*Look at the first letter, think of the sound, say the sound*) to prompt students to apply phonemic awareness knowledge and phonics skills. Although students have used the procedures when prompted, it remains to be seen whether the students use the procedures independently to decipher new words they encounter in nonprompted reading situations (Hoogeveen, Kouwenhoven, & Smeets, 1989).

O'Connor (2000) and O'Connor and Jenkins (1995) found that teaching spelling in conjunction with sound and/or symbol skills helped students generalize their knowledge to sound out and read new words. Additionally, Joseph and McCachran (2003) investigated a word-study technique to categorize printed words based on sounds and spelling patterns that was shown to help students with moderate disabilities build relationships between sounds and printed words.

Guidance on instructional tools that facilitate student learning is also emerging. Hoogeveen et al. (1989) studied the common practice of using word cards paired with pictures to teach both sounds and words. They found that students had more accurate sound and word recognition when presented with written words without picture cues, unless the picture or graphic mark had a direct meaning to the student. Another promising instructional tool involves interactive technology that highlights words as a story is read aloud on the computer (Bourassa & Levy, 2001). Software that provides this interaction also supports vocabulary development and an awareness of the relationship between letters and sounds in words, and promotes fluent recognition of letter–sound relationships. Tjus, Heimann, and Nelson (1998) also investigated the use of computer-assisted instruction paired with regular classroom reading instruction for students with moderate disabilities. They found that computer-based practice activities matched to specific decoding skills being taught in regular classroom instruction was beneficial to the students.

For typically developing students, phonics becomes a tool that is honed by practice during the reading to learn stage. There are no studies to explore how students with moderate disabilities use decoding skills at this stage. However, given that students with moderate disabilities often require additional practice and support for maintenance of learning, teachers should continue to provide some level of phonics instruction, even as students become more independent readers. Teachers may find it helpful to continue to provide spelling instruction that will assist students with application of decoding skills to new words. It may also be beneficial to provide periodic practice for maintenance of skills to support generalization of decoding skills to new words.

Building Automaticity of Word Recognition: Fluency

Fluency is another key component at the learning to read stage. At the prereading stage, focusing on fluency is premature. However, making students aware of frequently encountered words in their environment can facilitate building toward automatic word recognition. These words may serve a function in the students' environment, such as labels on restroom doors, names of familiar words (e.g., colors, favorite animals), high-frequency Dolch words, or words that allow the students to make choices in their routines (e.g., the name of their favorite restaurant). An excellent source is the widely used *Fry's Teachers' Book of Lists* (Fry, Kress, & Fountoukidis, 2000).

Fluency includes increasing automatic word recognition and reading with expression. Several reviews of research have demonstrated the positive effects of sight-word training, but not all investigated the techniques to build a student's *automatic* word recognition (Browder & Xin, 1998; Connors, 1992). Two studies revealed that classwide peer tutoring resulted in an increased rate of words read correctly (Fuchs et al., 2001; Kamps, Leonard, Potucek, & Garrison-Harrell, 1995). Another study indicated that although students with moderate disabilities read slower than typically developing peers, the reading rate did not appear to negatively influence the comprehension of sentences read by the students (Kabrich & McCutchen, 1996). Developing decoding skills to any degree will provide strategies for the student to decipher unknown words. Even if the proficiency rate and speed for using decoding skills to read new words is slower than typically developing students, it creates the possibility of independent reading.

As students are building fluency, there will still be the need for them to learn functional sight vocabulary to function within their environment. Perhaps one way to bridge this gap is to use the student's targeted functional word list to identify words that can be used to teach decoding skills. For instance, *name* and *game* are typical functional words. These words could be incorporated into prac-

Table 5.4.   Materials for fluency practice

Title	Web site	Description
Great Leaps	http://www.greatleaps.com/	Provides words in lists, phrases, and passages from kindergarten to adult
Quick Reads	http://www.pearsonlearning.com/mcp/quickreads.cfm	Provides passages on social studies and science themes with reading levels from second to fifth
Read Naturally	http://www.readnaturally.com/	Provides passages from kindergarten through adult reading levels. Also a good source of multicultural passages and passages in Spanish

tice activities designed to build fluency, which would allow students to learn functional words and build on their decoding skills simultaneously. Of course, this is not practical with all functional words. However, overlapping the need to read functional words and build automatic recognition of words using decoding skills is worthy of investigation as a teaching strategy.

As students with moderate disabilities add to their reading vocabulary and encounter words that may challenge their decoding skills, instructional activities can facilitate fluency with those words. These instructional activities should provide multiple opportunities to practice reading the word in text. One potentially effective program, designed for students reading at about the second- through fifth-grade level, that combines fluency, vocabulary, and comprehension instruction is *QuickReads* (Hiebert, 2003). This program uses expository passages (social studies and science content areas) that are arranged thematically. For students reading at a second-grade level, for example, there are five passages with illustrations covering the topic "Water and Us." Vocabulary is repeated across the thematic unit. At the end of the unit, students categorize the vocabulary into a semantic web activity and answer questions that address word-level meaning as well as the main idea. Table 5.4 provides a list of three commercially available curricula, including *QuickReads*.

Building the Capacity to Read to Learn: Comprehension

The fifth component is reading comprehension, the ultimate goal of reading. Building vocabulary and verbal thinking skills involved in listening comprehension may be even more critical for reading for students with significant cognitive disabilities. Continual development of general language skills and vocabulary enhances the student's potential to understand what is read. In turn, these skills provide a base for future text comprehension. Activities such as the dialogic reading activities described in this chapter under the vocabulary section can have the additional benefit of building listening comprehension. Making a point of including daily story time and interactive reading allows students the opportunity to be read to and then retell stories they hear.

As their students learn to decode and recognize sight words, teachers may begin instruction of explicit reading comprehension strategies such as main idea, questioning, prediction, and summarization. It is important to support students' emerging reading comprehension by selecting text that is engaging but is also at the right readability level. A simple way to check the "fit" of a text for a student is to listen to them read aloud: If they can't accurately read 95% of the words in a text, it would be difficult for them to comprehend what they are reading independently. Thus, students with significant cognitive disabilities would likely benefit from initial comprehension in easy-to-read texts with controlled vocabulary that focuses on high-frequency Dolch words and easily decodable word families. Figure 5.1 provides a lesson plan that integrates phonemic awareness, phonics, fluency, vocabulary, and comprehension for an elementary-age student, such as Charlie.

Students with significant cognitive disabilities also should have daily opportunities to build comprehension skills in settings other than reading class, such as instructions for job-related tasks or functional words they encounter. We know that students with significant cognitive disabilities require more practice and opportunities to apply their skills in functional settings. Therefore, emphasizing reading comprehension in as many instructional and daily living activities as possible can facilitate additional practice opportunities.

Recall that the reading to learn stage begins to emerge when students can decode one- to two-syllable words, read basic words fluently, and read approximately 100 words per minute (Hasbrouck & Tindal, 1992). This level of reading emerges for typically developing students around third grade. Students who reach this stage still need explicit comprehension strategy instruction that would typically be a part of core reading programs. However, they would likely need more guided practice reading text at their own independent reading level. Providing supported practice using strategies such as peer tutoring has support in the literature. For example, peer tutoring with repeated reading was associated with improved recall and comprehension scores for students with moderate disabilities (Kamps, Barbetta, Leonard, & Delquadri, 1994).

Other aspects that affect the readability of text are structure and genre. Some evidence suggests it may be particularly important to consider these aspects for students with cognitive disabilities. For example, Wolman (1991) reported that students with moderate disabilities, as well as typically developing students, were better able to recall facts and make cause–effect statements when stories had a clear structure for events and details from start to finish. Bos and Tierney (1984) investigated the ability of students with moderate disabilities to make inferences from narrative reading passages. The students were able to make the same quantity and quality of inferences as typically developing students who had a similar level of reading ability (Bos & Tierney, 1984). However, when the reading passages were expository, students with moderate disabilities still were able to generate the same quantity of inferences, but the quality of these inferences was rated as lower than the typically developing students.

USING ASSESSMENTS TO GUIDE READING INSTRUCTION

The following section describes a problem-solving model of assessment that is being promoted for general education and special education under NCLB and the Individuals with Disabilities Education Act Amendments of 1997 (PL 105-17). This model could prove particularly supportive for teachers of students with significant cognitive disabilities as they begin to plan instruction, select appropriate texts, and monitor student learning. After considering a child's reading stage, teachers should first screen their students to get an idea of strengths and to decide where to place a student in a reading program. Next, teachers would use progress monitoring to determine whether students are making adequate growth. Third,

Lesson 10 objectives	Reflections and plans for next lesson
Phonological awareness: 15 minutes *Materials*: Lesson 7 sound play sheet from Kindergarten Peer-Assisted Learning Strategies (K-PALS; Fuchs et al., 2001) *Objectives*: When given a lesson sheet with pictures, Charlie will correctly identify the words that start with /t/ and /b/ such as *turkey* and *bug*. *Reinforcement plan*: Praise correct words; give 1 point on Charlie's point sheet. (For each 5 points, he may shoot a basket with the soft ball.)	Charlie ran through the first sounds in the sound play Lesson 7 with no problems. So we also did a flashcard game sorting 12 pictures by their initial sound (/m/, /t/, /b/, and /s/). Charlie did very well today, so we will add review and add more sounds in the next session.
Decoding: 15 minutes *Objectives:* Charlie will correctly name 8 of 10 letter sounds in isolation on the K-PALS lesson sheet. When given a CVC word composed of letter sounds previously practiced (i.e., *bat*), Charlie will say each sound, blend the sounds, and correctly pronounce the word. *Reinforcement plan:* 1 point per 2 letter sounds; 1 point per word correct	We also did K-PALS Lesson 7; he is getting very good at naming the letter sounds, blending them together, and pronouncing the word.
Sight-word fluency: 5 minutes *Materials:* Words will be presented in a flashcard sight-word card game. *Objectives:* Charlie will correctly read 30 familiar sight words per minute. *Reinforcement plan:* 1 point for each 2 correct; if he beats his time, he gets to choose a book for me to read to him.	Charlie really enjoyed the competition of this game and concentrated really hard with the words. He got most of the words but still consistently has trouble with the words *want* and *they*. I think I will play his favorite Concentration card game with several pairs of these words.
Vocabulary and comprehension: 20 minutes *Objectives:* Charlie will listen to me read two books of his choice to him. He will point and name familiar pictures; will read to familiar sight words in the text, and will correctly name three out of four rhymes. *Reinforcement plan:* 1 point for each correct sentence	Charlie enjoyed reading the book, *What Rhymes with Snake*. Charlie now is able to read almost the whole book by himself and only struggles with a few words. We started a new book this week called *Big Bird Follows the Signs*. Charlie enjoys reading what the signs say and seemed to really enjoy me reading this book to him, so we'll keep working on it next session!
Assessment: 5 minutes *Objectives:* Charlie will read the sight words and letter sounds for curriculum-based measurement (CBM) assessment. *Reinforcement plan:* 1 point and 2 "high fives" for each time he beats his last score	Charlie did CBM today with both letter sounds and sight words. Charlie improved his sight words by a little and he is also not so hesitant to do CBM, which was wonderful. Last week, Charlie scored extremely high on his letter sounds and this session he concentrated very hard and got the same score! He worked very hard on assessment today and it paid off!

Figure 5.1.   Example of a lesson plan for Charlie.

diagnostics measures would be used to fine tune instruction and allow teachers to determine their students' level performance in terms of percentile ranking.

Under NCLB in general education settings, authentic curriculum-based screening measures are used at the beginning of the year to quickly assess the major components of early reading and readiness for literacy instruction. One example of an efficient, widely used screening tool is the Dynamic Indicators of Basic Early Literacy Skills (DIBELS; Kaminski & Good, 1996). Many states have selected DIBELS as both a screening and progress monitoring measure because the subtests are closely related to high-quality reading instruction, are good predictors of later reading achievement, have alternate forms for monitoring progress, have multi-probe reliability exceeding 0.95, and are sensitive to responsiveness to early literacy interventions (Kaminski & Good, 1996). A video tutorial for DIBELS may be ordered commercially but is available in the public domain on at least two web sites (http://www.fcrr.org and http://dibels.uoregon.edu).

Good and colleagues (Kaminski & Good, 1996) developed several DIBELS subtests that are appropriate for students whose prereading or reading skills are at a kindergarten through sixth-grade level. The measures are easy, brief, and efficient to administer. The subtests may be downloaded at no charge on the DIBELS web site, which also offers useful benchmarks based on cutoff scores that indicate to teachers whether a child is at risk for future reading difficulty.

Teachers administer alternate forms of DIBELS as a quick way to determine whether children are making adequate progress toward these benchmarks. The web site also offers fee-based data management that provides teacher reports. For the kindergarten level, four DIBELS subtests are applicable. The first is Letter Naming Fluency, which assesses how many letters a child can name correctly in 1 minute. Teachers show children a sheet with upper- and lower-case letters presented in random order and ask the children to name as many letters as they can. The second is Initial Sound Fluency, which is a measure of beginning phonemic awareness. Teachers present children with pictures and ask them to point to or name the picture that starts with a target sound. The third is Phoneme Segmentation Fluency; this is another measure of phonemic awareness that assesses the number of sounds in a short word that children can pronounce in 1 minute. The fourth measure is Nonsense Word Fluency, which addresses phonics. Teachers present an array of made-up words like *sim* and *lut*, and children can either say each sound in the word individually or blend sounds together to read the whole word.

For students reading at roughly a first- or second-grade level, teachers continue to give the Nonsense Word Fluency test and also begin to administer Oral Reading Fluency, which measures how many words a child can read in 1 minute in connected text. Beyond a third-grade reading level, only Oral Reading Fluency is administered. Links to downward extensions of DIBELS created at other universities for preschool teachers are also available on the DIBELS web site. The following web sites are very helpful because they provide extensive information about assessments and also offer online tutorial sessions that demonstrate how to administer assessments to children:

Florida Center for Reading Research: http://www.fcrr.org/assessment/

Texas Primary Reading Inventory: http://www.tpri.org

University of Oregon: http://idea.uoregon.edu/assessment/index.html

In preschool, play and language may be screened and progress-monitored using Individual Growth and Development of Preschoolers (IGDIs). IGDIs may be accessed from the developers at the University of Minnesota web site (http://www.umn.edu/). Given the overall emphasis on language development for students with significant disabilities, the IGDI vocabulary measure may be of particular interest. An infant and toddler version was created by researchers at the University of Kansas; this web site is http://www.lsi.ukans.edu/jgprojects/igdi/. We have focused on assessment procedures for screening and progress monitoring in greater length than diagnostic testing because of its usefulness in designing instruction for students with significant cognitive disabilities.

NCLB also requires diagnostic tests that are more in-depth than progress monitoring assessments and are only administered for the specific purpose of helping teachers plan more individualized instruction or gauge student progress relative to national norms of typically developing children. Examples of potentially helpful information that could be gleaned from a diagnostic assessment might include answers to the following questions:

As a result of instruction, have my students improved in expressive vocabulary?

Has a student mastered the phonemic awareness skills typical for typical first graders?

Is a student relatively stronger in sight-word recognition than in decoding?

How does a student like Charlie compare with national norms in terms of reading comprehension?

See Table 5.5 for web sites for scientifically based reading research instruction and intervention and Table 5.6 for a more thorough description of diagnostic assessments that are being used in general education settings under NCLB.

Teachers can also supplement progress monitoring with additional teacher-made or informal assessments. For example, teachers can design individualized curriculum-based assessments to identify the student's current skill level and track progress over time. As an example, Figure 5.2 displays a graph of Charlie's progress in letter-sound and sight-word fluency using a curriculum-based assessment.

SUMMARY

Implications for Current Practice

Clearly there are gaps in the knowledge base about reading development and instruction for students with significant cognitive disabilities. However, there are accounts of adults with moderate disabilities who have learned to read with comprehension (Bochner et al., 2001; Carr, 1988; Moni & Jobling, 2001). There is also emerging research to indicate that students with moderate disabilities do benefit from comprehensive reading instruction. This information clearly points to the importance of providing students with significant cognitive disabilities the opportunity to develop reading skills.

Developing reading competencies expands opportunities to participate independently in school and community environments. When students with significant cognitive disabilities have skills that allow them to gain meaning from print at any proficiency level, this ability allows for independent learning. It also provides a tool for students to interact within the community, including leisure, future

Table 5.5.   Web sites for scientifically based reading research instruction and interventions

Web site	Description
http://www.fcrr.org	The Florida Center for Reading Research (FCRR) at Florida State University is a center for research and technical assistance to improve reading instruction and assessment. Faculty at the center conducts basic and applied research, while other staff provide technical assistance and support for the implementation of Reading First in Florida. The web site offers technical reports and reviews of core reading programs and interventions.
http://w-w-c.org/index.html	The What Works Clearinghouse was established by the U.S. Department of Education's Institute of Education Sciences to provide educators, policymakers, and the public with a central, independent, and trusted source of scientific evidence of what works in education.
http://novel.nifl.gov/	The National Institute for Literacy is a federal organization that shares information about literacy and supports the development of high-quality literacy services so all Americans can develop essential basic skills. Research is presented to help teachers be discerning consumers of interventions.
http://www.nochildleftbehind.gov/	On Jan. 8, 2002, President Bush signed into law the No Child Left Behind (NCLB) Act of 2001 (PL 107-110). This new law represents his education reform plan and contains the most sweeping changes to the Elementary and Secondary Education Act (ESEA) since it was enacted in 1965. It changes the federal government's role in kindergarten through Grade 12 education by asking America's schools to describe their success in terms of what each student accomplishes.
http://www.nifl.gov/partnershipforreading/	The Partnership for Reading is a collaborative effort by three federal agencies—the National Institute for Literacy (NIFL), the National Institute of Child Health and Human Development (NICHD), and the U.S. Department of Education—to bring the findings of evidence-based reading research to the educational community, families, and others with an interest in helping all people learn to read well. First established in 2000, The Partnership is now authorized by NCLB.

job opportunities, and independent living. To set the stage for developing reading competencies, teachers and families may need to shift their expectations to consider the possibilities that students with significant cognitive disabilities can acquire reading skills. Providing continual support for language development and experience with written text builds the foundation for reading with understanding. Teachers also may benefit from professional development to effectively incorporate systematic reading instruction into students' educational programs (Katims, 1999).

A firm understanding of typical reading development will provide a framework for designing reading instruction and understanding the differences that may exist for students with significant cognitive disabilities. Reading instruction for students with significant cognitive disabilities can be organized around the research base for effective reading instruction for typically developing students. This chapter provided examples of materials and strategies aligned with this research base that can be used to build reading skills for students with significant cognitive disabilities. However, it is reasonable to incorporate techniques that address specific characteristics and needs of this population of students, such as direct instruction, multiple exposures to information, and extended practice. Clearly, this instruction must be very explicit and more intense than is provided for most students. Individual and small-group instruction will almost certainly be required to help students with significant cognitive disabilities master critical skills.

Although the importance of teaching students with significant cognitive disabilities is becoming clear, the gaps that exist in complete understanding of reading development and effective instruction for these students make it critical to monitor the progress and growth of reading ability. Assessment and progress monitoring not only document student growth, but also provide teachers data on which to adjust instruction and determine when it is appropriate to adjust instructional strategies or move to the next skill. Teachers may find it useful to use both classroom assessment and formal assessment instruments to measure student learning. Formal assessments provide a general overview of a student's reading skill level compared with peers or students performing at the same ability level. Teachers can design individualized curriculum-based assessments to identify the student's current skill level and track progress over time.

Table 5.6. Description of diagnostic reading assessments used in general education settings

Assessment	Publisher	Description
Diagnostic Assessment of Reading (DAR)	Riverside Publishing (http://www.riverpub.com)	This test is designed for students in Grades 1–12 and has subtests that include Word Recognition, Word Analysis, Oral Reading, Silent Reading Comprehension, Spelling, and Word Meaning.
Early Reading Diagnostic Assessment (ERDA)	Harcourt Assessment (http://www.harcourtassessment.com)	This test is a battery of tests that evaluate the early reading skills of students in kindergarten, first, second, and third grades. Subtests include Concepts of Print, Phonological Awareness, Listening Comprehension, Letter Identification, Language Development, Reading Comprehension, and Oral Reading.
The Fox in a Box	CTB/McGraw-Hill (http://www.ctb.com)	This assessment includes subtests designed for children in grades K–3 and include Phonemic Awareness, Alphabetic Recognition, Alphabetic Writing, Spelling, Decoding, Sight Words, Reading, and Listening and Writing.

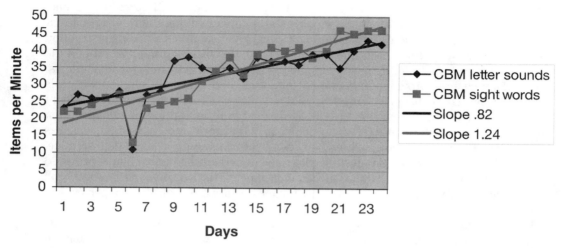

Figure 5.2. Student progress on curriculum-based measures.

The research emphasis on reading for all students will continue to provide new information to guide our understanding of reading development and to inform our instructional practice. Just as researchers, educators, and policy makers have attempted to establish appropriate growth guidelines for students with learning disabilities, additional work is needed to define "adequate yearly progress" in learning to read for students with significant cognitive disabilities. Over the coming years, new information will emerge from current research studies investigating reading for students with significant cognitive disabilities. As the body of knowledge grows with regard to effective reading development for students with significant cognitive disabilities, teachers will need to adjust both their thinking and strategies for reading instruction.

Directions for Future Research

One of the first issues to be addressed by future research is to document how and to what degree students with significant cognitive disabilities are able to develop reading skills. An understanding of potential for reading achievement for these students could be established through review of archival records to document the level of reading instruction that has been provided and the reading level achieved by the students. In addition, longitudinal studies would allow us to track students' reading development to determine whether there are differences in the expected age or developmental stage at which reading skills can be expected to develop.

We know that language development is critical to reading development for all students, particularly students with significant cognitive disabilities. Replication of the research on home literacy and the impact of different language development strategies on reading abilities using students who have significant cognitive disabilities can provide guidance to develop effective early language intervention programs. It will also be important to determine the most effective methods to support language development as students progress through each of the reading stages.

Additional research that applies evidence-based reading instruction (i.e., NICHD, 2000; Snow et al., 1998) to students with significant cognitive disabilities is critical. It is important to explore the sequence of reading skill development for students with significant cognitive disabilities and determine any implications for instruction. We must continue and expand our efforts to address questions that will lead to the identification of the most effective and efficient instructional strategies for teaching students with significant cognitive disabilities to read. Of particular interest is the benefit of phonemic awareness and phonics instruction for this population.

Finally, a potential research topic emerges from the heavy emphasis on accountability for reading development for all students. It will be important to analyze participation and reading achievement levels of students with significant cognitive disabilities in high-stakes reading initiatives, such as those required by NCLB. The information provided by research on reading development and students with significant cognitive disabilities also can be used to inform policy development for accountability in these initiatives.

REFERENCES

Adams, M.J. (1990). *Beginning to read: Thinking about learning and print.* Cambridge, MA: The MIT Press.

Adams, M., Foorman, B., Lundberg, I., & Beeler, C. (1998). *Phonemic awareness in young children: A classroom curriculum.* Baltimore: Paul H. Brookes Publishing Co.

Adams, G.L., & Engelmann, S. (1996). *Research on direct instruction: 25 years beyond DISTAR.* Seattle: Educational Achievement Systems.

Al Otaiba, S., & Fuchs, D. (2002). Characteristics of children who are unresponsive to early literacy intervention: A review of the literature. *Remedial and Special Education, 23*(5), 300–316.

Al Otaiba, S., & Hosp, M. (2004). Service learning: Training preservice teachers to provide effective literacy instruction to students with Down syndrome. *TEACHING Exceptional Children, 36*(4), 28–35.

Arnold, D.H., Lonigan, C.J., Whitehurst, G.J., & Epstein, J.N. (1994). Accelerating language development through picture book reading: Replication and extension to videotape training format. *Journal of Educational Psychology, 86*, 235–243.

Beck, I.L., & McKeown, M.G. (2004). *Elements of reading.* Austin, TX: Steck-Vaughn.

Beck, I.L., McKeown, M.G., & Kucan, L. (2002). *Bringing words to life: Robust vocabulary instruction.* New York: Guilford Press.

Blachman, B., Ball, E., Black, S., & Tangel, D. (1998). *Road to the code.* Baltimore: Paul H. Brookes Publishing Co.

Bochner, S., Outhred, L., & Pieterse, M. (2001). A study of functional literacy skills in young adults with Down syndrome. *International Journal of Disability, Development and Education, 48*(1), 67–90.

Bos, C.S., & Tierney, R.J. (1984). Inferential reading abilities of mildly mentally retarded and nonretarded students. *American Journal of Mental Deficiency, 89*, 75–82.

Bourassa, D., & Levy, B.A. (2001, June). *Developing reading skills in children with Down syndrome: Use of orthographic analogies.* Poster presented at the Society for the Scientific Study of Reading (SSSR) annual convention, Boulder, CO.

Bracey, S., Maggs, A., & Morath, P. (1975). The effects of a direct phonic approach in teaching reading with six moderately retarded children: Acquisition and mastery learning stages. *Exceptional Child, 22*(2), 83–90.

Browder, D.M., & Xin, Y.P. (1998). A meta-analysis and review of sight word research and its implications for teaching functional reading to individuals with moderate and severe disabilities. *The Journal of Special Education, 32*, 130–153.

Bus, A., & Van IJsendoorn, M. (1999). Phonological awareness and early reading: A meta-analysis of experimental training studies. *Journal of Educational Psychology, 91*, 403–411.

Carr, J. (1988). Six weeks to twenty-one years old: A longitudinal study of children with Down's syndrome and their families. *Journal of Child Psychology and Psychiatry, 29,* 407–431.

Chall, J.S. (1983). *Stages of reading development.* New York: McGraw-Hill.

Conners, F.A. (1992). Reading instruction for students with moderate mental retardation: Review and analysis of research. *American Journal on Mental Retardation, 96,* 577–597.

Cossu, G., Rossini, F., & Marshall, J.C. (1993). When reading is acquired but phonemic awareness is not: A study of literacy in Down's syndrome. *Cognition, 46,* 129–138.

Crain-Thoreson, C., & Dale, P.S. (1999). Enhancing linguistic performance: Parents and teachers as book reading partners for children with language delays. *Topics in Early Childhood Special Education, 19,* 28–39.

Dale, P.S., Crain-Thoreson, C., Notari-Syverson, A., & Cole, K. (1996). Parent-child book reading as an intervention technique for young children with language delays. *Topics in Early Childhood Special Education, 16,* 213–235.

Dorfman, C. (2003). *I knew you could.* East Rutherford, NJ: Grosset & Dunlap.

Ehri, L.C. (1998). Grapheme-phoneme knowledge is essential for learning to read words in English. In J. Metsala & L. Ehri (Eds.), *Word recognition in beginning reading* (pp. 3–40). Hillsdale, NJ: Lawrence Erlbaum Associates.

Ehri, L. (2002). Phases of acquisition in learning to read words and implications for teaching. In R. Stainthorp & P. Tomlinson (Eds.), *Learning and teaching reading* (pp. 7–28). London: British Journal of Educational Psychology Monograph Series II.

Ehri, L.C., Nunes, S.R., Willows, D.M., Schuster, B.V., Yaghoub-Zadeh, Z., & Shanahan, T. (2001). Phonemic awareness instruction helps children learn to read: Evidence from the National Reading Panel's meta-analysis. *Reading Research Quarterly, 36,* 250–287.

Elley, W.B. (1989). Vocabulary acquisition from listening to stories. *Reading Research Quarterly, 24,* 174–187.

Engelmann, S., & Osborn, J. (1999). *Language for learning.* Columbus, OH: SRA/McGraw-Hill.

Fitzgerald, J., Roberts, J., Pierce, P., & Schuele, M. (1995). Evaluation of home literacy environment: An illustration with preschool children with Down syndrome. *Reading and Writing Quarterly: Overcoming Learning Difficulties, 11,* 311–334.

Fry, E.B., Kress, J.E., & Fountoukidis, D.L. (2000). *The reading teacher's book of lists.* Upper Saddle River, NJ: Prentice Hall.

Fuchs, D., Fuchs, L.S., Thompson, A., Al Otaiba, S., Yen, L., Yang, N.J., et al. (2001). Is reading important in reading-readiness programs? A randomized field trial with teachers as program implementers. *Journal of Educational Psychology, 93,* 251–267.

Gersten, R., Williams, J.P., Fuchs, L., Baker, S., Koppenhaver, D., Spadorcia, S., et al. (1998). *Improving reading comprehension for children with disabilities: A review of research. Final report.* Washington, DC: Special Education Programs (ED/OSERS).

Gough, P.B. (1996). How children learn to read and why they fail. *Annals of Dyslexia, 46,* 3–20.

Hasbrouck, J.E., & Tindal, G. (1992). Curriculum-based oral reading fluency norms for students in grades 2 through 5. *TEACHING Exceptional Children, 24*(3), 41–44.

Hiebert, E.H. (2003). *QuickReads: A research-based fluency program.* Parsippany, NJ: Modern Curriculum Press.

Hockenberger, E.H., Goldstein, H., & Haas, L.S. (1999). Effects of commenting during joint book reading by mothers with low SES. *Topics in Early Childhood Special Education, 19,* 15–27.

Hoogeveen, F.R., Kouwenhoven, J.A., & Smeets, P.M. (1989). Establishing sound blending in moderately mentally retarded children: Implications of verbal instruction and pictorial prompting. *Research in Developmental Disabilities, 10,* 333–348.

Individuals with Disabilities Education Act Amendments of 1997, PL 105-17, 20 U.S.C. §§ 1400 *et seq.*

Joseph, L.M., & McCachran, M. (2003). Comparison of a word study phonics technique between students with moderate to mild mental retardation and struggling readers without disabilities. *Education and Training in Developmental Disabilities, 38,* 192–199.

Kabrich, M., & McCutchen, D. (1996). Phonemic support in comprehension: Comparisons between children with and without mild mental retardation. *American Journal on Mental Retardation, 100,* 510–527.

Kaminski, R.R., & Good, R.H. (1996). Toward a technology for assessing basic early literacy skills. *School Psychology Review, 25,* 215–227.

Kamps, D.M., Barbetta, P.M., Leonard, B.R., & Delquadri, J. (1994). Classwide Peer Tutoring: An integration strategy to improve reading skills and promote peer interactions among students with autism and general education peers. *Journal of Applied Behavior Analysis, 27,* 49–61.

Kamps, D., Leonard, B., Potucek, J., & Garrison-Harrell, L. (1995). Cooperative Learning Groups in reading: An integration strategy for children with autism and general classroom peers. *Behavioral Disorders, 21,* 89–109.

Katims, D. (1999). Standards fail to address literacy needs of individuals with mental retardation. *Council for Exceptional Children Today, 5*(9), 14.

Kay-Raining Bird, E., Cleave, P.L., & McConnell, L. (2000). Reading and phonological awareness in children with Down syndrome: A longitudinal study. *American Journal of Speech-Language Pathology, 9,* 319–330.

Kliewer, C., & Landis, D. (1999). Individualizing literacy instruction for young children with moderate to severe disabilities. *Exceptional Children, 66,* 85–100.

Lane, H.B., & Pullen, P.C. (2004). *Phonological awareness assessment and instruction: A sound beginning.* Boston: Pearson.

Lonigan, C.J., Burgess, S.R., & Anthony, J.L. (2000). Development of emergent literacy and early reading skills in preschool children: Evidence from a latent variable longitudinal study. *Developmental Psychology, 36,* 596–613.

Luftig, R.L., & Johnson, R.E. (1982). Identification and recall of structurally important units in prose by mentally retarded learners. *American Journal of Mental Deficiency, 86,* 495–502.

Marvin, C., & Mirenda, P. (1994). Literacy practices in head start and early childhood special education classrooms. *Early Education and Development, 5,* 289–300.

Mastropieri, M.A., & Scruggs, T.E. (1997). Best practices in promoting reading comprehension in students with learning disabilities: 1976–1996. *Remedial and Special Education, 18,* 197–213.

Mathes, P., Clancy-Menchetti, J., Allor, J.H., & Allen, S.H. (2000). *Kindergarten PALS (Peer-Assisted Literacy Strategies).* Longmont, CO: Sopris.

Mathes, P., Torgesen, J.K., Allen, S.H., & Allor, J.H. (2000). *First grade PALS (Peer-Assisted Literacy Strategies).* Longmont, CO: Sopris.

McFadden, T.U. (1998). Sounds and stories: Teaching phonemic awareness in interactions around text. *American Journal of Speech-Language Pathology, 7,* 5–13.

Mercer, C.D., Campbell, K.U., Miller, M.D., Mercer, K.D., & Lane, H.B. (2000). Effects of a reading fluency intervention for middle schoolers with specific learning disabilities. *Learning Disabilities Research and Practice, 15,* 179–189.

Meyer, M.S., & Felton, R.H. (1999). Repeated reading to enhance fluency: Old approaches and new directions. *Annals of Dyslexia, 49,* 283–306.

Mirenda, P., & Erickson, K.A. (2000). Augmentative communication and literacy. In A.M. Wetherby & B.M. Prizant (Eds.), *Autism spectrum disorders: A transactional developmental perspective* (pp. 225–250). Baltimore: Paul H. Brookes Publishing Co.

Moni, K.B., & Jobling, A. (2001). Reading related literacy learning of young adults with Down syndrome: Findings from a three year teaching and research program. *International Journal of Disability, Development and Education, 48,* 377–394.

National Institute of Child Health and Human Development (NICHD). (2000). *Report of the National Reading Panel. Teaching children to read. An evidence-based assessment of the scientific research literature on reading and its implications for reading instruction* (NIH Publication No. 00-4769). Washington, DC: U.S. Government Printing Office.

National Reading Panel. (2001). *Put reading first.* Retrieved November 1, 2004, from http://www.nationalreadingpanel.org/NRPAbout/Charge.htm

Nietupski, J., Williams, W., & York, R. (1979). Teaching selected phonic word analysis reading skills to TMR labeled students. *TEACHING Exceptional Children, 11*(4), 140–143.

No Child Left Behind Act of 2001, PL 107-110, 115 Stat. 1425, 20 U.S.C. §§ 6301 *et seq.*

O'Connor, R. (2000). Increasing the intensity of intervention in kindergarten and first grade. *Learning Disabilities Research and Practice, 15*(1), 43–54.

O'Connor, R.E., & Jenkins, J.R. (1995). Improving the generalization of sound/symbol knowledge: Teaching spelling to kindergarten children with disabilities. *The Journal of Special Education, 29,* 255–275.

O'Connor, R.E., Jenkins, J.R., & Slocum, T.A. (1995). Transfer among phonological tasks in kindergarten: Essential instructional content. *Journal of Educational Psychology, 87,* 202–217.

O'Connor, R.E., Notari-Syverson, A., & Vadasy, P.F. (1996). Ladders to literacy: The effects of teacher-led phonological activities for kindergarten children with and without disabilities. *Exceptional Children, 63,* 117–131.

O'Connor, R.E., Notari-Syverson, N., and Vadasy, P. (2005). *Ladders to literacy: A kindergarten activity book* (2nd ed.). Baltimore: Paul H. Brookes Publishing Co.

Pellegrini, A.D., Galda, L., Flor, D., Bartini, D., & Charak, D. (1997). Close relationships, individual differences and early literacy learning. *Journal of Experimental Child Psychology, 7,* 409–422.

Purcell-Gates, V. (1996). Stories, coupons, and the TV Guide: Relationships between home literacy experiences and emergent literacy knowledge. *Reading Research Quarterly, 31,* 406–428.

Rayner, K., Foorman, B.R., Perfetti, C.A., Pesetsky, D., & Seidenberg, M.S. (2001). How psychological science informs the teaching of reading. *Psychological Science in the Public Interest, 2,* 31–73.

Reitsma, P. (1983). Printed word learning in beginning readers. *Journal of Experimental Child Psychology, 75,* 321–339.

Robbins, C., & Ehri, L.C. (1994). Reading storybooks to kindergarteners helps them learn new vocabulary words. *Journal of Educational Psychology, 86,* 54–64.

Saint-Laurent, L., Giasson, J., & Couture, C. (1998). Emergent literacy and intellectual disabilities. *Journal of Early Intervention, 21,* 267–281.

Share, D.L., & Stanovich, K.E. (1995). Cognitive processes in early reading development: A model of acquisition and individual differences. *Issues in Education: Contributions from Educational Psychology, 1,* 1–57.

Singh, N.N., & Singh, J. (1988). Increasing oral reading proficiency through overcorrection and phonic analysis. *American Journal on Mental Retardation, 93,* 312–319.

Snider, V.E. (1995). A primer on phonemic awareness: What it is, why it's important, and how to teach it. *School Psychology Review, 24,* 443–455.

Snow, C. (1993). Literacy and language: Relationships during the preschool years. *Harvard Educational Review, 53,* 165–189.

Snow, C. (2002). *Reading for understanding: Toward an R&D program in reading comprehension.* Arlington, VA: RAND.

Snow, C.E., Burns, M.S., & Griffin, P. (1998). *Preventing reading difficulties in young children.* Washington, DC: National Academy Press.

Spear-Swerling, L., & Sternberg, R.J. (1996). *Off track: When poor readers become "learning disabled."* Boulder, CO: Westview Press.

Stanovich, K.E. (1985). Cognitive determinants of reading in mentally retarded individuals. *International Review of Research in Mental Retardation, 13,* 181–214.

Tjus, T., Heimann, M., & Nelson, K. (1998). Gains in literacy through the use of a specially developed multimedia computer strategy. *Autism, 2*(2), 139–156.

Torgesen, J.K., & Mathes, P.G. (1998). *What every teacher should know about phonological awareness.* Tallahassee, FL: Florida Department of Education.

Torgesen, J.K., Rashotte, C.A., & Alexander, A. (2001). Principles of fluency instruction in reading: Relationships with established empirical outcomes. In M. Wolf (Ed.), *Dyslexia, fluency, and the brain.* Parkton, MD: York Press.

Van Kleeck, A., & Vander Woude, J. (2003). Book sharing with preschoolers with language delays. In A. Van Kleeck, S.A. Stahl, & E.B. Bauer (Eds.), *On reading books to children* (pp. 58–94). Mahwah, NJ: Lawrence Erlbaum Associates.

Vaughn S., & Linan-Thompson, S. (2003). Group size and time allotted to intervention: Effects for students with reading difficulties. In B. Foorman (Ed.), *Preventing and remediating reading difficulties: Bringing science to scale* (pp. 299–324). Parkton, MD: York Press.

Wagner, R.K., & Torgesen, J.K. (1987). The nature of phonological processing and its causal role in the acquisition of reading skills. *Psychological Bulletin, 101,* 192–212.

Whitehurst, G.J., & Lonigan, C.J. (1998). Child development and emergent literacy. *Child Development, 69,* 335–357.

Whitehurst, G.J., & Lonigan, C.J. (2001). Emergent literacy: Development from prereaders to readers. In S.B. Neuman & D.K. Dickinson (Eds.), *Handbook of early literacy research* (pp. 11–29). New York: Guilford Press.

Wolman, C. (1991). Sensitivity to causal cohesion in stories by children with mild mental retardation, children with learning disabilities, and children without disabilities. *The Journal of Special Education, 25,* 135–154.

Wren, S. (2000). *The cognitive foundations of learning to read: A framework.* Austin, TX: Southwest Educational Development Laboratory.

Zevenbergen, A.A., & Whitehurst, G.J. (2003). Dialogic reading: A shared picture book reading intervention for preschoolers. In S. Stahl, A. Kleeck, & E. Bauer (Eds.), *On reading books to children* (pp. 177–203). Mahwah, NJ: Lawrence Erlbaum Associates.

Chapter 6

Balanced Literacy Classrooms and Embedded Instruction for Students with Severe Disabilities

Literacy for All in the Age of School Reform

Terri Ward, Cheryl A. Van De Mark, and Diane Lea Ryndak

Three of the most significant documents to change education in the United States in the last decade have been the reauthorization of the Individuals with Disabilities Education Act (IDEA) and amendments of 1997 (PL 105-17) and reauthorization of 2004 (PL 108-446), the No Child Left Behind (NCLB) Act of 2001 (PL 107-110), and the Report of the National Reading Panel (National Institute of Child Health and Human Development [NICHD], 2002). Each of these documents represents a nationwide alteration of our collective definition of the concepts of access to the general education curriculum, demonstration of adequate yearly progress, and instruction on literacy, including skills in reading, writing, speaking, and listening. Major concepts from these documents have been addressed in previous chapters because they have affected how schools meet the needs of students with severe disabilities as they access general education achievement benchmarks under their state's standard and/or alternate assessment systems. Although discussed briefly in this section, it is clear that the single-mindedness of the major concepts in these three documents has provided the foundation for instruction in literacy for students with severe disabilities in general education classrooms, focusing on both general education reading skills and functional use of literacy throughout the day.

During the same period of time as the inception of NCLB and the reauthorization of IDEA '97, the National Reading Panel conducted a meta-analysis of scientifically based research and outlined five components of reading instruction that are most directly linked to early reading success: 1) phonemic awareness, 2) phonics, 3) fluency, 4) vocabulary, and 5) text comprehension (see Table 6.1). In addition to identifying these five components of reading instruction, the National Reading Panel outlined competencies and methodologies that are essential for student achievement in reading. They further suggested that the most successful classroom teachers directly and explicitly teach specific literacy

Table 6.1.   Key components that are crucial for early reading success

Key component	Definition
Phonemic awareness	The ability to hear, identify, and manipulate the individual sounds (phonemes) in spoken words. Phonemic awareness is the understanding that the sounds of spoken language work together to make words. Children do not need print awareness to have phonemic awareness.
Phonics	The understanding that there is a predictable relationship between phonemes (the sounds of spoken language) and graphemes (the letters and spellings that represent those sounds in written language). Readers use these relationships to recognize familiar words accurately and automatically and to decode unfamiliar words.
Fluency	Fluency is the ability to read text accurately and quickly. It provides a bridge between word recognition and comprehension. Fluent readers recognize words and comprehend at the same time.
Vocabulary	Development of stored information about the meanings and pronunciation of words necessary for communication
Text comprehension	Strategies for understanding, remembering, and communicating with others about what has been read. Comprehension strategies are sets of steps that purposeful, active readers use to make sense of text.

Source: National Reading Panel, 2002.

skills, engage students in authentic learning tasks, and assist students with the development of metacognitive strategies that facilitate reading. The examples contained in this chapter align with the recommendations from the National Reading Panel (see Table 6.1).

Since this report and the inception of NCLB, the U.S. government has made available a formula grant aimed at improving the reading performance of all learners. In order to retool our teachers and schools, the U.S. Department of Education created the Reading First initiative, which provided funds to assist state and local school districts in eliminating the reading deficit in any minority subgroup by establishing high-quality, comprehensive reading instruction in kindergarten through third grade. In order to receive the funding, however, a state was required to use a solid research foundation and develop a comprehensive plan for improving students' reading performance. Although states had flexibility in choosing reading programs and strategies suitable to their needs, a clear mandate was that any reading program selected must meet the federal definition of "scientifically-based reading research practice" (U.S. Department of Education, 2002, pp. 4–6). In essence, a state was required to choose reading programs and strategies that aligned with the results from the Report of the National Reading Panel (NICHD, 2002). In addition, the state must outline how it would 1) implement the scientifically based reading program; 2) provide professional development so that teachers could use the reading program effectively; and 3) ensure accountability through ongoing valid and reliable screening, as well as diagnostic and classroom-based assessment (U.S. Department of Education, 2002).

Clearly, the IDEA 1997/2004, NCLB, Report of the National Reading Panel (NICHD, 2002), and the Reading First Guidance Document (U.S. Department of

Education, 2002) outlined instructional practices to be used for literacy instruction in classrooms across the United States. Increasingly, it has become common in elementary classrooms to see explicit and direct instruction in the key components of early reading success, to see students with severe disabilities receiving instruction alongside their classmates without disabilities during literacy blocks, and to see progress for all students being measured through ongoing data collection. Although phonemic awareness and phonics instruction fade as children progress through the grades, the upper elementary, middle, high school, and postsecondary schools continue to focus on fluency, vocabulary development, and text comprehension. Additionally, as children progress through grade levels, increasing amounts of time are spent on the writing process. The challenge for both general and special education teachers at each level of education is to provide effective and engaging instruction for all students that addresses both accountability standards and individual needs. The following sections discuss the practical organization of a literacy block at different grade levels, and how the needs of students with severe disabilities could be addressed along with the needs of their classmates without disabilities.

THE FOCUSED LITERACY BLOCK

Although there is no *one* widely accepted checklist of best practices used in a literature-rich classroom, many experts agree on a number of practices that provide high-quality literacy instruction within the general education classroom (Cunningham, 1995; Cunningham & Allington, 1999; Snow, Burns, & Griffin, 1998). Such practices include strategies that build phonemic awareness and decoding skills, increase fluency and comprehension, broaden vocabulary, improve spelling, and provide authentic writing opportunities. As students' skills develop, the amount of instructional time dedicated to these strategies typically is modified. Whether at the early elementary or the secondary level, however, the desired result is a focused literacy block of instruction that incorporates both simulated and natural reading and writing activities, as well as reliance on teachers to regularly monitor student performance. This naturally results in a literature-rich learning environment in which each student receives instruction that matches their literacy level and instructional needs.

Although there is no single approach to teaching reading, exemplary focused literacy blocks provide students with multiple opportunities to interact with text, as well as with one another, on a daily basis. This may be one of the most significant predictors of student success and it has direct major implications for students with severe disabilities. Fielding and Pearson (1994), for example, indicated that background knowledge is a reliable predictor (i.e., either positive or negative) of student comprehension of text. It can be argued, therefore, that for students with severe disabilities to develop text comprehension skills, they will need direct literacy instruction in a language-rich environment in which teachers expand the students' background knowledge and provide a clear purpose for reading. Students who are developing an understanding that symbols represent sounds and words (i.e., students who are emergent readers) have demonstrated literacy growth and an increased ability to construct meaning when they handle books, listen to books on tape or books presented orally, experiment with letters, and connect words to pictures in a given text. It is critical, therefore, that the materials used by students, both during focused literacy block instruction and across other instructional contexts, are conducive to these activities. It has been suggested that students be exposed to a variety of printed materials (e.g., books, newspapers, magazines, poetry, maps, flyers, and letters) at various reading levels. Consistent exposure to such materials helps to demonstrate and reinforce the functional uses of reading and writing in our society. Although these statements are widely accepted as applying to students without disabilities and students with mild disabilities, it must be noted that they also apply to students with severe disabilities.

Including Students with Severe Disabilities in the Focused Literacy Block

As students with severe disabilities increasingly have been included in general education classes, education teams have identified variables whose consideration is critical to providing effective instruction for them. In particular, three sets of variables are critical when considering literacy instruction for students with severe disabilities. Each of these sets is discussed briefly in the following sections.

Learning Characteristics   The first set of variables that an education team must consider includes learning characteristics demonstrated by many students with severe disabilities (Ryndak & Alper, 2003). For instance, students usually are identified as having severe disabilities at a very young age because they learn much more slowly than other students, even students with mild disabilities (e.g., learning disabilities, mild mental retardation). Because they learn so slowly, over time students with severe disabilities usually learn a lot less than other students. In addition, students with severe disabilities frequently have a difficult time 1) maintaining information they have learned; 2) generalizing across contexts (e.g., across settings, people, materials, and cues) the use of information they have learned; and 3) putting together skills that are components of one activity (e.g., communication, mobility, motor, and cognitive skills that, after being learned separately, cannot necessarily be used in conjunction with each other in a meaningful naturally occurring activity, such as ordering, obtaining, and eating lunch in the cafeteria with classmates who do not have disabilities).

Purpose of Education   The second variable that must be considered is the purpose of education. It has been argued that the purpose of education for students with severe disabilities is to assist each student to participate more fully, and be as independent as possible, in activities that occur naturally in contexts that comprise their present and future lives (Brown, Nietupski, & Hamre-Nietupski, 1976). When determining the content on which a student with severe disabilities should receive instruction, the education team uses an ecological approach (Brown & York, 1974). To do so, the team first identifies contexts in which students without disabilities of a given chronological age naturally participate (e.g., second-grade class, interior and exterior grounds of school building attended by sibling[s], home, community immediately around their home, community settings frequented by the family). Second, the team determines the activities in which students without disabilities of the same chronological age participate within those contexts. Third, the team determines the skills that are required to participate in those activities, and completes a discrepancy analysis to determine which of those skills has not yet been acquired by the student with severe disabilities. Instruction for the student with severe disabilities then occurs on those specific skills, during the naturally occurring activities within the naturally occurring contexts (Brown et al., 1976; Ryndak & Alper, 2003). This approach to identifying relevant instructional content for a student with severe disabilities emphasizes the student's need to participate in contexts with classmates who do not have disabilities while receiving instruction on the specific skills he or she needs to participate more fully with classmates, and to be more independent in meaningful activities that occur in current contexts while preparing the student for future contexts.

By adopting this purpose of education and using the ecological approach to identifying meaningful literacy content for students with severe disabilities, education teams will have a higher probability of providing effective literacy instruction. For instance, when identifying literacy content for a student with severe disabilities who attends seventh-grade classes, an education team would focus on the naturally occurring school-sponsored activities in which other seventh graders participate across the day and week, including activities during class sessions (e.g., answering questions on course content), between class sessions (e.g., locating the correct locker), and before and after school hours (e.g., reading track team schedule, publishing class newsletter). In addition, the education team would identify the naturally occurring activities that are not school-sponsored, but that compose the student's life with family (e.g., selecting a movie), friends (e.g., using a telephone number), and community members (e.g., using a bus schedule, reading a menu). When considering what the student might need to learn to participate more fully in those activities, or to be as independent as possible during those activities, the team must consider the literacy skills that are embedded within those activities and the ways in which classmate, family members, friends, and community members use those literacy skills. Then the education team can complete a discrepancy analysis of how the use of literacy skills by the student with disabilities during those activities compares with the use of literacy skills by classmates, family members, friends, and community members. This allows the education team to identify literacy skills that are specific to naturally occurring activities in the student's life both in and out of school, and to determine which skills require additional embedded instruction.

Components of Literacy   A third set of variables that must be considered includes the components of literacy and literacy instruction. Literacy has been conceptualized as ways of learning about and sharing information with others (see Chapter 3, this volume). As such, literacy encompasses the acts of reading, writing, speaking, and listening. Each of these acts allows an individual, either with or without disabilities, to participate more fully in naturally occurring activities across contexts that compose their current and future lives. For students with severe disabilities, literacy and effective communication are linked in numerous and complex ways (see Chapter 3 for a detailed discussion). However, literacy and literacy instruction will be different for each student with a severe disability, depending on 1) the student's cognitive, motor, and sensory abilities; 2) the findings of the ecological approach to identifying meaningful instructional content for the student; and 3) the family members' involvement with literacy experiences. There can be no doubt that literacy comprises a set of skills that assist a student with severe disabilities to participate more fully and function more independently in activities that occur naturally throughout contexts in current and future life. As such, literacy is at the heart of life for students with severe disabilities, and literacy instruction must be the heart of their educational experiences.

Summary

When considering IDEA and NCLB, there is a clear preference for students with disabilities to have access to and involvement in the general education curriculum and instruction, and a preference for all students to pursue general education standards through scientifically based practices. In addition, when considering the variables discussed above, it is clear that literacy instruction is critical for students with severe disabilities. What is not evident thus far is how an education team matches the instructional needs of a student with severe disabilities to the supports and services required for the student to be a successful learner, and then embeds that student's instruction within the focused literacy block in general education classes.

IDENTIFYING MEANINGFUL INSTRUCTIONAL CONTENT FOR STUDENTS WITH SEVERE DISABILITIES

During the 1970s and 1980s, the field moved from a largely *developmental* to a *functional* approach to identifying instructional content for students with severe disabilities. Initially it became clear that when students with severe disabilities were expected to follow the same developmentally sequenced curriculum as students without disabilities, one of two things happened—either the students did not maintain the skills initially taught, as they moved on to the next set of skills, or, if they did maintain the skills, the students never caught up to their peers without disabilities. Either way, the developmental approach caused students with severe disabilities always to be segregated from the instruction provided for their peers without disabilities, and always to be working on skills that were expected of young children. Once this was realized, the field moved to a functional approach to identifying instructional content but started to identify activities believed to be functional for everyone (Wilcox & Bellamy, 1987). It was then assumed, therefore, that this content should be included in a student's instructional program. Shortly after this, several commercial curriculum guides were developed, listing functional skill after functional skill (i.e., activities of daily living). It quickly became apparent, however, that such functional curriculum guides were inappropriate for identifying the unique needs of individual students with severe disabilities and their families, because the skills and activities identified as "functional" did not necessarily match the contexts that compose a student's life. Put another way, such lists of functional activities misinterpreted the word *functional* and assumed that if an activity was meaningful for one student, it would be meaningful for all students. This realization then led to a revisiting of the "functional" concept in the field of severe disabilities (Ferguson & Baumgart, 1991), reinforcing the concept that an activity was functional for a student with severe disabilities only if it had meaning to the student within naturally occurring contexts with peers who did not have disabilities.

The field then moved to a more thoughtful approach to identifying instructional content, focusing not so much on the assessment of students' strengths and weaknesses in selecting skills for instruction, but on the assessment of current, and most probable future, environments in which a student lived, worked, and spent leisure time. These assessments involved gathering information from many sources, particularly from the students and families, regarding those skills and supports that might provide the best preparation for positive quality-of-life changes in the student's natural contexts. Often, a formal process involving ecological or environmental inventories was applied. These processes used direct observation and interviews with significant individuals in a student's life to identify specific functional needs across school, home, work, and community settings.

Although use of the aforementioned practices resulted in instructional content that was more relevant to a student's individual functional needs than the prepackaged curriculum guide approach that preceded them, such practices still did not address the concepts of involvement and progress of students with severe disabilities in the general education curriculum, as supported by IDEA (1997/2004) and NCLB. In order to achieve these goals, it is imperative that education teams do not revert to a variation of the prepackaged curriculum approach and select items from the general education curriculum, reduce them to their simplest terms, and then teach them to students with severe disabilities. This method for determining instructional content would be very similar to that of pulling items from the commercial curriculum guides of two decades ago. Rather, the care and thought that were inherent in such processes as ecological inventories must be expanded to encompass the broader experiential base that our students encounter in inclusive school environments. The task of selecting instructional content, then, is not one of determining which of the skills that form the general education curriculum *can* be taught to students with significant disabilities. Instead, the task remains one of identifying instructional content and supports that are likely to lead to participation in valued roles during activities in natural environments, which include naturally occurring general education classes and contexts. In addition, education teams must determine how access to the general education curriculum and instruction can enhance the development of skills and activities that are meaningful (i.e., functional) for each individual student with severe disabilities.

The ecological inventory process remains valuable, and several slightly different processes have been outlined for determining what constitutes instructional content that is meaningful in the life of a student with severe disabilities, including *Choosing Outcomes and Accommodations for Children* (COACH; Giangreco, Cloninger, & Iverson, 1998), MAPS (Forest & Lusthaus, 1990), PATH (Pearpoint, O'Brien, & Forest, 1993), and the Osborn-Parnes Creative Problem-Solving method (Giangreco, Cloninger, Dennis, & Edelman, 2002). However, a more complex process is required because inclusive environments are more complex than segregated settings, and because intersections are sought between meaningful life outcomes and access to the general education curriculum (Jackson, Ryndak, & Billingsley, 2000). Much has been studied and written about creating inclusive classrooms while using accommodations and modifications to meet the individual needs of learners (Friend & Bursuck, 2002; Hamill & Everington, 2002; Peterson & Hittie, 2003; Ryndak, Morrison, & Sommerstein, 1999; Ryndak & Ward, 2003; Sands, Kozleski, & French, 2000; Vaughn, Bos, & Schumm, 1997). In addition, however, processes have been developed to incorporate meaningful involvement in the general education curriculum and instruction for students with severe disabilities (Ryndak & Alper, 2003). Inherent in such processes is a concern for blending content to meet a student's individual needs across life's contexts with content that reflects the general education curriculum and instructional contexts. These processes also focus on developing a shared vision for the student, both currently and in the future, and modifying educational systems as necessary to maximize the probability that the vision will be realized. Finally, there is an emerging focus on the role of assistive technology and universal design (Center for Applied Special Technology, 2004) in the educational process for students with severe disabilities.

As priority needs are identified for a student with severe disabilities, the education team also must consider whether instructional content will emphasize the student's independent or partial participation in naturally occurring activities across contexts with peers who do not have disabilities. The principal of partial participation suggests that even those students with extensive cognitive, motor, and sensory disabilities, who may not achieve total independence in activities, can learn to participate with peers in activities that are both valued and valuable (Baumgart et al., 1982; Ferguson & Baumgart, 1991). Of equal importance may be determining whether instructional time would most effectively be spent 1) providing opportunities for a student with severe disabilities to practice or maintain skills and activities which already are known, but now are being expected in additional contexts, or on increasing the student's behavioral repertoire (Ferguson & Baumgart, 1991); and 2) increasing *extension skills* (i.e., skills that extend core skills and include such elements as activity initiation, preparation, problem solving, and so forth), or on developing *enrichment skills* (i.e., skills that are not critical to the performance of a core skill, but add to its quality, such as communication, preference selection, and social behaviors). For a thorough discussion of extension and enrichment skills in the curriculum, see Brown, Evans, Weed, and Owen (1987) and Brown and Lehr (1993).

Regardless of the student's cognitive, motor, and/or sensory disabilities, espousing the principle of partial participation ensures that *all* students can take part in those activities that contribute to a rewarding quality of life, including literacy instruction and activities that require literacy skills. As the work of Lave and Wenger (1991) suggests, active participation is the basic and necessary condition for the future development of social relationships, skill development, and school and community membership.

Although all of these processes and concepts can be used to develop instructional goals and to identify the supports and services needed by a student with severe disabilities in inclusive settings, the remainder of this chapter will focus on two issues. First, it will describe one specific process for identifying relevant literacy content on which a student with severe disabilities could receive instruction within literacy instruction, as well as accommodations and modifications that would allow the student to benefit from the instruction. Second, it will provide examples of embedded literacy instruction for students with varying severe disabilities across three educational age levels—primary to early elementary years, intermediate to middle school years, and high school to postsecondary contexts.

IDENTIFYING MEANINGFUL LITERACY
CONTENT FOR STUDENTS WITH SEVERE DISABILITIES

As noted earlier, the accepted purpose of education services for a student with severe disabilities is to assist each student to participate more fully, and to be as independent as possible, in activities that occur naturally in contexts that comprise their present and future lives (Brown et al., 1976; Ryndak & Alper, 2003). To accomplish this purpose, an education team uses an ecological approach to determine the content on which a student with severe disabilities should receive instruction. This ecological approach includes identifying contexts that are meaningful to the student, activities that occur in those contexts, and skills that are required to participate in those activities. Although this approach assists in identifying content for greater participation and independence during activities in naturally occurring contexts with peers who do not have disabilities, it frequently ends without systematically considering either the academic knowledge addressed in the general education contexts or the activities that occur within those contexts. Only when an education team firmly believes that the general education classes are naturally occurring contexts for all students of a specific chronological age are they likely to consider the general education content and activities as relevant for a student with severe disabilities. Because of this, even when students with severe disabilities are included in general education classes, many of these students do not yet receive instruction on the content being taught to their classmates without disabilities. Instead, their instruction frequently occurs parallel to the instruction of their classmates, resulting in the student not having true exposure to the general education content.

To avoid this, education teams can use two methods. First, when completing analyses of the naturally occurring contexts in a student's life the education team should consider the general education content that typically is *used* by students without disabilities in those contexts. In relation to literacy, education teams should consider how and when students of the same chronological age use their literacy skills during activities that occur in those contexts. When doing so, the education team should identify which of those literacy skills the student with severe disabilities also can use, and which literacy skills the student needs to acquire. When preparing for lunch in the school cafeteria, for example, students may use a menu posted in the classroom to decide what they will order for lunch from the cafeteria worker, and then use speaking skills to order those items in the cafeteria. The same set of skills might be used at a fast-food restaurant in a shopping mall, or in a sit-down restaurant in the community. In this way the functional use of literacy becomes very salient to the education team. Second, when reviewing the literacy skills to be taught to the students without disabilities in a specific grade level, if it is expected that a student with severe disabilities will not acquire all of those skills, the education team should consider which components of that content would be most important to allow the student to participate more fully with classmates during the general education instructional activities, as well as be most relevant for the student's life in other school contexts, at home, and in the community. For example, there may be 10 new vocabulary words that fourth graders are learning for social studies. Three of those may be words that appear consistently across units in the social studies curriculum. As such, they might be words that a student with severe disabilities should learn to read (i.e., with pictures, line drawings, or words), write (i.e., with pictures, words written by hand, a computer, or another assistive technology device), say (i.e., with pictures, voice-output assistive technology, or verbally), or identify receptively (i.e., with pictures, voice-output assistive technology, or verbally). These skills, in this case vocabulary words, may or may not be the same as the literacy skills identified by considering the student's naturally occurring contexts.

When these two methods of identifying meaningful instructional content are used, most frequently education teams identify literacy skills that allow the student to listen, speak, read, and/or write across every activity of the day. Consistent with the concept of literacy as learning about and sharing information with others, the literacy skills identified are incorporated into communication with classmates, about content that the classmates are addressing, during activities that are meaningful to the classmates. The key is to focus on the aspects of literacy instruction provided for the students without disabilities and identify those aspects that are most meaningful and useful to the student with severe disabilities both currently (i.e., in general education contexts, in the school, at home, and in the community) and in the future (i.e., in adult life). Instruction on those literacy skills then can be embedded within the activities that occur naturally across settings throughout the day—activities that require the student with severe disabilities to use those literacy skills with classmates.

Another aspect of general education literacy instruction that should affect decisions regarding content that is meaningful for a student with severe disabilities is each state's standards. Some states have embedded standards for students with severe disabilities (1% of the population) within their general education standards, whereas other states have developed a separate set of standards for these students (see Chapter 1). Regardless, although a student's individual needs should drive the selection of literacy content for instruction, adaptive equipment, and instructional method, an education team also must consider the student's performance on and participation in state standards (i.e., standards for general education and separate standards for students with severe disabilities). The student's performance on the state's standards, and whether their performance reflects adequate yearly progress, will affect the literacy content from the general education standards that are reflected in the student's individualized education program (IEP). It is expected that all students, including those with severe disabilities, will demonstrate progress toward meeting their state's standards, whether through the use of the state and district assessments required to earn the general education diploma or through alternate performance strategies.

EMBEDDED MEANINGFUL LITERACY INSTRUCTION FOR STUDENTS WITH SEVERE DISABILITIES

Using the information in the previous section as the foundation for literacy instruction for students with severe disabilities, we consider meaningful examples of embedded literacy instruction. The sections that follow first describe three students traditionally identified as having severe disabilities but who demonstrate different levels of abilities. The students, Anthony, David, and Patty, initially are described in detail but then are revisited at different windows of time. Specifically, they will be revisited during literacy instruction representative of primary to early elementary years, intermediate to middle school years, and high school to postsecondary years. These windows of time were chosen because they are reflective of dramatic shifts in the focus of literacy instruction for general education students, while simultaneously providing opportunities to discuss age-appropriate practices across the educational careers of students with severe disabilities.

In addition to considering a student's use of literacy skills across contexts and the student's cognitive, motor, and sensory abilities, education teams systematically review types of accommodations and modifications that would maximize a student's learning when embedding instruction for a student with severe disabilities within general education contexts and activities. Accommodations and modifications might be used to 1) allow a student to participate during an instructional activity, using skills and demonstrating knowledge previously acquired; or 2) assist the student in acquiring new knowledge or skills (for detailed information about processes used to determine appropriate accommodations and modifications, see Ryndak & Ward, 2003).

The Students and School Setting

The following sections describe three students, each at a different stage of developing literacy skills (i.e., presymbolic to early symbolic stage, symbolic/emergent literacy stage, and use of literacy to learn stage). For each student, information is provided related to 1) the student's cognitive, motor, and sensory abilities; 2) findings of the ecological approach to identifying meaningful instructional content for the student; and 3) the family members' involvement with literacy experiences. Information also is provided related to how and when students of the same chronological age use their literacy skills during activities that occur across naturally occurring contexts. Finally, information is provided related to which components of the general education literacy content would allow the student to participate more fully with classmates during general education instructional activities, as well as to be meaningful for the student's life in other school contexts, at home, and in the community. For all three grade levels per student, the general education teacher has worked with other school-based professionals (i.e., special education teacher, speech-language pathologist, occupational therapist, physical therapist, counselor, psychologist, school administrator) and other education team members (i.e., family members, classmates who do not have disabilities, paraprofessionals) and identified meaningful instructional content and accommodations and/or modifications for the student. This same team collaboratively plans, implements, and evaluates the effectiveness of the student's instruction.

Each of the students introduced in the following scenarios is described as living in the same small city school district and attending the same neighborhood school. Sixty percent of the students in their school are from low socioeconomic status families and receive free lunches. The school also has a linguistically diverse population. Their State Department of Education has indicated that when last tested with statewide assessments, the scores for all of the students in the school demonstrated that students had made adequate yearly progress toward the achievement of state standards. Most of the classes in the school include 20–24 students and have similar compositions of students. For instance, in addition to students who are not identified as having any special needs, each class includes two to three students who have been identified as having either an emotional disability, behavioral disability, or learning disability, as well as one to two students identified as gifted.

Although Anthony, David, and Patty are described at the same age levels, it is assumed that they would not attend the same classes. For ease of comparison, however, it is assumed that the same general education literacy instruction would occur in each of their classes. The general education literacy instruction at each age level, therefore, is summarized in table format, accompanied by information about accommodations and/or modifications for each of the three students during that literacy instruction. It may seem that the growth in literacy skills of the students is minimal over time. However, it should be assumed that each student is making adequate yearly progress according to their IEPs and that literacy skills applied across age levels are occurring at increasing levels of sophistication in multiple contexts. These examples are not provided in an attempt to show growth across years for any of the students; rather, the intent of the examples is to demonstrate 1) how meaningful literacy skills can be identified for students with severe disabilities who demonstrate varying levels of literacy competence at various ages, and 2) how instruction to address the needs of students at various stages of developing literacy skills can be embedded within general education contexts.

Anthony   Anthony is labeled as having multiple disabilities, including severe to profound cognitive disabilities, physical impairments, and visual impairments. He is learning basic cause-and-effect relationships through the use of rudimentary assistive communication devices. Although previously in self-contained special education classes for students with multiple disabilities, Anthony's favorite activity was rolling a ball back and forth with either the special education teacher or paraprofessional. Since being included this academic year, Anthony refuses to roll a ball with an adult, but he consistently rolls balls with his classmates when on the playground. Anthony is very motivated to be with his classmates who do not have disabilities, and his classmates vie for the rotating honor of being his assistant for the day. Several students have formed meaningful relationships with Anthony and include him in all activities, both in school and out of school.

Listening and Speaking   Anthony's home language is Spanish. Because his parents speak and read only Spanish, Anthony's younger sister translates all written material for her parents. At school, however, instruction is provided only in English. It is his family's belief that their children must learn to function, and help their parents to function, in the English-speaking community in which they live. Because of the language differences, it has been difficult to determine the extent to which Anthony's responses, or lack thereof, are due to his difficulty listening and/or speaking or due to language barriers. Regardless, Anthony attends to people and activities in his immediate environment. In class sessions, he looks toward the person who is speaking, whether it is the general education teacher addressing the entire class, a classmate who is answering a question for the class, or a nearby classmate who is off-task. During these situations, Anthony's facial expression usually does not change—that is, his facial features usual remain flat and nonexpressive. Anthony does, however, respond appropriately (i.e., smiles and laughs briefly) to many situations and comments that are humorous, although his response frequently is a little delayed. Aside from such responses, Anthony is nonvocal. He makes a few of his wants known by pointing to, reaching for, or leaning toward people or objects, although he has not generalized this to self-care needs such as toileting. Anthony is learning to use assistive communication devices, each activated with gross motor skills and each with preprogrammed one-sentence comments, to respond to questions planned to be asked of his classmates during a given class session. Peers provide hand-over-hand support for him to use the devices at appropriate times during class activities.

Reading and Writing   Anthony is learning the relationship between pictures and their meanings. When asked to do so by his general education teacher during a class session, Anthony uses a chart containing pictures of his individual classmates to select a student to respond to a question from the teacher or to complete a task. He does so by pointing to a classmate's picture and then relying on his peer supporter to say the student's name aloud. Over time it has become clear that Anthony frequently was selecting specific students, resulting in the location of pictures being changed on the chart to determine whether he was selecting a student or a picture that happened to be in a preferred position. With this change of picture location, Anthony continues to call on the same classmates frequently. This reinforces the perception that Anthony is selecting specific students, rather than selecting the picture in a specific location on the chart. Most recently, he is required to scan the students in class, determine which of the students have their hands raised, and select the picture of one of those students. This reinforces the perception that Anthony is identifying and purposefully selecting students who are ready to answer the teacher's question. Anthony requires either hand-over-hand support or a splint with a strap to hold and use a writing implement, with which he makes random linear marks on chart paper or paper taped to a surface in front of him.

Motor Abilities   Overall, Anthony is hypotonic. He has a flaccid and flat facial expression, although his eyes are attentive and expressive. When seated on the floor, Anthony uses either a straight-legged or cross-legged position, with periodic peer support for balance. When seated in a chair or his wheelchair, Anthony requires straps to maintain an upright position when unattended. When on the floor, Anthony slowly scoots across small areas. For mobility between rooms or sections of a room, Anthony is reliant on others to push him in his wheelchair, to assist with his use of a walker, or to provide physical support on one arm as he walks. His level of participation while walking with support is dependent on his level of motivation to get to the next location or activity. For example, after Anthony's first few months of being included in general education classes, his classmates were scheduled to take a districtwide assessment. During this time period, Anthony returned to his former self-contained special education classroom, where he refused to participate in activities that he previously had preferred (e.g., rolling a ball in the classroom with an adult). When it was time to return to his second-grade room, a paraprofessional provided physical support for him to walk to the classroom. Instead of requiring multiple verbal cues to continue walking and responding by slowly following the paraprofessional, Anthony walked in front of the paraprofessional, leaning toward his general education classroom. In essence, he was pulling his paraprofessional so he could get to the second-grade classroom more quickly.

Sensory Abilities   Anthony has been identified as having visual impairments. It is unclear exactly what this means, however, because it is unclear what he can and cannot see. For instance, he appears to visually track people both close to him and across the room, as well as to respond to humorous events within the normal field of vision. In addition, he consistently scans the classroom for students who have their hands raised and selects the picture of one of those students from his "student selection folder." There is no indication of hearing loss either in Anthony's record or his behaviors.

   Ecologically Identified Instructional Content   After conducting relevant inventories (i.e., family inventory with a translator, peer inventory, community inventory, student preferences inventory, general education settings inventory [see Ryndak, 2003]) and reviewing both related services reports and general education standards for second grade, Anthony's education team identified three areas related to his use of literacy that consistently were identified as critical for his participation in naturally occurring activities across current and future contexts. First, Anthony needs a systematic way of communicating verbally with others in his environments through the use of one or more assistive communication devices (e.g., multiple BIGmacks, touch talker). This would maximize and extend his current listening abilities while providing him with a way to "speak" with others. Second, Anthony needs a way to provide written information to others through the use of a computer. Although his computer use initially will rely on selecting pictures that are programmed to type words in both Spanish and English, it is expected that his reading ability will progress, allowing him to choose words to speak from a set of words predetermined to be meaningful in given situations. Third, Anthony needs to have a way to demonstrate his acquisition of information from the general education curriculum. Initially, his assistive technology communication devices and his computer will provide ways for him to respond to yes/no questions that incorporate basic vocabulary from academic topics and tasks. It is expected that as Anthony's understanding of the relationship between words, presented either in pictures or letters, and their meanings develops, his ability to demonstrate acquisition of concepts presented through the general education curriculum also will evolve to the use of basic vocabulary for each subject area. In addition to these literacy skills, Anthony needs to develop independent mobility skills. Although continuing to develop walking skills, he also is being fitted for a motorized wheelchair that will facilitate his ability to control where he goes, and when.

   Family's Involvement with Literacy   Although he is from a Spanish-speaking household, Anthony has access to English-language materials through his younger sister, who speaks both Spanish and English well. Every night before bed, his sister reads to Anthony from her textbooks. Aside from this, there is little print matter in the household, and the print matter that is available is in Spanish.

   David   On his IEP, David is labeled as having moderate cognitive disabilities. He is considered an active student who enjoys interacting with peers. He completes simple 5-piece interlocking puzzles, feeds himself, opens his own milk carton, follows large-group routine activities without assistance (e.g., getting lunch, lining up for activities, returning books to the library), and enjoys being read to on a one-to-one basis. He has difficulty attending to large-group activities (e.g., read-alouds, lectures, art projects, large-group games during physical education) and may seek out inappropriate attention during those times by walking away, pushing a peer, or tossing materials to the floor. He is learning basic skills related to following large-group, small-group, and individual directions.

Listening and Speaking   David's native language is English and his receptive language skills are more developed than his expressive skills. He uses both nonsymbolic and symbolic communication with both peers and adults. Although he is considered to be verbal, his speech is best understood by those who know him. His sentences often are incomplete, with only major concepts stated (e.g., when relating an event that occurred over the weekend he might state, "Mom go shop mall me"), and may be accompanied by gestures, facial expressions, or simple sign language. David enjoys engaging others in conversation, even though he struggles with skills such as turn-taking, asking questions, entering and exiting conversations, and listening to his communication partners. He can answer "what" questions during a conversation, state one occurrence from a story, follow one-step directions, and follow social cues in a large group. David speaks in three-word utterances to relay information. These utterances, however, are not complete sentences; rather, they are multiple words related to the same topic (e.g., "me ball throw," or "movie mom home"). David has not yet demonstrated an ability to ask questions of others or engage in a meaningful three-exchange conversation.

Reading and Writing   David is best described as an early emergent reader. He enjoys short, repetitive picture books or books with simple phrases. He holds books appropriately, has some print awareness, and points to words on a page. David is developing initial sound–symbol relationships, although he reads high-interest, high-frequency words. He will answer factual questions about picture books that he has read independently. David uses left-to-right progression and can write the first letter of his first name, which he writes for his name on the top of his papers. To show that he has written a story, David will draw an unidentifiable picture and place lines or shapes under the picture. The general education teacher or paraprofessional will interpret David's verbal speech, facial expressions, gestures, and sign language to determine what is represented on the page, and then he or she will write a simple sentence under David's marks.

Motor Abilities   Overall, David is considered slightly hypotonic. He is, however, able to hold utensils independently to eat, use scissors to cut a straight line, use pencils to write some letters of his name in approximation of the real letter, and use a zipper to secure his pants most of the time. He needs assistance cutting food, starting a zipper, and tying his shoes. David also has good balance and gross motor coordination. He is within normal weight limits for his age, and his parents keep him involved in sporting activities such as martial arts and swimming.

Sensory Abilities   David has a mild-to-moderate bilateral hearing loss, with loss in the right ear benefiting from the use of a hearing aid. His eyesight is normal and he demonstrates some tactile sensitivity. For instance, he does not like tags on his shirts and often will rip out any tag that was not removed before he got dressed.

Ecologically Identified Instructional Content   After conducting relevant inventories (i.e., family inventory, peer inventory, community inventory, student preferences inventory, general education settings inventory) and reviewing both related services reports and general education standards, David's education team found three areas related to his use of literacy that consistently were identified as critical for his participation in naturally occurring activities across both current and future contexts. First, David needs a more effective means for understanding and using oral language in small- and large-group settings. This would improve his attention in those settings while also increasing his meaningful involvement in various academic activities. Second, David needs to improve understanding of sound–symbol relationships. This would enable him to develop greater word-attack skills, while simultaneously improving his speech intelligibility. Third, David needs to improve his writing ability in two ways: 1) he needs to view print as a means of communication, and 2) he needs to improve his fine motor writing skills. Currently, adults write for him and, thus, relieve him of opportunities to practice penmanship and sound-symbol writing, as well as limiting his participation in the writing process. It is expected that focused instruction on letter formation, vocabulary development, and practice with alphabetic principles will further David's understanding of the purpose of literacy. It is also expected that David will rely on pictures paired with words to develop reading and writing skills.

Family's Involvement with Literacy   David's mother reads with him every night before bedtime. His younger brother is in kindergarten and already is developing an understanding of literacy that is more advanced than David's. At times his brother will read to David when they play school at home.

Patty   Patty's formal testing indicates that she qualifies for special education services as a person with a moderate cognitive disability. However, her daily performance and level of independence exceed what formal testing would lead a person to expect. For instance, Patty makes her own breakfast at home, cleans up after herself, sings in the church children's choir, and answers the phone and summons the correct person. Patty's greatest difficultly relates to her social maturity and personal interactions, as she often is silly, engages in repetitive conversations, or is not able to accurately interpret the verbal and nonverbal communication of others. Academically, Patty continues to progress in reading and mathematics. This is demonstrated by her completion of assigned tasks and modified tests, although her performance on norm-referenced assessments has not changed concurrently.

Listening and Speaking   Patty is a symbolic communicator. Her articulation is understandable to strangers and she speaks in full sentences, although they are short sentences. She engages in one-to-one or small-group conversations but has difficulty when the group size exceeds four. Although very social, Patty often strays from the topic and task at hand and must be drawn back to focus on the topic or task.

Reading and Writing   Patty is a solid beginning reader. She can identify all of the letters in the alphabet; in fact, the education team believes that her phonemic awareness and phonics skills are her greatest strength. Patty can read her name and 200 other high-frequency, high-interest words (e.g., *Mom, Dad, Grandma, dog, school, toys*). She enjoys reading in the community by identifying the logos of stores, gas stations, and fast-food restaurants. Although Patty enjoys it when others read aloud to her, she struggles with independently reading any book beyond a simple picture book with two or three sentences per page. Patty can write words and simple sentences to describe pictures or ideas. If she encounters a new word she cannot read or spell, Patty requests help from her classmates or adults. Often, if given cues of letter sounds, Patty can write the new words. She answers simple fact-based questions about stories, but she could use additional work on such skills.

Motor Abilities   Patty is slightly hypotonic. The occupational therapist, special education teacher, and general education teacher provide many opportunities for Patty to use, and develop further, fine motor control. In particular, Patty uses an adapted pencil grip, raised-line paper, and a slant table for reading and writing activities.

Sensory Abilities   Patty is considered both legally blind and hard-of-hearing. All fonts of her textbooks and worksheets are enlarged to at least 14 points, and Patty wears hearing aids in both ears. Some gross motor activities are a challenge for Patty, although she completes them independently (i.e., descending stairs, playing basketball or softball).

Ecologically Identified Instructional Content   After conducting relevant inventories (i.e., family inventory, peer inventory, community inventory, student preferences inventory, general education settings inventory) and reviewing both related services reports and general education standards for second grade, Patty's education team found three areas related to her use of literacy that consistently were identified as critical for her participation in naturally occurring activities across both current and future contexts. First, Patty needs a way to improve her writing skills by increasing the speed of writing and expanding the length of writing on one topic. Although Patty enjoys writing, her motor and sensory limitations make writing a labor-intensive task that may require less effort with the use of assistive technology devices. Second, as Patty's sight-word vocabulary increases, her comprehension skills also must increase. Finally, Patty needs to develop a greater interest in topics that encourage more age-appropriate social interaction. For instance, she often writes about characters from children's cartoons or television shows. Although these programs are a source of entertainment for infants, toddlers, and preschoolers, Patty's peers discuss more mature topics (e.g., current age-appropriate movies, pop songs, and video games).

Family's Involvement with Literacy   Patty's grandmother lives with the family and is a retired elementary school teacher. Grandma and Patty practice reading and phonics skills after school each day. Patty's mother reads to her each night and, as discussed with the education team, encourages a variety of literacy experiences at home.

PRIMARY TO EARLY ELEMENTARY LITERACY BLOCK

In primary and early elementary classrooms, teachers often use a combination of instructional methods in whole-group, small-group, and individualized settings. Both the methods and grouping patterns are highly dependent on such variables as the teacher's philosophical approach to teaching, students' performance levels, time dedicated to literacy instruction, and materials available to the teacher. Tables 6.2, 6.3, and 6.4 describe an example of methods and grouping patterns used by a second-grade teacher during a 90–120-minute literacy block. These methods and grouping patterns are consistent with those most frequently observed during primary to early elementary literacy blocks. They also align with the Report of the National Reading Panel (NICHD, 2000) key elements of focused literacy instruction. Additionally, these literacy practices allow Anthony, David, and Patty to participate fully in the instructional activities while working on components of literacy that are relevant and important for them (see Tables 6.2–6.4).

In the instructional activities presented, the general education teacher conducts a whole-group literacy lesson that focuses on three areas of early literacy: 1) text comprehension, 2) vocabulary development, and 3) phonics. First, the teacher gathers the students to the floor and conducts a writing activity that incorporates the current events of the school day (i.e., daily news of school life). The students may volunteer statements or ideas about the school day ahead of them, and the teacher models for them the thought processes used when writing. As the teacher writes, she asks questions to the students regarding spelling, punctuation, and vocabulary (Cunningham, 1995). The teacher then moves the students into whole-group literacy instruction by conducting a read-aloud (Allen, 2000). During the whole-group read-aloud, the teacher focuses the students' attention on a book that encourages or reinforces pattern recognition in text, familiarizes students with circular stories, and engages students in discussions about the sequence of events in the story. Common books that address these objectives are *If You Give A Mouse A Cookie*, by Laura Joffe Numeroff (1985), and *The Napping House*, by Audrey Wood (1984).

Following the whole-group activities, students spend the majority of the literacy block at literacy centers in small groups of five to six students, with the membership of each group changing frequently. To support the instruction that occurred during the whole-group read-aloud, the literacy centers are organized to further enhance and expand on the book's theme. Each literacy center contains teacher- or student-directed instructional activities that incorporate materials chosen by the teacher based on the performance levels of the students in each group. For the elementary examples, the students' performance levels were assessed through ongoing formative and summative measures, including teacher observations, individualized conferences, written tasks, and criterion- or norm-referenced assessments (e.g., the Lexile; Basic Reading Inventory [BRI]). For each literacy center, the activities were designed to match the goals of the overall general education lesson while addressing the performance levels and needs of each group's members. Because Anthony, David, and Patty have unique learning needs that require either accommodations or modifications to the instructional materials and/or activities, or modifications to the instructional objectives, the education team used similar logic to design the activities in ways that support their participation and instruction during each literacy center.

The first literacy center uses teacher-directed guided reading. For three of the four small groups that rotate through this center, the teacher uses the district's basal series as the source of literature for instruction. For the fourth group, the teacher focuses instruction on the content of supplemental materials provided by the textbook publisher in the form of leveled reading books. During their participation in this teacher-directed literacy center, the students focus on reading fluency, vocabulary development, and targeted comprehension strategies. The teacher models strategies used by good readers (e.g., thoughtful questioning, inferring, chunking) and encourages the development of these strategies in the students. Guided reading lessons rely on explicit, focused instruction and conferencing that incorporate a collection of resources, such as graphic organizers, word walls, dictionaries, books, technology, and peer support (Fountas & Pinnell,

1996). As noted in the tables, when Anthony, David, and Patty are members of this class, each is involved in a different teacher-directed guided reading group, because of their unique learning objectives and characteristics. For instance, during their participation in this literacy center, Anthony focuses on objectives that are different from classmates in his group, David focuses on phonics within the act of reading, and Patty participates using her decoding skills as she and her group members read for comprehension.

As students transition to the other three literacy centers, they have the opportunity to extend and expand their ability to play with word sounds, to write, and to develop word connections. Two of these structured literacy centers provide students opportunities to "work with words." It is during these portions of the instructional block that students are encouraged to experiment with words by using some of the skills they have learned during whole-group instruction. One might suggest that a balanced reading instructional model requires phonics instruction to be both explicitly taught and embedded throughout regular classroom instruction. When students are given the opportunity to work with words in literacy centers they are encouraged to test the rules they have learned by manipulating letters, looking for what makes sense, chunking, and applying the construct that sounds are determined by patterns in words and not individual letters (Cunningham, 1995; Cunningham & Allington, 1999). Anthony, David, and Patty participate in these two structured literacy centers with varying objectives, materials, and assistive technology, based on their individual needs. For instance, David's words may be fewer and accompanied by pictures, whereas Anthony might select pictures that represent words that his classmates make. In contrast, Patty might need only a slightly modified learning objective for each center. The final small-group literacy center is self-selected reading. During this center, both Anthony and David are required to choose a book that is accompanied by a tape. Anthony uses a switch to activate a tape recorder to listen to his story, whereas David uses a more traditional manner to activate a tape recorder. In contrast, Patty chooses a book on her level and reads silently without the need for accommodations.

At the end of the literacy block, the teacher returns to the whole-group structure and engages the students in the writing process with a brief lesson that encourages them to think like a writer. Students are asked to retell a story, evaluate interactions of characters, or create new endings to a shared story. Writing is a daily activity focused on increasing the efficiency of student expression and fluency. As such, it is done with a specific purpose in mind, and Anthony, David, and Patty are involved in writing and journaling based on their unique needs.

It should be remembered that Anthony, David, and Patty are not included in the same class. Rather, the same instructional activities have been used here to demonstrate how, regardless of their reading level (i.e., nonsymbolic through symbolic/emergent reading), any student with significant disabilities can participate in a traditional English Language Arts block while meeting individualized objectives.

INTERMEDIATE TO MIDDLE SCHOOL LITERACY INSTRUCTION

At the intermediate to middle school level the focus of literacy instruction turns toward increased skill in comprehension of a variety of genres, skill in the use of written and oral language to communicate with various audiences, and increased

Table 6.2. Anthony's participation in a second-grade English language arts block (90–120 minutes)

Objectives and structure	Sample activity	Anthony's participation
Structure: Whole group **Objective:** Develop students' knowledge of the writing/editing process, expand vocabulary through oral and written modeling **Anthony's objective:** *Select pictures on computer, programmed to type words in response to questions*	**Daily news practice** Students are seated around chart paper or whiteboard sharing ideas about the daily schedule or special events. The teacher models the writing/editing process. Students record sentences in a personal journal.	*Anthony will use a touch screen to select pictures of items related to the daily schedule, or a key topic from school or community current events that will have an impact on his life. Anthony will touch pictures that are correct responses to questions, some repeated daily for several weeks or months (e.g., related to daily schedule), some repeated daily for a period covering the current event.*
Structure: Whole group **Objective:** Develop students' vocabulary, fluency, and text comprehension through reading aloud **Anthony's objective:** *Answer yes/no questions that incorporate basic words from activity or book*	**Read aloud** The teacher previews the book, begins reading, models comprehension strategies as she reads, and questions students about the predictable word patterns or vocabulary.	*Anthony will use two assistive communication devices (e.g., two BIG-macks), each programmed with one response (i.e., one yes and one no) and with a corresponding picture on it. On being asked a yes/no question about either the activity itself (e.g., "Is your friend, Bobby, sitting beside you today?") or the book being read (e.g., "Is today's book about a dog?"), Anthony will respond correctly by activating the switch with the correct answer.*
Structure: Whole group **Objective:** Develop students' vocabulary, fluency, and text comprehension through reading aloud **Anthony's objective:** *Read a section of the book aloud by activating a switch for a prerecorded section*	**Word wall practice** Students select 8 words off the word wall and write them on their BINGO grid (middle space is free).	*Anthony's switch is hooked to the All-Turn It™. He picks 5 words for a different peer each day this activity occurs. The peer picks 3 words. When the game begins, Anthony activates a switch connected to a tape that states words preprogrammed by the aide, a student, or the teacher.*
Structure: Four rotating small-group literacy centers: one teacher-directed, three cooperative; Anthony joins and rotates to centers with Group 1 **Objective:** Extend skills in the areas of fluency, phonics, text comprehension, and vocabulary development. Each center focuses on a slightly different literacy skill.	**Teacher-directed center** Group 1 reads book together, identifies high-frequency words, and discusses events of the story (main idea); Groups 2–4 read Maps and Journeys in basal and discuss main idea/details within the story.	*At a small table in his wheelchair, Anthony has two tasks: he activates his switch to begin a audiotape that states his part of the story; he holds his book with two hands for two continuous minutes.*

144

Anthony's objective: Read a section of the book aloud by activating a switch for a prerecorded section; select pictures on computer, programmed to type words in response to questions; motor control for holding large objects, pointing to pictures, and using assistive technology

Skill practice center

Folder games to reinforce and practice skills, including placing words in ABC order by first and second letter, compound words, beginning digraph sounds, long vowels, and words that end with silent e

Anthony is paired with a peer and is in a prone stander with a tray. Anthony's materials are made of heavyweight paper for ease of grasp, and include key words from the class list. From a two-item array he selects a picture that matches a picture-word combination. His peer alphabetizes the words that match the pictures. Example: Anthony selects a picture of a cake, while the group is working on silent e.

Making words center

With the vowel /e/, students use letters a, n, y, w, h, e, r, e to create as many words as possible. Students record words in composition books.

Continue in prone stander with tray: Anthony works with peer to move large letters on his tray. Focus is on grasp and movement, listening to directions from peer, and sustaining attention.

Self-selected reading

Students choose a book to read from the leveled class library and summarize their book in reading/language journals.

Anthony returns to his wheelchair. With a peer, Anthony uses eye gaze to choose a book. He then holds the book so he and his partner can see it, while his partner reads it aloud.

Writing/spelling work

Review process used by good writers; brainstorm what people might want to write about, using words from word wall and from today's stories, thinking about fiction, and studying pictures. Each child records notes in a writing journal.

Teacher assists Anthony in showing the class pictures of topics that the students generate for writing topics.

Structure: Whole group, with some individuals recording in writing journals

Objective: Develop knowledge about the characteristics of a good story. Expand specific writing skills as essays begin to enter the first draft.

Anthony's objective: Motor control for holding pictures

Table 6.3. David's participation in a second-grade English language arts block (90–120 minutes)

Objectives and structure	Sample activity	David's participation
Structure: Whole group **Objective:** Develop students' knowledge of the writing process, expand vocabulary through oral and written modeling. *David's objective: Communicate orally in large groups. Apply the rule of capitalization to his writing task.*	**Daily news practice** Students are seated around chart paper or whiteboard sharing ideas about the daily schedule or special events. The teacher models the writing/editing process. Students record sentences in a personal journal.	*Just prior to this activity, David was prompted to find a picture of an activity about which he might like to speak. When called on David shares the information in a sentence. The teacher writes his sentence on the board and places his picture next to it. David returns to his seat and writes the one word activity in his journal.*
Structure: Whole group **Objective:** Develop and reinforce sight-word recognition *David's objective: Increase fine motor skills by manipulating Velcro cards. Reinforce sight-word vocabulary.*	**Word wall practice** Students select 8 words off the word wall and write them on their BINGO grid (middle space is free). Teacher gives clues and students "cover up" word on grid	*David picks words from his word wall for BINGO card. His squares have Velcro for placing the picture/word cards. He pulls off words to work on pincer grasp and motor strength.*
Structure: Whole group **Objective:** Develop students' vocabulary, fluency, and text comprehension through reading aloud. *David's objective: Develop listening skills and understanding and use of oral language.*	**Read aloud** The teacher previews the book, begins reading, models comprehension strategies as she reads, and questions students about the predictable word patterns or vocabulary.	*David is provided special seating that ensures good visual contact with the teacher and the text. David is asked questions related to who, what, when, where, why.*
Structure: Four rotating small-group literacy centers: one teacher-directed; three cooperative; David joins Group 2 **Objective:** Extend students' skills in the areas of fluency, phonics, text comprehension, and vocabulary development *David's objective: Improve comprehension of stories read independently or by an adult.*	**Teacher-directed center** Groups 1–3 read *Maps and Journeys* in basal, discussing main idea/details within the story. Group 4 reads level 6/7 Rigby books identifying high-frequency words, then discussing what is happening in the story (main idea).	*David participates in Group 2. Teacher sets a purpose for reading by asking questions and conducting a "book-walk." David answers literal level questions about the story that could be answered by viewing pictures. While the story is read, David follows along by listening, turning the page, and identifying any known words.*

146

Objective	Center / Activity	David's Accommodation
Improve fluency while reading high-interest words from an individualized sight-word vocabulary list.	**Skill practice center** Folder games (skills reinforced and practiced include placing words in ABC order by first and second letter, compound words, beginning digraph sounds, long vowels, and words that end with silent e)	*All students have individual folders. David is provided folders that address spelling his name, high-frequency, high-interest words that have pictures to match.*
Develop alphabetic principles by practicing letter-sound skills and patterning.	**Making words center** Vowel /e/: use letters a, n, y, w, h, e, r, e to create as many words as possible. Record words in composition books.	*David works with a small group of peers with assistant guiding peers to model writing for David. Words might be written and then copied by David or number of total words is reduced. He may also use rubber stamps if writing is tiring for him.*
Develop independent reading skills. Develop comprehension abilities through journal writing and reflection.	**Self-selected reading** Students choose a book to read from the class library; books in the library are leveled. Students must summarize the selection in their reading/language journals.	*David chooses a book that represents his current instructional level. He may also read along with a peer. The two may summarize, each recording thoughts in separate journals. The teacher is looking for some sound-symbol matches for David.*
Structure: Whole group with some individual recording in writing journals **Objective:** Develop knowledge about the characteristics of a good story. Expand specific writing skills as essays begin to enter the first draft. *David's objective: Communicate ideas through oral and written language. Learn to organize ideas as part of a writing process.*	**Writing/spelling work** Review process used by good writers. Brainstorm a list of things that people might want to write about (idea generation leads to producing a rough draft)	*David is involved in the large-group discussion. The teacher has pictures that might supplement ideas that David expresses. His short chunks of expression are restated and modeled back to him as full sentences.*

Table 6.4. Patty's participation in a second-grade English language arts block (90–120 minutes)

Objectives and structure	Sample activity	Patty's participation
Structure: Whole group **Objective:** Develop students' knowledge of the writing/editing process, expand vocabulary through oral and written modeling. ***Patty's objective:** Same as peers*	**Daily news practice** Students are seated around chart paper or whiteboard sharing ideas about the daily schedule or special events. The teacher models the writing/editing process. Students record sentences in a personal journal.	*Patty's work is enlarged in a notebook. She does not copy from the board but rather edits and participates in large group as other students.*
Structure: Whole group **Objective:** Develop and reinforce sight-word recognition. ***Patty's objective:** Reinforce sight-word vocabulary alongside peers.*	**Word wall practice** Students select 8 words off the word wall and write them on their BINGO grid (middle space is free). Teacher gives clues; students "cover up" word on grid.	*Patty has the same BINGO card as other students in class. She participates in the activity as peers.*
Structure: Whole group **Objective:** Develop students' vocabulary, fluency, and text comprehension through reading aloud. ***Patty's objective:** Improve listening comprehension and application of active reading comprehension strategies.*	**Read aloud** The teacher previews the book, begins reading, models comprehension strategies as she reads, and questions students about the predictable word patterns or vocabulary.	*Patty is provided special seating to accommodate hearing and visual impairments.*
Structure: Four rotating small-group literacy centers: one teacher-directed, three cooperative; Patty joins high reading group. **Objective:** Extend students' skills in the areas of fluency, phonics, text comprehension, and vocabulary development. Each center focuses on a slightly different literacy skill. ***Patty's objective:** Improve comprehension of stories read independently or by an adult.*	**Literacy Workshop** **Teacher-directed center** Groups 1–3 read *Maps and Journeys* in basal discussing main idea/details within the story. Group 4 reads level 6/7 Rigby books identifying high-frequency words, discuss what is happening in the story (main idea).	*Patty participates in Group 4 because her decoding skills are strong. The teacher demonstrates a comprehension strategy that works for all students, especially Patty.*

148

Reinforce decoding skills through individual folder games.	**Skill practice center** Folder games (skills reinforced and practiced include: placing words in ABC order by first and second letter, compound words, beginning digraph sounds, long vowels, and words that end with silent e).	*All students have individual folders. Patty is given her slant table as needed and provided folder games that address blends and diagraphs.*
Develop alphabetic principles by practicing letter-sound skills and patterning.	**Making words center** Vowel /e/: use letters a, n, y, w, h, e, r, e to create as many words as possible. Record words in composition books.	*Patty participates with a peer on the computer with an adapted keyboard and word prediction software. The generated list is printed and added to by other classmates.*
Develop writing skills by targeting two on-topic sentences.	**Self-selected reading** Students choose a book to read from the class library; books in the library are leveled. Students must summarize the selection in their reading/language journals.	*Patty chooses a book from a bin that represents her instructional level. Her notebook contains question prompts (e.g., who, what, when, where). Patty writes two summary sentences that will later lead to greater paragraph structure.*
Structure: Whole group with some individual recording in writing journals **Objective:** Develop knowledge about the characteristics of a good story. Expand specific writing skills as essays begin to enter the first draft. ***Patty's objective:*** *Communicate ideas through oral and written language. Learn to organize ideas as part of the writing process.*	**Writing/spelling work** Review process used by good writers. Brainstorm a list of things that people might want to write about (idea generation leads to producing a rough draft).	*Patty is involved in the large group discussion. The teacher supplements discussions with pictures for the whole class. She has consistent access to adaptive materials as needed.*

use of study strategies across content areas. Instruction is based on the premise that students have developed word-attack skills as a foundation for engaging in a variety of reading experiences across subjects, as well as engaging in the writing process. Because students achieve these reading and writing standards at different levels of sophistication, teachers of adolescent literacy must balance a variety of factors that influence literacy achievement, including student skill level for both reading and writing, state curriculum standards, district-selected materials, additional resources available, and time allotted in each student's schedule for explicit literacy instruction (Shanklin, 2002). It often is at this level of education that educators feel the gap is too great between the performance of learners with severe disabilities and their classmates who are achieving their state's curriculum standards for the students with disabilities to participate effectively in the same general education contexts. When intermediate and middle school literacy instruction aligns with best practice, however, education teams need only view the instructional strategies used to determine how the individual learning needs of students similar to Anthony, David, and Patty can be met.

Traditionally, little consideration has been given to the developmental differences of adolescent readers and writers; therefore, reading, writing, speaking, or listening tasks often are conducted as whole-group activities in which all students are expected to reach a similar level of proficiency (Ivey, 2002). In recent years, however, the focus of discussion regarding middle school literacy has shifted to include topics such as differentiated methods of instruction (Tomlinson, 1999, 2003), ongoing assessment that informs both the teacher and the child about progress (Wiggins, 1998), exposure to various types of literature (Langer, 2004; Moore, Bean, Birdyshaw, & Rycik, 1999), and the need for improved comprehension skills across content areas (Harvey & Goudvis, 2000; Tovani, 2004; Tovani, Keene, & Stratton, 2000). As with younger children, adolescents often need multiple instructional strategies to learn new skills as well as to apply those skills across curriculum areas. To address this need, the International Reading Association's (IRA) Position Statement on Adolescent Literacy (Moore et al., 1999) stated that all content area teachers should embed reading and writing strategies within instruction on a daily basis. Specifically, the IRA stated that these strategies should be taught explicitly, as well as modeled by both the language arts and content area teachers. Students then should practice these skills in small-group, large-group, and individual contexts throughout the day (Langer, 2004).

Just as in the elementary scenario, it is impossible to capture the complexity of literacy instruction that occurs within an intermediate or middle school classroom. The examples in this chapter, however, are based on best practices in the area of literacy instruction, while also confining an example to one 45–60-minute block of instruction at the sixth-grade level. The intermediate to middle school literacy instruction described in Tables 6.5, 6.6, and 6.7 is meant to provide a snapshot of activities during one day of instruction in one subject area (i.e., language arts). The students begin the period with a quick review of vocabulary terms using a random, whole-group review strategy that incorporates question and answer vocabulary cards. Previously, students created the cards and, wherever possible, represented the term through an accompanying picture. This activity is meant to activate students' prior knowledge while also requiring the involvement of 100% of the students for 2–4 minutes. Anthony, David, and Patty are able to take part in this whole-group activity with ease. Anthony often starts the activity by activating a switch that states a vocabulary question for the class; David completes the task with a preselected card that represents a vocabulary term with both words and pictures; and Patty is given a choice of two or three cards with the vocabulary words she is learning (see Tables 6.5–6.7).

After the review is completed, the teacher shifts the students into literacy circles (Day, Spiegel, McLellan, & Brown, 2002) where small groups are reading different novels related to the current topic (i.e., how prejudice or preconceived ideas about people can affect daily life). Each student has an individual reading journal, and each group has a recording sheet on which the group describes their daily discussions about the passages read. These literacy circles have been designed based on the instructional reading level of the students, student interest, and each student's individual learning needs. For instance, Patty is a member of a group that is reading *Number the Stars*, by Lois Lowry (1989). This particular piece of historical fiction has a lower readability level than the other texts written by Lowry (1999, 2000), yet it is supportive of the teacher's overall focus on the impact of prejudice. Although Patty still may need the book on tape for fullest understanding of the story as a whole, the text can be used to increase her decoding and reading comprehension skills. David could participate in any of the groups, as long as the literature being read lends itself to picture representation. Although David may not comprehend the entire book, he could grasp an understanding of the positive characteristics of one of the book's main characters (e.g., Annmarie or Ellen in *Number the Stars*). As David expands his picture-based whole-word reading vocabulary, he also could learn the interaction skills required for solving problems. In contrast, Anthony could participate in any of the circles by activating the book on tape, selecting pictures on his computer that represent characters or events in the book, or listening to his classmates discuss their understanding of the vocabulary. In each of the groups, regardless of the book being read, the general education students are applying active reading strategies to draw conclusions and make predictions and generalizations to the larger society, while Anthony, David, and Patty fully participate with adapted materials, purposeful grouping strategies, and individualized learning outcomes.

As the instructional time closes, the teacher asks students across groups to share information about characters and main ideas through the use of a compare-contrast graphic organizer. In this situation, Anthony and David could share the pictures they used in their small groups. A classmate could add their pictures to the graphic organizer, providing visual representations of characters or main ideas for the entire class. As an alternative, the groups might use graphic organizer software that can add pictures (e.g., Inspiration Software, 2003).

Tables 6.5, 6.6, and 6.7 illustrate that Anthony, David, and Patty have become more skilled in literacy than during their elementary scenarios. Although each of these students with severe disabilities continues to make educational gains, however, the gap between the general education curriculum standards and their individualized progress becomes more pronounced. In spite of this, each of the students is involved in the general education instructional activities in a meaningful way, while they benefit from instructional activities that match their own unique needs (see Tables 6.2–6.4).

Table 6.5. Anthony's participation in a sixth-grade English language arts class (45–60 minutes)

Objectives and structure	Sample activity	Anthony's participation
Structure: Whole group **Objective:** Reinforce previously introduced vocabulary ***Anthony's objective:*** *Select pictures on computer, programmed to type words in response to questions.*	**Whole-group vocabulary review** Each student has a card with a question and an answer, related to vocabulary. Students ask and answer questions in a random whip.	*Anthony starts and completes the vocabulary warm-up activity by activating a switch that begins a prerecorded question. Multiple switches can be used to also provide him opportunities to answer.*
Structure: Small groups with predictable reading routine **Objective:** Apply active reading comprehension strategies to the reading selection. Identify major themes and conflicts in the selection. ***Anthony's objective:*** *Read a section of the book aloud by activating a switch for a prerecorded section; select pictures on computer, programmed to type words in response to questions; motor control for holding large objects, pointing to pictures, and using assistive technology.*	**Guided reading/book clubs** Three groups read chapter books that are associated with the theme. They develop an understanding of characters as they relate/interact with one another. Group 1: *The Giver* (Lowry, 1999) Group 2: *Gathering Blue* (Lowry, 2000) Group 3: *Number the Stars* (Lowry, 1989) *evolve into an author study	*Anthony uses a switch to "read aloud" a prerecorded section of his book. He uses pictures on his computer that represent characters and events in the book to answer questions.*
Structure: Teacher-created pairs; students already learned the comprehension strategy in previous classes. **Objective:** Increase identification and use of vocabulary in context while applying a comprehension strategy. ***Anthony's objective:*** *Motor control for holding large objects, pointing to pictures, and using assistive technology*	**Classwide peer tutoring** In pairs, students identify difficult words in the text and record them in the group journal. Students then use strategies in the group to define unknown words and hand in their work to the teacher later. These words will be incorporated into the daily vocabulary review. Students also record information on worksheets for their individualized growth.	*Anthony is the third member of a pair. His classmates work on the assignment, then audiotape 2 words and their definitions so he can use them in later vocabulary lessons. Andrew hands in his audiotape to the teacher, just as other students hand in their work. His 2 words should be concrete and part of his picture vocabulary list. The words may be the same or different from his classmates'.*

Structure / Objective	Activity	Anthony's adaptation
Structure: Whole group **Objective:** Improve ability to draw conclusions and integrate information across time periods and cultures by sharing all texts. *Anthony's objective: Motor control for holding large objects, pointing to pictures, and using assistive technology.*	**Graphic organizer** Complete the Venn diagram by recording the similarities/differences between the community where the characters from the story live and their own community	*Anthony has a completed Venn diagram on his computer using Inspiration or PowerPoint. At the close of the activity, Anthony must activate the switch at least 5 times to help students check their work. Essentially, he reveals answers to students in his group for self-checking after the group has brainstormed.*
Structure: Whole group **Objective:** Continue to develop students' abilities to write essays based on a single thesis statement and defend the position. *Anthony's objective: Answer yes/no questions that incorporate basic words from activity or the book; select pictures on computer, programmed to type words in response to questions; motor control for holding large objects, pointing to pictures, and using assistive technology.*	**Writer's workshop** Community, family, diversity: brainstorm the impact that our prejudice and preconceived notions have on how we view our place and the place of others in the community. If time permits, begin writing stories from a personal perspective focusing on the importance of diversity in our lives.	*Anthony answers yes/no questions about his family and his life in the community. Classmates assist him in developing a picture journal on his computer by selecting pictures. Later, he can share his story with his classmates.*

Table 6.6. David's participation in a sixth-grade English language arts class (45–60 minutes)

Objectives and structure	Sample activity	David's participation
Structure: Whole group **Objective:** Reinforce previously introduced vocabulary ***David's objective:*** *Improve listening and turn-taking in the large group. Improve oral communication.*	**Whole-group vocabulary review** Each student has a card with a question card and an answer relating to vocabulary. Students ask and answer questions in a random whip.	*David has 2 vocabulary words. He starts the class by reading his card and listening to the answer. He ends the activity by listening for his vocabulary definition and providing the answer. His cards may have picture cues.*
Structure: Small groups with predictable reading routine **Objective:** Apply active reading comprehension strategies to the reading selection. Identify major themes and conflicts in the selection. ***David's objective:*** *Improve listening in the small group by making on-topic statements or posing questions.*	**Guided reading/book clubs** Three groups read chapter books that are associated with the theme; develop understanding of characters as they relate/interact with one another. Group 1: *The Giver* (Lowry, 1999) Group 2: *Gathering Blue* (Lowry, 2000) Group 3: *Number the Stars* (Lowry, 1989) Evolve into an author study.	*During other times in his day or at home, Number the Stars has been previewed by listening to the book on tape or viewing a video. David participates by answering only one or two factual questions (who, what, when, where, and why questions). He may answer some questions related to one main character (Ellen or Annmarie).*
Structure: Teacher-created pairs; students were already taught the comprehension strategy in previous classes. **Objective:** Increase identification and use of vocabulary in context while applying a comprehension strategy ***David's objective:*** *Increase sight-word vocabulary.*	**Classwide peer tutoring** In pairs, students identify difficult words in the text and record them in the group journal. Use strategies to define unknown words in the group and give to teacher later (these will be incorporated into the daily vocabulary review).	*David is the third member of a pair. He listens to the vocabulary peers identify as new and, with peer assistance and adult guidance, chooses one new word that could be represented by a concrete picture. He records the word on his worksheet and a definition may be written by a peer or adult (i.e., the word community or home might align with the texts). However, David tries to state the definition on his own. Students in his group may have the same or slightly different words than David. Students in his group also record information on worksheets for their individualized growth.*

154

Structure: Whole group

Objective: Improve ability to draw conclusions and integrate information across time periods and cultures by sharing all texts.

David's objective: Increase sight-word vocabulary and connections between sight words and meanings (facts).

Structure: Whole group

Objective: Continue to develop students' abilities to write essays based on a single thesis statement and defend the position.

David's objective: Increase use of sight-word vocabulary and facts in sentences.

Graphic organizer

Complete the Venn diagram by recording the similarities/differences between the community where the characters in the story live and our own community.

Writer's workshop

Community, family, diversity: brainstorm the impact that our prejudice and preconceived notions have on how we view our place and the place of others in the community. If time permits, begin writing stories from a personal perspective focusing on the importance of diversity in our lives.

David completes this Venn diagram, capturing at least one fact on either side of the diagram.

David now uses his one vocabulary word from the pair activity and one fact from his Venn diagram to write and/or draw his understanding of community or home. When sharing their work, peers help him think more about how to write or illustrate his reflective piece on his level.

Table 6.7. Patty's participation in a sixth-grade English language arts class (45–60 minutes)

Objectives and structure	Sample activity	Patty's participation
Structure: Whole group **Objective:** Reinforce previously introduced vocabulary. ***Patty's objective:*** *Improve listening and turn-taking in the large group. Improve oral communication.*	**Whole-group vocabulary review** Each student has a card with a question and an answer relating to vocabulary. Students ask and answer questions in a random whip.	*Patty is given the same card from the middle of the deck of cards each day this activity occurs. She listens to the word and reads the card as other students. The print is enlarged.*
Structure: Small groups with predictable reading routine **Objective:** Apply active reading comprehension strategies to the reading selection. Identify major themes and conflicts in the selection. ***Patty's objective:*** *Improve listening in the small group by making on-topic statements or posing questions.* *Make on-topic responses in two full sentences with correct punctuation.*	**Guided reading/book clubs** Three groups read chapter books that are associated with the theme; develop understanding of characters as they relate/interact with one another. Group 1: *The Giver* (Lowry, 1999) Group 2: *Gathering Blue* (Lowry, 2000) Group 3: *Number the Stars* (Lowry, 1989) *evolve into an author study	*Because Patty has a great deal of home support, the family has previewed the section of the book read today and answered some comprehension questions that the students will answer. Patty participates in the group discussion using her notes from home reading. She writes one prediction on her own. Her recording sheet allows for larger writing and she is required to write all her responses in full sentences with proper punctuation.*
Structure: Teacher-created pairs; students were already taught the comprehension strategy in previous classes. **Objective:** Increase identification and use of vocabulary in context while applying a comprehension strategy. ***Patty's objective:*** *Increase sight-word vocabulary.*	**Classwide peer tutoring** In pairs, students identify difficult words in the text and record them in the group journal. Use strategies to define unknown words in the group and give to teacher later (these will be incorporated into the daily vocabulary review).	*Patty is the third member of a pair. She listens to the vocabulary the peers identify as new and, with peer assistance, chooses two new words, that can be paired with words she uses in her speech but might not be able to read. For instance, the word diversity could be paired with the word different, and similar could be paired with the word same. The words diversity and similar are words the general education students are learning to decode and use in writing.*

Structure: Whole group
Objective: Improve ability to draw conclusions and integrate information across time periods and cultures by sharing all texts.
Patty's objective: Still needed

Graphic organizer
Complete the Venn diagram by recording the similarities/differences between the community where the characters in the story live and our own community.

Patty writes at least one fact on each side of the Venn diagram.

Structure: Whole group
Objective: Continue to develop students' abilities to write essays based on a single thesis statement and defend the position.
Patty's objective: Still needed

Writer's workshop
Community, family, diversity: brainstorm the impact that our prejudice and preconceived notions have on how we view our place and the place of others in the community. If time permits, begin writing stories from a personal perspective, focusing on the importance of diversity in our lives.

Patty uses her Venn diagram and her vocabulary words (diversity and similar) to write at least two sentences on topic. Peers exchange ideas about writing, she listens to and exchanges thoughts about writing and the books being read in class.

HIGH SCHOOL OR COLLEGE-LEVEL LITERACY INSTRUCTION

Similar to the intermediate to middle school levels, it often is stated that students with severe disabilities should be excluded from general education literacy classes at the high school and college levels because the perceived gap in performance levels seems too large for the student with a severe disability to benefit. While this may be true when analyzing some high school and college content areas or instructional methods, course selection procedures at this level of education usually are more flexible than at the earlier levels. The availability of more elective courses, as well as a range of liberal education courses, provides students with severe disabilities opportunities to select coursework that matches their individual needs, strengths, and desired life outcomes. For example, older students with severe disabilities often need continued expansion and improvement of reading, writing, speaking, and listening skills; within the field of special education, however, these skills frequently are referred to as socialization and/or communication skills. This difference in terminology frequently interferes with communication across grade levels, as well as between general and special education personnel.

Several courses at the high school and college levels can support the further development of literacy skills, including courses in theater (e.g., drama and set design, beginning acting, Shakespeare for the stage), literature (e.g., poetry, modern literature), and composition (e.g., freshman English). Courses offered in high school to college assume that students who are pursuing standard curriculum outcomes already have developed the required literacy skills. Short- and long-term assignments, therefore, rely on those literacy skills in very direct ways. For instance, a professor might require students to defend a thesis statement by integrating information from one class with content taught in another (e.g., writing about toxic chemicals and the impact those chemicals have on the reproductive habits of a particular species). Such assignments often are graded for scientific accuracy, degree of depth regarding the content, and the sophistication of language. Although reading and writing skills are not explicitly taught, it is assumed that students already developed those skills and are prepared to apply them to novel and higher level tasks.

Recently, students with severe disabilities have begun to enjoy the benefits of college-level education opportunities. Students with severe disabilities, usually ages 18–21, have extended their public school special education services to include support for transitioning to a college campus. Although there are a number of ways in which students with severe disabilities have participated in college life, research suggests that involvement in college-level coursework is an important component of the college experience for individuals with severe disabilities (Doyle, 2003; Grigal, Newbert, & Moon, 2002; Ryndak et al., 1999). Access to and participation in college-level coursework and activities is viewed as an avenue for students with severe disabilities to further develop their literacy skills through reading, writing, speaking, and listening across contexts that naturally occur in their lives. Because the participation of students with severe disabilities in college-level coursework is a relatively new endeavor, little literature exists concerning best practices. However, it is assumed that students with severe disabilities will extend their literacy skills by 1) completing modified short-term and semester-long assignments, 2) participating in weekly support sessions for review and preview of course content, and 3) participating in small- and large-group discussions.

As individuals such as Anthony, David, and Patty engage in the person-centered planning process (Mount & Zwernick, 1988), it becomes clear which courses might align with their interests, personal learning styles, and desired life outcomes. For instance, if David expressed a desire to work with people in the human services arena (e.g., employment at a child care center, assisted living center, hospital), then a developmental psychology course might be a worthwhile course for him. If Patty expressed an interest in science, or a desire to work in a lab, it would be appropriate to consider a laboratory science class. Whether a student is participating in an introductory or advanced course, the opportunity to engage in literacy development is present. Specifically, when Anthony, David, or Patty decides to attend college, each of them will have opportunities to practice reading (e.g., choosing a course from a catalog, reading signs on campus, referring to a calendar for important dates), complete writing tasks (e.g., registering for class on computer, completing adapted assignments), communicate with a variety of people (e.g., advocating for a particular course, presenting in class, making appointments with study partners, working on campus), and listen to a variety of individuals across contexts (e.g., in class sessions, on the job, at social events on campus).

When considering the opportunities for developing literacy skills discussed previously, it is critical to identify the supports and services that students with severe disabilities will require to benefit from those opportunities, both on and off campus. Early each semester, those supports and services must be identified for each student with severe disabilities, ensuring their success in high school and college life. Such supports and services must consider the accommodations and modifications that will be required for the students to benefit from the courses selected, based on the student's individual strengths and instructional needs. As indicated earlier, the education team identifies appropriate accommodations and modifications with information gathered through ecological inventories. Figures 6.1 and 6.2 provide a framework for determining accommodations and modifications for an individual student in specific courses. Figure 6.1 considers accommodations and modifications to the coursework so that the student will benefit, and Figure 6.2 considers how the student will participate in each of the course requirements. As an example, each of these forms has been completed for David. These forms illustrate a course modification outline and course participation agreement. Both are meant to be completed by David, the faculty member who will be teaching the course, David's special education teacher, and David's advocate. Collectively, this team should ensure that David is practicing self-advocacy skills and self-determination. Through these activities, the high school or college student with severe disabilities uses literacy skills prior to registering for a specific course, as well as throughout the course as requirements and activities change (see Figures 6.1 and 6.2).

A liberal education course commonly selected by college freshman is developmental psychology. Because the professor who teaches this course at the local college uses a variety of media (e.g., video case studies, WebQuests, film documents of young children's drawings) during each class session, this course frequently is considered appropriate for students like Anthony, David, and Patty. Tables 6.8, 6.9, and 6.10 provide examples of these students being actively engaged in each of the course's assignments.

Student: David
Course title:
PSY 150 Child and Adolescent
Development

Semester: Spring 05
Day/time/location:
Tu & Th 9:30–10:45

Professor:
Dr. Ward

Course-related goals

- Students will develop observational assessment skills based on principles and theories of child development through class assignments, readings, and field-based observations.
- Students will assess the impact of family and social factors on early development through class assignments, readings, and field-based observations.

David's course-related goals

David will participate in class discussions and activities by making on-topic comments, recording reflections about class in a journal, and creating computerized slide presentation about child development.

Teaching tips	Expected participation
During class involvement	
Lectures	David enjoys listening. He should attend to the lecture but will not take notes. A peer will review notes during a study session. Supplementing lectures with visuals is helpful.
Tests and quizzes	David is provided an adapted test using pictures that parallel 1 or 2 concepts from class and lead to functional literacy.
Small groups (including labs)	During class observations, David will need a peer group to work with to gain the most from observations.
Long-term assignments	
Research paper	David is creating his paper using pictures from his observations. This will take the form of an electronic slide portfolio. Peer study partners will develop this with him.
Group presentations	David can read simple sentences on an overhead, from note cards or on a screen. He can be a member of a group.

Peer supports   **Contact information**   **Role**

Figure 6.1. Coursework modification form.

In keeping with previous examples, Anthony, David, and Patty have continued to make adequate yearly progress on individualized curriculum goals and objectives. During small-group activities, Anthony uses various assistive technology with picture cues to participate in content-based instruction. Vocabulary words are selected that can be represented in pictures and that are meaningful to him. David's involvement in small groups focuses more on his listening and turn-taking skills than on acquisition of course content. Patty is able to make progress in reading, writing, speaking, and listening by both interacting with peers and learning the "big ideas" of child development. As the remainder of the class unfolds and the professor outlines the long-term assignment, Anthony, David, and Patty's individualized outcomes and participation are different. Supports are provided to each of these learners based on their IEP objectives and long-term outcomes.

Student: David
Course title:
PSY 150 Child and Adolescent
  Development

Semester: Spring 05
Day/time/location:
Tu & Th 9:30–10:45

Professor:
Dr. Ward

Course expectations	My participation
Lectures and discussions	• I will listen and take notes. ☑ I will listen but do not take notes. • I will volunteer for an activity. • I need a few seconds to answer questions. ☑ Before class I will give you a notecard for a question I've prepared to answer.
Readings, tests, and quizzes	• I can read passages in class. ☑ I prefer not to read aloud in class. • I can read all of the text. • I can listen to a book on tape or use peer notes. ☑ I am not able to read the text but a peer study partner or my family will help me summarize the information for class. • I can take tests and quizzes like everyone else. ☑ I will make arrangements through the student support center to take my tests. ☑ I can take an adapted version of the test. ☑ I will not take tests but will demonstrate my learning other ways.
Small groups (including labs)	• I can participate in small groups. ☑ Sometimes, I need to watch my peers in a group but not be an active member.
Research paper	• I can write all required papers. • I can write _____ paper(s). • I can write one paper that is focused on a specific topic. ☑ I will create a modified paper on a topic through the use of a slide presentation. I will need to ask a peer to help me. • I can dictate my thoughts to someone. • I will not write papers but demonstrate my learning other ways.
Group presentations	• I can complete my own presentation. ☑ I would prefer to present with a partner.
Grading	☑ I would like you to grade my work according to my adapted learning outcomes. • I do not want a grade for the course.
Arrival/departure from class	☑ I can travel to and from class alone. • I would like a peer to walk with me.

Figure 6.2. Course participation form. (From Diane Lea Ryndak and Sandra Alper, *Curriculum Instruction for Students with Significant Disabilities in Inclusive Settings,* 2e [p. 313]. Published by Allyn & Bacon, Boston, MA. Copyright © 2003 by Pearson Education. Adapted by permission of the publisher.)

Table 6.8. Anthony in the developmental psychology course (1 hour, 15 minute class)

Objective and structure	Sample activity	Anthony's participation
Structure: Small groups at tables **Objective:** Review and apply previously presented theories of child development to observable behavior. ***Anthony's objective:*** *Select pictures on computer, programmed to type words in response to questions; motor control for holding large objects, pointing to pictures, and using assistive technology.*	**Warm-up** Envelopes on each table contain cards with Piaget and Erickson's developmental stages, including definitions, expected age ranges, and a child activity. Students align the theorist, developmental stages, ages, and corresponding child example. This is a 10–15-minute activity.	*Anthony has two tasks during this activity: to select pictures on his computer that represent specific answers (e.g., individuals at various ages to represent children's activities); to hold cards that have other components on them, from which his classmates select correct answers*
Structure: Whole group **Objective:** Develop and improve observation skills related to child development. ***Anthony's objective:*** *Motor control for holding large objects, pointing to pictures, and using assistive technology; answer yes/no questions that incorporate basic words from activity or the book*	**Lecture** Discusses how Piaget's and Erickson's theories of development serve as a foundation for some aspects of developmental psychology. The lecture focuses on developing observational skills based on those theories.	*During the lecture, Anthony selects pictures that represent specific concepts addressed in class, and responds to yes/no questions about the topic in general.*
Structure: Whole group **Objective:** Develop skill in the use of a developmental inventory for use in field-based observations ***Anthony's objective:*** *Motor control for selecting pictures; answer yes/no questions that incorporate basic behaviors observed and basic concepts from the lecture.*	**Class simulation** The professor distributes directions on how to conduct a structured observation of an infant, toddler, or preschooler. Students watch a video to simulate real observations. The video is stopped at various points to ensure students are observing and recording information accurately.	*During each stop of the videotape, Anthony responds to yes/no questions about content on the videotape, and selects pictures that represent specific behaviors reflected on the videotape.*
Structure: Students can collaborate but each is expected to hand in an individual product **Objective:** Produce a comprehensive report that integrates all learning from the semester. ***Anthony's objective:*** *Motor control for pointing to pictures, and using assistive technology; answer yes/no questions that incorporate possible behaviors observed and basic concepts from the course.*	**Summative assignment** Students are expected to observe three children outside of class, write observation summaries that are grounded to theoretical concepts from class, and embed digital photos of child examples into the paper.	*With a team from class Anthony will conduct observations of one child. With assistance, Anthony will develop a written summary of the observation by responding to yes/no questions and selecting pictures that represent specific behaviors he observed.*

Table 6.9. David in the developmental psychology course (1 hour, 15 minute class)

Objective and structure	Sample activity	David's participation
Structure: Small groups at tables **Objective:** Review and apply previously presented theories of child development to observable behavior. *David's objective: Listen and respond to peers in the small group. Ask clarifying questions if needed.*	**Warm-up** Envelopes on each table contain cards with Piaget and Erickson's developmental stages, including definitions, expected age ranges, and a child activity. Students align the theorist, developmental stages, ages, and corresponding child example. This is a 10–15-minute activity.	*David is the third member of a pair and moves pieces as suggested and discussed by classmates. This requires listening and thinking. If he is confused he questions classmates to clarify where the piece should be placed.*
Structure: Whole group **Objective:** Develop and improve students' observation skills related to child development. *David's objective: Attend to the lecture within the large group. Highlight key words presented by the professor*	**Lecture** Discusses how Piaget's and Erickson's theories of development serve as a foundation for some aspects of developmental psychology. The lecture focuses on developing observational skills based on those theories.	*The lecture is accompanied by an electronic slide presentation that can be accessed prior to class through the internet access supplementing the course. David, during a study group session outside of class, accessed the notes on the Internet and placed them in his notebook for class. He attends to social cues and opens notebook when peers do so. Note taking is not necessary, but listening is expected.*
Structure: Students can collaborate but each is expected to hand in an individual product **Objective:** Produce a comprehensive report that integrates all learning from the semester. *David's objective: Create a slide presentation concerning his observations. Write short sentences describing observations.*	**Summative assignment** Students are expected to observe three children outside of class, write observation summaries that are grounded to theoretical concepts from class, and embed digital photos of child examples into the paper.	*The professor, peers from class, and the college placement office work with David's personal supports to get him both a job experience and field observation hours at the college preschool. He not only works with the children for future job skills, he takes pictures of activities he completes with the children and creates a modified book through the use of an electronic slide presentation. This is developed with peer support during outside of class tutoring sessions.*

Table 6.10. Patty in the developmental psychology course (1 hour, 15 minute class)

Objective and structure	Sample activity	Patty's participation
Structure: Small groups at tables **Objective:** Review and apply previously presented theories of child development to observable behavior. *Patty's objective: Listen to peers and ask clarifying questions. Identify major theorists and at least one stage of development.*	**Warm-up** Envelopes on each table contain cards with Piaget and Erickson's developmental stages, including definitions, expected age ranges, and a child activity. Students align the theorist, developmental stages, ages, and corresponding child example. This is a 10–15-minute activity.	*Patty is the third member of a pair and moves pieces as suggested and discussed by classmates. This requires listening and thinking. If she is confused she questions classmates to clarify where the piece should be placed.*
Structure: Whole group **Objective:** Develop and improve students observation skills related to child development. *Patty's objective: Attend to the large-group lecture. Take notes for at least 3 slides from the lecture.*	**Lecture** Discusses how Piaget's and Erickson's theories of development serve as a foundation for some aspects of developmental psychology. The lecture focuses on developing observational skills based on those theories.	*The lecture is accompanied by an electronic slide presentation that can be accessed prior to class through the Internet access supplementing the course. Patty is able to get on the computer independently using a laminated card with her security sign-on. With only verbal guidance, she prints out the notes and places them in her binder for class. She attends to social cues and opens notebook when peers do so. At least 3 slides are highlighted to visually cue her to note-take during those slides, even if only one word.*
Structure: Whole group **Objective:** Develop skill in the use of a developmental inventory for use in field-based observations *Patty's objective: Identify stage of development with correct term on accompanying worksheet.*	**Class simulation** A handout outlines how to conduct a structured observation of an infant, toddler, or preschooler. Students watch a video to simulate real observations. The video is stopped at various points to ensure students are observing and recording accurately.	*All students are provided a 3-page handout that is divided into quadrants on each page (behavior alone, behavior with an object, behavior with others, overall use of language and motor skills). Each page addresses a different level of development (infant, toddler, preschool). Students watch the video and write in observations. Patty watches the video and*

164

Structure: Students can collaborate but each is expected to hand in an individual product

Objective: Produce a comprehensive report that integrates all learning from the semester.

Patty's objective: *Create a slide presentation of observations using at least 5 vocabulary terms from the class. Short sentences describe each picture.*

circles a word (college peers are writing all observations, not selecting words) that matches what is presented. This is repeated for each stage of development. Patty is encouraged to advocate for herself and asks the professor if she can view the video at home to review the material.

Summative assignment

Students are expected to observe three children outside of class, write observation summaries that are grounded to theoretical concepts from class, and embed digital photos of child examples into the paper.

The professor, peers from class, and the college placement office work with Patty's personal supports to get her both a job experience and field observation hours at the college preschool. She works with the children for future job skills, takes pictures of activities she completes with the children and creates a modified book through the use of an electronic slide presentation. This is developed with peer support during outside of class tutoring sessions.

SUMMARY

In the last decade, legislation stemming from the standards-based reform movement in education has altered current practices regarding literacy instruction and the involvement of students with disabilities in general education curriculum, instruction, and accountability measures. As with other students with disabilities, this legislation has had a profound effect on services for students with severe disabilities. In addition, however, we are beginning to see the long-term effects of receiving special education services in inclusive general education contexts on the quality of life for students with severe disabilities (Fisher & Meyer, 2002; Ryndak et al., 1999). These effects are evident not only in the students' quality of life during and after school, but also in the students' access to instructional content that previously had been denied them.

Just as is the case for general education students, the development of literacy skills for students with severe disabilities is critical if they are to participate in naturally occurring, real-life activities with their friends, neighbors, and family members who do not have disabilities. Just as is the case for general education students, the development of literacy skills for students with severe disabilities is critical if they are to be as independent as possible during, and to have meaningful involvement in, a variety of activities across naturally occurring, real-life contexts. Although students with severe disabilities may not acquire all of the content required for a general education diploma in their state, continued meaningful exposure to that content is essential if they are 1) to have experiences and knowledge base in common with members of society, so that these common experiences can lead to mutual understanding and respectful interactions; 2) to have meaningful relationships across the stages of their lives with members of society who do not have disabilities; and 3) to be contributing and valued members to society.

To achieve these long-term outcomes, collaborative education teams that rely on the active involvement of the student, family members, and peers without disabilities strive to determine the most functional and meaningful curriculum content for annual goals, as well as identify the most effective supports and services for students with severe disabilities. Their use of ecological assessments for determining both curriculum content and progress speaks to the importance of the student's use of skills throughout daily life. When applied to the development of literacy skills, these strategies emphasize each student's use of literacy skills in meaningful activities. This allows instruction on literacy skills to be pervasive across contexts and activities, thus allowing education teams to address the learning characteristics that partially define this population. By doing so, education teams assist students with severe disabilities to engage in literacy development, and to use literacy skills, across their lifetime.

REFERENCES

Allen, J. (2000). *Yellow brick roads: Shared and guided paths to independent reading.* Portland, ME: Stenhouse Publishing.

Baumgart, D., Brown, L., Pumpian, I., Nisbet, J., Ford, A., Sweet, M., et al. (1982). The principle of partial participation and individualized adaptations in educational programs for severely handicapped students. *The Journal of The Association for Persons with Severe Handicaps, 7*(2), 17–27.

Brown, F., Evans, I.M., Weed, K.A., & Owen, V. (1987). Delineating functional competencies: A component model. *The Journal of The Association for Persons with Severe Handicaps, 12*, 117–124.

Brown, F., & Lehr, D. (1993). Making activities meaningful for students with severe multiple disabilities. *TEACHING Exceptional Children, 25*(4), 12–16.

Brown, L., Nietupski, J., & Hamre–Nietupski, S. (1976). The criterion of ultimate functioning and public school services for severely handicapped students. In M.A. Thomas (Ed.), *Hey, don't forget about me: Education's investment in the severely, profoundly, and multiply handicapped.* Reston, VA: Council for Exceptional Children.

Brown, L., & York, R. (1974). Developing programs for severely handicapped students: Teacher training and classroom instruction. *Focus on Exceptional Children, 6*(2).

Center for Applied Special Technology. (2004). *Universal designs for learning.* Retrieved March 16, 2005, from http://www.cast.org/research/udl/index.html#Underlying%20Premises

Cunningham, P.M. (1995). *Phonics they use: Words for reading and writing* (2nd ed.). New York: HarperCollins.

Cunningham, P.M., & Allington, R.L. (1999). *Classrooms that work: They can all read and write* (2nd ed.). New York: Addison Wesley Longman.

Day, J.P., Spiegel, D.L., McLellan, J., & Brown, V.B. (2002). *Moving forward with literature circles: How to plan, manage, and evaluate literature circles that deepen understanding and foster a love of reading.* New York: Scholastic.

Doyle, M.B. (2003). Supporting students with significant disabilities in college. In D.L. Ryndak & S. Alper (Eds.), *Curriculum and instruction for students with significant disabilities in inclusive settings* (2nd ed.). Boston: Allyn & Bacon.

Ferguson, D.L., & Baumgart, D. (1991). Partial participation revisited. *The Journal of The Association for Persons with Severe Handicaps, 16*, 218–227.

Fielding, L.G., & Pearson, P.D. (1994). Reading comprehension: What works. *Educational Leadership, 51*(5), 62–68.

Fisher, M., & Meyer, L.H. (2002). Development and social competence after two years for students enrolled in inclusive and self–contained educational programs. *Research and Practice for Persons with Severe Disabilities, 27*, 165–174.

Forest, M., & Lusthaus, E. (1990). Everyone belongs with the MAPS action planning system. *TEACHING Exceptional Children, 22*(2), 32–35.

Fountas, I.C., & Pinell, G.S. (1996). *Guided reading: Good first teaching for all children.* Portsmouth, NH: Heinemann.

Friend, M.P., & Bursuck, W.D. (2002). *Including students with special needs: A practical guide for classroom teachers* (3rd ed.). Boston: Allyn & Bacon.

Giangreco, M.F., Cloninger, C.J., Dennis, R.E., & Edelman, S.W. (2002). Problem solving methods to facilitate inclusive education. In J.S. Thousand, R.A. Villa, & A.I. Nevin (Eds.), *Creativity and collaborative learning: A practical guide to empowering students, teachers, and families* (2nd ed., pp. 111–134). Baltimore: Paul H. Brookes Publishing Co.

Giangreco, M.F., Cloninger, C.J., & Iverson, V.S. (1998). *Choosing outcomes and accommodations for children (COACH): A guide to educational planning for students with disabilities* (2nd ed.). Baltimore: Paul H. Brookes Publishing Co.

Grigal, M., Newbert, D.A., & Moon, S.M. (2002). Post-secondary options for students with significant disabilities. *TEACHING Exceptional Children, 35*(2), 68–73.

Hamill, L.B., & Everington, C. (2002). *Teaching students with moderate to severe disabilities: An applied approach for inclusive environments.* Upper Saddle River, NJ: Prentice Hall.

Harvey, S., & Goudvis, A. (2000). *Strategies that work: Teaching comprehension to enhance understanding.* Portland, ME: Stenhouse Publishing.

Individuals with Disabilities Education Act (IDEA) Amendments of 1997, PL 105-17, 20 U.S.C. §§ 1400 *et seq.*

Individuals with Disabilities Education Improvement Act of 2004, PL 108-446, 20 U.S.C. §§ 1400 *et seq.*

Inspiration Software, Inc. (2003). Inspiration (Version 7.5) [Computer software]. Portland, OR: Author.

Ivey, G. (2002). Meeting, not ignoring, teen literacy needs. *The Education Digest, 68*(2), 23–25.

Jackson, L., Ryndak, D.L., & Billingsley, F. (2000). Useful practices in inclusive education: A preliminary view of what the experts in moderate and severe disabilities are saying. *The Journal of The Association for Persons with Severe Handicaps, 25,* 129–141.

Langer, J.A. (2004). *Effective literacy instruction: Building successful reading and writing programs.* Urbana, IL: National Council of Teachers of English.

Lave, J., & Wenger, E. (1991). *Situated learning: Legitimate peripheral participation.* Cambridge, England: Cambridge University Press.

Lowry, L. (1989). *Number the stars.* New York: Houghton Mifflin.

Lowry, L. (1999). *The giver.* New York: Bantam Books.

Lowry, L. (2000). *Gathering blue.* New York: Houghton Mifflin.

Moore, D.W., Bean, T.W., Birdyshaw, D., & Rycik, J.A. (1999). *Adolescent literacy: A position statement for the commission on adolescent literacy of the International Reading Association.* Newark, DE: International Reading Association.

Mount, B., & Zwernick, K. (1988). *It's never too early, it's never too late: An overview of personal futures planning.* St. Paul, MN: Governor's Planning Council on Developmental Disabilities.

National Institute of Child Health and Human Development. (2002). *Report of the National Reading Panel. Teaching children to read: An evidence-based assessment of the scientific research literature on reading and its implications for reading instruction* (NIH Publication No. 00–4769). Washington, DC: U.S. Government Printing Office.

No Child Left Behind (NCLB) Act of 2001, PL 107-110, 115 Stat. 1425, 20 U.S.C. §§ 6301 *et seq.*

Numeroff, L.J. (1985). *If you give a mouse a cookie.* New York: Laura Geringer.

Pearpoint, J., O'Brien, J., & Forest, M. (1993). *PATH: A workbook for planning positive possible futures.* Toronto: Inclusion Press.

Peterson, J.M., & Hittie, M.M. (2002). *Inclusive teaching: Creating effective schools for all learners.* Boston: Allyn & Bacon.

Ryndak, D.L. (2003). The curriculum content identification process: Rationale and overview. In D.L. Ryndak & S. Alper (Eds.), *Curriculum and instruction for students with significant disabilities in inclusive settings* (2nd ed., pp. 86–115). Boston: Allyn & Bacon.

Ryndak, D.L., & Alper, S. (2003). *Curriculum and instruction for students with significant disabilities in inclusive settings* (2nd ed.). Boston: Allyn & Bacon.

Ryndak, D.L., Morrison, A.P., & Sommerstein. L. (1999). Literacy before and after inclusion in general education settings: A case study. *The Journal of The Association for Persons with Severe Handicaps, 24,* 5–22.

Ryndak, D.L., & Ward, T.A. (2003). Adapting environments, materials, and instruction to facilitate inclusion and learning. In D.L. Ryndak & S. Alper (Eds.), *Curriculum and instruction for students with significant disabilities in inclusive settings* (2nd ed., pp. 382–410). Boston: Allyn & Bacon.

Sands, D.J., Kozleski, E.B., & French, N. (2000). *Inclusive education for the 21st century: A new introduction to special education.* Stamford, CT: Wadsworth Publishing.

Shanklin, N.J. (2002). *Adolescent literacy: Encouraging the development of adolescent readers.* National Council of Teachers of English. Retrieved January 28, 2004, from http://www.ncte.org

Snow, C.E., Burns, M.S., & Griffin, P. (Eds.). (1998). *Preventing reading difficulties in young children.* Washington, DC: National Academy Press.

Tomlinson, C.A. (1999). *The differentiated classroom: Responding to the needs of all learners.* Washington, DC: Association for Supervision and Curriculum Development.

Tomlinson, C.A. (2003). *Fulfilling the promise of the differentiated classroom: Strategies and tools for responsive teaching.* Washington, DC: Association for Supervision and Curriculum Development.

Tovani, C. (2004). *Do I really have to teach reading?: Content comprehension, grades 6–12.* Portland, ME: Stenhouse Publishing.

Tovani, C., Keene, E.O., & Stratton, P. (2000). *I read it, but I don't get it: Comprehension strategies for adolescent readers.* Portland, ME: Stenhouse Publishing.

U.S. Department of Education, Office of Elementary and Secondary Education. (2002). *Guidance for the Reading First program.* Washington, DC: Government Printing Office.

Vaughn, S., Bos, C.S., & Schumm, J.S. (1997). *Teaching mainstreamed, diverse, and at-risk students in the general education classroom.* Boston: Allyn & Bacon.

Wiggins, G. (1998). An exchange of views on "Semantics, psychometrics, and assessment reform: A close look at authentic assessments." *Educational Researcher, 27*(6), 20–21.

Wilcox, B., & Bellamy, T. (Eds.). (1987). *A comprehensive guide to the activities catalogue: An alternative curriculum for youth and adults with severe disabilities.* Baltimore: Paul H. Brookes Publishing Co.

Wood, A. (1984). *The napping house.* New York: Harcourt.

Chapter 7

Enhancing Numeracy

Diane M. Browder, Lynn Ahlgrim-Delzell,
David K. Pugalee, and Bree A. Jimenez

> Today in Alex's math class, his teacher's goal is to extend students' understanding of geometric patterns by introducing the concept of symmetry. She gives the class half of a symmetric figure (e.g., half a heart or star). Students find the person with a matching half to form partners for the math lesson. Alex, who is nonverbal and has a significant cognitive disability, and Chondra, a classmate who is nondisabled, find that they have matching halves. The teacher then gives several cut-out shapes to each student pair. She tells the students to fold each shape in half to see if the two halves match exactly. Alex and Chondra work together to sort the patterns that do and do not have matching halves. Alex uses his Boardmaker symbol for *same* to confirm each match or communicates *no* for those that do not create a match as Chondra folds each one. Chondra then accepts the teacher's bonus challenge to determine whether more than one line of symmetry can be drawn for each shape. That night, Alex's parents help him with his homework to find at least three common objects that have symmetry. Chondra's homework will involve drawing lines of symmetry for several complex shapes. *(This illustration is adapted from the lesson plan of Tucker, Singleton, & Weaver, 2002, pp. 39–42.)*

Teachers often use concrete objects such as those in this geometry lesson to illustrate concepts such as symmetry. Even with these illustrations, some students find mathematical concepts difficult to grasp. Rivera (1997) notes that as many as 25% of students with learning disabilities need support for math in school and continue to struggle with math in postsecondary settings and everyday life-related activities. Because mathematics can be challenging, educators have sometimes narrowed instruction to the basics of computation. For students with significant cognitive disabilities, instruction has often been narrowed further to focus solely on the use of money or telling time.

In contrast, reform initiatives within mathematics education seek to broaden educators' approach to mathematics to include problem solving while developing and maintaining procedural and computational proficiency. The National Council of Teachers of Mathematics (NCTM) also advocates broadening mathematics education to be responsive to all students. One of the organization's six principles for school mathematics is equity in mathematics education with high expectations and strong support for all students. The NCTM equity principle states that

> All students, regardless of their personal characteristics, backgrounds, or physical challenges must have opportunities—and support to learn—mathematics. Equity

does not mean that every student should receive identical instruction; instead, it demands that reasonable and appropriate accommodations be made as needed to promote access and attainment for all students. (NCTM, 2000, p. 12)

The focus of this chapter is on how to create access to a broad array of mathematics concepts for students with significant cognitive disabilities. To work toward *numeracy* is to acquire an understanding of mathematical concepts encountered in adult life in order to apply them in a variety of settings. Students need more than knowledge of a few facts or functions in mathematics. Students also need to acquire problem-solving strategies.

Teaching problem solving and the reasoning involved in mathematics can be a difficult challenge. Miller and Mercer (1997) summarize the types of difficulties that may be exhibited by students with disabilities:

- Memory and strategic deficits have differential performance results, with some students experiencing problems with conceptualization of mathematical operations, representation and recall of mathematics facts, and the conceptualization and learning of algorithms, or mathematical problem solving.

- Communicative disorders interfere with students' performance when they engage in tasks that involve reading, writing, and discussing mathematical ideas.

- Process and strategy deficiencies associated with solving mathematical word problems can interfere with conceptual understanding of the problem situation and how to address the situation mathematically.

- Low motivation, poor self-esteem, and a history of academic failure may affect how students value mathematics.

For students with significant cognitive disabilities, educators may also discover that students have had minimal exposure to mathematical concepts in prior schooling and lack adequate communication symbols for the expression of math concepts.

To promote the principle of equity, the NCTM (2000) identifies some specific adaptations that can assist in meeting the needs of students with disabilities. These include increased time to complete assignments, the use of oral rather than written assignments, and additional support (including after-school tutoring, and mentoring). The use of technologies such as voice creation and recognition software, as well as the use of subject matter software, also may be important adaptations for students with disabilities. The use of ongoing progress monitoring can also help teachers know where students need extra support. This chapter offers ideas for creating adaptations in mathematics. Some of these adaptations can be surmised from current research; others will be provided based on practical experience of the authors.

GUIDELINES FROM RESEARCH ON HOW TO TEACH MATHEMATICS
Research with Students with Mild Disabilities

Mathematics research with special populations has focused predominantly on the development and maintenance of basic skills by students with learning disabilities and other high-incidence disabilities. A meta-analysis of 58 studies focusing on mathematics interventions for elementary students with special needs found that most studies focused on basic skills and in general found interventions in this domain to be more effective than those in preparatory mathematics and problem solving (Kroesbergen, 2003). Among the studies reviewed, direct instruction and self-instruction were found to be more effective than mediated instruction. Direct instruction was considered to be most effective for basic math facts, whereas self-instruction was quite effective for problem-solving skills. The studies also suggested that interventions with teachers are more effective than computer-assisted instruction and peer-oriented tutoring. Consistent with this research, Carnine (1998) has recommended that math instruction

1. Focus on the big ideas—generalizable concepts rather than individual details

2. Teach conspicuous strategies, neither too broad nor too specific for conducting math operations and solving problems

3. Make efficient use of time in prioritized objectives

4. Communicate strategies in a clear and explicit manner

5. Provide practice and review to promote retention

Although direct instruction of basic skills in mathematics has the strongest research support to date (Kroesbergen, 2003), emerging studies report gains for students with disabilities in problem-solving strategies which align with reform-oriented mathematics. Concerns have been raised about the appropriateness of reform-oriented mathematics for students with disabilities; however, students with disabilities who are given authentic and challenging tasks may perform better than students with and without disabilities who receive less challenging tasks (King, Schroeder, & Chawszczewski, 2001).

For example, Cichon and Ellis (2003) compared the use of MATH *Connections* and a matched-comparison group using traditional curricula. MATH *Connections* is a 3-year sequence based on teaching students to be critical thinkers and problem solvers through an integrated curriculum with topics from algebra, geometry, statistics, and discrete mathematics. Students with and without disabilities performed as well or better on standardized tests of mathematics performance, including the Connecticut Academic Performance Test, Preliminary Scholastic Aptitude Test, and the Scholastic Aptitude Test, with MATH *Connections* compared with the traditional curricula. In contrast, students with disabilities needed more time to master subchapter units. During Year 1 on 35 subchapter unit quizzes, there was a significant difference on seven of the measures favoring non–special education students. During Year 2, there was no statistical significance in the mean score differences. The author posited that some students with special needs required more time to assimilate to the new classroom environment.

In a comparative year-long case study involving several students with learning disabilities, Woodward, Monroe, and Baxter (2001) found that ad hoc tutoring enhanced students' strategic knowledge of how to solve problems and communicate dimensions related to the problem tasks. The author reported that the learning environment in the study had a math reform orientation in which students worked on only one or two problems during a session. The approach promoted verbal collaboration that contributed to scaffolding and peer mediation. The authors concluded that "the combined focus on problem solving in the ad hoc tutoring sessions and the classwide practice on performance assessment tasks led to positive effects over time" (p. 47). Their results also indicate that teachers were able to assess special education students with some adaptations while maintaining the level of the tasks.

Summary of Research for Students with Mild Disabilities

As noted in Kroesbergen's (2003) meta-analysis, strong research exists for teaching students with high-incidence disabilities the basic facts of math using a direct instruction approach. Some research also exists for the application of self-instruction strategies to promote problem solving. A few studies have found benefits for using more extensive problem-solving approaches that are comparable to the reform-oriented approach of general education. Students with disabilities may experience difficulty with reform math curricula, particularly due to challenges with processing and distinguishing relevant information, deficits in computational capabilities, and inefficiency in reasoning and problem-solving skills (Pugach & Warger, 1993). Cognitive strategy instruction and assistive technologies hold promise for the teaching and assessment of this mathematics understanding.

Research on Teaching Math to Students with Moderate and Severe Disabilities

Although most of the research with students with mild disabilities has focused on basic skill instruction, much of the research with students with moderate and severe disabilities has targeted teaching the functional skill of money management. In a comprehensive review, of 55 studies involving math skills and students with moderate and severe disabilities since 1975, almost half (27) involved some type of money-management skill (Browder, Spooner, Ahlgrim-Delzell, Flowers, & Algozzine, 2005). Chapter 8 provides an overview of the functional math research and describes how this work is applicable to addressing state standards in mathematics. This chapter focuses on other math skills typically contained in national and state standards. Similar to the research with students with mild disabilities, most of these studies have focused on the basic skills of counting and computation. In contrast, the research on teaching students to self-manage their own behavior and learning also reflects strategies to teach math skills such as frequency tallying, one-to-one correspondence, charting/graphing, using math tools (ruler, calculator, counter, stopwatch), use of number line, and comparing numbers (1 more than, same/higher/lower).

In most of these math studies with students of moderate and severe disabilities, educators used a form of direct instruction called *systematic instruction*, in which students received repeated (massed) trials to practice the target response. This instruction typically has been designed to minimize students' errors through the use of systematic prompting and feedback. The application of these strategies to math instruction is described in more detail in Chapter 8. In some studies, educators used special stimulus prompts; that is, cues embedded in the instructional materials themselves. Examples of stimulus prompts used were picture cues, dice or cards with the corresponding number of dots to represent numbers, color cues highlighting the correct response, reduction in the size of the number to be matched so that it equaled the size of the number on a telephone, and increase in the number of numerals to be matched in a number sequence.

Most of the research on math instruction has demonstrated skill acquisition by students with moderate cognitive disabilities. Browder et al. (2005) found eight studies with students with severe cognitive disabilities, but only three of these targeted skills other than money management. These studies involved counting, matching numbers to learn to dial a telephone, and one-to-one correspondence in self-monitoring number of tasks completed (Lagomarcino & Rusch, 1989; Lalli, Mace, Browder, & Brown, 1989; Morrison & Rosales-Ruiz, 1997).

Summary of Research on Teaching Math to Students with Moderate and Severe Disabilities

Table 7.1 provides a summary of the studies on teaching math skills to students with moderate and severe disabilities. Similar to the research with students with mild disabilities, only a limited scope of mathematics concepts and skills have been addressed in the research to date. The problem-solving approach of reform-oriented instruction is notably absent in this research. In contrast, research does exist that students with moderate and severe disabilities can learn problem-solving skills (Agran & Hughes, 1997). For example, Hughes and Rusch (1989) taught individuals with severe mental retardation to solve problems that occurred in their job context, such as the need to replace missing materials. The students learned to follow a problem-solving sequence to state the problem, state the solution, provide self-report, and reinforce themselves. Although problem solving strategies have been applied with students with mild disabilities in mathematics (Bottge & Hasselbring, 1993), the need exists to adapt strategies such as those of Hughes and Rusch (1989) to teach math skills to students with significant cognitive disabilities (see Table 7.1).

TEACHING ALL COMPONENTS OF MATHEMATICS

To move beyond the limited scope of past mathematics instruction for students with significant cognitive disabilities, it is important to understand the basic components of math. The National Council for Teachers of Mathematics has articulated principles and standards for school mathematics (http://www.nctm .org) that provide a useful framework for understanding the scope of mathematics. The NCTM content standards focus on numbers and operations, algebra, geometry, measurement, and data analysis/probability. The NCTM note that the amount of coverage given to these components varies across years. For example, students may learn patterns and other pre-algebra content in the early grades, but spend more time on number concepts. Many state standards reflect similar categories of math content.

The NCTM also emphasizes the processes of mathematics including problem solving, reasoning and proof, communication about mathematics, making connections, and representation. Table 7.2 summarizes the components of mathematics. Following are descriptions of each math component and examples of skill instruction for students with significant cognitive disabilities (see Table 7.2).

Table 7.1. Research studies on teaching math skills to individuals with moderate and severe disabilities

Author(s)	Purpose	Skill being taught	Instructional procedures
Ackerman and Shapiro (1984)	Examine whether work productivity would be maintained with self-monitoring.	Frequency tally Graphing	Systematic instruction Verbal modeling, physical modeling response prompt Reinforcement
Baroody (1996)	Determine whether students could spontaneously invent and apply efficient addition strategies.	Addition	Massed trial Addition cards, dice, blocks stimulus prompts Verbal and physical modeling, physical guidance response prompts Repeat trial error correction
Bracey, Maggs, and Morath (1975)	Determine whether structured instructional programs provide significant gains in arithmetic skills.	Counting Number ID Math symbol ID	DISTAR computer program Reinforcement
Coleman and Whitman (1984)	Evaluate effectiveness of a physical fitness program with self-directed and external control components.	Compare numbers (higher/lower, one more than)	Systematic instruction Verbal and physical model response prompt Reinforcement
Copeland, Hughes, Agran, Wehmeyer, and Fowler (2002)	Examine effectiveness of an intervention package to improve classroom performance.	Use number line Match numbers	Systematic instruction Physical modeling response prompt Reinforcement
Kapadia and Fantuzzo (1988)	Teach children to self-monitor and self-reinforce sustained attention to schoolwork.	Counting Match numbers	Massed trial Ribbon, timer stimulus prompts Reinforcement
Karsh, Dahlquist, and Repp (1994)	Determine effects of adding dynamic presentation features to a validated fading program for teaching discrimination skills.	Measurement	Massed trial Stimulus shaping Repeat trial error correction Reinforcement

Study	Purpose	Skill	Instructional methods
Kircaali-Iftar, Birkan, and Uysal (1998)	Compare effects of structural and rational language in teaching color and shape.	Shape identification Color identification	Massed trial Direct instruction
Koller and Mulhern (1977)	Demonstrate effectiveness of calculator use instruction on arithmetic skills.	Addition Subtraction	Verbal and physical modeling, physical guidance response prompts Repeat trial, prompt hierarchy error correction
Lagomarcino and Rusch (1989)	Identify self-management strategies that teach independent performance.	1:1 correspondence	Systematic instruction Coinboard stimulus prompt Verbal modeling response prompt Constant time delay prompt fading Reinforcement
Lalli, Mace, Browder, and Brown (1989)	Compare efficacy of the Dial-A-Phone package plus prompts and a least intrusive prompt hierarchy in teaching phone-dialing skills. Evaluate adaptations to the Dial-A-Phone.	Match numbers	Massed trial Color, picture stimulus prompts Verbal and physical modeling response prompts Least intrusive prompt fading Repeat trial, prompt hierarchy error correction Reinforcement
Lovett and Haring (1989)	Examine maintenance effect of self-management training on task completion.	Use calculator Graphing	Systematic instruction Verbal modeling response prompt Reinforcement
Mace, Shapiro, West, Campbell, and Altman (1986)	Examine role of reinforcement in reactive self-monitoring.	Use counter Grouping	Systematic instruction Physical model response prompt Prompt hierarchy error correct Reinforcement
Mackay, Soraci, Carlin, Dennis, and Strawbridge (2002)	Teach matching to sample.	Matching shape	Massed trial Repeat trial error correction Reinforcement

(continued)

177

Table 7.1 *(continued)*

Mank and Horner (1987)	Determine whether a relationship exists between maintenance of work rate and use of self-recruited feedback.	Use counter, stopwatch, ruler Read graph	Systematic instruction Verbal and physical modeling, physical guidance response prompt Repeat trial, prompt hierarchy, teacher demonstration error correction Reinforcement
Matson and Long (1986)	Teach calculator use and shopping skills.	Addition Subtraction	Forward chaining Physical model response prompt Reinforcement
Maydak, Stromer, Mackay, and Stoddard (1995)	Determine whether sequencing skill training increased matching skills and vice versa.	Match to sample Sequencing	Massed trial Touch screen computer program stimulus prompts Reinforcement
McEvoy and Brady (1988)	Evaluate use of contingent access to free time as a reinforcer.	Addition Match objects to number	Systematic instruction Repeated trial error correct Reinforcement
Morin and Miller (1998)	Determine whether concrete- representational-abstract sequence (CSR) and strategy instruction are effective in teaching multiplication facts and related word problems.	Multiplication	Direct instruction Practice with feedback Repeat trial error correction Reinforcement
Morrison and Rosales-Ruiz (1997)	Analyze degree to which preferred objects evoke differential rates of stereotyping and alter accuracy of counting.	Counting	Massed trial Verbal modeling, physical modeling response prompts Prompt hierarchy error correction Reinforcement
Repp, Karsh, and Lenz, (1990)	Compare effects of the task demonstration model to the standard prompting hierarchy.	Number ID	Massed trial Verbal and physical modeling, physical guidance, picture cues response prompting Least intrusive prompt fading Repeat trial, prompt hierarchy error correction Reinforcement

Author	Purpose	Skills	Techniques
Rosine and Martin (1983)	Examine efficacy of self-control procedures in reducing challenging behaviors.	Use counter Graphing	Systematic instruction Verbal response prompt Prompt hierarchy error correct Reinforcement
Shapiro and Ackerman (1983)	Examine use of self-monitoring as a technique to increase work productivity.	Frequency tally Graphing Compare numbers (same)	Systematic instruction Arrow marker stimulus prompt Verbal and physical model response prompt Reinforcement
Vacc and Cannon (1991)	Examine the effectiveness of cross-age tutoring.	Counting Number word ID Number ID Match numbers	Systematic instruction
Wheeler, Ford, Nietupski, Loomis, and Brown (1980)	Describe effectiveness of a technique to teach shopping skills.	Subtraction	Total task chaining Verbal and physical modeling, picture cue response prompting Stimulus shaping Prompt hierarchy error correct
Young, Baker, and Martin, (1990)	Distinguish effects of a program based on discrimination learning theory on academic engagement and DISTAR on academic engagement and mastery.	Counting Number ID Symbol ID Addition	Distar computer program
Zegiob, Klukas, and Junginger (1978)	Investigate reactive effects of self-monitoring and examine its effectiveness in decreasing challenging behavior.	Frequency tally	Systematic instruction Reinforcement

Table 7.2.   Standards for preK–12 mathematics from the National Council of Teachers of Mathematics

Content standards

   Numbers and operations

   Algebra

   Geometry

   Measurement

   Data analysis and probability

Process standards

   Problem solving

   Reasoning and proof

   Connections

   Communication

   Representation

Numbers and Computation

Students need to understand numbers, ways of representing numbers, relationships among numbers, and number systems (NCTM, 2000). Not only is this the beginning of math, but also a goal which must be introduced in order to proceed with high-level mathematical thinking. Some components of this mathematic strand include identifying numbers, showing one-to-one correspondence, understanding place value, and numerical order. It is important to remember that whole numbers can be represented using concrete, pictorial, and symbolic representations. For example, the concept of *seven* can be represented with the numeral 7, with seven objects, with a manual sign for *seven*, or with seven pictures. Students can learn to apply entry-level number sense in increasingly complex contexts across the grade-level content of mathematics. For example, numbers can be used to identify the date, street addresses, phone numbers, locker numbers, and recipe additions. A young student may learn to match *three* to three pictures of balls. An older elementary student may be learning that *three* can describe the three parts of a whole (denominator of a fraction). A high school student may be learning that *three* is the number needed to complete the set of an algebraic equation. Even if the students' number recognition and counting skills remain limited (e.g., numbers to 20), the student may learn increasingly sophisticated number sense across the grade levels. With this increasing understanding of number sense, adaptations such as computer software, calculators, and other materials may be used to manage larger numbers. Numbers can be used to manage everyday tasks such as counting down the initiation of a self-care routine (count to 3 before lift from wheelchair), tracking tasks completed, and organizing materials (e.g., put items in the number 5 bin).

Number sense also includes computation skills such as addition, subtraction, multiplication, and division. Two studies have found positive outcomes using the commercial program Distar that is based on direct instruction principles (Bracey, Maggs, & Morath, 1975; Young, Baker, & Martin, 1990). Promoting improvements in computation is especially important in the lower grades. As students with significant cognitive disabilities move through the grade levels of the general curriculum, it will be important not to hold back on introducing other concepts because math facts or other computation skills are incomplete. For example, students who still struggle with addition facts may grasp principles of geometry.

Geometry

Geometry and spatial sense is a second mathematical strand that is essential to developing numeracy. Sometimes educators have questioned the functional use of geometry for students with significant cognitive disabilities. If instruction is limited to discriminating between basic shapes (circle versus triangle) with no further concepts or applications introduced, this may be a fair criticism of this component of mathematics. In contrast, everyday life includes rich applications of geometric concepts that may be taught across the grade levels. Through geometry, for example, students learn directional vocabulary and how to draw the path between two points using a straight line. They learn concepts such as *parallel* and *perpendicular* in order to compare and contrast objects and figures. They learn to manipulate shapes—to rotate them and measure them. Some jobs (e.g., machine technology) require having excellent understanding of these spatial relations. Geometry can also be related to orientation and mobility, arts and crafts, and building projects. In contrast, the research to date for students with moderate and severe disabilities has only focused on the beginning skills of shape discrimination (see Table 7.1). Until additional research is available, resources such as state curriculum guides related to alternate assessment may be useful for generating ideas in this area of mathematics. The Massachusetts Department of Education (2001) curriculum frameworks, for example, provide an illustration of students applying geometric principles through developing a map of streets that are parallel and perpendicular (http://www.doe.mass.edu/mcas/alt/rg/math).

Graphing and Data Display   In the 1980s, educators became increasingly interested in teaching students with disabilities to manage their own behavior and learning. Although not described in the literature as "mathematics," the instruction in data collection, comparison, and graphing that was part of this self-management research provides an important resource on how to teach this component of mathematics. As shown in Table 7.1, several researchers taught students with moderate and severe disabilities to tally data and use graphs or other means of data comparison. As part of a comprehensive math program, students need the opportunity to learn graphing and data display in general, not just as a component of a behavior support plan. For example, students may learn to tally and compare different attributes of their class. Students could paste pictures of male and female classmates in two columns to determine which group has more. They might learn to interpret data displays such as bar graphs of a school fundraiser or a pie chart with the largest "slice" showing which group collected the most cans for food drive. One of the most basic ways to introduce a graph might be in the form of an elimination graph with small blocks affixed using Velcro on a bar graph for each day of the school week. Students might remove a block after each task is completed and then compare days at the end of the week to determine the best days (fewest blocks).

Algebra: Patterns and Sequences   Finding and creating patterns, correcting errors in patterns, and translating patterns into different forms extend understanding and build an early foundation for algebra. Students also learn to use symbols to represent known and unknown numbers ($3 + 2 = x$). At a basic level of understanding, students may use simple patterns to make predictions. For example, if a job task or art project is laid out as blue, white, green, blue, white . . . what's next? At later grades, students begin to use symbols to describe how they combine sets. For example, if they have three napkins for the table, but five people are coming, how many more are needed ($3 + x = 5$)? Little to no research exists on teaching algebraic concepts to students with moderate and severe disabilities. This may reflect past low expectations for academic learning. In contrast, as educators begin exploring how to include students with significant cognitive disabilities in algebra, it will be important to create meaning for the skills acquired. Being able to repeat a pegboard pattern, for example, may have minimal usefulness either in real life or for future development of mathematics unless related directly to both contexts.

PROMOTING PROCESSES FOR LEARNING AND APPLYING MATHEMATICS

Although number sense, algebra, geometry, measurement, and data analysis are areas of mathematics content, educators also need to consider the processes students use to acquire and apply content knowledge. The NCTM (2000) identified five processes of mathematics including problem solving, reasoning and proof, communication, connections, and representation. With further understanding of these processes, educators may glean new ideas for developing mathematics education for students with significant cognitive disabilities that is both meaningful and challenging.

Problem Solving

Agran and Wehmeyer (1999) define a problem as a *task, activity, or situation for which a solution is not immediately known.* Mathematics can provide a format for learning problem strategies that students may be taught to generalize to other contexts. To promote problem solving, the teacher can set up a context that presents a problem and provide instruction on a strategy to identify a solution. Most strategies will include at least these three steps: 1) problem identification, 2) problem analysis, and 3) problem resolution. For example, in working with supported employees, Hughes and Rusch (1989) taught them to first state the problem (missing material). Next, they learned to state a solution (where to get material). Then they noted when the problem was solved (found material) and self-reinforced (good).

Traditionally, students have been taught problem solving through reading a paragraph, identifying the computations required, and performing the computations accurately. Fuchs and Fuchs (2002) found that students with reading problems had poorer mathematical problem-solving skills. For students with significant cognitive disabilities, problem solving may be more accessible if presented within the context of a familiar activity. For example, the student might be given a worksheet or other material to pass to each person in a small-group activity, but with two short of the number needed. The teacher could prompt the student to identify the problem (e.g., not enough) and then the solution (more). The teacher might ask, "How many more?" The student could then count how many more (1–2). The student then gets this number, distributes them, and communicates *enough*. The teacher might then use this as a teachable moment to translate what just occurred into symbols. She might show five people in the group (pictures or line drawings) and three papers. Drawing a line from each paper to a person shows two left out. Next, she can put the numbers beside the illustration to introduce the equation: $3 + x = 5$. Using differentiated instruction, she might have some students in the group now write the word problem for what just occurred and others show how to solve for x. The student who needs more concrete applications might create an illustration that summarizes what occurred (e.g., drawing a line from the picture of a paper to the picture of the students and circling the numbers).

Although this illustration focuses on the problem of not having enough for each person, other problems can be developed from the mathematics materials for the grade level. Another type of problem is the one presented in the illustration at the beginning of this chapter in which the student determines which item represents the mathematical concept. The problem-solving strategy the teacher used for symmetry was folding the items in half (and drawing lines of symmetry for more advanced students). Students might solve problems such as how to determine the necessary container size to store particular items, what is the shortest route to the cafeteria, and in what direction to move a picture to make it parallel to another.

Reasoning and Proof

Through reasoning and proof, students gain insights and begin to realize that mathematics makes sense. For students with significant cognitive disabilities, the application of mathematics in everyday activities may promote this reasoning. In setting a table in different ways or stocking shelves, for example, can the student discover the pattern by the third item? Can he or she create a pattern for the teacher to follow? In doing computation with a calculator, the teacher might also have the student "prove" the answer with manipulatives to check for understanding. A beginning point for teaching students to gain meaning from their experiences with mathematics in their everyday lives may be to teach recognition of current concepts being addressed. For example, in the classroom or school, in how many places can the student find the number *3* or in how many places can the student identify collections of three like items? What items in the classroom are parallel? Then, the teacher can extend this information by asking questions such as "How can we move these pictures to be parallel?" to model reasoning.

One strategy that has been effective in promoting the acquisition of new information for students with significant cognitive disabilities is instructive feedback (Werts, Wolery, Holcombe, & Gast, 1995). Using systematic instruction in which students practice a target response with prompting and praise, the teacher adds additional information with the praise statement (e.g., "Yes, the word is *milk*; it comes from the dairy section"). To extend this research to mathematical reasoning, the teacher might use systematic instruction for a target response (e.g., finding the square) and then provide instructive feedback ("It has four corners. All the sides are the same."). Then, the teacher might ask the student to recall and apply this extra information. For example, "Why is this a square (or not a square)?" The student could then be prompted to apply the "proof" for a square: 1) Does it have four corners? and 2) Are the sides the same?

Communication

Through mathematical communication, individuals share ideas and clarify understanding. In mathematics education, students learn to use clear, convincing, and precise mathematical terms. Mathematics communication includes both the unique symbols used in this field (e.g., +, %, ×) and the vocabulary for various concepts (e.g., congruence, slope, equal). Students with significant cognitive disabilities may not have had exposure to, or mastered, the mathematical symbols or comprehend the vocabulary. An important step in making mathematics accessible is teaching these symbols and vocabulary. Students using augmentative communication systems will need access to symbols to be able to express concepts such as equals (=) and greater than (>). Using these symbols in multiple daily contexts can enhance their meaning. For example, the Boardmaker (Mayer-Johnson, Inc., 1998) symbol for *is* looks like an equals sign (=). By learning to use the symbol for general communication, its use in mathematics may be easier to understand. Similarly, the symbol (>) can be paired with the concept of *more* in a variety of daily activities such as leisure and meals. Other Boardmaker math symbols include fractions, coins, graph and graph paper, percent, pie charts, algebraic formula, addition, subtraction, multiplication, and division.

Introducing mathematical vocabulary for concepts such as slope and symmetry are part of setting higher expectations for students with significant cognitive disabilities. Educators may look for ways to embed the concepts in everyday experiences to promote their meaning. For example, while assisting a student on a wheelchair ramp the teacher might talk about slope. To help students understand zero and null sets, the teachers might use these terms as the opportunity arises. For example, "There are zero pencils left in my pencil holder today" or "There are no books left on this shelf" are examples of null sets. Some students might be able to learn to read key mathematical terms as sight words. Chapter 4 provides information on how to teach sight words. Mathematical symbols might also be taught using flash cards. If using these strategies to drill for recognition of the word or symbol, it will be important also to promote their meaning through various problems and everyday applications to mathematics problems.

Connections

Although mathematics is typically taught as a distinct content area, the concepts of mathematics permeate many content areas and daily experiences. Making these connections explicit for students with significant cognitive disabilities will be key to mathematics having functional applications in daily life. Music is one way to make connections for mathematics that can be highly motivational for some students. Some songs incorporate counting forward and backward. In the song *Doubles*, students learn to add items together (e.g., three kittens and three chicks for six animals).

Unfortunately, some of the music that focuses on mathematics concepts is not age-appropriate for elementary level and older students. Popular music can be adapted for mathematics applications. For example, students may learn to recognize patterns by clapping the beat for a specific line of a song. Students may count how many times a recurring phrase is sung. Students may also learn to count notes (whole notes, half notes) that are sung or played on an instrument.

Some educational music is available that is specifically designed to teach mathematics concepts. *The Ordinal Song, Herman the Worm* (measurement), and *Learning How to Tell Time* are songs that can be used to teach these basic skills. Test-taking strategies can even be learned through music by using Jeff Schroeder's song *Solving "Real Life" Problems*. This song's lyrics outline a problem-solving strategy: "When you read the words fewer, more or less, when you take a test . . . you subtract! But when you read the words and, in all, and altogether too . . . Add is what you'll do."

Whereas music is one area for making mathematics connections, students may also find meaning for their current academic skills in cooking or construction projects. Teachers may adapt the instructions to include current concepts. A recipe may be adapted for counting, measuring, using fractions, and matching large numbers (oven temperature). Instructions for building a bird house may include references to shape, angles, measurement of length, and slope (roof).

Representations

Mathematical ideas can be represented in many different ways. A worksheet with rows of number problems may be the most familiar representation associated with mathematics, but it is only one of numerous ways to present and assess mathematics. Pictures, concrete materials, spreadsheet displays, graphs, and words are all other options for representation. Students with significant cognitive disabilities may be able to gain understanding of concepts such as division or volume of a cone if given real materials to manipulate to see the concept displayed. For example, dealing cards can be used to illustrate the principle of division. For example, using a subset of the deck of cards, the student finds out how many each of 4 people receive when there are 20 cards. The teacher can then illustrate this on a board or worksheet (20 cards divided by 4 people = 5 cards each or 20 / 5 = 4). Using a cylinder and cone with the same base and height, the student may fill the cone with water or sand, then pour this into the cylinder to discover that the cone only fills a third of the cylinder, which is illustrated by the formula $V = 1/3$ Bh.

Computer software provides another important resource for representing math in ways that are accessible to students with significant cognitive disabilities. Software such as *Millie's Math House* by Riverdeep (http://www.riverdeep.net) or Davis A. Carter's *How Many Bugs in a Box?* (http://www.smartkidssoftware.com) address math computational skills including number identification, addition, subtraction, sequencing, and shapes. The use of IntelliTools adaptive keyboards and IntelliKeys software can also be used to help students access technology to practice skills such as typing their phone number, lunch number, social security number. This software can also be set up as a calculator.

PLANNING AND ADAPTING
MATHEMATICS LESSON AND UNIT PLANS

To create access to the general curriculum, the beginning point to plan mathematics lessons is the curriculum for the student's assigned grade level. To illustrate, a student with significant cognitive disabilities who is 10 years old will
likely be a fifth grader. The foundation for this student's math instruction should
be the fifth-grade curriculum and state standards for this grade level. In contrast,
the student's current skills in mathematics can create a challenge for educational
planning at the fifth-grade level. The student may not have learned mathematical
symbols and may not have the counting or number recognition skills typically
acquired in preschool. In a *remedial* curricular approach, the teacher would
focus all instruction on the sequence of skills that begin at this preschool level
with no exposure to fifth-grade mathematics. In a purely *functional* approach,
the teacher might give up on the student acquiring numeracy and focus instead
on skills needed for daily living, such as telling time and making purchases. In the
general curriculum access approach promoted in this chapter, the teacher uses
what might be called *dual instruction*—direct instruction in the sequence of
skills needed to achieve numeracy within the mathematics activities and concepts typical of fifth grade. The teacher also uses functional applications to give
these skills meaning. Figure 7.1 illustrates this approach and provides examples
of how the student applies current skills in the context of fifth-grade concepts.

Adapting Objectives for Student Mastery

The first step in adapting a lesson plan from the general curriculum for students
with significant cognitive disabilities is to identify what the student is expected
to learn. For example, in Gordon's fifth-grade class (see Figure 7.1), the grade-
level expectation is for students to be able to read and compare graphs found in
written text. Students might be given four bar graphs showing comparative information, such as the income level for four professions or the amount of electricity used across 4 years, and be expected to compare and contrast the data in
several ways (e.g., which has more, number for a specific entry). They might also
be given data and asked to create the graph. Gordon is a student who is nonverbal and is learning to use an augmentative communication system with an array
of four Boardmaker symbols presented at one time. Gordon has not had much
prior mathematics instruction. He is beginning to learn to name numbers and
count by using manual signs. In his fifth-grade class, Gordon will be working on
interpreting graphs like his classmates, but the specific expectation is for Gordon to use his new symbol for greater than ($>$) to indicate which graph has more.
The fifth-grade–level expectation for learning place values is to be able to identify place to 100,000. Gordon's objective will be to name the first number in 6-digit
figures and then use a preset switch (e.g., BIGmack) to "read" the full number. He
also will work with numbers that are rounded to the nearest 100,000.

There are several guidelines that can be followed to identify this alternate
level for achievement for students. First, the objective is directly related to the
content and is not just a general communication or motor skill. For example,
although Gordon has individualized education program (IEP) objectives to greet
his peers with a smile and grasp objects, these are insufficient by themselves to
promote the learning of mathematics. Second, the objective relates directly to
the state standard and type of math activities presented in general education for

the student's assigned grade level. When the unit on graphing is addressed, Gordon works on graphs. When other fifth-grade students work on geometric patterns, so does Gordon. This creates opportunities for Gordon to learn from the general education context and ensures that he has access to the full fifth-grade curriculum. In contrast, the objectives also target mastery of basic math skills that will build toward numeracy. Gordon is at an early point in the journey toward numeracy. He currently needs to master identifying numbers, counting, and basic math symbols. These can be embedded in the fifth-grade activities; Table 7.3 summarizes the criteria.

Adapting Materials and Representation

The second way to create access to the general curriculum lesson is to identify ways to adapt the materials and representation so that the concept is understandable to the student. This may involve using pictures, objects, computer software,

---

THE FORMULA FOR ACCESSING GRADE-LEVEL CONTENT

Instruction in...

Basic numeracy skills (e.g., concept of number)

+ Applications to functional contexts

+ Applications to priority concepts from the grade-level content

= Access to the general math curriculum for students with significant cognitive disabilities

---

AN EXAMPLE OF APPLYING THE FORMULA

Student's IEP Goal: *Gordon will increase use of beginning math symbols (e.g., =, +) and concepts (e.g., equals, zero) within the context of applying these to fifth-grade mathematics activities and functional activities.*

Grade-level achievement	Alternate achievement for Gordon for applications to fifth-grade math	Functional applications
Test conjectures about polygons; compute sum of angles	*Guess (conjecture) if shape is triangle/square; count angles to verify*	Use shapes for communication and other organizational purposes (e.g., put these away in the folder marked with a square)
Interpret bar graph	*Create picture bar graphs by pasting pictures of familiar item* *Use symbol to determine which of two has more (use of symbol >)*	Create bar graph with football stickers to compare which team got the most touchdowns; use bar graph with dollars to compare which cinema charges more for movies
Extend geometric pattern	*Create or extend a three-figure pattern*	Make a border for bulletin board or as part of art project that uses a pattern
Extend knowledge of place value to hundred thousands	*Identify first number of 4–6-digit numbers rounded (e.g., "2" in 200,000); then use AAC to state number ("200,000")*	Identify price of homes in area; identify number of people who live in a city or town

Figure 7.1.   A general curriculum access approach to mathematics for a fifth-grade student, Gordon, who has significant cognitive disabilities.

Table 7.3.   Criteria for adapting lesson objectives to reflect alternate achievement in mathematics

---

1.   The alternate learning outcome relates directly to the content area.

   A math skill is targeted, not just a general motor or communication skill.

2.   The alternate learning outcome is in the same category or unit of the content and relates closely to the grade-level expectations.

   In math, the alternate learning outcome is from the same content standard (e.g., geometry, algebra, measurement) and the same math construct (e.g., slope, comparison of sets, volume).

3.   The alternate learning outcome builds on the student's current skill level to promote longitudinal attainment of numeracy.

   Students learn basic skills such as number identification, symbol use, recognition of shapes, comparison of sets, problem solving that build toward a meaningful knowledge of the use of mathematics in daily life.

Rule of thumb: A teacher of mathematics recognizes the objective as mathematics.

---

or other alternative materials. When Gordon's math class worked on graphing, the teacher used both the textbook and computer software that generated graphs. Because Gordon could not read the text or software prompts, these materials had little meaning to him. The teacher decided to use one of his strong preferences (basketball) to motivate him to learn about graphing. She found basketball stickers and had Gordon create graphs for two of his favorite teams based on the number of points each scored in the prior week's game. She gave him the number, prompted him to count out stickers for each number, and then showed him how to line them up on two sheets of paper to create his two graphs. He then put the one with *more* first and pasted his sign for *greater than* to show that one was greater than the other. After this activity, she had Gordon work with a peer on creating a graph in software with these basketball data for exposure to this activity. When the class worked on geometric patterns, the teacher used worksheets with reoccurring patterns of letters and numbers. These were too complex for Gordon, but he could learn the concept of patterns using a sequence that he helped create for a craft project.

   When planning the use of alternative materials, it is important to use the general education class materials whenever possible. For example, Gordon might be able to practice identifying numbers using the textbook and class worksheets. Sometimes the student may be given the opportunity for exposure to the general education materials, even when alternative materials are used to promote mastery (e.g., Gordon's exposure to the computer-generated graph). When alternative materials are used, care should be taken not to compromise the mathematical concept being addressed. If Gordon simply places basketball stickers on a page, he loses the opportunity to learn about how to generate and interpret a graph.

Planning Participation in Activities

In reform-oriented classrooms, teachers often use a variety of activities to engage students in mathematical learning. Planning may be needed to determine how the student with significant cognitive disabilities can participate in meaningful ways.

Alex's vignette at the beginning of this chapter illustrates a lesson that was developed from the onset with differentiated instruction. That is, the teacher planned the activity so that students with varying levels of skill could succeed. Having students work with a partner made it possible for those who already had some understanding of the concept of symmetry to help those for whom the concept was new (the teacher arranged who would be paired together). By using a concrete application (folding shapes), students could learn the concept without being challenged by reading deficits. To challenge students who knew the concept, the teacher introduced lines of symmetry and asked them to find if the shape had more than one line of symmetry. When teachers are using differentiated instruction, finding ways to adapt the activity may be easier. For Alex, the only adaptation needed was that he would communicate about symmetry using his AAC device. He also needed alternative homework.

In contrast, when the lesson plan has less differentiation, the challenge becomes planning meaningful alternatives that are still as close as possible to general education activities. For example, Samantha's class will be applying formulas to compute the volume of various objects using examples in the textbook. Samantha does not have the skill to read the textbook or write answers on a worksheet. In contrast, Samantha can learn about volume using actual containers. A peer might help her summarize her experiment using an IntelliKeys keyboard to copy the formula. Samantha might also create a worksheet in which she matches pictures of each container to the volume the peer helps her compute.

Opportunities for Practice and Skill Acquisition

The general education curriculum often moves at a rapid pace, with teachers introducing new concepts and skills each day. Although teachers may review material, it is not typically done with sufficient repetition for students with significant cognitive disabilities. As noted earlier in this chapter, most of the research on the acquisition of mathematics skills by students with significant cognitive disabilities has used systematic instruction methods with repeated opportunities to practice the target response across days using prompting and feedback (e.g., Karsh, Dahliquist, & Repp, 1994). If a student such as Gordon is to learn to use manual signs to identify numbers to 10 (an IEP objective to build numeracy), he will need many opportunities to do so each day with systematic prompting and feedback. This review might be embedded in the day's activity. For example, the unit on place value yields many opportunities for Gordon to identify numbers. In contrast, when the class works on the geometry unit focusing on polygons and patterns, there may be fewer opportunities for Gordon to identify numbers in the materials used for each day. On these days, the teacher may create opportunities for Gordon to practice (e.g., using numbers in the environment or practice flash cards) while also giving him the opportunity to work on the geometry activities.

Because of the pacing of general curriculum, it may be more feasible to develop objectives for mastery for each unit of the grade-level mathematics curriculum rather than for each day's lesson plan. For example, Gordon's objective for mastery during the geometry unit is to identify angles and shapes. This objective can be embedded in many of the daily activities while providing him with exposure to many other topics.

Assessment of Student Mastery

The assessments used to determine mastery of each standard for the grade level are often paper-and-pencil tests with limited accessibility for students with significant cognitive disabilities. Many states have teachers collect portfolios of student work samples and data on student performance to document learning of the academic content. For ongoing assessment, it is important to plan how to measure mastery of the objectives developed for each mathematics unit to monitor ongoing progress. One option is to use ongoing data collection for the target objectives related to specific mathematics skills, with student work samples providing additional evidence for the acquisition and generalization of broader concepts. For example, the teacher might use a data sheet to record the numbers Gordon correctly signs without prompting. A data sheet for this might have the following entries. The teacher might assess the different numbers in random order rather the sequential order shown here:

1. Signs *one*

2. Signs *two*

3. Signs *three*

4. Signs *four*

5. Signs *five*

The teacher might also use task analytic data for Gordon's use and interpretation of graphs. The task analysis might be

1. Identify the first data entry.

2. Count out items for the first entry.

3. Arrange items vertically to form first graph.

4. Identify the second data entry.

5. Count out items for the second entry.

6. Arrange items vertically to form second graph.

7. Select which graph has more.

8. Place graph with more to the left of other graph.

9. Enter > sign between the two graphs.

Similarly, a task analysis might be used to assess Gordon's conjectures about polygons. In this example, Gordon's first answer is not scored as incorrect because it is his initial guess. He has a later step when he can correct his answer.

1. Guess if the figure is a triangle or a square.

2. Touch and count first corner "1."

3. Touch and count second corner "2."

4. Touch and count third corner "3."

5. If applicable, touch and count fourth corner "4."

6. State the rule ("triangle 3; square 4").

7. Decide whether to change answer for triangle or square.

Permanent products might be used to illustrate Gordon's generalization. For example, he might label a set of digital pictures of familiar items as triangles or squares. His portfolio might also include the varied types of squares and triangles that he did or did not identify correctly. His work might include a chart of the types of items he counted correctly using manual signs and digital pictures of him signing. It might also include some of the graphs he creates.

Example of an Adapted Lesson in Algebra

Figure 7.2 shows a lesson plan from a high school algebra unit with adaptations for a student with significant cognitive disabilities that is adapted from one taught to students by Bree Jimenez. Tyler is a high school student with Down syn-

---

Student's name

Tyler

Objective

Grade-level objective: The learner will perform operations with numbers and expressions to solve problems. (North Carolina Standard Course of Study Competency Goal 1 Algebra 1)

Objective 1.01: Write equivalent forms of algebraic expressions to solve problems.

Alternate objective: *Given an algebraic equation and manipulatives, Tyler will use counting, number recognition, and problem-solving skills to find the missing number by performing all steps of the task analysis correctly for 4 of 5 problems.*

Materials

General curriculum materials: Paper, pencil, and equation on board ($4 + x = 6$)

Adapted materials: *Number line, red marker, green marker, manipulative to move along number line, Velcro number board (#s 1–9), equation at desk*

Teaching activities

Activities planned for general education class: Students are guided through task analysis as a large group on solving for x. They will review with the teacher and then complete the task on their own.

Adaptations for participation and parallel activities: *Tyler will identify the addition symbol, identify the beginning number by marking it with the green marker (for go), and the final number by marking it with red (for stop). He will count from the green number to the red number and identify that number on the Velcro number chart. Finally, he will replace the x on the equation with the number chosen, completing the algebraic equation.*

Opportunities for practice

How students will practice or apply the concept/skill: *Practice will occur when Tyler is given a vocational task where he is to finish filling the fruit baskets. There are already four apples in the basket, but he needs to have six in each basket. Using the algebraic equation, Tyler needs to solve for x.*

Additional systematic instruction of student's adapted objective: *Once this objective is mastered, Tyler can learn how to apply this skill to other forms of algebraic equations. He can learn how to solve for x using subtraction and multiplication to complete various other functional jobs. Subtraction equations could be used to complete tasks where there are too many in each bag, and multiplication can be used to complete baking tasks where Tyler needs to find out how many cookies are on the sheet by counting the number of rows and how many are in each row.*

Assessment

General class assessment: Paper and pencil test

Alternate assessment: *Task analysis of the steps needed to complete the functional task using an algebraic formula*

Figure 7.2.   Adaptation of a high school algebra lesson.

Data Sheet

Student: Tyler Burgh Academic component: Math		Given an algebraic equation and manipulatives, Tyler will use counting, number recognition, and problem-solving skills to find the missing number by performing all steps of the task analysis correctly for 4 of 5 problems. Example of equation: $4 + x = 9$							
Steps: ↓	**Date:** →								
1. Student points to sum on equation									
2. Moves red marker to sum on chart									
3. Counts number of items in container and finds number on equation									
4. Moves the green marker to number on chart									
5. Leaps to the sum									
6. Selects the number counted									
7. Puts correct number in for x in for formula									
8. Puts correct number needed in container									
9. Solves for x (writes number)									
Total independently correct:									

Student response codes: I, independent; V, verbal prompt; P, physical prompt

Figure 7.3. Task analysis for an algebraic equation.

drome who has had minimal exposure to mathematics instruction. Although Tyler can count to 10, he does not currently identify written numbers consistently. Although Tyler needs to build basic numeracy skills, Ms. Jimenez also wants him to participate in the grade-level standards for algebra. Her goal is for Tyler to learn number recognition and adding on using concrete materials that represent beginning algebraic equations. In doing so, she promotes not only the acquisition of basic skills, but a problem-solving strategy as shown in the steps in Figure 7.3.

SUMMARY

Students with significant cognitive disabilities have often had limited exposure to mathematics. To broaden this instruction, educators can begin by understanding the content and process standards of mathematics. Mathematics has five broad content areas including number and operations, algebra, geometry, measurement, and data analysis and interpretation. Most of the research to date with students with significant cognitive disabilities has focused on purchasing skills; fewer studies have targeted other math components. In contrast, for access to the general curriculum to occur, students need the opportunity to learn this broader content. This chapter has provided ideas for how to teach content in these broader areas. Students also need instruction in the processes of mathematics, including problem solving, reasoning and proof, communication, connections, and representations. Research on problem solving for students with significant cognitive disabilities provides a methodology that may be extended to mathematics. Reasoning, proofs, and connections may be taught through functional applications. Students will also need to acquire the symbols and vocabulary to communicate about mathematics. Representing mathematical concepts with concrete objects and pictures may increase students' understanding. Once the standards of mathematics are understood, educators can focus on adapting the grade-level content for students with significant cognitive disabilities. This chapter provides examples of how to adapt lessons or units by modifying objectives, materials, activities, and assessments and creating opportunities for systematic instruction.

Some educators may question whether teaching students skills such as conjectures about polygons or solving simple equations has functional use for daily life. The answer lies in the level of expectation for the future of students with significant cognitive disabilities. If the only expectation is that students will go to the store or a restaurant, then purchasing skills may be adequate. If the expectation is for students to access the many environments of our world through travel, the internet, the media, and their jobs, then students need the opportunity to learn to notice patterns in their lives, solve problems, make comparisons, and comprehend mathematical concepts. The ongoing challenge is to be sure that as mathematics is learned, students also are taught to make connections to their daily lives so that these skills have meaning and utility.

REFERENCES

Ackerman, A.M., & Shapiro, E.S. (1984). Self-monitoring and work productivity with mentally retarded adults. *Journal of Applied Behavior Analysis, 17,* 403–407.

Agran, M., & Hughes, C. (1997). Problem solving. In M. Agran (Ed.), *Student-directed learning: Teaching self-determination skills* (pp. 171–198). Pacific Grove, CA: Brooks/Cole Thomson Learning.

Agran, M., & Wehmeyer, M. (1999). *Innovations: Teaching problem solving to students with mental retardation.* Washington, DC: American Association on Mental Retardation.

Baroody, A.J. (1996). Self-invented addition strategies by children with mental retardation. *American Journal on Mental Retardation, 101(1),* 72–89.

Bottge, B.A., & Hasselbring, T.S. (1993). Taking word problems off the page. *Educational Leadership, 50,* 36–38.

Bracey, S., Maggs, A., & Morath, P. (1975). Teaching arithmetic skills to moderately mentally retarded children using direct verbal instruction: Counting and symbol identification. *Australian Journal of Mental Retardation, 3(7),* 200–204.

Browder, D.M., Spooner, F., Ahlgrim-Delzell, L., Flowers, C., & Algozzine, B. (2004, May). A comprehensive literature review of data-based studies investigating access to the general curriculum: 1975–2003. In F. Spooner (Chair), *Accessing the general curriculum for students with significant disabilities.* Symposium presented at the annual meeting of the Association for Behavior Analysis, Boston.

Carnine, D. (1998). Instructional design in mathematics for students with learning disabilities. In D. Rivera (Ed.), *Mathematics education for students with learning disabilities* (pp. 119– 138). Austin, TX: PRO-ED.

Cichon, D., & Ellis, J.G. (2003). The effects of MATH *Connections* on student achievement, confidence, and perception. In S.L. Senk & D.R. Thompson (Eds.), *Standards-based school mathematics curricula* (pp. 345–374). Mahwah, NJ: Lawrence Erlbaum Associates.

Coleman, R.S., & Whitman, T.L. (1984). Developing, generalizing, and maintaining physical fitness in mentally retarded adults: Toward a self-directed program. *Analysis and Intervention in Developmental Disabilities, 4,* 109–127.

Copeland, S.R., Hughes, C., Agran, M., Wehmeyer, M.L., & Fowler, S.E. (2002). An intervention package to support high school students with mental retardation in general education classrooms. *American Journal on Mental Retardation, 107,* 32–45.

Fuchs, L.S., & Fuchs, D. (2002). Mathematical problem-solving profiles of students with mathematical disabilities with and without comorbid reading disabilities. *Journal of Learning Disabilities, 35,* 563–574.

Hughes, C., & Rusch, F.R. (1989). Teaching supported employees with severe mental retardation to solve problems. *Journal of Applied Behavior Analysis, 22,* 365–372.

Kapadia, S., & Fantuzzo, J.W. (1988). Training children with developmental disabilities and severe behavior problems to use self-management procedures to sustain attention to pre-academic/academic tasks. *Education and Training in Mental Retardation, 23,* 59–69.

Karsh, K.G., Dahlquist, C.M., & Repp, A.C. (1994). A comparison of static and dynamic presentation procedures on discrimination learning of individuals with severe or moderate mental retardation. *Research in Developmental Disabilities, 15,* 167–186.

King, M.B., Schroeder, J., & Chawszczewski, D. (2001). *Authentic assessment and student performance in inclusive schools.* Research Institute on Secondary Education Reform for Youth with Disabilities Brief No. 5. Madison, WI: Wisconsin Center for Educational Research.

Kircaali-Iftar, G., Birkan, B., & Uysal, A. (1998). Comparing the effects of structural and natural language use during direct instruction with children with mental retardation. *Education and Training in Mental Retardation and Developmental Disabilities, 33,* 375–385.

Koller, E.Z., & Mulhern, T.J. (1977). Use of a pocket calculator to train arithmetic skills with trainable adolescents. *Education and Training of the Mentally Retarded, 12,* 332–335.

Kroesbergen, E.H. (2003). Mathematics interventions for children with special educational needs. *Remedial and Special Education, 24*(2), 97–115.

Lagomarcino, T.R., & Rusch, F.R. (1989). Utilizing self-management procedures to teach independent performance. *Education and Training of the Mentally Retarded, 24,* 297–305.

Lalli, J.S., Mace, F.C., Browder, D., & Brown, D.K. (1989). Comparison of treatments to teach number matching skills to adults with moderate mental retardation. *Mental Retardation, 27,* 75–83.

Lovett, D.L., & Haring, K.A. (1989). The effects of self-management training on the daily living of adults with mental retardation. *Education and Training in Mental Retardation, 24,* 306–323.

Mace, F.C., Shapiro, E.S., West, B.J., Campbell, C., & Altman, J. (1986). The role of reinforcement in reactive self-monitoring. *Applied Research in Mental Retardation, 7,* 315–327.

Mackay, H.A., Soraci, S.A., Carlin, M.T., Dennis, N.A., & Strawbridge, C.P. (2002). Guiding visual attention during acquisition of matching-to-sample. *American Journal on Mental Retardation, 107,* 445–454.

Mank, D., & Horner, R. (1987). Self-recruited feedback: A cost effective procedure for maintaining behavior. *Research in Developmental Disabilities, 8,* 91–112.

Massachusetts Department of Education. (2001). *Resource guide to the Massachusetts curriculum frameworks for students with significant disabilities.* Malden, MA: Author. Retrieved January 10, 2005, from http://www.doe.mass.edu/mcas/alt/rg/math

Matson, J.L., & Long, S. (1986). Teaching computation/shopping skills to mentally retarded adults. *Journal of Mental Deficiency, 91,* 98–101.

Maydak, M., Stromer, R., Mackay, H.A., & Stoddard, L.T. (1995). Stimulus classes in matching to sample and sequence production: The emergence of numeric relations. *Research in Developmental Disabilities, 16,* 179–204.

Mayer-Johnson, Inc. (1998). Boardmaker for Windows [Computer software]. Solana Beach, CA: Author.

McEvoy, M.A., & Brady, M.P. (1988). Contingent access to play materials as an academic motivator for autistic and behavior disordered children. *Education and Treatment of Children, 11,* 5–18.

Miller, S.P., & Mercer, C.D. (1997). Educational aspects of mathematic disabilities. *Journal of Learning Disabilities, 30,* 47–56.

Morin, V.A., & Miller, S.P. (1998). Teaching multiplication to middle school students with mental retardation. *Education and Treatment of Children, 21,* 22–36.

Morrison, K., & Rosales-Ruiz, J. (1997). The effect of object preference on task performance and stereotyping in a child with autism. *Research in Developmental Disabilities, 18,* 127–137.

National Council of Teachers of Mathematics. (2000). *Principles and standards for school mathematics*. Reston, VA: Author.

Pugach, M.C., & Warger, C.L. (1993). Curriculum considerations. In J. Goodland & T. Lovitt (Eds.), *Integrating general and special education* (pp. 125–148). New York: Merrill.

Repp, A.C., Karsh, K.G., & Lenz, M.W. (1990). Discrimination training for persons with developmental disabilities: A comparison of the task demonstration model and the standard prompting hierarchy. *Journal of Applied Behavior Analysis, 23*, 43–52.

Rivera, D.P. (1997). Mathematics education and students with learning disabilities: Introduction to the special series. *Journal of Learning Disabilities, 30*(1), 2–19.

Rosine, L.P., & Martin, G.L. (1983). Self-management training to decrease undesirable behavior of mentally handicapped adults. *Rehabilitation Psychology, 28*, 195–205.

Shapiro, E.S., & Ackerman, A. (1983). Increasing productivity rates in adult mentally retarded clients: The failure of self-monitoring. *Applied Research in Mental Retardation, 4*, 163–181.

Tucker, B.F., Singleton, A.H., & Weaver, T.L. (2002). *Teaching mathematics to all children: Designing and adapting instruction to meet the needs of diverse learners*. Upper Saddle River, NJ: Prentice Hall.

Vacc, N.N., & Cannon, S.J. (1991). Cross-age tutoring in mathematics: Sixth graders helping students who are moderately handicapped. *Education and Training in Mental Retardation, 26*, 89–97.

Werts, M.G., Wolery, M., Holcombe, A., & Gast, D.L. (1995). Instructive feedback: Review of parameters and effects. *Journal of Behavioral Education, 5*, 55–75.

Wheeler, J., Ford, A., Nietupski, J., Loomis, R., & Brown, L. (1980). Teaching moderately and severely handicapped adolescents to shop in supermarkets using pocket calculators. *Education and Training of the Mentally Retarded, 15*, 105–112.

Woodward, J., Monroe, K., & Baxter, J. (2001). Enhancing student achievement on performance assessments in mathematics. *Learning Disability Quarterly, 24*, 33–46.

Young, M., Baker, J., & Martin, M. (1990). Teaching basic number skills to students with a moderate intellectual disability. *Education and Training in Mental Retardation, 25*, 83–93.

Zegiob, L., Klukas, N., & Junginger, J. (1978). Reactivity of self-monitoring procedures with retarded adolescents. *American Journal of Mental Deficiency, 83*, 156–163.

Chapter 8

Addressing Math Standards and Functional Math

Belva C. Collins, Harold L. Kleinert, and Lou-Ann E. Land

Teachers of students with moderate and severe disabilities often struggle with relating the "access to the general curriculum" requirements of Individuals with Disabilities Education Act (IDEA '97) Amendments of 1997 (PL 105-17) to the need for their students to develop functional, generalized real-life skills. For teachers, this disconnect may appear great indeed, especially in the area of math. At the secondary level, for example, how are students with moderate and severe intellectual disabilities to participate in learning age-appropriate standards in algebra and geometry? Does it even make sense for these students to perhaps study these subjects at the expense of instruction in community living or vocational skills? This chapter will address those questions by showing how instruction in real-life math skills for students with moderate and severe disabilities can be related to the math standards identified as important for *all* students. We will also show how students with moderate and severe disabilities can be included in age-appropriate general education classes and curricular activities, while simultaneously ensuring that their individualized education program (IEP) objectives are addressed. To do so, we will first turn our attention to the seminal work of The National Council on Teachers of Mathematics (NCTM, n.d.) and the relationship of its Principles for School Mathematics to research-based practices for students with moderate and severe disabilities.

RELATIONSHIP OF EFFECTIVE INSTRUCTIONAL PRACTICES IN MATHEMATICS TO RESEARCH-BASED PRACTICES FOR STUDENTS WITH SIGNIFICANT COGNITIVE DISABILITIES

The NCTM defines six essential principles for the instruction of mathematics for students of all ages. Those principles are

- The Equity Principle

- The Curriculum Principle

- The Teaching Principle

- The Learning Principle

- The Assessment Principle

- The Technology Principle

We will relate each of these principles, in turn, to research-based practices for students with moderate and severe disabilities.

First, the Equity Principle states that "Excellence in mathematics education requires equity—high expectations and strong support for all students" (*Overview of Principles and Standards for School Mathematics;* NCTM, n.d.). Specifically,

> All students, regardless of their personal characteristics, backgrounds, or physical challenges, must have opportunities to study—and support to learn—mathematics. This does not mean that all students should be treated the same. But all students need access every year they are in school to a coherent, challenging mathematical curriculum that is taught by competent and well-supported mathematics teachers. (p. 1)

The Equity Principle is closely aligned with the principle of *individualization* in special education, in which a student's educational objectives are chosen carefully to reflect valued life outcomes for that student. Within the Equity Principle, strategies such as peer mentoring, cross-age peer tutoring, and collaborative teaching all have been shown to be effective in enabling students to attain their objectives. Indeed, as we delineate later in this chapter, peer-delivered instruction can be as reliable as teacher-delivered instruction in teaching academic skills to students with moderate to severe disabilities (Miracle, Collins, Schuster, & Grisham-Brown, 2001).

Second, the Curriculum Principle states that a "curriculum is more than a collection of activities. It must be coherent, focused on important mathematics, and well articulated across the grades" (p. 2). This relates directly to the component of *longitudinal programming* for students with severe disabilities that we discuss later in this chapter. The Curriculum Principle further states that mathematics must "prepare students for continued study and for solving problems in a variety of school, home, and work settings" (p. 2). This relates directly to the importance of instruction in real-life skills, with opportunities for *generalization* across life domains, identified as an essential practice for students with severe disabilities. Again, we present these components in greater detail later in this chapter.

Third, the Teaching Principle acknowledges that "selecting and using suitable curricular materials, using appropriate instructional tools and techniques to support learning, and pursuing continuous self-improvement are actions that good teachers take everyday" (p. 2). The Teaching Principle is related directly to the research-based practice of *systematic instruction* for students with severe disabilities (Wolery, Ault, & Doyle, 1992), which has been used effectively across a variety of studies to teach math skills to students with moderate and severe disabilities.

Fourth, the Learning Principle that "students must learn mathematics with understanding, actively building new knowledge from experience and prior knowledge" (p. 3) acknowledges that a deeper understanding allows students to deal with novel problems and settings. Again, this relates directly to the essential practice of teaching for generalization for students with severe disabilities. The Learning Principle also notes that the "students learn more and better when they take control of their own learning" (p. 3). This echoes the fundamental principle of *self-determination*, which has been related directly to the quality of post-school outcomes for students with significant disabilities (Wehmeyer & Palmer, 2003;

Wehmeyer & Schwartz, 1998). Indeed, as we will show in one of our classroom examples in this chapter, the teaching of mathematics can actually enhance self-determination skills for students with moderate and severe disabilities.

Fifth, the Assessment Principle notes that "assessment should be an integral part of instruction that guides and enhances student learning" (p. 3). Kleinert and Kearns (2004) have noted the essential relationship of good instruction with continuous assessment for students with severe disabilities as well. The Assessment Principle further states that "because different students show what they know and can do in different ways, assessments should also be done in multiple ways, and teachers should look for a convergence of evidence from different sources" (p. 4). This same principle guides the development of *alternate assessments* for students with moderate and severe disabilities (see Chapter 11, this volume).

Last, the Technology Principle notes that "technology is essential in teaching and learning mathematics" (p. 4). For students with significant disabilities, the applications of technology and assistive technology can make even difficult mathematical applications accessible, be it through the simple use of a calculator in making purchases (Slaton, Schuster, Collins, & Carnine, 1994) or the use of money management software in managing a checkbook (Davies, Stock, & Wehmeyer, 2003).

Our purpose in beginning this chapter with the NCTM Principles of Mathematics Education is to illustrate the integral relationship of effective instruction in mathematics to research-based instructional practices for students with moderate and severe disabilities and to show the commonalities of effective instruction in each of these educational disciplines. Next, we turn our attention to how the NCTM Standards in Mathematics for all students can be applied to meet the instructional needs of students with significant disabilities.

The NCTM Standards are divided into five specific content areas, each of which extends across prekindergarten through Grade 12. Those five content areas are

- *Number and Operations*, which include a sense of numbers and how to represent them, the meaning of operations, and fluency in computation

- *Algebra*, which includes recognizing patterns, using algebra to represent mathematical situations, and constructing mathematical models to solve problems

- *Geometry*, including an understanding of two- and three-dimensional shapes, using representational systems such as coordinate geometry, and using spatial reasoning to solve problems

- *Measurement*, including an understanding of basic measurement units and how to apply formulas for measurement purposes

- *Data Analysis and Probability*, including developing questions that can be answered with data and collecting and organizing those data, developing predictions based on data, and applying basic ideas of probability

Table 8.1 illustrates an example of a standard from each of the five NCTM content areas, the grade-level expectation for that standard, and how that standard and grade-level expectation might be applied to a student with a moderate or severe disability. It is key to note that the NCTM standards can be applied to

Table 8.1. Examples of National Council of Teachers of Mathematics standards and grade-level expectations for all students and specific applications for students with moderate and severe disabilities

Content area	Age level	NCTM standard	Example of grade-level expectation for that standard	Application for a student with a significant disability
Number and operations	PreK–Grade 2	Understand numbers, ways of representing numbers, relationships among numbers, and number systems.	Count with understanding and recognize "how many" in sets of objects.	Count out sets of 1 to 10 items (e.g., passing out snacks, counting game pieces, solving single-digit addition problems with manipulatives).
Measurement	Grades 3–5	Apply appropriate techniques, tools, and formulas to determine measurements.	Select and apply appropriate standard units and tools to measure length, area, volume, weight, time, temperature, and the size of angles.	Use a ruler to measure length of different items in a class science experiment; keep temperature chart of daily temperatures for 1 month.
Data analysis and probability	Grades 3–5	Formulate questions that can be addressed with data, and collect, organize, and display relevant data to answer them.	Collect data using observations, surveys, and experiments.	Do classroom survey of students' favorite type of music (e.g., rock, country, pop, classical). Chart results and make PowerPoint presentation to class.
Geometry	Grades 6–8	Use visualization, spatial reasoning, and geometric modeling to solve problems.	Recognize and apply geometric ideas and relationships in areas outside the mathematics classroom, such as art, science, and everyday life.	Identify geometric patterns in print design in art class; create basic print using at least three geometric shapes.
Algebra	Grades 9–12	Represent and analyze mathematical situations and structures using algebraic symbols.	Use symbolic algebra to represent and explain mathematical relationships.	Develop a linear equation to determine how much money the student will have made after 2 weeks on the job.

all students, and that students with significant disabilities can participate in learning activities based on these standards. These same learning activities can address prioritized IEP objectives for the student within the context of functional, real-life applications (see Table 8.1).

In the next part of this chapter, we focus more in depth on those best practices in teaching functional academics, such as math, to students with moderate to severe disabilities. We will review the existent literature on teaching functional math skills to these students, and provide examples of how functional skill instruction can be embedded in the context of national and state math standards, the general curriculum, and general education class activities.

FUNCTIONAL MATH FOR STUDENTS WITH MODERATE TO SEVERE DISABILITIES

As mandated by law, students with moderate to severe disabilities have IEPs that are developed by a team that includes the teachers (general and special education), related service delivery personnel (e.g., speech-language pathologist, physical therapist), parents or guardians, and the student. Each IEP contains goals and objectives based on the student's strengths and areas of need that lead to an outcome of a normalized and productive life in the least restrictive environment when the student transitions from the school setting to adulthood. To meet this outcome, students must learn functional skills, which are those skills that are needed to perform frequently demanded tasks in everyday life. Functional academic skills include basic math concepts, such as number recognition, counting, and computations that can be applied to such skills as telling time, managing money, and performing measurements. There is a wealth of research-based evidence that students with moderate to severe disabilities can learn these skills through the application of direct systematic instruction (e.g., response-prompting strategies) and that the embedding of instruction across settings can lead to generalization (e.g., application of skills in activities and settings where they are needed). The first section of this chapter provides an overview of the general education math skills across age levels and ties this to best practices used in working with students with moderate to severe disabilities. This section will elaborate on those best practices within the context of teaching functional math instruction, citing specific examples from the professional research literature. This section will be followed by sample lesson plans that illustrate ways in which functional math skills can be taught to students with moderate to severe disabilities at the elementary, middle, secondary, and postsecondary levels within the context of general education math classes, with additional practice embedded across the curriculum to facilitate generalization.

There are several components to best practices in teaching functional academics, such as math, to students with moderate to severe disabilities. First, instruction must be individualized because there is a large variance across the abilities and needs of students with moderate to severe disabilities. Second, instructional programming must be longitudinal so that one skill builds on another as students transition from early childhood to adulthood. Third, the phases of learning must be addressed to ensure that students will be able to use the skills they have been taught in activities and settings where they are needed. Finally, systematic instructional procedures, such as response prompting strategies, should be used to ensure that instruction will be both effective and efficient. These components are described in the following sections. In addition, examples from the research base are provided to illustrate ways in which these components have been applied in the instruction of functional math skills.

Individualized Instruction

Functional math skills for students can be determined by compiling data from a variety of sources that include 1) an ecological inventory of the math skills needed in the student's current and future community, residential, and vocational settings (Brown et al., 1979); 2) assessment data compiled by service delivery personnel in related areas such as communication (Mar & Sall, 1999) and assistive technology (Parette & Brotherson, 1996); 3) adaptive behavior scales such as the *AAMD Adaptive Behavior Scales* (Lambert, Winmiller, Taringer, & Cole, 1981) and the *Vineland Adaptive Behavior Scale* (Sparrow, Balla, & Cicchetti, 1984); 4) parent surveys using instruments such as *Impact (A Functional Curriculum Handbook for Students With Moderate to Severe Disabilities;* Neel & Billingsley, 1989) or *Choosing Outcomes and Accommodations for Children (COACH;* Giangreco, Cloninger, & Iverson, 1998); and 5) published functional curricula such as *The Syracuse Community-Referenced Curriculum Guide* (Ford, Schnorr, et al., 1989) or *A Functional Curriculum for Teaching Students with Disabilities* (Valletutti, Bender, & Sims-Tucker, 1996). Once chronological-age–appropriate skills are targeted for instruction, the IEP can be written to specify each student's individual goals and objectives.

Steere and Cavaiuolo (2002) recommend that IEP goals and objectives be tied to long-term community, residential, and employment outcomes that will be needed for a seamless transition to adulthood, as in the following examples. If a long-term residential outcome is for a student to transition to living in an apartment with minimal support, a short-term specific objective might be for the student to estimate monthly expenses and compose a budget. If a long-term vocational outcome is for a student to be employed in a supermarket, a short-term specific objective might be for the student to compile a list of activities to be completed within a specified amount of time and write the "clock face" time beside each activity. On the IEP, these short-term objectives can be listed under chronological-age–appropriate goals within the general education math curriculum, thus enabling students to work toward national math standards.

Once the IEP is written, the next step is to determine when and where math instruction will take place. This is done by creating a matrix (Siegel-Causey, McMorris, McGowan, & Sands-Buss, 1998), such as the one shown in Table 8.2. In addition to working on functional math objectives within the context of a general education math class, math objectives can be embedded across the curriculum and the school day, such as in a general education science class, during lunch in the cafeteria, or while shopping for school supplies while participating in community-based instruction (see Table 8.2).

Longitudinal Programming

The functional math curriculum of students with moderate to severe disabilities should include instruction in basic math concepts (e.g., one-to-one correspondence, numeral identification, simple addition and subtraction) as well as in spe-

Table 8.2. Matrix of student's individualized education program objectives embedded across the curriculum

Class schedule	Math objectives			
	Performing computations	Telling time	Managing money	Performing basic measurement
8:00 Homeroom	Compute class attendance	Make daily schedule	Pay for school supplies	
9:00 Language Arts	Compute reading progress	Record date in daily journal	List prices for class project	Create bulletin board
10:00 Math	Work on basic math facts	Work on basic time skills	Work on basic money skills	Work on basic measuring skills
11:00 Lunch*	Compute fat grams or calories	Monitor length of break	Pay for lunch	Weigh serving ounces
12:00 Physical Ed.*	Compute physical progress	Record time for walking laps	Shop for class project materials	Measure distance in activities
1:00 Science	Compute total cost of science project items	Record calendar of season	List prices for science project	Measure daily temperature
2:00 Social Studies		Estimate travel time to site	Compile travel budget	Measure distance between sites
3:00 Dismissal		Make homework schedule	Purchase snack from machine	

*Community-based instruction occurs during lunch and physical education two times per week.

cific math applications related to telling time, managing money, and performing measurements that are clearly related to national and state standards in math. Several functional curricula have addressed the scope and sequence of functional math skills from preschool through postsecondary levels. For example, *A Functional Curriculum for Teaching Students with Disabilities: Functional Academics* (Vallettuti et al., 1996) lists functional math goals of acquiring basic math skills needed for independence, participating in cash transactions, performing measurement activities, and managing time and provides specific objectives and activities under each of these goals to be performed in the school and home settings at the preschool, primary, intermediate, and secondary levels. In another example, *The Syracuse Community-Referenced Curriculum Guide for Students with Moderate to Severe Disabilities* (Ford, Schnorr, et al., 1998) compares functional math skills for students with disabilities with those taught in the general education curriculum across the age levels of primary elementary school, intermediate elementary school, middle and high school, and postsecondary school in the areas of money handling (Ford, Davern, Schnorr, Black, & Kaiser, 1989) and time management (Ford, Black, Davern, & Schnorr, 1989). In using these curricula, always ensure that functional math skills are aligned with national and state standards for all students. This can be done by first obtaining copies of state and national standards for a student's age level, reviewing the text used by the student's peers, and planning in collaboration with the general education math teacher.

Using a longitudinal approach, the following objectives might be appropriate for students with moderate to severe disabilities across age levels based on individual needs. Telling time might consist of 1) teaching students in elementary school to tell time on a clock face to the hour and half hour; 2) teaching students in middle school to tell time by additional intervals of 5, 10, and 15 minutes; and 3) teaching students in secondary school to apply telling time to scheduling activities and using a personal calendar. Managing money might consist of 1) teaching students in elementary school to identify coins; 2) teaching students in middle school to add coin and dollar bill combinations; and 3) teaching students in secondary school to estimate budgets, make change, and compare prices. Again, it is essential to consider how each of these skills within a longitudinal approach is related to the math standards and grade-level core content for typical peers.

Phases of Learning

At each age level, it is crucial that teachers address the four phases of learning (Wolery, Ault, & Doyle, 1992) in teaching functional math skills. These include 1) acquisition, 2) fluency, 3) maintenance, and 4) generalization. Acquisition is the learning of a new skill. This can be done through direct instruction on basic math skills within the context of a math class. Fluency is the ease and speed with which a student performs an acquired skill. Again, this can be the focus of repeated practice within a math class. Maintenance is a student's ability to use a skill over time. Maintenance can be facilitated by repeated overlearning within a math class as well as using the skill in applied activities where it is needed. Generalization is the student's ability to use a skill across settings, activities, materials, and persons. This can be facilitated in the math classroom by teaching with real materials and practicing the skill in realistic simulations as well as in practicing the skill across a variety of settings, activities, and people where the skill is required.

Systematic Instruction

A number of systematic instructional strategies have been effective in teaching math skills to students with moderate to severe disabilities (Brown, McDonnell, & Billingsley, 1997; Wolery & Schuster, 1997). Among the numerous direct instructional practices documented in the research literature as resulting in effective and efficient instruction across academic areas (including math) are 1) response prompting strategies, 2) the inclusion of nontargeted information in the form of instructive feedback or observational learning, 3) the addition of accommodations and adaptations, 4) instructional trials embedded within the context of ongoing activities, 5) video- and computer-assisted instruction, and 6) delivery by peer tutors. These components of direct instruction as they relate to teaching functional math skills are described in the following sections.

Response Prompting Strategies   Response prompting strategies are considered nearly errorless and consist of the addition of a prompt that is inserted following the task direction and prior to the student's response (Wolery et al., 1992). As the student acquires the target response, the prompt is faded in

Table 8.3.   Overview of response prompting procedures

Response prompting strategy	Description of procedure	Math-based example of procedure
System of least prompts	If needed, increasingly intrusive prompts from a predetermined hierarchy are delivered within a trial until the student is able to perform the correct response.	Instructor provides opportunity for student to count money with next-dollar strategy. If the student needs assistance, the instructor first tells the student how to respond before showing the student how to respond, or physically guiding the student in the response.
Progressive time delay	Across sessions, the interval of time allotted for a student to respond independently before a predetermined prompt is delivered is increased in small increments until the student can respond independently without the prompt.	Instructor identifies various coins for the student. Over a number of subsequent trials, the teacher provides an increasing interval of time for the student to identify each coin before providing a prompt.
Constant time delay	Following a session of immediately prompting a student with a predetermined prompt, remaining sessions allot a standard interval of time for the student to respond independently before being prompted.	Instructor shows the clock and tells the student the time. In subsequent trials, the teacher waits for 3 seconds before stating the time, giving the students time to respond first.
Simultaneous prompting	Following trials to determine whether a student can respond independently, instructional trials are delivered in which the student is immediately prompted with a predetermined prompt.	Instructor asks the student to measure at the beginning of each instructional session. If the student cannot perform the response, the teacher then prompts the student in the response.

intensity, in intrusiveness, or over a dimension of time. A number of response prompting strategies have been effective and efficient in teaching math skills to students with disabilities. An overview of these procedures is presented in Table 8.3.

A constant time-delay procedure has been used to teach multiplication facts to elementary-level students with learning disabilities (Williams & Collins, 1994); to teach purchasing skills to elementary-level students with moderate disabilities (Morse & Schuster, 2000); to teach reading numerals in the information on prescription labels (i.e., dosages, telephone numbers, prescription numbers) to middle school students with moderate disabilities (Cromer, Schuster, Collins, & Grisham-Brown, 1998); and to teach telling time to secondary school students with moderate disabilities (Jones, 2004). In addition, a system of least prompts procedure has been used to teach the next dollar strategy to elementary school students with mild to moderate disabilities (Colyer & Collins, 1996), a progressive time-delay procedure has been used to teach selection of change and identification of telephone numbers to elementary and secondary school students with moderate disabilities (Collins, Stinson, & Land, 1993), and a simultaneous prompting procedure has been used to teach addition facts to middle school students with moderate disabilities (Fickel, Schuster, & Collins, 1998).

Nontargeted Information The efficiency of instruction can be increased by adding nontargeted information to instructional trials. This can be in the form of inserting instructional feedback with additional information within the task direction, prompt, or consequence of an instructional trial or through setting up students for observational learning of nontargeted information by using small-group instruction in which students are exposed to skills targeted to be taught to other members of the group.

At the elementary level, Wolery and colleagues (1992) used instructive feedback when they taught elementary-level students with moderate disabilities to read words on restaurant menus and included the comparative costs of items on restaurant menus (i.e., more or less than 1 dollar) as one of the prompt levels within the system of least prompts procedure. The authors found that all of the students acquired some of the nontargeted information. In addition, Smith (1998) taught students to identify the parts of a check and used instructive feedback showing various calendar dates and dollar amounts as she presented the task direction. The author found that the students learned to read various dates and dollar amounts written as numbers and as number words.

At the middle school level, Fickel and colleagues (1998) facilitated observational learning when they taught different tasks with different stimuli to a heterogeneous group of four middle school students (no disability, mild disability, moderate disability, severe disability). Although the instructor taught basic addition facts to the student with moderate disabilities, the student also learned the manual signs and some of the tasks taught to other students in the group.

At the secondary level, Jones (2004) facilitated observational learning when she taught different discrete tasks with different stimuli to a group of three secondary school students and also included instructive feedback on related nontargeted chained tasks in each instructional trial. One of the students learned the targeted task of telling time through direct instruction as well as the nontargeted information of setting a watch to the correct time. In addition, the other members of the group also acquired the ability to tell time and set a watch through observational learning.

Adaptations and Accommodations Sometimes students with disabilities need adaptations or accommodations to complete a functional math task that is appropriate for their chronological age. These are individually determined. An example of an accommodation might be to provide extended time for testing on a math test (Elliott & Marquart, 2004). The professional literature contains a range of data-based math adaptations for students with moderate to severe disabilities, especially in the area of money management. These include teaching students to match a sequence of numbers on a telephone card to a sequence of numbers on a telephone in placing a telephone call (Collins et al., 1993), teaching students to use a next dollar strategy in paying for purchases by either adding an extra dollar for change at either the beginning (Test, Howell, Burkhart, & Beroth, 1993) or the end (Colyer & Collins, 1996) of counting out 1 dollar bills or inserting a requirement to "say-back" the price before paying (Test et al., 1993), teaching students to use an adapted number line in comparing prices (Kleinert, Guiltinan, & Sims, 1988; Sandknop, Schuster, Wolery, & Cross, 1992), and teaching students to respond to telling time on a clock face by using response cards that state the time (Horn, 2002).

Embedded Skill Instruction   Embedding the instruction of math skills within other instructional activities can facilitate the maintenance and generalization of math skills that have been taught through direct instruction. Siegel-Causey et al. (1998) provided an example of how a middle school student with severe disabilities might work on math skills during activities in home room, earth science class, home economics, computer applications, community instruction, and vocational experiences. Specifically, math skills in the earth science class might include recording and graphing wind speed, humidity level, and barometric pressure. Examples of functional math skills embedded in community-based instruction include paying for purchases in teaching elementary-level students with moderate disabilities to shop for groceries (Morse & Schuster, 2000) and coin identification and numeral recognition in teaching elementary and secondary school students with moderate disabilities to use a public pay telephone (Collins et al., 1993). Examples of functional math skills embedded in leisure activities include number recognition and number matching in teaching secondary school students with moderate disabilities to play UNO with peers without disabilities (Collins, Hall, & Branson, 1997) and number sequencing in teaching secondary school students with moderate disabilities to play Solitaire (Seward, 2000).

Video- and Computer-Based Instruction   In recent years, technology has become an efficient way to provide individualized instruction to students with disabilities. Video-anchored instruction can facilitate generalization by providing realistic situations in which math skills can be applied (Bottge, 2001; Hess, 2004). For example, a student may watch a video of other students shopping and then be required to compute the amount of time they have to shop (based on the time they arrive at the mall and the time their parents will arrive to take them home) and the cost of their purchases with taxes or tips added. Technology also can be used as a tool to assist students in acquiring new math skills. When Spear (2002) compared teacher-delivered instruction with computer-delivered instruction (both employing a simultaneous prompting procedure) in teaching coin values to elementary school students with mild to moderate disabilities, the author found that both delivery formats were effective. Technology also can be a permanent adaptive tool for performing activities requiring math skills. For example, money management software can be used to assist students in managing a checkbook (Davies, Stock, & Wehmeyer, 2003).

Peer-Delivered Instruction   There is evidence that systematic instruction delivered by same-age peers without disabilities can be as reliable as teacher-delivered instruction in teaching academic skills to students with moderate to severe disabilities (Miracle et al., 2001). In regard to math, Calhoun and Fuchs (2003) found that secondary school students without disabilities were effective in teaching math computation skills to their peers with disabilities. The use of peer tutors has the advantage of providing assistance to teachers when classes are large or diverse.

EXAMPLES OF FUNCTIONAL MATH INSTRUCTION EMBEDDED WITHIN THE GENERAL EDUCATION MATH CURRICULUM

Although none of the research investigations referenced in the previous sections was conducted in inclusive general education settings, there is no reason why general education math classes cannot be the context for teaching functional math skills to students with disabilities. First, research has shown that the presence of students with disabilities does not adversely affect the learning of students without disabilities ("Study: Special Education Helps Boost Math Scores," 2003). Second, there is evidence that students with moderate and severe disabilities can learn other academic tasks (e.g., sight words, writing, social studies facts, health and safety rules) within general education classes (Collins, Branson, Hall, & Rankin, 2001; Collins, Hall, Branson, & Holder, 1999; Collins, Hendricks, Fetko, & Land, 2002). Third, there is evidence that students with disabilities benefit from instruction in heterogeneous groups because observational learning can occur (Fickel et al., 1998). Finally, the skills acquired by students in the general education math class do not have to be limited to functional math but can include other embedded skills (e.g., reading, writing, communication, social, motor) as well (Bottge, 2001; Siegel-Causey et al., 1998).

Including students with moderate and severe disabilities in general education classes requires finding ways to include the teaching of functional skills within the context of the general education curriculum. To provide a link between the objectives for functional math skills listed on the IEP and the general education math curriculum, functional goals for students with disabilities must be tied to national math standards. Assuming that the general education math curriculum is linked to national math standards, an additional matrix for planning can be compiled in which IEP math objectives are listed along the left side of the page and the general education curriculum appropriate for the student's chronological age can be listed across the top of the page as shown in Table 8.4.

It is up to the educational team to determine how and when functional skills will be covered within the general education curriculum. The format can vary. For example, functional math skills can be taught through direct instruction 1) within the context of a large-group lesson teaching the same or different math skills to students in the group; 2) within the context of a small-group hands-on activity in which functional math skills can be embedded; or 3) within the context of independent practice under the guidance of a teacher, paraprofessional, or peer. Regardless of the format, all phases of learning should be addressed. This requires planning for acquisition and fluency within the general education math class as well as maintenance and generalization in activities that take place in other settings across the school day (e.g., other academic classes, lunch and breaks, community-based instruction, extracurricular school activities, vocational exploration). The next sections provide lesson plans designed to illustrate ways in which functional math skills can be taught to students with moderate or severe disabilities across age levels within general education math classes and supplemented by embedded practice across settings. In each example, we have linked the skill to national math standards and an example of state standards from the Kentucky core content. In planning lessons, it is especially critical that teachers ensure that functional math skills are aligned with state standards. When typical students are learning skills related to time, money, and measure-

Table 8.4.   Matrix of student's functional math objectives embedded in general education math class

IEP objectives	Weekly unit of study				
	Monday	Tuesday	Wednesday	Thursday	Friday
Computing using basic addition	Count up to 5 objects in set	Demonstrate simple addition to 5 with objects	Demonstrate simple addition to 5 with numerals	Practice simple addition to 5 with flash cards and seatwork	Apply simple addition to 5 in real-life word problems
Telling time to hour and half-hour	Identify time math class begins	Identify time math class begins	Identify time math class begins	Identify time math class begins	Identify time math class begins
Identifying values of coins	Count up to 5 pennies in set	Add combinations of up to 5 pennies	Match pennies to numerals in problems	Practice simple addition problems counting pennies	Apply simple addition to 5 in real-life problem using pennies
Performing linear measurements	Count up to 5 objects in straight line	Add objects in straight line	Place objects on number line to add	Place objects on number line to add	Apply simple addition to 5 in real-life problem using number line

ment, there are naturally occurring opportunities to teach the same content, although this may be at a different performance level. In contrast, the majority of general math content focuses on other math standards as described in Chapter 7. In the examples that follow, functional skills are taught in ways that access these varied standards.

Primary Elementary School Example

In the following sections, we provide a lesson plan that focuses on teaching telling time to the hour for students with moderate or severe disabilities in a primary elementary nongraded kindergarten through second-grade classroom. The lesson is linked to the NCTM standards and more specifically to the Kentucky core content for primary students. In addition, the long-term goal is drawn from *The Syracuse Community-Referenced Curriculum Guide* (Ford, Schnorr, et al., 1989). The lesson is to be taught in a small-group instructional format during center time. Although the plan focuses on instruction for two students with moderate to severe disabilities, Kaia and Spenser, other students may join the group based on interest. Kaia is a 6-year-old female student with Williams syndrome and severe mental retardation. She demonstrates rote memory skills by singing simple repetitive songs and a functional receptive vocabulary through her ability to follow simple directions; however, Kaia does not have functional expressive language skills. Thus, her objective is to demonstrate receptive acquisition of telling time. Spenser is a 7-year-old male student with autism spectrum disorder and moderate mental retardation. Although he is often echolalic, Spenser has an expressive language vocabulary commensurate with same-age peers. Thus, his objective is to demonstrate expressive acquisition of telling time.

Students: Kaia and Spenser

Target Skill   Telling time to the hour

NCTM Number and Operations Standard   Understand numbers, ways of representing numbers, relationships among numbers, and number systems

NCTM Expectation   Develop a sense of whole numbers and represent and use them in flexible ways

Kentucky Core Content Skills   Students will perform mathematical operations and procedures accurately and efficiently, explain how the skills work in real-world or mathematical situations, and be able to

MA-E-1.2.1: Read, write, and rename whole numbers

Long-Term Instructional Goal   The student will "use clock time on the hour and half-hour to comment on the time, estimate time needs, and solve real-life problems" (Ford, Schnorr, et al., 1989, p. 151)

Long-Term Instructional Objectives   1) When presented with a variety of timepieces throughout the day, Kaia will match the time shown on the timepiece to the clock picture beside activities on her daily schedule. 2) When presented with a variety of timepieces throughout the day, Spenser will state the time shown on the timepiece and then identify the corresponding activity on his daily schedule.

Short-Term Instructional Objectives   1) When presented with a picture of a clock face and an analog timepiece that represents time to the hour, Kaia will match the timepiece to the correct clock picture with 100% accuracy for 5 days. 2) When presented with an analog timepiece that represents time to the hour, Spenser will state the correct time with 100% accuracy for 5 days.

Settings   Direct instruction will occur at the time-telling learning center time in the K–2 classroom during center time. Generalization probes will occur on the hour throughout the day during regularly scheduled activities (e.g., lunch, language arts, music, recess, dismissal).

Materials   Instructional materials at the learning center to be used during direct instruction include 1) a variety of clocks, watches, and timepieces that represent those that would be found in the students' natural environments which are labeled with cardinal numbers; 2) laminated cards showing pictures of clock faces with times to the hour from 1:00 to 12:00; and 3) daily schedules for Kaia and Spenser with pictures of clock faces showing times beside corresponding activities.

Instructional Procedures   The instructor will begin the session by telling the target students that it is time to work at learning centers and that they may choose a second center if they first complete instruction at the time-telling center. There will be a minimum of five random trials per student, and other interested students in the class will be welcome to join in the small-group instructional session. The instructor will then conduct the session using a constant time-delay instructional procedure. During the first two sessions, the instructor will wait for a delay interval of 0 second before providing a prompt. On all subsequent sessions, the instructor will wait for a delay interval of 3 seconds before providing a prompt. Each trial will consist of delivering 1) a general attention cue (i.e., "Look"), 2) the task direction, 3) the appropriate delay interval, 4) the prompt (if needed), and 5) the consequence (i.e., praise or error correction). For Kaia, the task direction will be "It is __ o'clock; point to the same" when presented with a timepiece set to the hour and a choice of two pictures of clock faces, and the controlling prompt will be a physical model. For Spenser, the task direction will be "What time is it?" when presented with a timepiece set to the hour, and the controlling prompt will be a verbal model. When delivering praise or correcting errors, the instructor will add nontargeted information consisting of naming the activity that takes place at the targeted time (e.g., "We eat lunch at 12:00").

Maintenance   When a student reaches criterion of 100% correct responses before the prompt for 2 days, the instructor will fade praise to the end of the session for 3 days.

Generalization   In addition to using multiple exemplars of timepieces during direct instruction, the instructor will conduct probes for generalization on the hour throughout the day. For Kaia, the instructor will show the student the time on a timepiece and her schedule and then deliver a task direction (e.g., "It is 12:00, and you are at lunch. Show me 12:00 on your schedule"). For Spenser, the instructor will show the student the time on a timepiece and deliver the task direction (e.g., "What time is it?"). After the student has an opportunity to respond, the instructor will show him his schedule, point to the corresponding picture of the clock face, and state the nontargeted information (e.g., "It is 12:00, and you are at lunch").

Data Collection   During instructional trials, the instructor will record whether the student 1) gives a correct response before or after the prompt, 2) gives an incorrect response before or after the prompt, or 3) fails to respond after the prompt. During generalization trials, the instructor will record whether the student 1) gives a correct response, 2) gives an incorrect response, or 3) fails to respond within 3 seconds following the task direction. A sample data sheet is shown in Figure 8.1.

Intermediate Elementary School Example

In the following sections, we provide a functional math lesson that focuses on teaching measuring units in inches for a student with a moderate disability in an intermediate elementary classroom (i.e., fourth grade). The lesson is linked to the NCTM standards and, more specifically to the Kentucky core content for primary students. In addition, the long-term goal is drawn from *A Functional Curriculum for Teaching Students with Disabilities* (Valletutti et al., 1996). Instruction will occur during independent seatwork time in a general education math class. Eun-bi is a 10-year-old female student with Down syndrome and moderate mental retardation. Although Eun-bi is nonverbal, she has an expressive vocabulary of 75–100 manual signs and can follow the majority of directions that are given to her. Her motor skills are adequate for working with small objects. In addition to using linear measurement as a personal tool, the ability to measure will enable Eun-bi to participate in a number of inclusive activities with her peers.

Skill: Telling time to the hour

Directions: In the appropriate column for each instructional trial, record a + for each correct response, a – for each incorrect response, or a 0 for each failure to respond. Use the same symbols to record the student's response beside each generalization probe time.

Kaia				Spenser			
Stimulus	Before	After		Stimulus	Before	After	
1.				1.			
2.				2.			
3.				3.			
4.				4.			
5.				5.			
Total correct				Total correct			
Total incorrect				Total incorrect			
Total no response				Total no response			
Generalization probes							
8:00: 9:00: 10:00: 11:00:				8:00: 9:00: 10:00: 11:00:			
12:00: 1:00: 2:00: 3:00:				12:00: 1:00: 2:00: 3:00:			
Total correct:				Total correct:			

Figure 8.1. Constant time-delay data sheet for teaching telling time to the hour.

Student: Eun-bi

Target Skill   Measuring in inches

NCTM Measurement Standard   Understand measurable attributes of objects and the units, systems, and processes of measurement

NCTM Expectation   Understand the need for measuring with standard units and become familiar with standard units in the customary and metric systems

Kentucky Core Content Skills   Students will perform mathematical operations and procedures accurately and efficiently, explain how the skills work in real-world or mathematical situations, and be able to

MA-E-2.2.5: Use nonstandard and standard units to measure weight, length, perimeter, area (figures that can be divided into rectangular shapes), and angles

MA-E-2.2.9: Choose appropriate tools (e.g., protractors, meter sticks, rulers) for specific measurement tasks

Long-Term Instructional Goal   "The student will acquire functional measurement skills that facilitate independence in various measurement activities" (Valetutti et al., 1996, p. 256).

Long-Term Instructional Objectives   Within the context of an activity, Eun-bi will measure materials in inches with 100% accuracy for 5 days. Activities may include measuring lengths of border for a bulletin board in social studies, measuring lengths of materials (e.g., ribbon, yarn, paper strips) for an art project, measuring results in projects in science class, and measuring uniform segments in constructing a graph to monitor personal progress.

Short-Term Instructional Objectives   When asked to construct a number line that is a set number of inches in length, Eun-bi will draw the number line with 100% accuracy for 5 days.

Settings   Direct instruction will occur at the beginning of independent seatwork time in the fourth-grade classroom during math time. Generalization probes will occur during activities (e.g., bulletin board construction, art project, science project, behavior monitoring) in other inclusive classes.

Materials   Instructional materials to be used during direct instruction at the student's desk include 1) a variety of writing implements (e.g., color pencils, graphite pencils, ink pens, fine point markers), 2) strips of heavy paper in various colors cut in 12-inch lengths, 3) a variety of rulers (e.g., wood or plastic varying in color), and 4) worksheets with addition and subtraction problems from 1 to 10.

Instructional Procedures   The instructor will begin the session by telling the class that it is time for independent seatwork. When Eun-bi takes a seat at her desk, the instructor will give her a math computation worksheet and tell her to select a writing implement, a paper strip, and a ruler. The instructor will then give the task direction, "Make a number line that is __ inches long." Instruction will follow using a system of least prompts procedure to teach the steps of the task analysis for measuring the set number of inches in the following manner. If the student fails to perform the first step independently within 5 seconds, the instructor will give a verbal prompt (e.g., "Put the ruler on the paper horizontally"). If the student fails to perform the step within 5 seconds following the verbal prompt, the instructor will give a model prompt (e.g., show the student where to place the ruler on the paper). If the student fails to perform the step within 5 seconds following the model prompt, the instructor will give a physical prompt (e.g., physically guide the student in placing the ruler on the paper). The instructor will then wait 5 seconds for the student to perform the next step of the task analysis before repeating the prompting sequence. Instruction will proceed in this manner until the task is completed.

Maintenance   When a student reaches criterion of 100% correct independent responses for 2 days, the instructor will fade praise to the end of the task analysis for 3 days.

Generalization   In addition to using multiple exemplars of materials during instruction, the instructor will give Eun-bi the opportunity to measure inches during inclusive activities in other classes throughout the day, as specified in the long-term instructional objective.

Data Collection   During instructional trials, the instructor will record the degree of assistance the student needed to perform each step of the task analysis correctly (i.e., independent, verbal prompt, model prompt, physical prompt). During generalization activities, the instructor will record whether the student

Student: Eun-bi	
Skill: Measuring in inches	
Directions: For each step of the task analysis during instruction, record the degree if assistance needed using *I* for independent, *V* for verbal prompt, *M* for model prompt, and *P* for physical guidance. During generalization probes, record whether or not the entire measurement task was completed independently with correct responses.	
1.　Place ruler horizontally on strip of paper.	
2.　Place a tic mark at 0 inches.	
3.　Place a tic mark at the terminal number of inches.	
4.　Draw a line from the 0 tic mark to the terminal tic mark.	
5.　Make tic marks that designate each inch between 0 and the terminal tic mark.	
6.　Write the corresponding numeral above each tic mark.	
Summary　　　　　　　　　　　　　　Number of independent responses:	
Number of verbal prompts:	
Number of model prompts:	
Number of physical prompts:	
Generalization probes	
Activity:　　　　　　　　　　　　　　　　　　　　Response:	
Activity:　　　　　　　　　　　　　　　　　　　　Response:	
Activity:　　　　　　　　　　　　　　　　　　　　Response:	
Activity:　　　　　　　　　　　　　　　　　　　　Response:	
Total independent correct generalization responses:	

Figure 8.2.　System of least prompts data sheet for teaching measuring inches.

was able to measure the correct number of inches independently. A sample data sheet is shown in Figure 8.2.

Middle School Example

The eighth-grade class is studying order of operations, a standard for calculating expressions that have more than one arithmetic operation. The class is learning how equations are expressed and solved, using the order of operations. Andrea is a 13-year-old eighth grader with a moderate cognitive disability. She can count with one-to-one correspondence to 100, recognizes numbers to at least 100, and uses a calculator to perform addition, subtraction, and multiplication problems. She primarily reads and communicates using picture symbols and a voice output device and follows directions well with the use of social stories and/or pictorial steps of an activity. She is participating in the typical eighth-grade math class. Her math IEP objectives include learning to use a calculator to solve problems using addition, subtraction, multiplication and division, and to use her calculator in solving real-life problems (e.g., shopping for groceries, solving calculator problems in other classes). In addition, Andrea is learning higher-order thinking and organizational skills (in the use of order of operations and graphic organizers) that can be generalized to problems encountered in daily life. The lesson is aligned with national math standards, as well as with the Kentucky core content for middle school students.

Student: Andrea

Skill   Using a calculator to solve equations

NCTM Standards Addressed in the Lesson   The following NCTM standards are addressed for all students in this instructional unit:

- Content standard (numbers and operations): Understand meanings of operations and how they relate to one another

- Process standard (problem-solving): Apply and adapt a variety of appropriate strategies to solve problems

- Process standard (communication): Communicate their mathematical thinking coherently and clearly to peers, teachers, and others

- NCTM grade-level expectations (sixth through eighth grade): Understand the meaning and effects of arithmetic operations with fractions, decimals, and integers

Kentucky Core Content Skills   Students will perform mathematical operations and procedures accurately and efficiently, explain how the skills work in real-world or mathematical situations, and be able to

MA-M-1.2.1: Add, subtract, multiply, and divide rational numbers (fractions, decimals, percents, integers) to solve problems

MA-M-1.2.2: Compute (e.g., estimate, use pencil and paper, use calculator, round, use mental math) large and small quantities and check for reasonable and appropriate computational results

MA-M-1.2.5: Apply order of operations

Long-Term Instructional Goal   Use a calculator to perform addition, subtraction, multiplication, and division operations involving real-life applications in school and community settings

Long-Term Instructional Objective   When presented with a real-life problem that can be solved through a series of operations (addition, subtraction, multiplication, and division), Andrea will solve the problem.

Short-Term Instructional Objective   When presented with a problem that can be solved through a series of operations (addition, subtraction, multiplication, and division) and a graphic organizer on the correct order of operations, Andrea will solve the problem correctly for 9 of 10 problems for 3 consecutive days.

Settings   Instruction will occur in the typical class setting. Andrea will receive assistance from her collaborating special education teacher in learning to use her graphic organizer to solve order of operation problems.

Materials   The special education teacher has adapted a graphic organizer (see Figure 8.3) for Andrea to use. She also will use her calculator.

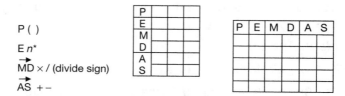

P ( )

E n^*

$\overrightarrow{MD}$ × / (divide sign)

$\overrightarrow{AS}$ + −

Figure 8.3. Sample graphic organizers for learning to use order of operations.

Instructional Procedures   The class is introduced to equations that contain multiple operations and students are asked to solve them. Andrea will use a calculator to solve the math problems. In the introduction to the lesson, the teacher gives the whole class the following problems to solve:

$8 - 3 \times 2 = $ ___

$6 \times 3 + 4 / 2 - 1 = $ ___

The teacher then has the members of the class share their answers—including Andrea. As might be expected, the teacher gets a variety of answers depending on which operations each student performed first! The teacher then gives the class the correct answers (i.e., 2 and 19, respectively) and asks why everyone got different results.

The teacher next introduces the *order of operations*:

1.   Solve the parenthesis

2.   Solve the exponents

3.   Multiply and/or divide in the order they appear left to right

4.   Add and/or subtract in the order they appear left to right.

She demonstrates with the equations she had introduced earlier:

$8 - 3 \times 2$

$8 - 6$

2

$6 \times 3 + 4 / 2 - 1$

$18 + 4 / 2 - 1$

$18 + 2 - 1$

$20 - 1$

19

Finally, she introduces the acronym *PEMDAS* (Parenthesis, Exponent, Multiply/Divide, Add/Subtract) as a way for students to remember the order of operations. As indicated in Figure 8.3, a variety of graphic organizers can be used with the acronym PEMDAS to assist students in remembering to use all steps in the correct order. After the teacher explains each graphic organizer, Andrea chooses the graphic organizer that works best for her (although this might take some experimenting!). She will learn to use the order of operations by following task-analyzed steps. The teacher uses a chained constant time-delay procedure with the following task analysis to teach Andrea the order of operations:

Summary of Basic Steps

1. Write the problem.

2. Refer to the PEMDAS organizer to determine which operation to perform first.

3. Highlight the operation within the problem to perform.

4. Use the calculator to solve that operation.

5. Rewrite the problem with the answer in place of the problem solved.

6. Refer to the PEMDAS organizer to determine which operation to perform next.

7. Highlight the operation within the problem to perform.

8. Use the calculator to solve that operation.

9. Rewrite the problem with the answer in place of the problem solved.

10. Refer to the PEMDAS organizer to determine which operation to perform next.

11. Continue until the problem is solved.

Within the constant time-delay procedure, the teacher performs the first three problems using 0-second delay interval. At the 0-second delay, Andrea is expected to follow the teacher's model for each step for each problem. The teacher has chosen a *controlling prompt* of a verbal and model demonstration (e.g., "First we write the problem" as the teacher is demonstrating writing the problem). Andrea then copies the problem herself. Next, the teacher points to the visual organizer to determine that operations within parentheses must be performed first. Andrea follows her model and points to her own visual organizer to the first box (P for parentheses). The teacher then highlights the part of her problem within parentheses and proceeds to solve that part (e.g., $8 - 4 = 4$). Andrea follows her model and solves the part of her problem in parentheses as well. Following the prompt delivered at a 0-second delay, Andrea has 5 seconds to initiate her response and 15 seconds to complete it. If she does not initiate her response within 5 seconds or complete it within 15 seconds, the teacher repeats her direction and model prompt.

On the fourth problem, the teacher introduces a 5-second delay interval. For each step, the teacher now waits 5 seconds for Andrea to complete each step. If Andrea correctly initiates the step within 5 seconds and completes it within 15 seconds, the teacher records a *correct "before" response* on the data sheet and verbally reinforces her for correctly completing that step. If Andrea makes an error, the teacher interrupts her response and says "No, watch me" and she then models and verbalizes the correct response while recording an *incorrect "before" response*. If Andrea does not initiate her response within 5 seconds, the teacher provides the prompt (verbal and demonstration) for that step. If Andrea then initiates that step correctly within 5 seconds and completes it within 15 seconds, the teacher praises her for her response and records a *correct "after" response*. If Andrea still does not respond, or responds incorrectly after the teacher's prompt, the teacher immediately interrupts Andrea, once again models and verbalizes the step, and records an *incorrect "after" response*. An example of one of Andrea's problems is presented here.

$25 / 5 - 3 + (\boxed{8 - 4})^2 \times 2$

$25 / 5 - 3 + \boxed{(4)^2} \times 2$

$\boxed{25 / 5} - 3 + 16 \times 2$

$5 - 3 + \boxed{16 \times 2}$

$\boxed{5 - 3} + 32$

$\boxed{2 + 32}$

34

Data Collection   Data collection consists of the completed problems, and the time-delay data sheet that the teacher has constructed to record Andrea's progress in mastering this skill, as described in the previous section. An example of that data sheet is presented in Figure 8.4.

Maintenance   Andrea uses her calculator throughout a range of in-school and community activities, which increases her opportunities to perform real-life problems related to addition, subtraction, multiplication, and division.

Generalization   Andrea also is learning to use her calculator to solve real-life problems throughout the day. In her home economics class, for example, Andrea and two of her classmates are responsible for purchasing the groceries for cooking. Every other week, they shop with the class's instructional assistant at a local store. Andrea uses her calculator to consecutively subtract the cost of each item as it is purchased to ensure that there is sufficient money. One day, for example, Andrea starts with $15.00. Because her state has a 6% sales tax, she applies a "tax formula" to subtract the potential amount of tax beforehand:

$\$15.00 \times 0.94 =$ the cost of her first item

Using the order of operations, Andrea has learned that she first multiplies $\times$ .94 to obtain the amount she has available after tax, and then she subtracts the cost of her first item. She proceeds to shop for the items on her list until she has spent all of her money (indicated by a minus sign [–] on her calculator at the point at which she has selected an item for which there is not sufficient money).

Andrea also uses her calculator in science class in a unit on weather, in which the students are charting the daily variability of daily temperatures in their community. Each day, Andrea checks the weather section of the newspaper to record the high temperature and the low temperature for that day, and subtracts the difference. She then uses a chart to graph the difference between the high and low temperature—the higher the bar on her chart for each day, the greater the temperature variability for that day. Using the addition and division functions of her calculator, she calculates the average temperature difference between the daily high and low temperatures. With a peer, she presents her chart to the class in a PowerPoint presentation.

Secondary School Example

Chad is a 16-year-old sophomore with a moderate cognitive disability. He is able to count with one-to-one correspondence to 100, can recognize numbers to 500, and uses a calculator to perform addition, subtraction, and multiplication prob-

Student: Andrea		
Skill: Using a calculator to perform order of operations		
Steps of task analysis	Before	After
1. Write the problem.		
2. Refer to PEMDAS organizer to determine operation to perform.		
3. Highlight operation to perform.		
4. Use calculator to solve operation.		
5. Rewrite problem with answer in place of problem solved.		
6. Refer to PEMDAS organizer to determine operation to perform.		
7. Highlight operation to perform.		
8. Use calculator to solve operation.		
9. Rewrite problem with answer in place of the problem solved.		
10. Refer to PEMDAS organizer to determine operation to perform.		
11. Continue until problem solved.		
Summary Total correct:		
Total incorrect:		
Total response:		
Generalization probes		
Activity:	Response:	
Activity:	Response:	
Activity:	Response:	
Total correct generalization responses:		

Figure 8.4. Constant time-delay data sheet for learning the order of operations.

lems. He is able to read approximately 150 sight words, communicates clearly verbally, and follows directions well. Two days a week, he has a paid after-school job for 2 hours each day. He is participating in the typical high school algebra class. His math IEP objectives include learning to manage a budget (e.g., budgeting for rent, food, clothes) and learning to use basic equations and measurement strategies to solve problems encountered in life. Although algebraic equations typically have not been considered a topic of study for students with moderate and severe disabilities, his collaborating special education teacher has developed a creative strategy for teaching Chad how he can apply these equations to real-life problems. The lesson is aligned with national math standards as well as with the Kentucky core content for secondary school students.

Student: Chad

Skill   Budgeting money for personal needs.

NCTM Algebra Standard   Represent and analyze mathematical situations and structures using algebraic symbols.

NCTM Problem-Solving Standard   Apply and adapt a variety of appropriate strategies to solve problems.

NCTM Communication Standard   Communicate their mathematical thinking coherently and clearly to peers, teachers, and others.

NCTM Expectation   Use symbolic algebra to represent and explain mathematical relationships.

Kentucky Core Content Skills

MA-H-4.2.1: Students will solve linear equations and linear inequalities.

MA-H-4.2.2: Students will graph the equation of a line.

MA-H.4.2.3: Students will solve systems of linear equations (two equations in two variables), including systems that arise from real-world problems.

Long-Term Instructional Goal   Applies basic operations to handle money when purchasing items, banking, paying bills, and budgeting

Long-Term Instructional Objective   Chad will compute a budget based on his income to meet his personal needs.

Short-Term Instructional Objective   When computing a budget to meet his personal needs, Chad will use a linear equation to determine the amount of money he will need to save each week with 100% accuracy.

Setting   The lesson takes places during a general education algebra class. The class is studying linear algebraic equations of the form $y = a(x) + b$, where a = the slope of the linear equation, and b = the y intercept (the value of y when $x = 0$). The class is learning how everyday problems can be expressed and solved through linear equations.

Materials   Chad will need paper, a pencil, and a calculator.

Procedures   As the class is introduced to linear algebraic equations, Chad is given the following problem from his own life:

> You already have $50 saved in your banking account. Every day that you work, you are able to save $10. How much money will you have saved after 1 day, 2 days, 3 days, 4 days, and 5 days of work?

As shown in Figure 8.5, the teacher helps Chad construct a table that he fills in by using his calculator, indicating how much money he will have saved through the first 5 days that he has worked. Chad then completes the table independently for Days 6–10. Next (as shown in Figure 8.6), Chad and a peer graph how much money he is making with a graph that employs the x-axis (days worked) and the y-axis (amount of money saved). They then connect the points to form a straight line, which Chad uses (extrapolates) to estimate how much money he will have earned on Day 15 and Day 20. This problem is used as the basis for a discussion of the formula that describes this algebraic line:

y (money earned) = $10 per day (x) + $50

where x = the number of days worked, and $50 equals the money that Chad originally had. Chad then uses his calculator to solve the equation for 15 days and 20 days to see if the formula produces the same result that he had estimated through extrapolation on his graph.

Days worked	Money made that day	Total money saved
Day 0 (before he starts work)	0	$50
Day 1 (first day on job)	$10	$60
Day 2	$10	$70
Day 3	$10	$80
Day 4	$10	$90
Day 5	$10	$100
Day 6		
Day 7		
Day 8		
Day 9		
Day 10		
Day 15		
Day 20		

Days worked	Money made that day	Total money saved
Day 0	0	$50
Day 1	$15	$65
Day 2	$15	$80
Day 3	$15	$95
Day 4	$15	$110
Day 5	$15	$125
Day 6		
Day 7		
Day 8		
Day 9		
Day 10		
Day 15		
Day 20		

Figure 8.5.   Tables constructed by Chad during budgeting lesson.

As a variation of the problem, Chad and a peer again complete a table to see how much he would have saved each day if he were making $15 per day. Again, they graph their results and extend the line for 15 and 20 days, as shown in Figure 8.6. This second problem is used as a basis for a discussion of the formula that describes this line:

y (money earned) = $15 per day ($x$) + $50

The slopes of the two lines are compared, and Chad determines with his calculator how much more he would have saved at 10, 15, and 20 days by making $15 per day as compared with $10 per day.

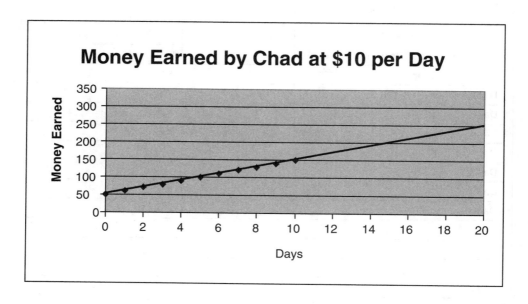

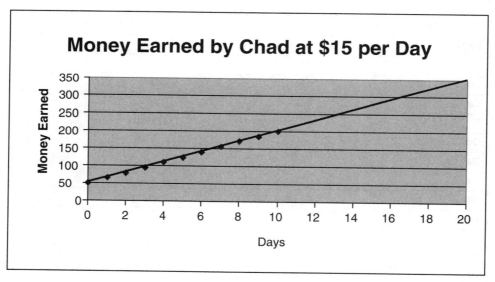

Figure 8.6.   Graphs constructed by Chad during budgeting lesson.

As the peer works with Chad, he uses a system of least prompts strategy in which he offers the least assistance necessary to help Chad perform the correct response. The peer has been taught to first allow Chad to perform a step independently. If he cannot do this, the peer tells him what to do next (i.e., verbal prompt). If he still cannot do this, the peer models the step for him (i.e., model prompt).

Data Collection   Data collection consists of the completed products, including the data tables that Chad has completed, the linear graphs he has drawn, and his solutions to the equation for extended data points (e.g., at 15 and 20 days). In addition to these products, the teacher might ask the peer who is assisting Chad to take data directly on the data chart or template by indicating in each cell the prompt level that Chad required to complete that step (i.e., I, independent; V, verbal prompt; M, model prompt).

Maintenance   Chad uses his calculator throughout a range of in-school and community activities, which increases his opportunities to maintain his calculator skills. In addition, he uses graphs to solve other problems in his algebra class; his teacher always insures that these problems are based on real-life situations that Chad will encounter.

Generalization   Chad is learning to use his calculator to perform a wide range of functional math problems encountered in everyday life. For example, he is using his calculator in home economics class to maintain a monthly budget for the future in which he will have to purchase his own groceries, pay his rent, and account for his other expenses; this is a unit on "life budgeting" that all of the students in the class are learning. He is also using his calculator to maintain his own checkbook, a skill that he indicated at his last IEP meeting that he really wanted to learn. Finally, he uses his calculator in such community-based instructional tasks as shopping for his own groceries, clothing, and other personal items. As did Andrea in the previous example, Chad uses a consecutive subtraction method, consecutively subtracting the cost of each item as it is purchased to ensure that there is sufficient money. For example, one day at a local discount store, Chad started with $30.00 to purchase work clothes. Because his state has a 6% sales tax, he applied a tax formula to subtract the potential amount of tax beforehand ($30.00 × .94) to ensure that he had sufficient money after tax to make his purchases. He then consecutively subtracted the cost of each item to ensure that he had sufficient funds to cover what he had purchased.

SUMMARY

In this chapter, we have described how functional math skills (e.g., time, money, measurement) can be taught to students with moderate and severe disabilities, based on the professional research base and our experiences. In doing this, we demonstrated how functional math skills can be referenced to general education math standards and provided sample lesson plans for students with moderate and severe disabilities across age levels (i.e., elementary, middle, and secondary school). Although this is considered best practice in the field of special education, there are a number of issues worthy of consideration in linking functional math skills to state and national standards:

1. *Episodic versus longitudinal programming.* General education often uses an episodic unit approach (e.g., a course in algebra followed by a course in geometry). It is not unusual for students with moderate and severe disabilities to require a number of years to acquire and generalize a single concept. Thus, an episodic lesson approach may not be appropriate. The challenge is how to work on skills over time with these students in an inclusive setting while their peers are progressing to new topics.

2. *Concrete versus abstract content.* A large number of math concepts require abstract thinking, and a number of students with moderate or severe disabil-

ities do not progress beyond dealing with concrete activities. Thus, creativity is required to translate abstract concepts into applied activities.

3. *Direct versus embedded approach.* Direct instruction is needed for acquisition to occur. This can be in the form of massed trials during a direct instruction lesson or through distributed trials in an embedded approach. Although massed trials result in more rapid acquisition, distributed trials are more likely to result in generalization.

4. *Math versus related-skill focus.* Whereas some students with moderate or severe disabilities acquire functional math skills within general education math classes, others may fail to grasp math concepts but may benefit more from a focus on related skills (e.g., motor, communication, or social skills) within math activities. This has been referred to as a curriculum-overlapping approach (Giangreco et al., 1998).

5. *Postsecondary versus secondary instruction.* Although students with moderate and severe disabilities may remain in the school setting until the age of 21 years, their peers exit secondary school by the age of 18. Thus, there are no standards for students past Grade 12. Therefore, students in the 18–21-year age range should focus on applying functional math skills in direct, real-life opportunities.

CONCLUSION AND FUTURE RESEARCH

For teachers of students with moderate and severe disabilities, there is a delicate balance in addressing functional math skills (i.e., frequently demanded, longitudinally relevant, applied across school, home, and community settings) and ensuring that these students have full access to the general curriculum and to the national math standards and grade-level expectations on which these standards are based. In the previous section, we have presented 10 considerations in addressing this balance. Clearly, we want both functional skill instruction and access to the general mathematics curriculum for our students. Yet, we also realize that the definition of this balance must be individualized for each student, carefully crafted by his or her IEP team to reflect the skills that he or she will need to live a full, productive, and inclusive life in the community. Thus, we offer the following guidelines for teaching functional math skills to students with moderate and severe disabilities in a collaborative setting:

1. Create the IEP by linking functional skills to national or state standards.

2. Collaboratively evaluate the lessons that will be used to teach math concepts or skills.

3. Select systematic instructional procedures to teach functional math skills within the context of the math unit.

4. Determine who will conduct the functional math instruction (e.g., general or special education teacher, paraprofessional, peer).

5. Collect formative and/or summative data on the functional math skill.

6. Identify activities throughout the student's day in which generalization of the functional math skill can be assessed.

7. Collect data during the generalization probes.

8. Analyze data on a regular basis to determine when criterion has been met within the math class and across activities.

We recognize the power of systematic instruction in providing students with moderate and severe disabilities with the critical skills required for community inclusion. Yet, we also recognize that the rich research base that we have described in this chapter has been carried out almost exclusively in self-contained settings and that the majority of students with moderate and severe disabilities continue to be served within separate classes. There is an essential need for researchers, in collaboration with teachers, to take research on systematic instructional procedures "to the next level" to show how teachers can apply such procedures as constant time delay and simultaneous prompting in inclusive settings, in ways that both increase students' functional, age-appropriate skills and simultaneously address both national and state math standards and provide access to the general curriculum. This is not an easy task and will take a great deal of teacher creativity. Without this research, we fear that students with moderate and severe cognitive disabilities may gain physical access to general education mathematics classrooms but not the intensive and structured instructional access that they need to succeed.

We have attempted, through the examples that we have provided in this chapter, to show how teachers might be able to provide this instruction, yet we acknowledge that our examples have pushed the envelope of our research base. We also believe that systematic instructional procedures, provided in the context of the general education classroom, can benefit other students as well. Although there is limited research in this area, heterogeneous instructional groups have been shown to be beneficial for students with and without disabilities (Fickel et al., 1998). Clearly, expanding the research base of systematic instruction on functional math skills into the general education classroom may provide both special and general educators with a key strategy in addressing the national math standards for all students.

REFERENCES

Bottge, B.A. (2001). Building ramps and hovercrafts—and improving math skills. *TEACHING Exceptional Children, 34*(1), 16–23.

Brown, F., McDonnell, J., & Billingsley, F.F. (1997). Responses to Wolery and Schuster. *Journal of Special Education, 31*, 80–83.

Brown, L., Branston, M.B., Hamre-Nietupski, S., Pumpian, I., Certo, N., & Gruenwald, L. (1979). A strategy for developing functional curricular content for severely handicapped adolescents and young adults. *The Journal of Special Education, 13*, 81–90.

Calhoun, M.B., & Fuchs, L.S. (2003). The effects of peer-assisted learning strategies and curriculum-based measurement on the mathematics performance of secondary students with disabilities. *Remedial and Special Education, 24*, 235–245.

Collins, B.C., Branson, T.B., Hall, M., & Rankin, S.W. (2001). Teaching secondary students with moderate disabilities in an inclusive classroom setting. *Journal of Developmental and Physical Disabilities, 13*, 41–59.

Collins, B.C., Hall, M., & Branson, T.A. (1997). Teaching leisure skills to adolescents with moderate disabilities. *Exceptional Children, 63*, 499–512.

Collins, B.C., Hall, M., Branson, T.A., & Holder, M. (1999). Acquisition of related and unrelated factual information delivered by a teacher within an inclusive setting. *Journal of Behavioral Education, 9*, 223–237.

Collins, B.C., Hendricks, T.B., Fetko, K., & Land, L. (2002). Student-2-Student learning in inclusive classrooms. *TEACHING Exceptional Children, 34*(4), 56–61.

Collins, B.C., Stinson, D.M., & Land, L. (1993). A comparison of in vivo and simulation prior to in vivo instruction in teaching generalized safety skills. *Education and Training in Mental Retardation, 28*, 128–142.

Colyer, S.P., & Collins, B.C. (1996). Using natural cues within prompt levels to teach the next dollar strategy to students with disabilities. *Journal of Special Education, 30*, 305–318.

Cromer, K., Schuster, J.W., Collins, B.C., & Grisham-Brown, J. (1998). Teaching information on medical prescriptions using two instructive feedback schedules. *The Journal of Behavioral Education, 8*, 37–61.

Davies, D.K., Stock, S.E., & Wehmeyer, M.L. (2003). Utilization of computer technology to facilitate money management by individuals with mental retardation. *Education and Training in Developmental Disabilities, 38*, 106–112.

Elliott, S.N., & Marquart, A.M. (2004). Extended time as a testing accommodation: Its effects and perceived consequences. *Exceptional Children, 70*, 349–367.

Fickel, K.M., Schuster, J.W., & Collins, B.C. (1998). Teaching different tasks using different stimuli in a heterogeneous small group. *Journal of Behavioral Education, 8*, 219–244.

Ford, A., Black, J., Davern, L., & Schnorr, R. (1989). Time management. In A. Ford, R. Schnorr, L. Meyer, J. Black, & P. Dempsey (Eds.), *The Syracuse community-referenced curriculum guide for students with moderate and severe disabilities* (pp. 149–170). Baltimore: Paul H. Brookes Publishing Co.

Ford, A., Davern, L., & Schnorr, R., Black, J., & Kaiser, K. (1989). Money handling. In A. Ford, R. Schnorr, L. Meyer, J. Black, & P. Dempsey (Eds.), *The Syracuse community-referenced curriculum guide for students with moderate and severe disabilities* (pp. 117–148). Baltimore: Paul H. Brookes Publishing Co.

Ford, A., Schnorr, R., Meyer, L., Davern, L., Black, J., & Dempsey, P. (1989). *The Syracuse community-referenced curriculum guide for students with moderate and severe disabilities*. Baltimore: Paul H. Brookes Publishing Co.

Giangreco, M.F., Cloninger, C.J., & Iverson, V.S. (1998). *Choosing Options and Accommodations for Children (COACH): A guide to planning inclusive education* (2nd ed.). Baltimore: Paul H. Brookes Publishing Co.

Hess, J.M. (2004). *A comparison of two models of web-based professional development in the implementation of an online contextualized math environment in general education inclusive classrooms*. Unpublished doctoral dissertation, University of Kentucky, Lexington.

Horn, C. (2002). *A study on the use of response cards to teach telling time to students with moderate to severe disabilities*. Unpublished master's thesis, University of Kentucky, Lexington.

Individuals with Disabilities Education Act Amendments of 1997, PL 105-17, 20 U.S.C. §§ 1400 et seq.

Jones, K. (2004). *Presenting chained and discrete tasks as non-target information (NTI) when teaching discrete academic skills through small group instruction*. Unpublished master's thesis, University of Kentucky, Lexington.

Kleinert, H.L., Guiltinan, S., & Sims, L. (1988). Teaching students with moderate and severe handicaps to select lower-priced items in shopping activities. *TEACHING Exceptional Children, 20*(3), 18–21.

Kleinert, H., & Kearns, J. (2004). Alternate assessments. In F. Orelove, D. Sobsey, & R. Silberman (Eds.), *Educating children with multiple disabilities: A collaborative approach* (4th ed., pp. 115–149). Baltimore: Paul H. Brookes Publishing Co.

Lambert, N., Winmiller, M., Taninger, D., & Cole, L. (1981). *American Association on Mental Deficiency adaptive behavior scales*. Monterey, CA: CTB/McGraw-Hill.

Mar, H.H., & Sall, N. (1999). Profiles of the expressive communication skills of children and adolescents with severe cognitive disabilities. *Education and Training in Mental Retardation and Developmental Disabilities, 34*, 77–89.

Miracle, S.A., Collins, B.C., Schuster, J.W., & Grisham-Brown, J. (2001). Peer versus teacher delivered instruction: Effects on acquisition and maintenance. *Education and Training in Mental Retardation and Developmental Disabilities, 36*, 375–385.

Morse, T.E., & Schuster, J.W. (2000). Teaching elementary students with moderate intellectual disabilities how to shop for groceries. *Exceptional Children, 66,* 273–288.

National Council of Teachers of Mathematics. (n.d.). *Overview of principles and standards for school mathematics.* Retrieved June 8, 2004, from http://www.ntcm.org/standards/principles.htm

Neel, R.S., & Billingsley, F.F. (1989). *Impact: A functional curriculum handbook for students with moderate to severe disabilities.* Baltimore: Paul H. Brookes Publishing Co.

Parette, H.P., & Brotherson, M.J. (1996). Family participation in assistive technology assessment for young children with mental retardation and developmental disabilities. *Education and Training in Mental Retardation and Developmental Disabilities, 31,* 29–43.

Sandknop, P.A., Schuster, J.W., Wolery, M., & Cross, D.P. (1992). The use of an adaptive device to teach students with moderate mental retardation to select lower priced grocery items. *Education and Training in Mental Retardation, 27,* 219–229.

Seward, J. (2000). *Comparison of simultaneous prompting and constant time delay in teaching chained tasks.* Unpublished master's thesis, University of Kentucky, Lexington.

Siegel-Causey, E., McMorris, C., McGowan, S., & Sands-Buss, S. (1998). In junior high, you take earth science: Including a student with severe disabilities into an academic class. *TEACHING Exceptional Children, 31*(1), 66–72.

Slaton, D.B., Schuster, J., Collins, B., & Carnine, D. (1994). A functional approach to academics instruction. In E.C. Cipani & F. Spooner (Eds.), *Curricular and instructional approaches for persons with severe disabilities* (pp. 322–346). Boston: Allyn & Bacon.

Smith, A. (1998*). The effect of constant time delay and instructive feedback when teaching check writing skills to students with mild to moderate disabilities.* Unpublished master's thesis, University of Kentucky, Lexington.

Spear, A. (2002). *A comparison of simultaneous prompting presented by a teacher versus a computer to teach coin values to students with mild to moderate disabilities.* Unpublished master's thesis, University of Kentucky, Lexington.

Steere, D.E., & Cavaiuolo, D. (2002). Connecting outcomes, goals, and objectives in transition planning. *TEACHING Exceptional Children, 34*(6), 54–58.

Sparrow, S.S., Balla, D.A., & Cicchetti, D.V. (1984). *Vineland Adaptive Behavior Scales.* Circle Pines, MN: American Guidance Service.

Study: Special education helps boost math scores. (2003, January). *Special Education Report.*

Test, D.W., Howell, A., Burkhart, K., & Beroth, T. (1993). The one-more-than technique as a strategy for counting money for individuals with moderate mental retardation. *Education and Training in Mental Retardation, 28,* 232–241.

Valletutti, P.J., Bender, M., & Sims-Tucker, B. (1996). *A functional curriculum for teaching students with disabilities: Functional academics.* Austin, TX: PRO-ED.

Wehmeyer, M., & Palmer, S. (2003). Adult outcomes for students with cognitive disabilities three years after high school: The impact of self-determination. *Education and Training in Developmental Disabilities, 38,* 131–144.

Wehmeyer, M., & Schwartz, M. (1998). The relationship between self-determination and quality of life for adults with mental retardation. *Education and Training in Mental Retardation and Developmental Disabilities, 33,* 3–12.

Williams, D.M., & Collins, B.C. (1994). Teaching multiplication facts to students with learning disabilities: Teacher-selected versus student-selected materials prompts within the delay procedure. *Journal of Learning Disabilities, 27,* 589–597.

Wolery, M., Ault, M.J., & Doyle, P.M. (1992). *Teaching students with moderate to severe disabilities: Use of response prompting strategies.* New York: Longman.

Wolery, M., & Schuster, J.W. (1997). Instructional methods with students who have significant disabilities. *Journal of Special Education, 31,* 61–79.

Chapter 9

Science Standards and Functional Skills

Finding the Links

Fred Spooner, Warren Di Biase,
and Ginevra Courtade-Little

T he years following the launching of Sputnik in 1957 were known as the golden age of science education reform. In many respects, this event woke a sleeping giant. Realizing it was behind in science, the United States made reform in science education a top priority. To help achieve this goal, the National Science Foundation (NSF) funded numerous curriculum projects, such as the so-called alphabet soup textbook series for high school science and kits for the elementary science classroom. The goal of this reform movement was to improve students' achievement in science. Unfortunately, the full potential of this movement was never realized.

The report titled *A Nation at Risk* (National Commission on Excellence in Education, 1983) issued a clarion call for reform in science education.

> Our Nation is at risk. Our once unchallenged preeminence in commerce, industry, science, and technological innovation is being overtaken by competitors throughout the world. . . . If an unfriendly power had attempted to impose on America the mediocre educational performance that exists today, we might well have viewed it as an act of war. As it stands, we have allowed this to happen to ourselves. We have even squandered the gains in achievement made in the wake of the Sputnik challenge. (¶ 2 and 3)

Furthermore, the report asserts that

> All, regardless of race or class or economic status, are entitled to a fair chance and to the tools for developing their individual powers of mind and spirit to the utmost. This promise means that all children by virtue of their own efforts, competently guided, can hope to attain the mature and informed judgment needed to secure gainful employment, and to manage their own lives, thereby serving not only their own interests but also the progress of society itself. (¶1)

In response to *A Nation at Risk* (National Commission on Excellence in Education, 1983), the American Association for the Advancement of Science (AAAS) began an initiative titled *Project 2061: Science for All Americans* (SFAA) in 1985—the year Halley's comet was last visible from the Earth. The project calls for a scientifically literate society by the year 2061, the year Halley's comet once again passes near the Earth. According to SFAA,

> [E]ducation has no higher purpose than preparing people to lead personally fulfill-ing and responsible lives. Science education should help students to develop under-standings and habits of mind they need to become passionate human beings and to think for themselves and to face life head on. (p. xiii)

Although not specifically delineated in the respective reports, it is important to note that *A Nation at Risk* used the inclusive term *all* when referring to being educated, and Project 2061 used the slogan "science education for *all*."

The National Science Education Standards (NSES), published by the Na-tional Research Council (NRC) in 1996, is the living document underpinning the current reform in science education. The NSES affirms that the nation has estab-lished a goal that all students should achieve scientific literacy. In defining *all students*, the NSES relays that the "Standards apply to all students, regardless of age, gender, cultural or ethnic background, disabilities, aspirations, or interest and motivation in science" (NRC, 1996, p. 2). In addition, the NSES goes on to re-port that different students will achieve understanding in different ways and that different students will achieve different degrees of depth and breadth of under-standing depending on their interest, ability, and context.

Science learning is contingent on two factors—the learner's prior knowl-edge and the meaning or understanding the learner constructs. A learner's prior knowledge is influenced by previous learning experiences, whereas the meaning constructed is subject to a number of factors including, but not limited to, the developmental appropriateness of the experience and the developmental abili-ties of the learner. As a result, different students achieve both different levels of understanding and different degrees of depth and breadth of understanding. In other words, all students can learn given the developmental appropriateness of the learning experience. As such, learners with developmental disabilities are included in the NSES discussion of *all students*.

Both SFAA and the NSES call for the development of individuals who are scientifically literate. In defining scientific literacy, the NSES lists the following criteria:

- Competence in scientific inquiry

- Sense of wonder about the natural world

- Understandings of humans, other constituent parts of the universe, and their interactions and transformations

- Facility for synthesizing and applying the big ideas of science for the purpose of problem-solving and evidence-based decision making

- A functioning perspective on the interrelations between and among the sci-entific endeavor, society, and technology

The NSES calls for the science curriculum to be composed of a number of strands, which include the nature of science, scientific inquiry, science knowledge, sci-ence technology and society (STS), and the history of science. The nature of sci-ence invites learners to develop an understanding of the nature of science which encompasses the understanding and the practice of scientific inquiry. Science knowledge includes both an understanding of the content, concepts, and relationships in and among the various science disciplines and the ability to apply skills and knowledge to daily life experiences. The STS strand requires an understanding of science and technology in the context of social and personal perspectives. In learning the history of science, students develop an understanding that science is a human endeavor. In addition, they realize the contributions of diverse cultures, past and present scientists, and society in general.

Inquiry is a set of interrelated processes by which scientists and students pose questions about the natural world and investigate phenomena. In doing so, students acquire knowledge and develop a rich understanding of concepts, principles, models, and theories. The process of inquiry is not a uniform series of predetermined steps. Instead, students follow innumerable paths in seeking new knowledge about natural and human-made phenomena. Nevertheless, certain patterns in the methods of successful scientists are evident in the students during inquiry; for example, in their capacity to recognize problems, ask relevant questions, formulate working hypotheses, figure out the best way to observe phenomena, handle data with accuracy, reach tentative conclusions consistent with what is known, and express themselves clearly about the significance of findings.

The process of inquiry promotes development of scientific attitudes as well as a scientific habit of mind. Through inquiry, learners construct their own understanding about the natural and designed world. In addition, the process of inquiry will provide for the development of process skills such as observing, inferring, communicating, experimenting, questioning, analyzing, predicting, classifying, and concluding. Development of the process skills not only helps learners construct knowledge but also assists them in the development of important management and work skills.

Inquiry is the instructional strategy advocated by the NSES. Inquiry learning experiences are generally structured in a learning cycle format. The learning cycle is composed of a set of interrelated phases including preassessment, exploration, concept development, concept application, and assessment. Much is written in the literature about inquiry, the learning cycle, and teaching science to gifted, regular education, and special needs learners. On the one hand, Colburn (2000), Staver (1998), and Treagust (1996) have described inquiry and science learning for typically developing learners, and Doran and Sentman (1994) and Scruggs and Mastropieri (1994) have illustrated the process of inquiry in special education. On the other hand, there is a significant lack of research in the area of teaching science to learners with significant cognitive disabilities. In preparing to develop this chapter, we conducted a comprehensive review of the research on teaching science to this population and found only one study in the last 28 years (Utley et al., 2001). Briefly, Utley et al. (2001) trained five students with developmental disabilities on health and safety facts. Given the lack of research in teaching science to students with developmental disabilities, this chapter introduces a foundation for science by considering potential links between the research on functional skills and science concepts. The fact that our review uncovered only one study since 1975 is not totally shocking in that the focus for imparting content to students with significant disabilities across the course of the existence of the subdiscipline has been on teaching functional skills (Brown et al., 1979; Brown, Nietupski, & Hamre-Nietupski, 1976).

APPLICATIONS OF TEACHING SCIENCE TO STUDENTS WITH SIGNIFICANT COGNITIVE DISABILITIES

Based on information from The National Research Council (1996), there are content standards that have been developed in the area of science. Generally speaking, these content standards cover seven overarching areas: 1) science as inquiry, 2) physical science, 3) life science, 4) earth and space science, 5) science and technology, 6) science in personal and social perspectives, and 7) history and nature of science. Given the lack of research illustrating how to teach science to students with significant cognitive disabilities, an alternative is to consider what functional skills have been taught that may contain science concepts. The pitfall of trying to find science concepts in the research on functional skills is that the constructs of science may be lost or distorted. For example, professionals, paraprofessionals, teachers, and parents in the area of severe disabilities have been working on how to teach basic self-care skills to students and adults with significant cognitive disabilities at least since the 1960s (e.g., Bensberg, 1965; Bensberg, Colwell, & Cassel, 1965; Minge & Ball, 1967). Few would have considered these skills science. To try to find science concepts in skills such as handwashing and toothbrushing detracts from the rich science content available in general education and may lead to teaching these important personal skills in ways that do not respect the students' privacy. In contrast, some functional skills are more closely linked to general education science content (e.g., health and safety). To consider whether functional activities provide a good context for science content, the planning team may consider two criteria: 1) would general education teachers impart this content, and 2) would a content specialist (e.g., science teacher) concur that the science construct is clearly presented (i.e., Is it really science?). Researchers in the area of mental retardation and severe disabilities have also done work in the area of safety since the mid-1980s (e.g., Agran, 1997, 2004; Agran, Marchand-Martella, & Martella, 1994; Bannerman, Sheldon, & Sherman, 1991; Collins, Wolery, & Gast, 1992; Gast, Wellons, & Collins, 1994; Katz & Singh, 1986; Spooner, 1994; Spooner, Stem, & Test, 1989). For example, from the area of science in personal and social perspectives (Content Standard F), students in kindergarten should have a variety of experiences that provide initial understandings for personal care and that enable them to take responsibility for their own health. Student understandings should include following safety rules for all their school experiences as well as at home: preventing abuse and neglect, avoiding injury, and when and how to say "no."

Although little research exists on how to teach science to this population, besides what may be inferred from research on functional skills, what does exist are state resources on assessing science. In our collective work in the area of alternate assessment (e.g., Browder et al., 2004; Browder, Spooner, Ahlgrim-Delzell, et al., 2003; Browder, Spooner, Algozzine, et al., 2003), and specifically in the area of alignment of alternate assessments and state content standards (Browder et al., 2004), we discovered that, in most cases, states have created what are called *extended standards* or *performance indicators* (PIs) that allow a link to be made from these overarching content standards to specific components in the state's alternate assessments for students with significant cognitive disabilities. For purposes of this discussion, a PI is defined as a specific skill used to document progress toward meeting a state content standard. For example, this might be a state standard: *Students will develop, demonstrate, and practice positive health behaviors, skills, and choice making.* An extension of that state standard to an alternative assessment for a student with a significant cognitive disability, a PI, might be performing a task such as choosing snacks based on their nutritional value. When PIs in the area of science were analyzed as to the degree to which they are linked to the seven categories of science (e.g., science as inquiry, science and technology, and science in personal and social perspectives), it was found that of the 50 states, 29 (58%) had state standards for science, and of those 29 states, 23 states had PIs (Spooner & Browder, 2005). These facts suggest that states are well on their way to responding to the mandates of science content in No Child Left Behind (NCLB) Act of 2001 (PL 107-110) for students with significant cognitive disabilities. Science as indicated by NCLB is to be implemented in 2006 and evaluated in 2007.

In general, data-based research on teaching science to students with significant cognitive disabilities has been extremely limited, with the exception of Category 6, science in personal and social perspectives, and other categories such as Content Standard D, earth and space sciences, which includes weather. For example, Browder and Shear (1996) taught students with moderate mental retardation and severe behavior disorders to learn sight words related to the daily newspaper weather report. I am sure that many of us have either taught or observed a morning lesson on weather, involving Velcro-backed images (i.e., type of day, sunny or rainy; temperature, hot or cold) to be taken from their storage compartment and strategically placed on a super-sized calendar indicating type of day and temperature. Based on a component of personal care and safety items (e.g., toilet training, first aid) in Content Standard F, the subfield of severe disabilities has an extensive number of studies across almost 30 years to demonstrate that students with significant cognitive disabilities can master these skills.

COMPONENTS OF SCIENCE AND APPLICATIONS FOR STUDENTS WITH SIGNIFICANT COGNITIVE DISABILITIES

Although both functional skills research and the content of current alternate assessments provide some clues to teaching science, the most important resources will be the general education curriculum. By beginning with the general curriculum, the planning team can address the content and activities that will be addressed in the students' current assigned grade level. A good beginning point would be the state standards for science and any grade-level expectations for the students' assigned grade. The science textbook and teachers' guide provide an additional resource for planning science instruction. To help teams begin thinking about planning science instruction for this population, the following are categories typically found in science curriculum. Examples are provided in Table 9.1 for how each science concept might be applied to this population.

Content Standard A: Science as Inquiry

Through this standard, students should learn abilities necessary to do scientific inquiry. Those abilities include asking questions about objects, organisms, and events in the environment; planning and conducting simple investigations; employing simple equipment and tools to gather data and extend the senses; using data to construct a reasonable explanation; and communicating investigations and explanations.

Table 9.1.   Examples of activities for science content standards for students with significant disabilities

Content standards	Elementary examples	Middle school examples	High school examples
Science as inquiry	Bryanna will point to similarities and differences of people and animals.	Nina will record observations during an experiment using AAC.	Alex will use a spreadsheet program to display results from class science experiments.
Physical science	Eddie will choose the correct tool to measure his weight.	Wendy will observe and record information about phase changes (ice melting) using an augmentative communication device.	Rick will conduct an experiment using bleach and cloth to determine what may happen during incorrect laundering of clothing.
Life science	Leslie will match picture symbols to plants or animals to indicate what they need to survive (air, water, sun, food).	Seth will identify plants that are poisonous to eat or touch.	Karen will sort foods by their nutrient level (carbohydrates, fats, proteins) and develop meals that contain a balanced diet.
Earth and space Science	Jason will sort rocks according to their physical characteristics (e.g., size, shape, texture).	Brad will relate pictures of objects to the words hot and cold (e.g., lit stove, ice, steam).	Jenny will create a picture symbol safety brochure for inclement weather (e.g., hurricanes, tornadoes).
Science and technology	Brian will match simple tools to their functions (e.g., scissors, rulers, watches, straws).	Sonja will match cause-and-effect pictures of simple machines (e.g., can opener, pencil sharpener).	Using a computer program, Joyce will develop a map of her school and home.
Science in personal and social perspectives	Brett will recycle aluminum cans and newspapers.	Robin will identify common illnesses and ways to keep herself healthy (e.g., washing hands, washing food, cooking food thoroughly).	Mike will identify methods to stop pollution (no littering, no dumping).
History and nature of science	Laura will identify jobs in science.	Don will scan the newspaper for articles relating to current science events (identifying keywords such as *science*, *technology*).	Diane will sample science jobs and record her experiences in a picture journal.

Investigations conducted with students with significant disabilities that fall into this standard generally reflect the ability to employ simple equipment and tools to gather data and extend the senses. This area closely aligns with math; for example, using a watch to measure time (see Chapter 7).

Content Standard B: Physical Science

While studying this standard, students should develop an understanding of properties and objects. Three major components are covered:

1. Properties of objects and materials and using tools to measure the properties

    Describing objects by the properties from which they are made

    Materials existing in different states (i.e., solid, liquid, gas)

2. Position and motion of objects

    Position can be described relative to other objects

    Motion can be described by tracing and measuring position over time

    Sound is produced by vibrating objects

3. Light, heat, electricity, and magnetism

    Light travels in a straight line and can be reflected

    Heat can be produced in different ways

    Electricity can produce light, heat, and sound

    Magnets attract and repel

Content Standard C: Life Science

Concepts that students will learn about through this standard include

1. The characteristics of organisms

    Animals and plants need air, water, food, light

    Plants and animals have different structures for different purposes

    Organisms have senses that help them detect internal and external changes

2. Life cycles of organisms

    Plants and animals have life cycles

    Plants and animals closely resemble their parents

    Characteristics can be inherited or result from interactions with the environment

3. Organisms and their environments

    Animals depend on plants

    Organisms can cause changes in the environment

    Humans depend on natural and constructed environments

Content Standard D: Earth and Space Science

In the area of earth and space science, students study

1. Properties of earth materials

    Rocks, soil, water, gases

    Fossils provide evidence of the nature and environment from that time

2. Objects in the sky

    Sun, moon, stars, clouds

    Objects in the sky have properties and movements that can be observed

3. Changes in the earth and sky

    The surface of the earth changes

    Weather changes

    Objects in the sky have patterns of movement

One research study was found that can be linked with the earth and space science content standard which includes weather. Browder and Shear (1996) taught three students with moderate disabilities and severe behavior disorders to read 10 new weather words using an interspersal drill sequence. The students also made progress reading a daily weather report from the newspaper.

Content Standard E: Science and Technology

Through the science and technology standard, students should discover how technological objects and systems work, including discovery of

1. Abilities of technological design

    Identifying a problem

    Proposing a solution

    Implementing a proposed solution

    Evaluating a product or design

    Communicating a problem, design, and solution

2. Understanding about science and technology

    Science answers questions and explains the world

    People have had problems and invented tools and techniques to solve
      problems

    Tools help scientists to make better observations

3. Ability to distinguish between natural and human-made objects

    Some objects occur in nature, others are designed by humans

    This is another area of science in which investigators in the area of severe disabilities have done some work. One research-based study was found that dealt with teaching persons with significant disabilities how to use tools. Ivancic and Schepis (1995) taught 25 adults with mental disabilities ranging from moderate to profound to locate and use keys. The participants were first taught to locate keys to their lockers using a method that included praise, reinforcement, and the use of key-carrying devices. On the average, the ability of the participants to locate their keys increased by 59% from baseline to treatment. The same participants were then taught to use their keys to obtain items from their lockers using a task analysis and least-to-most prompt sequence. Approximately 80% of the participants learned to use the keys during the activity period; however, maintenance trials were necessary for almost 65% of the participants at some time during the study. Although this study did not teach a science concept per se, this activity could be used to introduce concepts such as defining technology (technology includes artifacts and hardware) or identifying human needs that are subject to technological solutions (keeping your home or belongings safe using locks and keys).

Another type of study that might be used to introduce science and technology constructs is a study that introduces assistive technology. Examples of teaching people with severe disabilities to use assistive technology can be found in a literature review completed by Lancioni, O'Reilly, and Basili (2001). This review addresses studies which used microswitches and speech output systems with people with severe/profound intellectual disabilities or multiple disabilities. Many of the participants involved in the studies were children or young adults. Findings for the increased use of microswitches and speech output systems were generally positive, although some failures occurred. To embed science content when introducing an assistive technology device, the teacher might have the student evaluate the usability of different devices during different science experiments.

Content Standard F: Science in Personal and Social Perspectives

Students studying in this content area should develop understanding of the following:

1. Personal health

    Safety, avoiding injury

    Dental hygiene

    Exercise, nutrition

    Licit and illicit drug use

2. Characteristics and changes in population

    Size of human population can increase and decrease

3. Types of resources

    Some resources are basic materials, some are produced from basic resources

    Supply of many resources is limited

4. Changes in the environment

    Changes can be natural or influenced by humans

    Some changes are good, some are bad (pollution)

    Some changes occur rapidly, some slowly

5. Science and technology in local challenges

    People continue to invent new ways of doing things

    Science and technology have improved lives

    All benefits are not available to all people

As noted, most of the researched-based studies that fall under the broad heading of science relate to the science in personal and social perspectives content standard. A sampling of the vast amount of research has been shared in the areas of first aid, safety, and exercise.

First Aid   Spooner et al. (1989) used a social modeling procedure (instructions, modeling, feedback, rehearsal, and social reinforcement) to teach three students with moderate disabilities first aid/safety skills. The four skills taught were communicating an emergency, taking care of a minor injury, applying a plastic bandage, and applying first aid for choking. All skills were acquired rapidly by the students and maintained during follow-up probes.

Gast and Winterling (1992) measured the ability of four high school students to learn to apply first aid to three simple injuries (a minor cut, a burn, and an insect bite). The students were taught each skill using a backward chaining procedure with a treatment package consisting of a lecture and a constant time-delay procedure. All students successfully learned to apply first aid for the three types of injuries.

Marchand-Martella and Martella (1992) evaluated the effects of two training programs used to teach treatment of abrasions to four students with disabilities (one with moderate mental retardation). They used a social modeling procedure, similar to that of Spooner et al. (1989), in addition to a partial sequential withdraw phase during which the model and practice components were withdrawn. The participants practiced on puppets or themselves. Participants in both programs learned to treat abrasions. First aid training can provide a functional context for introducing science concepts such as the respiratory system (CPR), how bones and muscles are connected and the movement of the body (broken bones and torn muscles), and how drugs and alcohol affect the body (drug overdoses).

Safety   Utley and colleagues (2001) used a classwide peer-tutoring method (including error correction, immediate feedback, and team competition) to teach five elementary-level students with developmental disabilities safety and health education facts (i.e., facts about body parts and their functions, poisons, drugs and their effects, and dangerous situations) via a BAB single-subject design. The tutors used flash cards with pictures of the science curriculum on one side and correct answers to the questions on the other side. All students improved their knowledge of the safety and health skills to 85% or higher on weekly tests.

Collins and Griffen (1996) taught four elementary school students with moderate disabilities to read key words from product warning labels. The study used a time-delay procedure and actual products whose labels contained the words. Students learned to read all target words and to provide appropriate motor responses when they saw the words (i.e., give the product to the teacher, and put the product on a storage shelf).

Watson, Bain, and Houghton (1992) taught seven elementary-age students with moderate to severe mental retardation to use appropriate strategies to respond to inappropriate invitations from strangers. The students were taught three target behaviors: *No, Go,* and *Tell.* A direct instruction method using guided discussion, modeling, and role play was used to teach the students to define and identify a stranger, the dangers of strangers, and target behaviors. Six of the seven students mastered the self-protective behavior sequence.

Exercise   Zhang, Gast, Horvat, and Datillo (1995) taught four high school students with severe to profound intellectual disabilities to perform three sports skills. A constant time-delay procedure was used to teach one-step bowling, overhand throwing, and short-distance putting. All of the students learned each age-appropriate skill and continued to perform the skills with about 85% accuracy approximately 3 months after the instruction was terminated. To embed science content in exercise instruction, students could learn to identify the parts of the body (specifically muscles) they are working on and how each muscle is connected to other muscles and bones. Students could also learn to identify whether their muscles are expanding or contracting with the movements they are making during exercise. Students could also learn about the overextension of muscles and bones and what types of exercise could cause problems for the body (too much weight, using equipment the wrong way).

Content Standard G: History and Nature of Science

The final content standard teaches students that science is a human endeavor. Through activities for this standard, students will learn: 1) science and technology have been practiced for a long time; 2) contributions to science and technology have been made by many men and women; 3) science will never be finished; and 4) many people choose science as a career.

A traditional way to teach science, particularly in upper elementary and secondary science classrooms, is the textbook approach (Mastropieri & Scruggs, 1994). Although textbooks can be good resources for teachers, the literacy level needed by the students to read the text is often quite high. So, for teachers of students with significant disabilities, teaching science using textbooks may not be appropriate unless the texts are made accessible through principles of universal design. For example, digital textbooks that involve the use of picture symbols and modified text could be used to teach the same science concepts to students with disabilities. A fifth-grade science textbook teaches students about factors that affect motion (e.g., force, friction, inertia, momentum). A universally designed textbook could provide movie clips that provide examples of each of these factors. The examples would not only benefit the students with significant disabilities, but would be useful for all students in the class.

A more appropriate method for teaching science to students with significant disabilities may be a hands-on approach that emphasizes the use of process/inquiry skills as opposed to accumulation of facts and theories (Polloway, Patton, & Serna, 2001). Salend (1998) made recommendations for teaching using a hands-on approach. Two of his guidelines may work well for students with significant disabilities. The first is to organize instruction around *big ideas.* Big ideas are concepts that help students see the connection between material that they are learning and their lives. Interdisciplinary themes, such as current events, may be a way to develop big ideas.

A second recommendation from Salend (1998) is to use real-life situations to teach science. For example, teaching a student simple circuitry using a CD player or toy he or she likes may be more effective than showing a circuit that is not connected to an object the student recognizes.

When teaching science to students with significant disabilities, it is important to maintain functionality for the student and not just teach science to teach it. Consider the big ideas or concepts of science and how to teach students about those concepts with functional applications for real-life situations. The following is an example of a student with a significant disability, Ieshia, and ideas of a physical science curriculum that could be made functional for her.

Ieshia is an elementary school student with severe mental retardation. Ieshia is able to walk and has a good grasp, but she cannot write. She has limited verbal skills and communicates mostly through gestures and a small array of picture symbols. Ieshia's teacher is designing a long-range adapted science curriculum for Ieshia. The teacher is currently planning the physical science section.

IDEAS FOR THE CURRICULUM

Elementary School

Under the big idea of *time:*

1. Ieshia will discriminate between night and day. She will categorize activities in her life that take place during the day (i.e., school) and at night (i.e., sleeping).

2. Ieshia will learn to look on a weather calendar in the newspaper to determine the next day's weather.

Middle School

Under the big idea of *hygiene/appearance:*

1. Ieshia will learn to read the temperature indoors and outside and choose clothes that are appropriate to wear for the temperature in either location.

High School

Under the big idea of *current events:*

1. Ieshia will identify the characteristics of worldwide weather occurrences (e.g., tornadoes, tsunamis, blizzards).

2. Ieshia will learn proper safety procedures for inclement weather in her area of the country (e.g., hurricanes, tornadoes).

SUMMARY

Science as a content area to be imparted to school-age children has been an important academic content area in the United States since 1957, the year in which Sputnik was launched. Learning science content, in the typical sense, relies on two factors: 1) the learner's prior knowledge and 2) the meaning and understanding of learner constructs. The NSES (National Professional Board, 1996) were predicated on the foundation that all students could achieve scientific literacy. For the most part, students with disabilities, at all levels, were not included in the grand scheme of scientific literacy. It was not until the mid-1990s that investigators and authors in the area of special education, outside the area of gifted and talented students, began to address how to teach science to students with milder disabilities (e.g., Colburn, 2000; Scruggs & Mastropieri, 1994; Staver, 1998; Treagust, 1996). The passage of NCLB in 2001 changed the landscape; science is now one of the content areas, along with reading and math, that is to be taught to *all* students, including those with significant cognitive disabilities, and annual progress must be evaluated.

The work of one component of our research group investigating access to the general curriculum suggests that only one study (e.g., Utley et al., 2001) was discovered in a comprehensive literature review for teaching science tasks to students with significant cognitive disabilities spanning the time period from 1975 to 2003. On the other hand, a closer examination of science content standards (e.g., science and inquiry, earth and space science, science in personal and social perspectives) suggests that some of these content areas (e.g., science in personal and social perspectives, earth and space science) have indeed been investigated and students with significant cognitive disabilities have been participants in those studies (e.g., first aid training and safety [Bannerman et al., 1991; Spooner et al., 1989]; weather words [Browder & Shear, 1996]). However, investigators in the area of severe disabilities have not been classifying these studies as science. The implementation of NCLB has created, among other things, an intersection between science content and academic instruction for students with significant cognitive disabilities.

Currently, it appears that states are well on the way toward imparting science content to students with significant cognitive disabilities. Many states have already established state science standards (58%), and 46% have delineated performance indicators (PIs), the link between the overarching content standards and the respective alternate assessment for students with significant cognitive disabilities (Spooner & Browder, 2005). Science content is to be implemented in 2006 and evaluated in 2007.

When each of the seven content standards for science is examined, it would appear that there have been investigators who have had an interest in examining the degree to which students with significant cognitive disabilities can acquire these skills in many of these areas (e.g., science as inquiry, earth and space science, science and technology). For the record, however, we have not been calling these investigations *science*. Now with the advent and continuation of NCLB, it will be prudent for us to continue our work and begin to classify these data-based investigations as science. From a practical perspective, it will be important for administrators and teachers in general and special education, including those who are responsible for and work with students with significant cognitive disabilities, to be aware of the seven content standards for science. We are all now in a mode and operating under a set of contingencies (i.e., NCLB) in which we must teach skills through PIs that link to the science curriculum. Awareness of the categories of science will help us think outside of current practices. It may not change what we do, but it will certainly help us think about what we do in a larger context—that of accessing the general curriculum.

REFERENCES

Agran, M. (1997). Health and safety. In P. Wehman & J. Kregel (Eds.), *Functional curriculum for elementary, middle, and secondary age students with special needs* (pp. 283–308). Austin, TX: PRO-ED.

Agran, M. (2004). Health and safety. In P. Wehman & J. Kregel (Eds.), *Functional curriculum for elementary, middle, and secondary age students with special needs* (2nd ed., pp. 357–383). Austin, TX: PRO-ED.

Agran, M., Marchand-Martella, N.E., & Martella, R.C. (Eds.). (1994). *Promoting health and safety skills for independent living.* Baltimore: Paul H. Brookes Publishing Co.

American Association for the Advancement of Science. (1990). *Project 2061: Science for all Americans.* New York: Oxford University Press.

Bannerman, D.J., Sheldon, J.B., & Sherman, J.A. (1991). Teaching adults with severe and profound retardation to exit their home upon hearing the fire alarm. *Journal of Applied Behavior Analysis, 24,* 571–578.

Bensberg, J.G. (1965). *Teaching the mentally retarded: A handbook for ward personnel.* Atlanta, GA: Southern Regional Education Board.

Bensberg, J.G., Colwell, B. S., & Cassel, R.H. (1965). Teaching the profoundly retarded self-help activities by behavior shaping techniques. *American Journal of Mental Deficiency, 69,* 574–579.

Browder, D.M., Flowers, C., Ahlgrim-Delzell, L., Karvonen, M., Spooner, F., & Algozzine, R. (2004). The alignment of alternate assessment performance indicators to academic and functional curricula. *Journal of Special Education, 37,* 211–223.

Browder, D.M., & Shear, S.M. (1996). Interspersal of known items in a treatment package to teach sight words to students with behavior disorder. *Journal of Special Education, 29,* 400–413.

Browder, D.M., Spooner, F., Ahlgrim-Delzell, L., Flowers, C., Karvonen, M., & Algozzine, R. (2003). A content analysis of the curricular philosophies reflected in states' alternate assessment performance indicators. *Research and Practice for Persons with Severe Disabilities, 28,* 165–181.

Browder, D.M., Spooner, F., Algozzine, B., Ahlgrim-Delzell, L., Flowers, C., & Karvonen, M. (2003). What we know and need to know about alternate assessment. *Exceptional Children, 70,* 45–62.

Brown, L., Bronston, M.B., Hamre-Nietupski, S., Pumpian, I., Certo, N., & Gruenewald, L. (1979). A strategy for developing chronological-age-appropriate and functional curricular content for severely handicapped adolescents and young children. *Journal of Special Education, 13,* 81–90.

Brown, L., Nietupski, J., & Hamre-Nietupski, S. (1976). Criterion of ultimate functioning. In M.A. Thomas (Ed.), *Hey, don't forget about me! Education's investment in the severely, profoundly, and multiply handicapped* (pp. 2–15). Reston, VA: Council for Exceptional Children.

Colburn, A. (2000). Constructivism: Science education's "grand unifying theory." *Clearing House, 74,* 9–12.

Collins, B.C., & Griffen, A.K. (1996). Teaching students with moderate disabilities to make safe responses to product warning labels. *Education & Treatment of Children, 1,* 30–45.

Collins, B.C., Wolery, M., & Gast, D.L. (1992). A national survey of safety concerns for students with special needs. *Journal of Developmental and Physical Disabilities, 4,* 263–276.

Doran, R.L., & Sentman, J.R. (1994). Special and special education: A science education perspective. *Remedial and Special Education, 15,* 128–133.

Gast, D.L., Wellons, J., & Collins, B.C. (1994). Home and community safety skills. In M. Agran, N.E. Marchand-Martella, & R.C. Martella (Eds.), *Promoting health and safety: Skills for independent living* (pp. 11–32). Baltimore: Paul H. Brookes Publishing Co.

Gast, D.L., & Winterling, V. (1992). Teaching first-aid skills to students with moderate handicaps in small group instruction. *Education & Treatment of Children, 15*, 101–124.

Ivancic, M.T., & Schepis, M.M. (1995). Teaching key use to persons with severe disabilities in congregate living settings. *Research in Developmental Disabilities, 16*, 415–423.

Katz, R.C., & Singh, N.N. (1986). Comprehensive fire-safety training for adult mentally retarded persons. *Journal of Mental Deficiency Research, 30*, 59–69.

Lancioni, G.E., O'Reilly, M.F., & Basili, G. (2001). Use of microswitches and speech output systems with people with severe/profound intellectual or multiple disabilities: A literature review. *Research in Developmental Disabilities, 22*, 21–40.

Marchand-Martella, N.E., & Martella, R.C. (1992). Teaching first aid to students with disabilities using two training programs. *Education & Treatment of Children, 15*, 15–31.

Mastropieri, M.A., & Scruggs, T.E. (1994). Text-based *vs.* hands-on science curriculum: Implications for students with disabilities. *Remedial and Special Education, 15*, 72–85.

Minge, M.R., & Ball, T.S. (1967). Teaching of self-help skills to profoundly retarded patients. *American Journal of Mental Deficiency, 71*, 864–868.

National Commission on Excellence in Education. (1983). *A nation at risk.* Retrieved February 16, 2005, from http://www.goalline.org/Goal%20Line/NatAtRisk.html

National Professional Board for Teaching Standards. (1998). *Science standards.* Southfield, MI: Author.

National Research Council. (1996). *National science education standards.* Washington, DC: National Academy Press.

No Child Left Behind (NCLB) Act of 2001, PL 107-110, 115 Stat. 1425, 20 U.S.C. §§ 6301 *et seq.*

Polloway, E.A., Patton, J.R., & Serna, L. (2001). *Strategies for teaching learners with special needs.* Upper Saddle River, NJ: Prentice Hall.

Salend, J.S. (1998). *Effective mainstreaming: Creating inclusive classrooms* (3rd ed.). Upper Saddle River, NJ: Prentice Hall.

Scruggs, T.E., & Mastropieri, MA. (1994). The construction of scientific knowledge by students with mild disabilities. *Journal of Special Education, 28*, 307–321.

Spooner, F. (1994). Foreword. In M. Agran, N.E. Marchand-Martella, & R.C. Martella (Eds.), *Promoting health and safety: Skills for independent living* (pp. ix–x). Baltimore: Paul H. Brookes Publishing Co.

Spooner, F., & Browder, D.M. (2005, February). *Current alignment of national science standards and performance indicators: What this means for students with severe disabilities.* Invited address presented at the annual meeting of the North Carolina Association for Behavior Analysis, Wrightsville Beach, NC.

Spooner, F., Stem, B., & Test, D.W. (1989). Teaching first aid skills to adolescents who are moderately mentally handicapped. *Education and Training in Mental Retardation, 24*, 341–351.

Staver, J.R. (1998). Constructivism: Sound theory for explicating the practice of science and science teaching. *Journal of Research in Science Teaching, 35*, 501–520.

Treagust, D.F. (Ed). (1996). *Improving teaching and learning in science and mathematics.* New York: Teachers College Press.

Utley, C.A., Reddy, S.S., Delquadri, J.C., Greenwood, C.R., Mortweet, S.L., & Bowman, V. (2001). Classwide peer tutoring: An effective teaching procedure for facilitating the acquisition of health education and safety facts with students with developmental disabilities. *Education & Treatment of Children, 24*, 1–27.

Watson, M., Bain, A., & Houghton, S. (1992). A preliminary study in teaching self-protective skills to children with moderate and severe mental retardation. *Journal of Special Education, 26*, 181–194.

Zhang, J., Gast, D., Horvat, M., & Datillo, J. (1995). The effectiveness of a constant time delay procedure on teaching lifetime sports skills to adolescents with severe profound intellectual disabilities. *Education and Training in Mental Retardation and Developmental Disabilities, 30*, 51–64.

Chapter 10

Developing Math and Science Skills in General Education Contexts

Karena Cooper-Duffy and Daniel G. Perlmutter

Mark is a 9-year-old boy who attends the fourth-grade general education class. During whole-group instruction Mark typically listens to the teacher and, points to switches and objects to show comprehension of his new vocabulary words with his classmates. During lab experiments, Mark's responsibilities to his lab partners are to use his object vocabulary list and bring all the needed materials to the work station (another comprehension task). He follows the directions of the lab experiment by measuring items and recording the results on graphs. Mark has shown a strong preference for both these science experiments and using functional math to observe how change occurs around him. Mark is a student with significant cognitive disabilities who is pursuing these interests through his access to the general curriculum in a typical fourth-grade class setting.

Jesse, a 30-year-old man with multiple disabilities who did not have this educational opportunity, taught me (Karena Cooper-Duffy) the importance of promoting inclusive science and math education for students like Mark. Jesse and I were talking about career options. I suggested working in a greenhouse, growing vegetables, cooking, or other opportunities. Jesse looked at me and asked how plants grow. He also wanted to know how to boil water. In that moment I was stunned to realize that Jesse left the public school system without receiving math and science instruction. I learned that Jesse spent 16 years in a self-contained classroom hearing about colors, preschool stories, making coffee, waiting for his turn, and coloring. Together, Jesse and I explored how to make plants grow, to boil water, and many other activities. Today, Jesse has a yearly garden and shares his flowers, fruit, and vegetables with his neighbors. One of the reasons for his successes is that he is careful about planting his seeds at the depth recommended on the seed packets. He uses stickers to match the number of inches recommended on the packet with the same number on his ruler. Then he uses the ruler to measure the depth of the soil so he can bury the seeds. Jesse also now marks his calendar and studies the weather and seasons to see when to plant different seeds and bulbs. Jesse has also learned to be very specific when he uses products like Miracle-Gro by making observations of his plants. Last year, Jesse talked about starting a business so he could sell his produce and use the money to buy seeds for the following year.

Jesse's pursuit of new science and math skills have also helped him develop as a cook, a talent he shares with his roommates. He learned to highlight each measuring cup and spoon and he matches the highlighted number with the recipe. He sets the timers, measures all ingredients, weighs ingredients, and problem solves when something is not right. His favorite part of cooking is watching ingredients change from one form to another (ice to water, water to vapor, powder to Hollandaise sauce, milk to pudding, flour and water into gravy).

Although Jesse has had the opportunity to develop some science and math skills for use in daily living as an adult, what he might have achieved with access to a comprehensive education in these subjects is unknown. In contrast, Mark and other students like him now have the right to general curriculum access. This chapter builds on Chapters 7–9 by describing how to promote math and science learning in general education classes.

TEACHING SCIENCE AND MATH TO ALL STUDENTS
Science

Science education evolved out of an effort to develop scientific literacy in the general population (Rutherford & Ahlgren, 1990). As National Science Education Standards (NSES) defines it

> Scientific literacy means that a person can ask, find, or determine answers to questions derived from curiosity about everyday experiences. It means that a person has the ability to describe, explain, and predict natural phenomena. Scientific literacy entails being able to read with understanding articles about science in the popular press and being able to engage in social conversation about the validity of the conclusions. Scientific literacy implies that a person can identify scientific issues underlying national and local decisions and express positions that are scientifically and technologically informed. A literate citizen should be able to evaluate the quality of scientific information on the basis of its source and the methods used to generate it. Scientific literacy also implies the capacity to pose and evaluate arguments based on evidence and to apply conclusions from such arguments appropriately. (National Research Council, 1996, p. 22)

Rutherford and Ahlgren (1990) suggest that science education should include developing an ability to deal with local and global problems of a social, environmental, and technological nature in addition to developing the ability to live in a mutually beneficial relationship with the natural environment. This requires being able to think sensibly, scientifically, critically, and independently about complex problems in daily life. The authors believe that an understanding of scientific principles will enable an assessment of consequences of technological applications. Along with an appreciation for and support of scientific endeavors, they feel that these skills and attitudes will lead to a desire to allow science to reach its full potential for human betterment. They suggest that curriculum should be purposely constrained to cover fewer significant scientific concepts in greater depth to provide a foundation for lifelong learning. Their criteria for concept inclusion are usefulness in terms of work and personal life and societal decision making. Significant scientific concepts are those that have pervasive influence in our culture and are useful for ethical and philosophical development. These concepts are also recognized for their value for enriching childhood.

An element of scientific literacy is appreciating and understanding the "culture" of science. Driver, Leach, Millar, and Scott (1996) propose teaching the nature of science rather than only science content. Understanding the nature of science can facilitate the use of technology in everyday life and allow participation in decisions that involve science and society. Other outcomes may be an appreciation for the nature of the scientific community and of science as part of our culture. Understanding the nature of science may reinforce the learning of science.

What is the goal for the general population: scientific literacy or science appreciation? Some science educators (Shamos, 1995) advocate abandoning high hopes for scientific literacy and more practically aiming for instilling some measure of science awareness and appreciation in students. This effort would focus on an integrated science curriculum at all grade levels that would 1) make the public feel a cultural imperative to support science, 2) focus on an understanding of technology and relate it to the student's self-interest, and 3) develop the public's ability to properly use expert scientific advice when necessary. In contrast, No Child Left Behind (NCLB) Act of 2001 (PL 107-110) requires states to show adequate yearly progress for all students in science. All students, including those with significant cognitive disabilities, will need more than awareness to show progress on state standards.

The NSES reflect both an empirical approach and a cultural or societal context for learning science. The NSES states that "students must become familiar with modes of scientific inquiry, rules of evidence, ways of formulating questions, and ways of proposing explanations" and emphasizes that "Science is a way of knowing that is characterized by empirical criteria, logical argument, and skeptical review" (NSES, 1996, p. 21). These new standards are also addressing the nature of science reflecting the concern that "students should develop an understanding of what science is, what science is not, what science can and cannot do, and how science contributes to culture" (NSES, 1996, p. 21). In Chapter 9, Spooner, Di Biase, and Courtade-Little provide a summary of the NSES for science.

Math

Just as teaching science is important for students, teaching math is also important for all students. According to the National Council of Teachers of Mathematics (NCTM, 2005) there are important standards for teaching mathematics. As described in Chapter 7, these standards include numbers and operations, algebra, geometry, measurement, data analysis and probability, problem solving, reasoning and proof, communication, connections, and representation (NCTM, 2005). The opportunity to experience mathematics in content is important. Students should connect mathematical concepts to their daily lives, as well as to situations from science, the social sciences, medicine, and commerce (NCTM, 2005). For example, high school students may work with a drug store chain to determine where it should locate a new pharmacy in their neighborhood on the basis of analyses of demographic and economic data.

It is important to encourage students to represent their mathematical ideas in ways that make sense to them, even if those representations are not conventional. At the same time, students should learn conventional forms of representation in ways that facilitate their learning of mathematics and their communication with others about mathematical ideas. The integration of technology into mathematics instruction further increases the need for students to be comfortable with new mathematical representations (NCTM, 2005).

Science Instruction for All Students

After reviewing the descriptions of what science and math education should be for all learners, it is easier to determine the purpose for this instruction for students with significant cognitive disabilities. In science, students with significant disabilities can 1) be exposed to information about the world around them, 2) learn to recognize key science words, 3) work collaboratively with other students to achieve science goals, 4) correctly manipulate tools, and 5) use technology to explore the world of science. Teaching students with significant disabilities science is important for at least four reasons. First, students can receive information about how the world around them works. For example, understanding that plants come from seeds, rain comes from the clouds, animals live in certain places, or bodies are made of certain parts that work together. Second, science provides the opportunity to learn about the world through direct manipulation of materials. Students have the opportunity to take things apart, see objects magnified, and use their senses to explore their world in science activities. For some students with physical or sensory challenges, science activities may provide a unique opportunity to manipulate items and learn more about their world. Third, science is a primary content area that teaches problem solving. Looking at a problem (e.g., the boat will not float) and generating possible solutions to address that problem are skills all students need. As problems are solved, students with significant disabilities may gain additional skills such as communicating a need or want, taking turns, completing a role in a task, or helping to obtain and return materials. Finally, science is a content area that stresses safety. For example, in the lab students can practice safety rules daily such as careful handling of poisonous products, avoiding fire, washing hands, cleaning a work area, and many other skills.

Math Instruction for All Students

In math, students with significant disabilities may learn a variety of skills that promote quality of life. The research literature in severe disabilities identifies ways of teaching functional math skills such as number recognition, money skills, telling time, and performance measurements (see Chapter 8, this volume; Ford et al., 1989; Westling & Fox, 2004). In contrast, all mathematics has the potential to be functional as students learn to use skills in their daily lives. Students can learn to recognize numbers so they can dial a phone number, point to an address or social security number. Students can learn vocabulary related to math to communicate with others about number quantities, prices, weights, medications, scales of pain they may be experiencing, bus schedules, temperatures, bank accounts, television channels, or amounts of soil they need to plant a garden. Learning geometry may promote understanding for activities like loading a dishwasher, setting the table, selecting the correct tool for a job, putting together a toy, changing batteries in an electronic device, planting bulbs, putting a puzzle together, or packing for vacation. Measurement skills can be used in cooking, cleaning, gardening, caring for pets, ordering items online, grocery shopping, doing laundry, and performing health care tasks. Math can also be beneficial for hobbies such as building models, collecting Yu-Gi-Oh cards (value and numbers of cards needed to complete the collection), and exercise (lifting a safe weight, counting jumping jacks, running for an identified time). Finally, math can be useful in learning to set and achieve goals. Students can learn to identify and set a goal, set up a data collection system, and graph results. Access to technology can help to make math useable in daily life. The use of calculators and online banking can enable students to complete math tasks more easily. Also, software programs that include math games provide options for use of free time.

HOW STUDENTS WITH SIGNIFICANT COGNITIVE DISABILITIES CAN BE PART OF GENERAL EDUCATION SCIENCE AND MATH LESSONS

When preparing to include a student with significant cognitive disabilities in the general education class it is critical to think of the process as a collaborative and ongoing process for both the general education and special education teachers. The collaborative journey requires that both parties 1) collaborate or labor together, 2) use the elements of effective team building, and 3) use collaborative problem solving and ongoing evaluation. Collaboration for inclusion of students with severe disabilities in science and math requires completing at least three steps. The first is to prepare the general education lesson plan using the general curriculum with consideration of the diverse learning needs of the class. The second is to identify the strengths and needs of the student with significant cognitive disabilities. The third part is to plan the specific strategies to include the student with significant cognitive disabilities as a full member of the class and lesson.

Strategies for Preparing the General Education Lesson to Include All Learners

PASS Variables   One strategy to prepare general education lessons was developed by Mastropieri and Scruggs (2004) and is called the PASS variables. PASS is an acronym for **P**rioritize objectives; **A**dapt instruction, materials, or the environment; use **S**ystematic instruction (SCREAM) variables during instruction; and implement **S**ystematic evaluation procedures. In *prioritizing objectives*, the team examines all the instructional objectives determining which are the most important for students with disabilities who are included in general education. For students with significant cognitive disabilities, this means identifying the objectives in the lesson that are relevant for the learner. *Adapting instruction* means that materials and the environment are used to accommodate the needs of the student with the disability. For a student with significant cognitive disabilities, for example, instead of learning the 15 new vocabulary words identified for the lesson on habitats, the student may be expected to point to a picture of a habitat instead of a picture of a dog. *Systematic teaching/systematic evaluation* means frequently measuring the students' progress toward the instructional objectives of the class and on individualized education programs (IEPs). A variety of assessment can be used to collect information on the learner's progress. For students with significant cognitive disabilities, this can mean daily data collection of specific responses the student makes during the lesson.

SCREAM Variables   Mastropieri and Scruggs (2004) also use the acronym SCREAM to summarize the strategies for systematic teaching. SCREAM stands for structure, clarity, redundancy, enthusiasm, appropriate rate, and maximum engagement. *Structure* is the organization of the lesson and the sequence the instructor will use when revealing the content. Structure can be provided by using an agenda (using the key content), an outline, a sequence of picture cards, a diagram or framework of what is coming next in the lesson, and highlights of the critical content for that day. Structure could even be a picture schedule for a student. *Clarity* is the specific manner in which the teacher addresses and reveals key concepts one at a time without distracting information. The teacher plans to address the specific point of each objective with definitions, examples and nonexamples, and logical sequences for presenting information. Graphic organizers can be used to enable the students to simply see the critical information needed in the lesson. Also, the student can see how the information is connected. Specifically, lessons with clarity provide precise cues that enable the learner to recall the key information and use it in the learning situation. *Redundancy* is the reemphasis of key terms and key concepts, behaviors, procedures, and rules. Redundancy or practice of key information and behaviors is critical for the maintenance and generalization of the information initially acquired. Redundancy can occur with homework, peer tutoring, software programs or Internet sites, lab experiments, or information presented in a variety of different formats (visually, auditorily, tactilely, or motorically). Redundancy also requires that learners have multiple opportunities to use the new skill or information in a manner that enables them to acquire it. Summarizing all the key points of the lesson at the end of the lesson can also provide redundancy. Classwide peer tutoring is an excellent way to provide practice opportunities for key concepts during class (e.g., Delquadri, Greenwood, Stretton, & Hall, 1983; Delquadri, Greenwood, Whorton, Carta, & Hall, 1986; Greenwood, Delquadri, & Hall, 1989). *Enthusiasm* is the process of creating exciting learning environments for both the teacher and the students. Enthusiastic teachers plan for lessons to be fun, challenging, promote curiosity, and enable thinking. The lessons should also be meaningful, motivating, and concrete. Videos, software, web sites, games, and real-life examples can keep lessons interesting and keep students interested. *Appropriate rate* is the pace at which the teacher plans to deliver the instruction. The teacher plans to use a slow rate of instruction when first introducing new information. As the students show an acquisition of information, the speed at which the teacher builds on new information can increase. Also, the teacher may plan to use a faster pace of instruction when he or she is reviewing previous content. Pacing for instruction is also needed when teaching children who show a slower rate of skill acquisition. Teachers may set time periods for devoting to specific areas of the lesson. *Maximized engagement* is the process of planning ways to actively involve the students in the learning process. The teacher may plan to use a variety of types of questioning, case studies, materials, role plays, games, cooperative learning activities, KWL charts (What I know?, What I want to Know? And What I learned?), learning centers, and peer tutoring.

Planning for Types of Learning

As the teacher is planning to include all students in the lesson, the teacher should also be sure to plan for the type of learning that is required in the lesson. Once the type of learning is planned, the teacher can include the specific strategies to ensure that type of learning in the lesson. The different types of learning can in-

Table 10.1. Planning for types of learning

Information taught	Type of learning	Strategy needed
Vocabulary on ecosystems	Factual	Peer-tutoring to practice vocabulary words during the first and last 5 minutes of class. Mnemonic devices. Constant time delay
Types of ecosystems	Discrimination	Present examples and nonexamples of the different types of ecosystems with the critical elements of each type of ecosystem highlighted. Teach the definitions of each type of system.
Making an ecosystem	Procedures	Teach the students to use a checklist, task analytic instruction, picture sequence of the steps, cooperative learning to learn roles and process in working together, or mnemonics.
The effect of pollution on ecosystems	Concept	Graphic organizers, role plays, case studies, if/then statements

clude discriminations, facts, rules, procedures, concepts and problem solving, and critical thinking (Mastropieri & Scruggs, 2004). In each lesson a teacher may be addressing multiple types of learning and may need to include multiple strategies to facilitate this type of learning. For example, if the teacher is planning a lesson on understanding ecosystems and she expects the students to acquire vocabulary (factual), types of ecosystems (discrimination), a method of making an ecosystem (procedures), and information on how pollution would effect an ecosystem (concepts), the teacher would need to ensure a variety of strategies were in place to facilitate this type of learning in the allotted time she had to teach this lesson (see Table 10.1).

Once the general education teacher has planned the lesson to include all learners, collaboration with the special education teachers is needed to ensure that the specific needs of the learners with disabilities will be met in the lesson. The learning experience for the student with significant cognitive disabilities in the general education lesson should be arranged so that the areas of skill development needed (IEP goals) for the learner are embedded in the general education lesson.

Knowing the General Education Curriculum

The first step in planning for the student's participation in the lesson is to understand the state standards and other outcomes the lesson will address. These standards may be written in the published teacher's guide, on the teacher's lesson plan, or available through the state's web site. The state standards that will be addressed in the lesson plan should be listed under the objectives in the lesson plan. The general education teacher takes the lead and shares with the special education teacher the lesson plan with the identified academic standards, using the PASS and SCREAM variables. This enables the special education teacher to identify the critical content the general education teacher needs to address in the class. The special education teacher can then identify specific concepts, parts of concepts, or ways the students with significant cognitive disabilities can participate in the lesson. The students with significant disabilities are taught the identified content using systematic instruction plans. Systematic instruction plans identify the specific skill the learner is to be taught, where the skill will be taught, what level of mastery is required, and how (with the necessary prompting) the learner will be taught. This information provides a predictable and consistent manner of teaching the student the skills in a variety of settings and with a variety of teachers.

Teaching to Grade-Level State Standards in Science and Math

Together, the special education teacher and the general education teacher will determine how the student with significant disabilities will address the standards for the grade level and the alternate achievement that will be expected. For Mark, one expectation is to show comprehension of living versus nonliving things by pointing to objects or pictures that represent that concept with 75% accuracy for three out of four trials. This connects to the fourth-grade standard: *1.01 Observe and describe how all living and nonliving things affect the life of a particular animal including: other animals, plants and weather.* During the general education lesson, the teacher will discuss with the class the characteristics of things that are living versus things that are not living. The teacher will ask the students to work in pairs to generate a list of things that are living and a list of things that are not living. Mark will work with a peer to generate his list by pointing to each object that is living. When the students have finished generating their own lists of living and nonliving things, the teacher will begin creating a whole-class list by calling on individual students to give examples of living things.

Setting differential expectations may also be needed in math. For example, if the teacher is teaching the class to add 2-digit numbers, some students in the class may still be practicing how to add single-digit numbers. The student with significant cognitive disabilities may be working on pointing to the correct digit on their communication board to say *I have 2 friends* and using Legos to build a graph of the number *2*. Another student may be using a timer to add up the total number of minutes he can hold a switch down to activate a tape player that reads a word problem to the class. The students in the class are all working on different levels of adding numbers.

Selecting the Inclusive Strategy

At this point in the planning it is important for both the general education teacher and the special education teacher to determine which types of inclusive strategies should be used to best meet the needs of all the learners in the lesson. The teachers can select co-teaching strategies (team and monitor, parallel teaching, station teaching, or team teaching), peer-tutoring strategies (classwide peer tutoring, same-age peer tutoring, cross-age peer tutoring), cooperative learning strategies (student teams, achievement divisions, team-assisted individualization, cooperative integrated reading and composition, jigsaw, group investigation) or curriculum modifications. When selecting an inclusive strategy it is important to have the general education content identified with a lesson plan and the IEP goals and accommodations for the student with the disability prepared in advance. Once these areas are identified, the general education teacher and the special education teacher can identify the strategies that are most effective. For example, if the teachers determine that the content would be better presented by dividing the class into two smaller groups and each teacher teaches the same lesson to half of the class, then parallel co-teaching is the best strategy. However, if the teachers agree that additional practice is needed on the content, then class-wide peer tutoring is best. Classwide peer tutoring could also be used in which the student with significant cognitive disabilities receives tutoring on a different set of vocabulary cards (e.g., cards may have photos of key concepts instead of words) than the rest of the class. Cooperative learning may be selected if the students need to work on applying information to a specific project.

Case Study Example for Elementary School Students   Mrs. Anderson is the science and math teacher for one of the fourth-grade classes at White Oak Elementary School. This example describes her plans for one science and math unit and how she worked with the special education team to include Mark, a student with significant disabilities. Mrs. Anderson prepared to teach the Life Science Unit called Looking at Ecosystems (Jones et al., 2000). This unit provided resources to address the fourth-grade science standards (see Appendix A for state standards identified to be taught in the unit).

During her preparation to teach the lesson to the entire class, she reviewed the lessons looking for the SCREAM variables. She found that the variables were present; however, she wanted to strengthen the areas of enthusiasm and maximum engagement by adding to the unit a scavenger hunt, a field trip to a nature trail and a botanical garden, and cooperative learning for the class activities such as making and observing an ecosystem. In addition, she set up peer-tutoring sessions that occurred for 10 minutes at various points of the science lessons. The peer-tutoring sessions were instrumental in assisting all the students to practice key vocabulary and concepts related to the unit. The teacher then identified the types of learning that were to occur during her lesson and the strategies that needed to be in the lesson plan to enable the types of learning to occur (see Table 10.1).

The special education teacher and the general education teacher planned for the specific needs of Mark, a student with special needs. Mark was a 9-year-old boy who enjoyed racing cars, being with peers, being outside, camping, playing with animals, listening to stories, and getting attention from adults. Mark had significant cognitive disabilities, Down syndrome, autism spectrum disorder, and a partial visual impairment that was corrected with glasses. He had had multiple surgeries and took a variety of medications daily. Mark had not learned to use symbolic communication consistently. He yelled "NO" to protest and said "yes" to request items. He also used smiles socially and loud vocalizations to gain attention, and he sometimes threw himself to the floor to protest. He was taught to use an object communication board that contained a juice box, spoon, book, and a switch that when pressed played a recording of "How am I doing?" Mark frequently touched the juice box to indicate thirst. Once this communication board was put into place, his challenging behavior rates dropped from 320 minutes of protesting per day to only 5 minutes of protesting per day. Also, he frequently touched a book that contained his vocabulary words. This book contained objects of his vocabulary words across all his subject areas. His science words included plants, soil, gravel, and sand.

During a person-centered planning meeting for using the McGill Action Planning System (Vandercook, York, & Forest, 1989), plans were made for positive behavioral support for Mark including increased use of an AAC system called a

Table 10.2.   Individualized education program goals for Mark relevant to math and science class

1. Mark will touch the correct object and word box on the communication device when asked comprehension questions about his vocabulary words for 4 out of 5 trials.

2. Mark will learn to show comprehension of three new science concepts by pointing to objects that represent that concept, with 75% accuracy.

3. Mark will follow science lab directions using an object checklist, with 75% accuracy.

4. Mark will use stickers and a measuring device (ruler) to measure an object, with 75% accuracy.

5. Mark will write his name using a stamper, with 80% accuracy.

6. Mark will graph data on a graph by placing stickers on the data points, with 70% accuracy.

Tech/Talk (Mayer-Johnson LLC). This device enabled cards with objects to be attached to the place on the board and when the objects are pressed the device plays a recorded message of the word. Mark's parents were also eager for him to increase his meaningful participation in general education science and math classes. The team targeted the IEP goals for Mark that could be addressed in these content areas (see Table 10.2).

After identifying and discussing the IEP goals, the teachers reviewed the unit that the general education teacher was preparing to teach on ecosystems and graphing. Together they looked at the lessons to determine which state standards related to Mark's IEP goals and what part of the state standards Mark could learn. Next, they discussed how Mark could participate in the lesson and where he could receive instruction for his IEP goals during the lesson. The teachers identified several ways many of the IEP goals could be taught during the lesson (see Appendix A). Figure 10.1 summarizes how the planning team incorporated Mark's participation into the lesson plan for the fourth-grade science class. The class will also be using a cooperative learning activity during this lesson. Figure 10.2 describes the specific way that Mark will participate as a member of the cooperative learning group. Mark also needs to receive some direct systematic instruction on his IEP objectives using systematic instruction plans and data sheets (Browder, Davis, Courtade-Little, Fallin, & Bohner, 2003). Examples of the objectives to be addressed during this science lesson are shown in Appendix A and Figures 10.3–10.6. A paraprofessional will provide Mark with this extra practice while his classmates generate lists of living and nonliving things in their communities (see Appendix A and Figures 10.3–10.6).

Case Study Example for Middle School Students

Bart, a 13-year-old boy, was a member of one of four seventh-grade teams at Crystal Creek Middle School. His interests included a love of nature, computers, and exploring how things work. Bart's disabilities included cerebral palsy and significant cognitive disabilities. He used a wheelchair for mobility and could communicate with simple sentences. He points using his right hand to large pictures to communicate other needs and was learning to follow a picture schedule. Bart, Mrs. Huyett, Mr. Bell, and Bart's mother conducted a person-centered plan using *Choosing Outcomes and Accommodations for Children* (*COACH;* Giangreco, Cloninger, & Iverson, 1998) to identify the IEP goals that Bart needs for the upcoming school year. Bart's planning team identified the following priorities for his IEP that are relevant to his science and math classes. He was learning communication, motor, and self-care skills that would also be addressed in all contexts of his school day.

Bart will follow a picture direction sheet to participate in the lab experiment.

Bart will point to 3–5 lab safety signs and state what they mean.

Bart will answer 3 questions based on the lab experiment using pictures or the actual objects.

Bart will sort 2 different types of items into the correct groups.

Bart will press a switch to active a search on the Internet and the Excel program using IntelliKeys.

The science teacher, Mr. Bell, was planning to teach a unit on classification. The specific lesson Mr. Bell selected, called *Leaf Classification,* was designed by Benson (1997) from the Utah Education Network (http://www.uen.org). Mrs. Huyett, the special education teacher, Bart's mother, and Mr. Bell discussed how Bart's learning needs could be addressed in this unit and specifically this lesson. Together they modified the lesson plan to include activities where Bart could work on his IEP goals during the science lesson and to specify how Bart would demonstrate classification (see Appendix B). They determined that Bart could label the different types of leaves and help to classify the different types of leaves using his sorting goal. In addition, they agreed that the whole class could benefit from a daily review of the safety rules in the lab using the safety signs around the room. Drew, a peer tutor earning Future Teacher of America (FTA) credits as a peer tutor, would be Bart's peer tutor and lab partner during science class. He used a peer-tutoring strategy to prompt Bart on the safety signs during the whole-class review. Each of the IEP goals that were on Bart's IEP were addressed with a systematic instruction plan and data sheets (Browder et al., 2003) that could be implemented during the general education lesson (see Figures 10.7–10.10).

Fourth-grade science standard: The learner will make observations and conduct investigations to build an understanding of animal behavior and adaptation.

Fourth-grade unit objective: Observe and describe how all living and nonliving things affect the life of a particular animal including: Plants

Expectations for Mark

The part or essence of the state standard Mark will learn is to identify the difference between living and nonliving things.

Fourth-grade math standard: The learner will understand and use graphs, probability, and data analysis.

Fourth-grade unit objective: Collect, organize, analyze, and display data (including line graphs and bar graphs to solve problems).

Expectation for Mark

The part of the math standard Mark will learn is to use stickers and a measuring device (ruler) to measure an object. He will place the sticker on the ruler to show the length of the object. Mark is collecting data for the graph. Also Mark will learn to graph data on a graph by placing stickers on the data points.

Figure 10.1.   Example of planning adaptations in science and math.

Purpose: Build a closed system with all the necessary parts.

The team will work together sharing the materials and problem solving.

Roles and responsibilities of team members:

Reader: this person will read the directions for the team

Recorder: this person will write all the needed information for the team, label items, record measurements, and so forth.

Getter: this person will take a list and go to the supply table and get all the materials the team needs to make the closed system.

Mark will be assigned the role of the getter. He will work with a peer. The peer will have an object list. Mark will use this list to get the needed items for his team. For example, the peer will hand Mark a basket and open a binder. On the first page of the binder, Mark will see an actual pair of scissors and the word scissors and a plastic bottle with the word bottle on the checklist. This is Mark's cue to go to the supply table and get the items and put them in the basket and take them to the team.

Doer: This person will follow the directions and put the system together based on the directions.

Process: The team will gather together and read the following directions.

1. The team should greet each other and state what they will be doing. Each member shows or states what their role is in the activity. *Mark will hold up the basket to show he is the getter. While Mark goes to the supply table, the peer tutor will prompt Mark to point to a living thing. He will then be prompted to point to a nonliving thing. Mark will look at his object list and select the first item on the list.*

2. Get a 2-liter soda bottle and a pair of scissors. Cut the top off of the soda bottle. *When Mark goes back to the supply table he will be asked to look at the second item on the list. He will need to use his communication board to push the button to identify the substance as gravel. Mark will be asked to get (measure out) the gravel. This process will be repeated for sand, and then he will take the two substances to the group.*

3. Get 1 cup of gravel and 1 cup of sand. Place the gravel in the bottom of the soda bottle and then pour the sand over the gravel. *Mark will return to the supply table and look at his object list. He will be prompted to use his communication board to identify the substance using his vocabulary words. After he presses the object/word soil, he will get (measure out) the soil and return it to the group.*

4. Get 2 cups of soil and pour it over the sand. *Mark will return to the supply table and be asked to point to a nonliving thing on the table. He will then be asked to point to a living thing. Next Mark will be prompted to point to the next item on his object list. He will use his communication board to touch the object/word plant. Next, he will count out 2 plants and take them to the group.*

5. Get 2 plants. Plant each of the plants in the soil. *Mark will use his object list and be asked to get the water bottle and take it to the group.*

6. Get a water bottle and spray the plants and soil with water. *Mark will return to the supply table and be asked to point to a living thing and then to a nonliving thing. He will use his object list to identify and get the next item on the list. He will take it to the group.*

7. Get a sheet of plastic wrap and 2 rubber bands. Place the plastic wrap over the soda bottle and pull the rubber bands around the plastic wrap to hold it on to the soda bottle.

8. Repeat this process, making a second terrarium.

9. Each student needs to write his or her name on two labels and stick the labels on each of the terrariums. *Mark will write his name using his stamper.*

10. Measure the height of each plant and record this information on a piece of paper. Also record the color of the leaves and the length of the leaves. Record the length of the roots. Date this information and post the paper on the wall next to the terrarium. Each team member should write his or her name on the paper. *Mark will use a stamper to write his name on his paper. He will use a ruler to measure the plant and place a sticker on the ruler where the top of the plant touches the ruler. Next Mark will take the ruler and place it on the graph so the ruler and the y-axis are parallel. He will then place a sticker on the graph at the same location as the sticker on the ruler saying the number of inches. He will then remove the sticker from the ruler.*

11. Place one terrarium in the sun and one in the dark.

12. Clean up the work area and replace all materials.

13. Students will use a rubric to rate their terrarium and how well they worked together.

14. Return to the whole group to summarize the lesson.

Figure 10.2.   Cooperative learning activity for the plant terrarium.

Student: _Mark_   Date plan started: _8/12/2004_

Target skill: _Collecting data_   Routine: _Math (academic)_

Specific objective: _Mark will use a measuring device (ruler) to measure objects (plants) and place a_
sticker on the ruler to identify the length of the object with 75% accuracy.

Materials: _Stickers, ruler, plants, objects to measure_

Setting and schedule for instruction: _During science class, and math class_

Number of trials: _One trial per day_

INSTRUCTIONAL PROCEDURE

Prompting

Specific prompt or prompts to be used (list in sequence):

1. _specific verbal_   2. _model prompt_   3. _partial physical_

4. _full physical prompt_

Type of prompt system (check which applies):

_X_ System of least prompts

____ Time delay ____ Constant OR ____ Progressive

____ Most to least intrusive prompts

____ Graduated guidance

____ Stimulus fading or shaping

____ Chaining ____ Backward OR ____ Forward

____ Other (describe): _____

Fading schedule for time delay: _3-5 second delay_

Feedback

Correct responses: _Super putting the sticker on the ruler_

Fading schedule for praise: _Natural praise given only with measuring plants_

Error correction: _Move to physical prompting_

Generalization and maintenance plan: _Mark will have the opportunity to measure_
a variety of objects all day long.

Figure 10.3.   Systematic instruction plan for Mark using a ruler or measure and graph.

SUMMARY

Providing meaningful instruction in inclusive science and math classrooms requires team planning to define expectations and supports for the student with significant cognitive disabilities. The general education teacher begins the process by preparing the lesson plan to be accessible to all students. In addition, the general education teacher identifies the state standards that are addressed in the lesson. At the same time, the special education teacher prepares for the process of including the student with significant disabilities by working with the person-centered planning team to identify the IEP goals for the student. The special edu-

Student: *Mark*			Task: *Mark will use a measuring device (ruler) to*

Task: *Mark will use a measuring device (ruler) to measure objects (plants) and place a sticker on the ruler to identify the length of the object with 75% accuracy.*

Student: *Mark*

Academic component:

☐ Reading   ☒ Math   ☐ Writing   ☐ Science

Steps: Dates:	3/4	3/6	3/11	3/13	3/18	3/20	3/22
1. Get ruler.	+	+	+	+	+	+	+
2. Put the number 1 of the ruler on the soil.	+	+	+	+	+	+	+
3. Place the ruler next to the plant.	–	–	–	+	+	+	+
4. Place the top of the plant against the ruler.	+	+	–	–	+	+	+
5. Place a sticker at the place on the ruler where the plant stops.	+	+	+	+	+	+	+
6. State the number of inches.	+	+	+	+	+	+	+
Total independent correct	5	5	4	5	6	6	6
Where	CL	CL	TR	CL	CL	TR	H
With whom	T	P	OT	P	T	OT	PA

Student response code	Where code	With whom code
(+) Independent correct	CL Classroom	T Teacher
(-) Incorrect	TR Therapy room	P Paraprofessional
NR No response/does not attempt	H Home	OT Occupational therapist
		PA Parent

Figure 10.4.   Data sheet to collect data on Mark's measuring skills.

cation teacher also works with the IEP team to identify any accommodations and modifications the student may need to be successful in the general education class. Next, the general education and special education teachers review the lesson plan with the state standards and the IEP goals of the student to determine how the student can be included in the lesson and have access to the state standards. The teachers will need to look at using peer tutoring, cooperative learning, co-teaching, or curriculum modifications, to effectively include the student with significant disabilities. Together the teachers will identify which IEP goals can effectively be addressed in the general education lesson. The special education teacher will also design a systematic instruction plan to ensure that the student will receive the specific prompting and motivators to acquire the information during the general education lesson. The special education teacher will also create a method of data collection to show that the student is making progress on the IEP goals, even in the general education lesson.

Student: _Mark_   Date plan started: _8/12/2004_

Target skill: _Science concepts_   Routine: _Science (academic)_

Specific objective: ___Mark will learn to show comprehension of 3 new science concepts by pointing to___ _objects that represent that concept with 75% accuracy (living and nonliving)_

Materials: _Stickers, ruler, plants, bottle_

Setting and schedule for instruction: _During science class, lunch, recess, hallways, all day long_

Number of trials: _5 trials @ zero delay for 3 days, 2 warm-up trials at zero delay and 3 trials at_ _5 second delay for 2 days, 5 second delay only for 1 day_

INSTRUCTIONAL PROCEDURE

Prompting

Specific prompt or prompts to be used (list in sequence):

1. _specific verbal_   2. _____   3. _____

4. _____

Type of prompt system (check which applies):

_____ System of least prompts

_X_ Time delay   _X_ Constant OR _____ Progressive

_____ Most to least intrusive prompts

_____ Graduated guidance

_____ Stimulus fading or shaping

_____ Chaining _____ Backward OR _____ Forward

_____ Other (describe): _____

Fading schedule for time delay: _5-second delay_

Feedback

Correct responses: _Yes, that plant is living._

Fading schedule for praise: _Natural praise given only with touching living things._

Error correction: _Return to zero delay. Stating correct response._

Generalization and maintenance plan: _Mark will have the opportunity to touch a variety of living_ _and nonliving things all day long._

Figure 10.5. Systematic instruction plan for Mark understanding science concepts.

Student: *Mark*					Task: *Mark will learn to show comprehension of new science concepts by pointing to objects that represent that concept with 75% accuracy (living and nonliving)*						
Academic component: ⊠ Reading ☐ Math ☐ Writing ☐ Science											
Dates:	11/05	11/14	11/21	12/5	12/12	12/19	1/09	1/16	1/23	1/30	2/06
Living	+	+	−	−	−	+	−	+	−	+	+
Living	−	−	+	−	+	-	+	−	+	−	+
Nonliving	−	−	−	−	−	+	+	−	+	+	+
Nonliving	+	+	+	+	+	+	+	+	−	−	+
Total independent correct	2	2	2	1	2	3	3	2	2	2	4
Where	CS	R	CS	H	C	CS	H	H	R	CS	C
With whom	GE	T	A	P	T	A	P	P	T	GE	A
Materials used	B S	P p	B P	B S	P S	P p	F S	F P	B P	P p	F P

Student response code

(+) Independent correct

(-) Incorrect

Where code

CS   Classroom Science

H   Home

C   Special education class

R   Recess

With whom code

T   Teacher

A   Assistant

P   Parent

GE   General education teacher

Materials

B   bug   S   Stapler

P   plant   p   pencil

F   flowers

Figure 10.6. Data sheet to collect data on Mark's science comprehension.

Student: _Bart_   Date plan started: _9/20/2004_

Target skill: _Sorting_   Routine: _Math skills_

Specific objective: _Bart will sort 2 different types of objects to discriminate different shapes,_
materials and learn classification skills with 80% accuracy

Materials: _Recycling, leaves, clothes, animals, foods, and so forth_

Setting and schedule for instruction: _During science class, lunch, prevocational instruction_

Number of trials: _5 trials @ zero delay for 3 days, 2 warm-up trials at zero delay and 3 trials at_
5-second delay for 1 day, 5-second delay only for 1 day.

INSTRUCTIONAL PROCEDURE

Prompting

Specific prompt or prompts to be used (list in sequence):

1. _Specific verbal and model (match to sample)_

Type of prompt system (check which applies):

_____ System of least prompts

_X_ Time delay   _X_ Constant OR _____ Progressive

_____ Most to least intrusive prompts

_____ Graduated guidance

_____ Stimulus fading or shaping

_____ Chaining _____ Backward OR _____ Forward

_____ Other (describe): _____

Fading schedule for time delay: _5-second delay_

Feedback

Correct responses: _Great matching the pine needles to the pine needle pile_

Fading schedule for praise: _Only praise after every 5 items sorted correctly_

Error correction: _No, that is a maple leaf; it goes with this pile of leaves. Return to zero delay._

Generalization and maintenance plan: _Bart will sort items for function reasons in science class and_
during his recycling job

Figure 10.7. Systematic instruction plan on Bart's sorting leaves in the general education lesson for classification purposes.

| Student: *Bart*
Portfolio #:

Academic component:
☐ Reading ☒ Math ☐ Writing ☐ Science | Task: *Bart will sort 2 different types of objects*
to discriminate different shapes, materials and
learn classification skill

────────────────────
*Essence 2 |

Trial:	Date:	8/12	8/14	8/20	8/23	8/27	8/29	9/4	9/6	9/10	9/12
3		1	1	1	1	1	1	2	2	2	2
2		1	1	1	2	1	2	2	2	2	1
1		1	2	1	2	2	1	2	1	1	1
Total independent correct		0	1	0	2	1	1	3	2	2	1
Where		CL	S	CA	S	CL	CL	S	CA	S	CL
With whom		T	P	T	P	T	P	PA	T	T	P

Student response code	Where code	With whom code
1 Verbal/model prompts	CL Classroom	T Teacher
2 Independent correct	CA Cafeteria	P Paraprofessional
	S Science class	PA Parent
	FT Field trip	

Figure 10.8. Data sheet to collect data on Bart's sorting skills.

Student: _Bart_____   Date plan started: _9/20/2004_____

Target skill: _Safety signs_____   Routine: _Safety in lab_____

Specific objective: _Bart will look at 5 safety signs and state what they mean with 100% accuracy for_
_   4 out of 5 days._____

Materials: _Personal picture set of the safety signs in the school. Signs can be in a small photo album that_
_   goes with him. Drew will be his peer tutor._____

Setting and schedule for instruction: _During science class whole-class review, lunch, prevocational_
_   instruction, hallway, all day long_____

Number of trials: _5 trials at zero delay for 3 days, 2 warm-up trials at zero delay and 3 trials at_
_   5-second delay for 1 day, 5-second delay only for 1 day_____

INSTRUCTIONAL PROCEDURE

Prompting

Specific prompt or prompts to be used (list in sequence):

1. _specific verbal and physical point to picture_   2. _____

3._____   4._____

Type of prompt system (check which applies):

_____ System of least prompts

_X_ Time delay _X_ Constant OR _____ Progressive

_____ Most to least intrusive prompts

_____ Graduated guidance

_____ Stimulus fading or shaping

_____ Chaining _____ Backward OR _____ Forward

_____ Other (describe):_____

Fading schedule for time delay: _5-second delay_____

Feedback

Correct responses: _Super stating fire, get burned._____

Fading schedule for praise: _Only praise after every other correct response_____

Error correction: _Return to zero delay, Stating correct response._____

Generalization and maintenance plan: _Bart will have the opportunity to point to and identify safety_
_   signs throughout the school_____

Figure 10.9. Systematic instruction plan to teach Bart the science lab safety signs.

| Student: *Bart*
 Portfolio #:

 Domain:
 ☒ Science   ☐ Math   ☐ Writing | | | Task: *Bart will look at 5 safety signs and state*
 what they mean. | | | | | | | | |

	Date										
Wash hands											
Acid											
Clear area											
Wear apron											
Poison											
Fire								+	+	+	+
Clean area			+	+	+	+	+	+	+	+	+
Wear glasses		+	+	+	+	+	+	+	+	+	+
Total independent correct	0	1	2	2	2	2	2	3	3	3	3
Where	CL	CL	H	SC	SC	SC	CL	H	CL	SC	SC
With whom	T	T	PA	A	A	SP	T	PA	A	T	SP
Materials used	Book	signs	Book	signs	signs	signs	Book	Book	Book	signs	signs

Student response code
(+)   Independent CORRECT
(-)   Incorrect

Where code
CL   Classroom
SC   Science class
H   Home
SCL   Speech

With whom code
T   Teacher
A   Assistant
PA   Parent
SP   Speech therapist

Figure 10.10.   Data sheet to collect data on Bart's knowledge of lab safety signs.

REFERENCES

Benson, K. (1997). *Leaf classification.* Retrieved December 1, 2004, from http://www.uen .org/Lessonplan/preview.cgi?LPid=1001

Browder, D., Davis, S., Courtade-Little, G., Fallin, K., & Bohner, E. (2003). *Finding the essences of literacy and math: A teacher training manual.* Unpublished manuscript, University of North Carolina at Charlotte.

Delquadri, J., Greenwood, C.R., Stretton, K., & Hall, R.V. (1983). The peer tutoring game: A classroom procedure for increasing opportunity to respond and spelling performance. *Education and Treatment of Children, 6,* 225–239.

Delquadri, J., Greenwood, C.R., Whorton, D., Carta, J.J., & Hall, R.V. (1986). Classwide peer tutoring. *Exceptional Children, 52,* 535–542.

Driver, R., Leach, J., Millar, R., & Scott, P. (1996). *Young people's images of science.* Buckingham: Open University Press.

Ford, A., Schnorr, R., Meyer, L., Davern, L., Black, J., & Dempsey, P. (1989). *The Syracuse community-referenced curriculum guide for students with moderate and severe disabilities.* Baltimore: Paul H. Brookes Publishing Co.

Giangreco, M.F., Cloninger, C.J., & Iverson, V.S. (1998). *Choosing Outcomes and Accommodations for Children (COACH): A guide to educational planning for students with disabilities* (2nd ed.). Baltimore: Paul H. Brookes Publishing Co.

Greenwood, C.R., Delquadri, J., & Hall, R.V. (1989). Longitudinal effects of classwide peer tutoring. *Journal of Educational Psychology, 81,* 371–383.

Jones, R., Krockover, G., McLeod, J., Frank, M., Lang, M., Van Deman, B., et al. (2000). *Science: Life Science Unit B* (pp. B1–B38). Orlando: Harcourt School Publishers.

Mastropieri, M., & Scruggs, T. (2004). *The inclusive classroom: Strategies for effective instruction* (2nd ed.). Upper Saddle River, NJ: Pearson Education.

National Council of Teachers of Mathematics. (2005). *Standards of school mathematics.* Retrieved March 2, 2005, from http://nctm.org/standards/standards.htm

National Research Council. (1996). *National science education standards.* Washington, DC: National Academy Press.

No Child Left Behind (NCLB) Act of 2001, PL 107-110, 115 Stat. 1425, 20 U.S.C. §§ 6301 *et seq.*

North Carolina State Board of Education and Department of Public Instruction. (2005). *North Carolina state standard course of study.* Retrieved March 2, 2005, from http://www.dpi .state.nc.us/curriculum/science/standard/042grade4.html

Rutherford, F.J., & Ahlgren, A. (1990). *Science for all Americans.* New York: Oxford University Press.

Shamos, M.H. (1995). *The myth of scientific literacy.* New Brunswick, NJ: Rutgers University Press.

Vandercook, T., York, J., & Forest, M. (1989). The McGill Action Planning System (MAPS): A strategy for building the vision. *The Journal of The Association for Persons with Severe Handicaps, 14,* 205–215.

Westling, D., & Fox, L. (2004). Teaching students with severe disabilities (3rd ed.). Upper Saddle River, NJ: Prentice Hall.

Example of Adaptations to a General Education Lesson Plan for Science

Unit: Looking at Ecosystems (Jones et al., 2000)
Fourth-grade Science lesson (1 hour and 30 minutes)
Lesson 1: What are systems?

Lesson objectives

Investigate how parts of a system work

Describe what makes up a system

Identify parts of an ecosystem

Learn about characteristics of systems

Work collaboratively to make a closed system

STATE STANDARD COURSE OF STUDY OBJECTIVES (NORTH CAROLINA STATE BOARD OF EDUCATION AND DEPARTMENT OF PUBLIC INSTRUCTION, 2005)

Science

1.01 Observe and describe how all living and nonliving things affect the life of a particular animal including: Plants

Math

The learner will understand and use graphs, probability, and data analysis.

4.01 Collect, organize, analyze, and display data (including line graphs and bar graphs to solve problems).

The learner will demonstrate an understanding of mathematical relationships.

5.01 Identify, describe, and generalize relationships in which: Quantities change proportionally

IEP Goals to Be Addressed During Lesson

1. Mark will touch the correct object and word box on the communication device when asked comprehension questions about his vocabulary words for 4 out of 5 trials.

2. Mark will learn to show comprehension of three new science concepts by pointing to objects that represent that concept with 75% accuracy (living and nonliving). (Science Objective 1.01)

3. Mark will follow science lab directions using an object checklist with 75% accuracy.

4. Mark will use stickers and a measuring device (ruler) to measure an object with 75% accuracy. He will place the sticker on the ruler to show the length of the object. (Math Competency Goal 4)

5. Mark will write his name using a stamper with 80% accuracy.

6. Mark will graph data on a graph, placing stickers on the data points with 70% accuracy. Mark will place a sticker on the graph, using the ruler to show the length of the object he measured. (Math Competency Goal 4)

Vocabulary

system

open system

closed system

plants*

soil*

gravel*

sand*

air

light

water

living

nonliving

terrarium*

Mark will learn 3 out of the 5 identified vocabulary words.

Procedures

1. Begin the lesson with some pictures of different systems and introduce the topic to the class. (whole group)

2. Introduce the new vocabulary to the class using a direct instruction approach with choral responding.

   Mark will have his communication device set up and when the teacher states the new vocabulary words, he will press the object and word that is the same as the new vocabulary word he is learning. For example, the teacher will say "soil," and the class will be describing it. As they are de-

scribing soil a peer or paraprofessional will be prompting Mark to locate the button on the communication device that has the soil glued to a card (also with the word soil) *using Velcro attached to the button. When the teacher asks the whole class to read the word* soil *Mark will press the button* soil *and "read" the word with the class.*

3. Present the term *systems* to the whole class using a graphic organizer. The class will define a system as a collection of parts that work together as a unit. Ask students to generate lists of examples of systems. Possible examples include: backyards, bikes, fish tanks, gardens, and so forth.

4. Explain parts of a system include plants, soil, air, water, and light. These are all parts of systems that exist in nature. Use a picture showing all these parts.

The teacher will call on Mark and ask what is one part of a natural system? He will use his communication device (with prompting from peer or paraprofessional if needed) to answer using his new vocabulary words.

5. Use a compare-and-contrast graphic organizer and describe the difference between open and closed systems. Open systems are systems such as the park, backyards, lake, and so forth. These systems take in things from outside the system—rain, sprinklers, hoses, sun, and so forth. Open systems also let things out of the system. Some water from a lake may leave the system by evaporating, getting splashed out of the lake by a boat. Birds could drink the water and then fly away. Pictures from the textbook can assist in clarification. What are some other examples? Introduce and compare a closed system. This is a system that that has no inputs or outputs, such as a fish tank, terrarium, hamster cage, and so forth. What are some examples of other kinds of closed systems? Students will do paired reading and read the sections of their textbook that describe open and closed systems. The students would then begin their peer tutoring activity in which they take out their vocabulary cards and tutor each other on the new vocabulary words. They are expected to read the word and state what it means. The tutors were trained to give each other feedback and record which words they get correct.

Mark will participate using his communication device and Systematic Instruction Plan on vocabulary (Figure 10.5). His tutor will show him the object and say, "The object is soil, *show me* soil *on your device."*

6. Explain that in both types of systems there are some things that are living and some things that are not living. Ask these questions: Looking at a picture of a lake, what things here are living? Living items move, breathe, eat, and excrete waste. What things here are nonliving? Explain: Nonliving things do not move, breathe, eat, or excrete waste. They are all part of a system. Each item in the picture can be labeled with the words *living* and *nonliving*.

To assist with this discrimination, Mark will be given a live worm to see and touch. The worm will be moving and slimy. Then he will be asked to put it in a box with other living things (caterpillars, frogs, leaves, bugs, and so forth). Then Mark will be given a pencil and be asked to put the pencil in a box marked nonliving things. *There will be other nonliving things such as erasers, crayons, paper, carpeting, and so forth. Mark and the other students can also help to sort five more items each into the correct boxes. To test Mark's comprehension of living and nonliving items, he will be presented with two items (worm and paper) and be asked to touch the item that is living.*

7. Say to class: "Now we will make a closed system and put both living and nonliving things in the system. We will watch the system over the next few days and watch to see how the different parts of the systems work together as a unit."

8. Break the students into cooperative learning groups. Each group will have 4–5 students in the team. The teacher will assign the teams. The team will use the attached sheet to follow the directions. A total of five different systems will be made: worm farm, two plant terrarium, fish tank, and tadpole aquarium.

9. Each team will view the systems each day for the next 2 weeks and record observations. Each student will record their data and record it on a graph to show the changes in the closed system. The students will also perform mathematic computations to show the change in their closed system from the time the system was made until the end of the 2-week period. The students will also compare the systems with all the necessary parts with systems that were missing necessary parts (sunlight or water).

Mark will use adapted measuring devices to measure his plants. He will use a large ruler and put stickers on the ruler at locations where the plant hits during the daily measuring sessions (see Systematic Instruction Plan for measuring [Figure 10.3]). He will then graph the growth or lack of growth of the plants on a graph. He will match the points on the graph to the points on the ruler where he put the sticker and verbally state the corresponding numbers (See Systematic Instruction Plan for graphing [Figure 10.3].) He will state if the plant is growing or shrinking.

Summary

Whole-class review with choral responding and pictures.

A system is made up of parts that interact together as a unit.

Open systems are systems that take inputs and give off outputs.

The parts of a system in nature are air, soil, water, light.

Closed system is a system with no outputs or inputs.

Each system can have living and nonliving things in it.

Adapted Lesson Plan on Leaf Classification to Include a Student with Significant Disabilities in a Seventh-Grade Science Lesson

Unit: Classification
Lesson: Leaf Classification
Time: 1 hour

Summary

All leaves possess numerous physical characteristics. These characteristics can be used to create a simple classification system.

Main Curriculum Tie

Seventh-grade science: Use and develop a simple classification system.

Materials

- Paper and pencil

- Set of 5–10 leaves for each group of two to three students. (Ideally, the set should include leaves from several evergreens and several deciduous trees; e.g., pine needles, spruce needles, juniper needles, oak leaves, elm leaves, maples leaves, and so forth.)

Background for Teachers

It is helpful if some understanding has been developed on classification systems where things are divided into categories and given names. Larger categories are divided into smaller categories and so on until everything that is different is in a group by itself.

Intended Learning Outcomes

- Develop and use categories to classify observations.

- Develop critical thinking skills.

- Use the language and concepts of science as a means of thinking and communicating.

STATE STANDARDS (NORTH CAROLINA STATE BOARD OF EDUCATION AND DEPARTMENT OF PUBLIC INSTRUCTION, 2005)

Science

1.03 Apply safety procedures in the laboratory and in field studies.

- Recognize potential hazards.
- Safely manipulate materials and equipment.
- Conduct appropriate procedures.

1.04 Students will understand that structure is used to develop classification systems.

- Classify based on observable properties.
- Use and develop a simple classification system.

1.05 Analyze evidence to

- Explain observations.
- Make inferences and predictions.
- Develop the relationship between evidence and explanation.

1.06 Use mathematics to gather, organize, and present quantitative data resulting from scientific investigations:

- Measurement
- Analysis of data
- Graphing
- Prediction models

1.08 Use oral and written language to

- Communicate findings
- Defend conclusions of scientific investigations

1.09 Use technologies and information systems to

- Research
- Gather and analyze data
- Visualize data
- Disseminate findings to others

Math

Competency Goal 1 **The learner will understand and compute with rational numbers.**

1.01 Develop and use ratios, proportions, and percentages to solve problems.

IEP Goals

Bart will follow a picture direction sheet to participate in the lab experiment.

Bart will point to 3–5 lab safety signs and state what they mean. (Science objective 1.03)

Bart will answer 3 science questions based on the lab experiment using pictures or the actual objects. (Science objective 1.08)

Bart will sort 2 different types of items into the correct groups. (Science objectives 1.04 and 1.08)

Bart will press a switch to activate a search on the Internet. (Science objective 1.09)

Bart will press a switch to select a pie chart using Excel to graph his proportion of leaves. (Math competency 1 and Science objectives 1.06 and 1.09)

Instructional Procedures

Whole class will review 5 safety signs present in the lab, prior to beginning any class experiments. *During this time Bart will point to his personal set of safety signs (same as the class) and state what each sign means to his lab partner, Drew. Drew will place the correctly identified cards in the correct envelope and the incorrectly identified cards in the incorrect envelope. See Systematic Instruction Plan for safety signs (Figure 10.9).*

1. Define classification as the systematic grouping or arranging of things into categories based on similar characteristics.

   Review previously gained knowledge pertaining to classification by asking students what they know about classification. How is it done? Why is it done? Who does it?

   Discuss as a class some ways that we use classification in our everyday lives to make keeping track of large numbers of things easier. Examples of classification systems that we use in our everyday lives may include: mailing addresses (country is divided into states, states into cities, cities into street addresses or Post Office Boxes, and so forth), finding items in a grocery store, finding a phone number of a particular individual or of a business in the yellow pages, a book in a library, and so forth. Make a list on the board or overhead of any examples the students can think of.

2. Introduce class activity. Divide the class into lab partners and give each group a leaf packet. Tell students that they will design a classification scheme that correctly identifies each leaf. (To facilitate communication, assign each of the leaves a number or a name. If the leaves are not identified in some way beforehand, the students will not be able to communicate their classification.)

Bart will pair up with Drew, his regular lab partner. Bart will use his lab direction in picture form to follow the lab experiment and participate in the lab experiment.

3. Brainstorm several physical traits that differentiate each leaf. Look at things like general shape, location of veins, shape of leaf edge, color, and so forth.

    Ask the question: *How could we make a classification system for these leaves?* Listen to student ideas.

4. Direct students to separate their leaves into two groups. Most likely the first grouping would be to separate the leaves into needles and broad leaf. Have the students calculate the ratio, proportions, and percentages of each type of leaf in relation to the whole sample. Record and report the results. Why do you think these percentages resulted? Ask the students to again separate the two groups into two more groups. Repeat the ratio, proportions, and percentages calculations. Record and report the results. Why do you think these percentages resulted? Listen to their suggestions on how the grouping be done. Instruct the students to continue separating the larger groups into smaller groups until each leaf is in its own separate category. What would be the ratio, proportion, and percentage of these samples? What does this mean? The students will graph their findings using pie charts and the Excel program.

    Bart will sort a pile of leaves into two separate piles of maple leaves and pine needles. The pine needles will go on a paper with a pine needle already on the paper. He will put all the maple leaves on the paper with a maple leaf already on the paper. See Systematic Instruction Plan on sorting (Figure 10.7). Bart will make a pie chart using Excel to show which portion of the maple leaves came from the sample and which part of the pine needles came from the sample. Note: Half of Bart's sample is pine and half is maple. Bart will enter the data and select the pie chart using using Excel software and a switch and the IntelliKeys assistive technology.

5. Instruct students to write down their classification systems. They should record the characteristics they used to separate the leaves at each level of the classification system.

6. Have a couple groups share their classification system. Point out that all the systems are not the same. Does that make one right and one wrong? (No, scientists often disagree about classification schemes. Also, many classification systems take different routes but end up with the same identification.) Classification schemes are valid if they are based on the observation of distinguishing characteristics and use a series of logical steps.

    Ask Bart and Drew about their classification system. Ask Bart 3 questions about the system. Bart can point or verbally answer questions: What did you sort? Show me the leaves that are green. Which leaf is big? What types of leaves did you sort?

7. Discuss the system (Five Kingdom system of classification) used by scientists to classify living organisms.

8. Use a plant key to identify the leaves that the students examined.

Web Sites

Animal Bytes (http://www.seaworld.org/AnimalBytes/animal_bytes.html)

Animal Bytes was specifically designed to help quickly find information about some of the unique creatures found in the animal kingdom. Most files include the scientific classification, fun facts, and biological value.

Bart and Drew will search for this web site. Drew will type in the address and Bart will hit the switch to begin the search.

Assessment Plan

1. Ask students to exchange classification schemes and see if they can correctly identify leaves using each other's schemes.

2. Give students rocks, bones, flowers, or some other set of objects and ask them to create a classification scheme to be used to identify those objects.

3. Give students a simple flower key and ask them to identify a flower using the key.

Author   Kendall Benson (http://www.MyUen.org/7866; 1997)

Modified by Karena Cooper-Duffy to include a student with significant disabilities.

Created Date   Jan 29 1997 17:30 PM Modified Dec 1, 2004.

Chapter 11

How Students Demonstrate Academic Performance in Portfolio Assessment

Jacqueline Kearns, Michael D. Burdge,
Jean Clayton, Anne P. Denham, and Harold L. Kleinert

This chapter will illustrate how grade-level content standards can be used to develop curriculum activities and materials that provide students with significant cognitive disabilities access to the general curriculum. In addition, we will demonstrate assessment strategies that can be used during instruction to gather data that provide both formative and summative information about student performance. These assessment strategies are best used within the context of a portfolio assessment in which multiple pieces of evidence provide a thorough picture of student performance. Moreover, with the requirements of the Individuals with Disabilities Education Act (IDEA) Amendments of 1997 (PL 105-17), the Individuals with Disabilities Education Improvement Act (IDEA) 2004 (PL 108-446), and the No Child Left Behind (NCLB) Act of 2001 (PL 107-110), for states to have in place alternate educational assessments for those students who cannot participate, even with modifications and accommodations, in regular educational assessments, many states have decided to include elements of portfolio and performance task assessments within their respective alternate assessments (Thompson & Thurlow, 2000). The use of these strategies may also result in enhanced student scores in these assessments (Kampfer, Horvath, Kleinert, & Kearns, 2001; Kleinert & Kearns, 2001).

WHY ACADEMIC STANDARDS?

Teachers of students with severe disabilities have long focused on developmental and functional skill instruction. Certainly an important part of our work is teaching students the skills they need to function as independently and productively as possible across a range of settings, both now and in the future. However, until recently, little thought was given to how or even *if* the curriculum we have traditionally provided our students relates to the general curriculum designed for all students. In fact, we have viewed a functional curriculum (e.g., activities of

This manuscript was supported, in part, by the U.S. Department of Education Office of Special Education and Rehabilitation Services (Grant H324U040001). However, the opinions expressed do not necessarily reflect the position or policy of the U.S. Department of Education and no official endorsement should be inferred.

daily living and basic or "access skills" such as social, communication, and motor in a developmental progression) for students with severe disabilities as an "alternate" or "substitute" curriculum, wholly separate from what is taught to other students. In addition, there is little attention to increasing the complexity of challenge or progression of skills. Students often work on the same skills within the context of the same activities year after year, even though classroom data indicate that the skills have often been mastered.

IDEA '97, IDEA 2004, and NCLB have changed our thinking about what students with disabilities should be learning in three very important ways. First, IDEA requires the individualized education program (IEP) team to determine how a student's disability affects his or her participation and progress in the general curriculum. Educators are required to identify measurable goals and short-term objectives (for students in the alternate assessment working toward alternate achievement standards), along with appropriate supports and modifications that will enable each student to progress in the general curriculum to the extent appropriate for that student. Second, IDEA requires that all students, including those with severe disabilities, be included in state and district educational assessments, as a direct indicator of what they have learned through their instruction. Third, NCLB requires that although alternate assessments may be based on alternate achievement standards, these assessments must align with grade-level content standards. This means that whereas the overall expectations (i.e., achievement standards) may describe student skills that are significantly below grade level or clearly differentiated in achievement, the assessment should include math and reading content that aligns with the standards, curriculum activities, and materials that are used by same-age/grade peers. Grade-level content standards should specify reading and mathematics skills that are to be measured. These skills in turn form the "skeleton" or framework for the curriculum lessons, activities, and materials.

Alignment of alternate assessments with grade-level content standards represents a fundamental shift in thinking about curriculum for students with significant disabilities. Whereas most states applied a functional mapping approach in their initial approach to the development of their alternate assessments (Browder et al., in press) by tying state standards for all students to "functional applications" for students with significant disabilities, the requirements of NCLB are clear that even alternate assessments must be aligned to grade-level content standards. Yet teachers have reported difficulty in understanding the relationship of alternate assessment outcomes to grade-level content standards (Flowers, Browder, Ahlgrim-Delzell, & Spooner, 2004), and it is not surprising that states have varied widely in the extent to which their alternate assessments have established clear links to math and reading content (Browder et al., 2004). The following example illustrates how a student, Aimy, who has significant cognitive disabilities, demonstrates performance on skills that align directly with the grade-level standard/benchmark for seventh-grade English language arts.

ALIGNING AND EVIDENCING GRADE-LEVEL CONTENT: AN EXAMPLE FROM SEVENTH GRADE ENGLISH LANGUAGE ARTS

The general education standard for Aimy's example has been taken from the International Reading Association (IRA)/National Council of Teachers of English (NCTE) standards for English language arts (2002):

Students conduct research on issues and interests by generating ideas and questions, and by posing problems. They gather, evaluate, and synthesize data from a variety of sources (e.g., print and nonprint texts, artifacts, people) to communicate their discoveries in ways that suit their purpose and audience.

The relevant seventh-grade standard/benchmark toward which all seventh graders work is

Students will conduct research on issues by posing questions, identifying appropriate sources, accessing information from a variety of sources, synthesizing and communicating findings in a variety of ways, and citing sources appropriately.

Although the standard for Aimy is from English language arts, her student work samples have come from social studies/history content, data from a variety of content areas, and the performance event from literature content. The samples have been developed, completed, and collected within the context of daily instruction across each of these areas. This embedded approach has the advantage(s) of

- Connecting instruction and assessment

- Being done in an authentic context

- Resulting from an age-appropriate, general education, grade-level curriculum activity in which all students have participated

Figure 11.1 is a student work sample that Aimy completed while working on a social studies/history unit on the Civil War. All seventh graders are expected to select a Civil War battle or major event of their choice to research. They are to use a graphic organizer to help them synthesize their research. As Aimy relies on picture symbols to help her understand content more effectively, the text and Aimy's research notes are supplemented with Mayer-Johnson Picture Symbols (Boardmaker) (2004a). Aimy's research notes, printed from Writing With Symbols 2000 (Mayer-Johnson, 2000), are cut apart and Aimy then pastes them into an adapted graphic organizer. The work sample, besides illustrating Aimy's performance, gives an idea of the supports (picture symbols), materials adaptation, and alternate means of performance (e.g., cutting and pasting versus writing) necessary for curriculum content to be accessible for Aimy. In addition, the teacher's description of this activity provides evidence for Aimy's increasing levels of self-determination (e.g., she chose this topic from several options and planned the content of her own entry; see Figure 11.2).

The student performance documented in this chart is based on the steps required to conduct research. The task analysis in this chart differs from more traditional, functional task analyses in that it involves broadly stated skills (e.g., *answer 2 questions correctly about read material*) that can be used across many different content areas and units of study, rather than a more discrete, task-analyzed activity (e.g., toothbrushing) which has fewer generalizable skills and no specific link to the general curriculum. This is not to say that skills such as toothbrushing may not be important for students to learn, but they do not represent the general curriculum content that alternate assessments are to measure under the requirements of NCLB. General skills such as this can and should be included

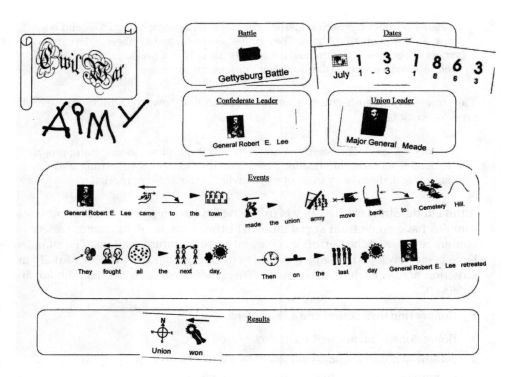

Figure 11.1. Data collection; adapted from graphic organizer used by all students. (Picture Symbols used with permission from Mayer-Johnson LLC.)

on the student's IEP; however, there is no requirement to assess them for the purposes of compliance with NCLB and IDEA '97.

In the previous example, data are collected on the five steps involved in conducting research. Because this skill can be applied over several content areas, the data points indicate that Aimy has increased her independence in these skills. The method of data collection and instruction gives information on not only her level of independent performance across steps, but also her responses within the systematic instructional strategy of system of least prompts. As the data are collected on a set of generic skills, the system can be used to document Aimy's performance on conducting research on a variety of topics ranging from language arts to science. This ensures that Aimy will have multiple opportunities to acquire the skills and demonstrate competence. Because the skill can also be applied over several units within a curriculum area, it allows Aimy to continue to work on improving her performance on the critical skill while allowing her to keep up with the pace of instruction of the general education curriculum. For example, the curriculum may support research on the Renaissance culture while reading a play by Shakespeare, and research on the depression while reading *Roll of Thunder, Hear My Cry* (Taylor, 1997).

Figure 11.3 is a performance task that corresponds to the same steps within the ongoing data collection task analysis shown in the preceding figure. A performance task is a single event to see how a student performs a skill in a novel situation. Although a performance task may be used very effectively as one element of a portfolio assessment, it differs from portfolio assessment in that portfolio assessment typically includes multiple evidences of performance, illustrating student growth over time and across settings and conditions. Alternatively, a performance task allows for a single-event examination of the critical skill targeted for instruction (*conducting research*), but examines how the student is able to transfer his or her performance on that skill in a new context. Although the skill is the same, the educational team can see how the student actually performs the steps when presented with a new learning activity (in this example, conducting research specifically about John Steinbeck) (see Figure 11.3).

The three types of evidence that we have presented thus far (student work, performance data, and performance task) serve to give a more complete picture of student learning than any one piece alone. This triangulation of evidence allows an alternate assessment portfolio to illustrate the complexities of student learning and performance toward a grade-level standard.

As illustrated in this example, assessment strategies used successfully with these students are direct observation of a skill in structured or unstructured contexts; performance events; recollection of student performance by individuals most familiar with the student (e.g., interviews, surveys, rating scales); and review of records, including anecdotal data and student work samples. Performance tasks may also be included in a portfolio (Colorado Enhanced Assessment Project, 2004; Kleinert & Kearns, 2004). Instructional observation data can be collected frequently (i.e., daily or twice weekly) using a single-observation coding system that is verified by another observer on a regular, ongoing basis. The data recording sheet is included in the portfolio along with other instructional products. Assessment strategies and their resulting types of evidence must be planned as an integral part of instruction, allowing direct, systematic observational data to be collected on specific skills through a variety of instructional activities.

Student Name: Aimy
Dates: November 1 – March 15
Objective: Aimy will conduct research by completing the task steps described with 80% accuracy for 3 out of 5 assignments

Task Steps ↓	Dates ⇒	Nov. 1	Dec. 3	Jan. 12	Jan. 30	Feb. 12	Feb. 28	March 15
1. Listen to information being read, demonstrated by pointing to familiar word in passage upon request	I	I	I	I	I	I	I	I
2. Answer 2 questions correctly about read material	V	I	V	V	I	V	I	I
3. Orally read summarized information written in picture symbol format	V	V	V	I	I	I	I	I
4. Paste cut apart information to correctly complete a graphic organizer	V	V	I	I	I	I	I	I
5. Sequence events by pasting picture symbols in correct order	V	V	V	V	V	V	V	V
6. Write 3 to 5 sentences using the graphic organizer as a model	I	I	I	I	I	I	I	I
Total	33%	50%	50%	67%	(83%)	67%	(83%)	(83%)

I = Independently   M = Model   V = Verbal Cue

Figure 11.2. Task analysis.

HOW CAN I BE SURE THE STUDENT'S WORK IS ALIGNED WITH GRADE-LEVEL CONTENT?

In order to be sure the student is receiving instruction that is aligned with grade-level content, review the content standards for the student's grade level (for more information on the concept of alignment, see Chapter 12). We recommend

---

Student Name: *Aimy*   Date: *March 30*

Performance Task for Research/Informational Reading

Steps	Directions for teacher	Task for Student
1. Listen to passage about John Steinbeck read aloud (demonstrated by pointing to familiar words upon request)	Stop and have student point to familiar words and match to a picture symbol	Words: __ born __ writer __ book __ truck __ America
2. Answer 2 questions correctly about read material	Following the reading of the short passage ask 2 questions	__ What did John Steinbeck do for a living? __ What did he ride in for a tour across America?
3. Orally read summarized information written in picture symbol format	Write a short passage in picture symbol format, summarizing the information and have student read orally	__ Missed words __ Total words in passage
4. Paste cut apart information to correctly complete a graphic organizer	Provide picture symbol material cut apart and a graphic organizer so the student can sort out the information	__ Name of person __ Date of birth __ What he did __ Special events
5. Write 3 to 5 sentences using the graphic organizer as a model	Have student copy from the graphic organizer to write 3 – 5 sentences about John Steinbeck	__ Used complete sentences __ Included at least 2 important facts __ Wrote at least 3 sentences

I = Independently   M = Model   V = Verbal Cue

Figure 11.3. Performance task.

a four-step process that begins with considering the grade-level standard, then translates the standard into outcomes for all learners, identifies instructional activities and the appropriate supports necessary for the student to access the learning activities, and finally considers opportunities to teach other skills from the student's IEP (Clayton, Burdge, & Kearns, 2002; Kearns, Burdge, & Kleinert, in press). This process is illustrated in the following example for Tim, who is learning about electrical circuits in his fourth-grade science class.

An Example from Science: A Fourth-Grade Unit on Electricity

The following example illustrates evidence of learning toward grade-level standards/benchmarks (fourth grade) for Tim, who has a cognitive disability. Tim is included in a general education science class with typical peers. All students are engaged in developing an understanding of science concepts and developing abilities of inquiry. Specifically, they are working toward the following science standard:

> Develop an understanding of light, heat, electricity and magnetism
> National Science Education Standards (1996)
> Center for Science, Mathematics, and Engineering Education (CSMEE)

All students are working on the corresponding grade-level standard/benchmark:

> Electricity in circuits can produce light, heat, sound, and magnetic effects. Electrical circuits require a complete loop through which an electrical current can pass.

As in the previous examples, possible documentation that can be used to support an alternate assessment entry include

- Student work sample

- Performance data to show progress toward an identified goal

- Video clip (approximately 3 minutes) of the performance task illustrating the process of creating a model, demonstrating a process, and sharing the results.

The unit includes information on electricity and circuits, and how this applies to the things the students see around them. Activities involve reading text (both as a group and individually), conducting experiments, making observations, and recording and sharing results.

Figure 11.4 illustrates the four steps that we have found helpful for teachers in linking student assessment activities to the grade-level content standards for all students.

- Link to both the state standard and the specific grade-level content standard

- Define the outcome of instruction

- Identify the instructional activities

- Target specific objectives from the IEP

The outcome for all students is that "they will understand that electrical circuits require a complete loop through which an electrical current can pass." The prioritized outcome for Tim is that "when the wires touch, the circuit works and the light comes on."

Tim is included in each aspect of the class activities. Some vocabulary words from the science unit are identified as important for Tim to learn (*circuit, bat-*

1. Link to the appropriate standard(s)	
State/district standard	**Grade-level standard(s)**
Physical science: Light, heat, electricity and magnetism.	Electricity in circuits can produce light, heat, sound, and magnetic effects. Electrical circuits require a complete loop through which an electrical current can pass.

2. Define the outcome(s) of instruction		
Outcomes for all students	**Prioritized outcomes**	**Supports**
Students will understand that electrical circuits require a complete loop through which an electrical current can pass.	When the wires touch, the circuit works and the light comes on.	• Simplified diagram • Content summary in simple text supported with graphics • Simplified directions • Modified table to record results

3. Identify the instructional activities	
Instructional activities	**Active participation**
1. Read chapter in textbook. 2. Students will work in pairs to build both a serial and parallel circuit with provided materials. 3. Students will observe and record differences in open and closed circuits.	1. Student will read printed text supported with graphics (summary of content material) with a peer. 2. Student will work with a partner to build a serial and parallel circuit. 3. Student will observe results of open and closed circuits and record observations using modified table.

4. Target specific objectives from the IEP		
Instructional activities	**Embedded standards-based objectives**	**Other embedded objectives**
1. Read chapter in textbook 2. Students will work in pairs to build both a serial and parallel circuit with provided materials 3. Students will observe and record differences in open and closed circuits	1. Improve reading skills 2. Work as a member of a group 3. Practice observation and enquiry	1. Read chapter in textbook 2. Improve fine motor skills; follow directions 3. Improve observation skills

Figure 11.4. Four-step process.

tery, closed, and *open*). These words are always paired with a graphic/symbol and are regularly presented to Tim in the form of summarized paragraphs, labels, and in a graphic word bank for writing. As the class goes over the textbook, Tim works on a summary of the text. Tim first reads the summary on the computer by using the text-to-speech feature of the software. He can see the word paired with the graphic and hear it. He then reads a printed version of the text with symbols with the support of a partner. Data are collected on targeted words as Tim reads. Both Tim's sample work and the data collected could be submitted within an alternate assessment entry. In this way, Tim also documents progress on his IEP objectives of *Improving reading skills* and *Working as a member of a group to achieve a common goal* (see Figure 11.4).

Figure 11.5 shows the summarized text that was available to Tim first on the computer, and then in printed form. The summary was created with Writing with Symbols 2000 (Mayer-Johnson, 2004b; see Figure 11.5). Figure 11.6 is a sample of the data collected from targeted words.

Addressing scientific inquiry, the class works in pairs to create circuits. Students gather materials, make predictions, test their predictions, and share results with the class. Again, Tim is included in each aspect of the inquiry using the same materials as the class, but with a modified chart. Tim works with his partner, records his prediction, makes careful observations, and records what he observes. The materials give further opportunity to practice his specific vocabulary through labeling, and the nature of the visuals on the chart cues Tim to use his eyes for observation. Tim circles his observation carefully, and the circuits are "opened" and "closed" repeatedly, yielding multiple opportunities for participation and observation.

Figure 11.7 illustrates the circuit created by Tim and his partner and Tim's modified chart with his observation recorded. Tim circled his observation using a marker. This process could be videotaped for submission in the assessment, which would identify Tim's level of independence, use of assistive technology, and natural peer support (see Figure 11.7).

As the unit progresses, students are tested on the material they have covered. Tim's test is modified significantly but still addresses the grade-level standard. Tim will complete sentences addressing the essence of the grade-level standard using a writing grid. The test is created through the use of the writing grid. The grid allows Tim to read the partial sentence and click independently on his answer (a choice of two words). He receives auditory feedback as he activates his selection. The sentence is then read again. Tim's test can be submitted as assessment documentation of his learning the standard, along with a short note explaining Tim's participation or a screen shot of his work illustrating the choice Tim made in addition to his completed sentence (see Figure 11.8).

By following the four-step process, Tim is able to demonstrate that he understands the science content standard for electrical circuits. Simultaneously, he is working on increasing his reading vocabulary and comprehension. Both of these skills are critical as Tim gains increasing access to the general curriculum.

How We Can Address Assessment for Learners with Complex Needs: A High School Math Example

Learners with complex needs, such as communication, motor, and even medical needs, present unique and often difficult challenges to both curriculum access

Figure 11.5. Summary of class text created with Writing with Symbols 2000. (Widgit Rebus symbols used with permission from Mayer-Johnson LLC.)

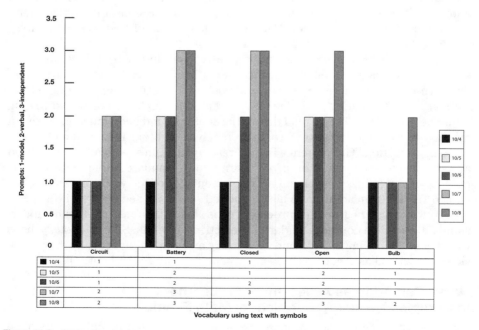

	Circuit	Battery	Closed	Open	Bulb
10/4	1	1	1	1	1
10/5	1	2	1	2	1
10/6	1	2	2	2	1
10/7	2	3	3	2	1
10/8	2	3	3	3	2

Vocabulary using text with symbols

Figure 11.6. Instructional data.

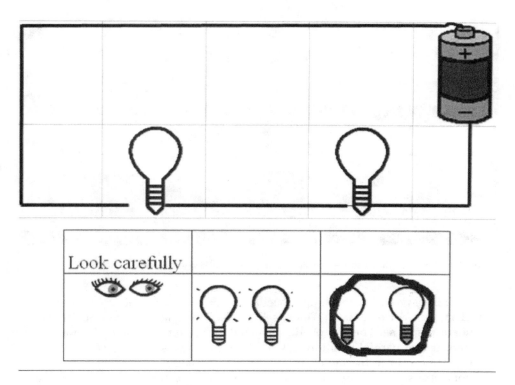

Figure 11.7. Student work sample.

and assessment, primarily because of their limited response repertoires, attentional deficits, and medical conditions. However, students who have limited verbal communication and motor skills, sensory impairments affecting vision and hearing, and/or attentional and health difficulties related to medical conditions (e.g., seizures) *can* be provided with access to grade-level curricular materials and activities.

Four things must be in place to adequately teach and assess these children and youth. First, the student must have a way to communicate a response. Studies by Wheatley (1993) and Kleinert, Kennedy, and Kearns (1999) found that augmentative communication systems became a priority once there was an alternate assessment requirement that students have a way to communicate. Coupled with the increasing availability of low-tech tools (e.g., photos, objects) and sophisticated electronic communication systems (e.g., scanning devices), many more students who previously were considered noncommunicative now have reliable and consistent ways to provide a response.

Second, curricular materials and activities need to be specially designed to provide meaningful access to the content for the widest array of possible users (CAST, 2003). Concrete materials, assistive technology, software packages, and digitally accessible materials are more readily available and serve to enhance access to academic curriculum that was previously unavailable. Moreover, content enhancements (such as graphic or visual organizers of more abstract concepts) and peer support (in which students have individualized learning goals within the same activity) have created greater access.

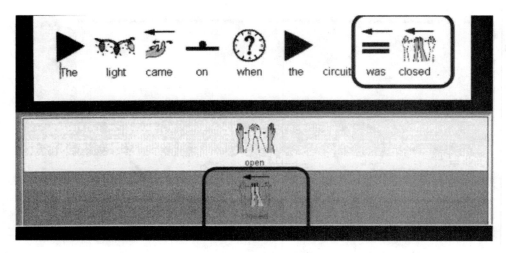

Figure 11.8. Tim's test. The student writing grid was created with Writing with Symbols 2000 (Widgit).

Third, systematic teaching procedures (see Chapter 8, this volume; see also Wolery, Ault, & Doyle, 1992; Wolery & Schuster, 1997) improve the consistency of student response. These procedures include precise response definitions, consistent use of careful positioning and attention cues, specified task directions, adequate response timing, clear and immediate feedback for both correct and incorrect responses, appropriate and meaningful positive reinforcement, and a consistent system for charting and monitoring the student's response behavior. Systematic instruction includes careful, formative evaluation of student performance based on daily or very frequent performance measures, with changes in instructional procedures tied directly to student progress (or lack thereof). Systematic instruction also includes a variety of near errorless instructional procedures, as noted in Chapter 8 by Collins et al. Finally, teachers who use systematic instruction carefully plan for each phase of student learning: *acquisition* (or initial learning of a targeted skill); *fluency* (or increasing and fluidity of responses to acceptable levels); *maintenance* (performance over time and after the unit of instruction is over); and, perhaps most critically, *generalization* to new settings, people, and activities.

This element of generalization is the fourth element that must be in place for students with significant disabilities to learn. Opportunities to practice skills that occur in multiple environments and/or skills that appear to motivate or cause an increase in the student's rate of response across settings increase the probability that the student will acquire useful and meaningful knowledge and skills. These four points are illustrated in the math example for Michelle.

Michelle has multiple disabilities, including significant cognitive disabilities and physical disabilities; she is nonverbal but communicates through tactile object cues and manual signs. Michelle is taking a general math class with her typical peers, working toward the following math standard:

Students will understand and apply basic concepts of probability
(National Council for Teachers of Mathematics; NCTM, n.d.).

All students are working on the corresponding grade-level standard/benchmark:

Students will make predictions and analyze accuracy by conducting simulations using theoretical and experiential probability.

Students are discussing probability and its importance in making informed decisions, from games of chance to important medical decisions. Probability is reflected in other curriculum areas, such as science, and this gives Michelle opportunity to work on a standard across the curriculum. The unit was introduced to the class by a traditional game of Rock, Paper, Scissors, with discussions focused on fairness, and the class created a tree diagram to illustrate theoretical probability. As the unit progresses, the math class is working on a modified version of the game in groups of three, and Michelle is an active member of a group. Students make predictions about what will occur and are now taking data to determine experiential probability. The group is conducting 27 trials and each member is taking turns recording data (the number of matches and nonmatches). Michelle uses objects to assist in the learning process and to actively participate in the game: Scissors, a small rock/stone, and a folded piece of paper are used instead of the hand shapes used by her peers. Michelle selects which item she will present from the choice of three, and she places her selection on the table as other group members present their hand shapes. Using concrete objects allows Michelle to participate in the simulation along with her peers. Michelle's group members assist her in identifying the match/nonmatch, using the terms *same* and *different* supported by text paired with symbols. This process could be videotaped for submission in the assessment, which would identify Michelle's level of independence, use of assistive technology, and natural peer support.

Possible documentation that can be used to support an alternate assessment entry includes

- Student work sample

- Performance data to show progress toward an identified goal

- Video clip (approximately 3 minutes) to illustrate the process of conducting an assessment (see Figure 11.9)

The group is responsible for collecting data using a frequency table; each member of the group collects data over 9 trials for a total of 27 trials. Michelle uses concrete objects to create her table. Using counters suitable for her grasp to represent trials, Michelle places a counter in the correct container (match/nonmatch) after each trial. Michelle's peers assist in numbering the counters as she collects her data for each trial. The numbers are laminated and mounted with a hook and loop anchor strip. When asked how many matches and nonmatches there were, Michelle touches the corresponding anchor strip so that the results can be tallied. Michelle's results could also be transcribed by a peer to be included in the assessment, but Michelle demonstrates a preference to be as independent as possible. The printed image provides a record of Michelle's results, which can be reviewed alongside the work of her peers. Michelle can view the image in paper form or on the computer monitor when results are dis-

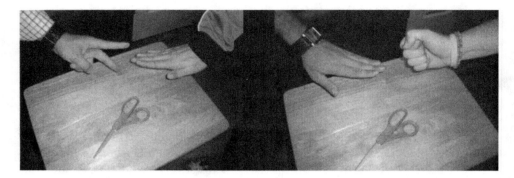

Figure 11.9. Experiment simulation. Left, during the modified simulation, this combination (scissors, scissors, paper) is identified as a match because scissors were presented by Michelle and one group member. Right, during the modified simulation, this combination (rock, paper, scissors) is identified as a nonmatch because Michelle's scissors and the hand shapes of her group members are all different.

cussed in class. Finally, Figure 11.11 illustrates the data sheet that the teacher uses to record Michelle's progress (i.e., level of prompt needed) in learning the steps necessary to make a prediction (see Figures 11.10 and 11.11).

Why Portfolios?

Portfolio assessment continues to be the most common form of alternate assessment that is based on alternate achievement standards used in states (Thompson & Thurlow, 2000). Yet teachers involved in portfolio assessment often report that they represent a paperwork burden (Kampfer et al., 2001; Kleinert et al., 1999). However, research on time, effort, and scores of alternate assessment portfolios suggests that the amount of time outside of instruction that a teacher spends preparing the portfolio has little impact on student results. The extent to which the teacher *embeds* the portfolio requirements into daily instruction *does* appear to be a predictor of student results (Kampfer et al., 2001). Another important predictor of student success in portfolio assessment is the degree to which the student is involved in the development of the portfolio (Kampfer et al., 2001). We have tried to demonstrate through the examples provided above that

- Good assessment is part and parcel of good instruction

- The best evidence for authentic alternate assessments comes from targeted skill instruction in alternate achievement standards that are based on grade-level content standards for all students, and that, whenever possible, that instruction should occur in the context of general education activities with typical peers

- Appropriate use of assistive technology and creative modifications matching preferred learner modalities enables students with significant disabilities to have access to grade-level content that may not have been available to them under more traditional presentation formats

- The best evidence of student learning in the context of those alternate achievement standards comes from a triangulation of evidence across systematic instructional data, student work sample, and performance events in novel settings

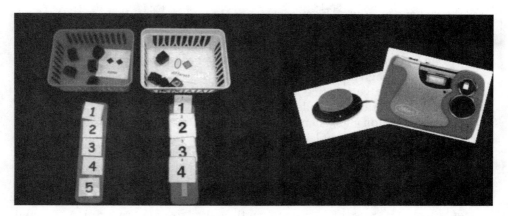

Figure 11.10.   Adapted frequency table. (a) Experiential probability. Michelle's adapted frequency table using concrete objects allows Michelle to collect data with a higher degree of independence. (b) Michelle uses a switch-operated digital camera to record her data collection so that her work may be printed and presented clearly in her assessment. Group members place or hold the camera to ensure the picture is aligned correctly while Michelle activates the switch independently.

Student: Michelle							
Objective:	Using two or three objects representing curriculum content, Michelle will make a prediction as demonstrated by completing the steps described with 80% accuracy for three of five trials across curriculum areas.						
Curriculum Area/date	Math 1/4	Math 1/18	Science 2/4	Statistics 2/26	Science 3/6	Math 3/27	Math 4/12
Task							
Use hands to explore each item presented	I	I	I	I	V	I	I
Return item to container	I	I	I	I	I	I	I
Visually scan items from left to right	V	V	V	I	I	I	I
Touch each item from left to right	PP	PP	PP	M	M	M	V
Make a clear prediction by placing item (scissor, paper, rock) in the container	M	V	I	I	I	I	I
Total	40%	40%	60%	80%	60%	80%	80%

PP – Partial Physical   M – Model   V – Verbal   I – Independent

Figure 11.11.   Data collection.

- Portfolio assessment allows students with significant disabilities to both document and enhance critical skills of self-determination, including self-assessment, choice making, and control over their own learning process.

CONCLUSION

A primary purpose for using a portfolio is so that student learning or skill demonstration can be assessed in a formative way from daily instruction. Portfolios historically have been used as an instructional tool in a formative assessment system. Indeed, writing and even mathematics portfolios continue to be used in some state *general* education assessment systems. The formative process entailed in a portfolio lends itself to the instruction of students who experience severe disabilities, because progress is often measured in small incremental steps. As discussed previously, effective practice in teaching students with severe disabilities suggests that the systematic collection of ongoing performance data results in increased acquisition and generalization of skills (Browder, 1989; Wolery, Bailey, & Sugai, 1988). As the examples in this chapter illustrate, instructional data can be collected, displayed, and stored easily within the context of a portfolio.

The population of students who take part in alternate assessments aligned with alternate achievement standards includes the widest diversity of students in terms of our current ability to measure and quantify their respective achievements, in part because of their significantly limited response repertoires (i.e., ability to communicate what they know). However, with the advent of assistive technology (e.g., switches, electronic communicators), educators are beginning to see a wider array of response repertoire possibilities. Still, traditional large-scale assessments (e.g., multiple-choice formats) are not accessible for this population as they are currently constructed. A portfolio can accommodate a wider array of response repertoires that may be customized for individual students. A portfolio can accommodate a variety of student demonstration techniques including systematic instructional data collection systems, student work samples, and video- or audiotaped performance events. Finally, portfolio assessment can enable students with significant disabilities to demonstrate what they are learning in the context of daily instruction aligned with grade-level content standards, and to take greater control over both the process and documentation of that learning. For teachers, portfolio assessment can provide a broader array of strategies to use to incorporate their students' performance into their state's large-scale alternate assessment.

REFERENCES

Browder, D.M. (1989). *Assessment of individuals with severe disabilities.* Baltimore: Paul H. Brookes Publishing Co.

Browder, D.M., Ahlgrim-Delzell, L., Flowers, C., Karvonen, M., Spooner, F., & Algozzine, R. (in press). How states implement alternate assessments for students with disabilities. *Journal of Disability Policy Studies.*

Browder, D.M., Flowers, C., Ahlgrim-Delzell, L., Karvonen, M., Spooner, F., & Algozzine, R. (2004). The alignment of alternate assessment content to academic and functional curriculum. *Journal of Special Education, 37,* 211–223.

Center for Applied Special Technology (CAST). (2003). *Underlying premises: Universal design for learning.* Retrieved February 16, 2005, from http://www.cast.org/udl/index .cfm?i=7#Underlying%20Premises

Clayton, J., Burdge, M., & Kearns, J. (2002). *Accessing the general curriculum.* Unpublished manuscript, University of Kentucky at Lexington.

Colorado Enhanced Assessment Project. (2004). *Instructionally embedded assessment: Educator manual.* Unpublished manuscript, University of Kentucky at Lexington.

Flowers, C., Browder, D., Ahlgrim-Delzell, L., & Spooner, F. (2004). *Teachers' perceptions of alternate assessments.* Manuscript submitted for publication.

Individuals with Disabilities Education Act (IDEA) Amendments of 1997, PL 105-17, 20 U.S.C. §§ 1400 *et seq.*

Individuals with Disabilities Education Improvement Act of 2004, PL 108-446, 20 U.S.C. § 1400 *et seq.*

International Reading Association/National Council of Teachers of English. (2002). *Read-WriteThink*. Retrieved February 16, 2005, from http://www.readwritethink.org/standards/index.html

Kampfer, S., Horvath, L., Kleinert, H., & Kearns, J. (2001). Teachers' perceptions of one state's alternate assessment portfolio program: Implications for practice and preparation. *Exceptional Children, 67*, 361–374.

Kearns, J., Burdge, M., & Kleinert, H. (in press). *INNOVATIONS: Practical strategies for conducting alternate assessments*. Washington, DC: American Association on Mental Retardation.

Kleinert, H., & Kearns, J. (2001). *Alternate assessment: Measuring outcomes and supports for students with disabilities*. Baltimore: Paul H. Brookes Publishing Co.

Kleinert, H., & Kearns, J. (2004). Alternate assessments. In F. Orelove, D. Sobsey, & R. Silberman (Eds.), *Educating children with multiple disabilities: A collaborative approach* (4th ed., pp. 115–149). Baltimore: Paul H. Brookes Publishing Co.

Kleinert, H., Kennedy, S., & Kearns, J. (1999). Impact of alternate assessments: A statewide teacher survey. *Journal of Special Education, 33*, 93–102.

Mayer-Johnson LLC. (2000). Boardmaker 2000 for Windows (Version 1.0) [Computer software]. Solana Beach, CA: Author.

Mayer-Johnson LLC. (2004a). Boardmaker (Version 5.0) [Computer software]. Solana Beach, CA: Author.

Mayer-Johnson LLC. (2004b). Writing with Symbols 2000 [Computer software]. Solana Beach, CA: Author.

National Council for Teachers of Mathematics (NCTM). *Principles and standards for school mathematics*. Retrieved February 16, 2005, from http://standards.nctm.org/document/chapter7/data.htm

National Research Council. (1996). *Standards for science content, in National Science Education Standards*. Retrieved February 16, 2005, from http://www.nap.edu/readingroom/books/nses/html/6e.html

No Child Left Behind Act of 2001, PL 107-110, 115 Stat. 1425, 20 U.S.C. §§ 6301 *et seq.*

Taylor, M.D. (1997). *Roll of thunder, hear my cry*. London: Penguin Books.

Thompson, S., & Thurlow, M. (2000). State alternate assessments: Status as IDEA alternate assessment requirements take effect. *NCEO Synthesis Report 35*. Retrieved February 15, 2005, from http://www.education.umn.edu/nceo/OnlinePubs/Synthesis35.html

Wheatley, S. (1993). *Communication systems for students with intellectual disabilities: A state-wide survey*. Unpublished manuscript, University of Kentucky at Lexington.

Wolery, M., Ault, M.J., & Doyle, P.M. (1992). *Teaching students with moderate to severe disabilities: Use of response prompting strategies*. New York: Longman.

Wolery, M., Bailey, M., & Sugai, G. (1988). *Effective teaching: Principles and procedures of applied behavior analysis with exceptional students*. Boston: Allyn & Bacon.

Wolery, M., & Schuster, J.W. (1997). Instructional methods with students who have significant disabilities. *Journal of Special Education, 31*, 61–79.

Chapter 12

Promoting the Alignment of Curriculum, Assessment, and Instruction

Claudia P. Flowers, Diane M. Browder,
Lynn Ahlgrim-Delzell, and Fred Spooner

In 1994, the Improving America's Schools Act (PL 103-382) and Title I of the Elementary and Secondary Education Act (PL 89-10) required states to set high expectations for student learning, to develop assessments that measure those expectations, and to create systems that hold educators accountable for student achievement. States' expectations, or standards, specify what students should be able to know or do and how good is good enough. Standards-based educational reform aims to focus educational resources, efforts, and energy toward students' achievement.

Large-scale state assessments have become an important component of standards-based education. Results of assessments inform policymakers of the progress that students and educational systems are making toward meeting their goals. Student achievement assessments are one of the most powerful levers for influencing what happens in schools and classrooms (Huebert & Hauser, 1999). These assessments are used to focus public attention on educational concerns and to motivate school administrators, teachers, and students to work harder and achieve higher standards (Haertel, 1999; Linn, 2000). Because of the importance policymakers place on assessment results and the high-stakes consequences of these results, students, teachers, and schools are experiencing increased pressure to meet state standards.

In most states, the first wave of standards-based reform excluded students with disabilities from large-scale assessments. Educators like Thurlow, Elliott, and Ysseldyke (1998) argued that inclusion of students with disabilities in large-scale assessments could help schools have an accurate picture of the students' education, avoid the unintended consequences of exclusion, and promote high expectations for all students. One reason students were excluded from early standards-based reforms was the lack of focus on the general curriculum for this population. For students with severe disabilities, curricular priorities were often functional skills and social inclusion with few or no academic priorities (Browder et al., 2003). As Wehmeyer, Sands, Knowlton, and Kozleski (2002) noted, promoting access to the general curriculum does not preclude providing additional functional skills instruction or academic remediation. Such access does require moving beyond *only* teaching a separate, special curriculum.

Accurate inferences about student achievement and growth over time can only be made when there is alignment between the standards (expectations) and assessments; from this perspective, alignment has both content and consequential validity implications (Bhola, Impara, & Buckendahl, 2003). This chapter provides a conceptual overview of alignment procedures and how they can be applied to the consideration of whether there is a match between alternate assessments, general curriculum, and instruction for students with significant cognitive disabilities. Because the focus on alignment procedures is fairly recent, some educators do not yet have familiarity with these procedures and their emerging importance. For this reason, the chapter begins with a detailed description of alignment procedures used in general education. We then describe how researchers have applied these methods to evaluate the alignment of alternate assessments with state content standards. Next, we provide practical examples of how to align instruction with state academic content standards by considering the role of the individualized education program (IEP). Finally, we conclude by considering some overall recommendations for teaching academic content that is aligned to state standards.

OVERVIEW OF ALIGNMENT PROCEDURES USED IN GENERAL EDUCATION

The ultimate goal of standards-based reform is to improve student learning and teacher instruction. For this to occur, there must be a high degree of *alignment* between the standards, state assessments, and ongoing classroom instruction. Educators have sometimes assumed that instructional systems are driven by content standards, which are translated into assessment, curriculum materials, instruction, and professional development (Porter, 2002). Teachers may understand what content is wanted and believe they are teaching that content when, in fact, they are not (Cohen, 1990). Improvements in student learning will depend on how well assessment, curriculum, and instruction are aligned and reinforce a common set of learning goals, and on whether instruction shifts in response to the information gained from assessments (Pelligrino, Chudowsky, & Glaser, 2001).

Alignment is simply the match between the written, taught, and tested curriculum. It can be formally defined as the degree of agreement, overlap, or intersection between standards, instruction, and assessments. The idea of alignment has existed since the beginning of the use of formal tests to aid decision making (Bhola et al., 2003). Alignment is often difficult to achieve because educational decisions are often made at different levels of the educational agency (Pelligrino et al., 2001). For example, states may have one set of experts to develop written standards, a second set of experts to develop the assessments, and a third set of experts to train teachers in standards-based instruction. Procedures for evaluating the alignment of standards, instruction, and assessments—and research into the effectiveness of these alignment procedures—are still emerging (Achieve, 2001; Herman, Webb, & Zuniga, 2002; Porter, 2002; Project 2061, 2002; Webb, 1997).

Although still emerging, current alignment procedures provide systematic procedures and common languages for describing the match between curricu-

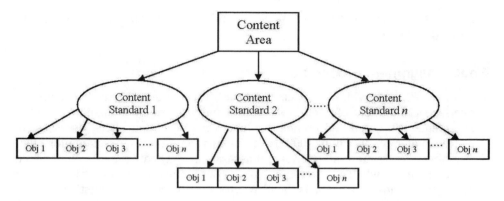

Figure 12.1. The levels of specificity for academic standards.

lum, assessment, and instruction. To evaluate this match, the procedures rely on statistical measures that describe the degree of alignment between two components of the standards-based educational system (e.g., state assessment and state standards). Using these alignment procedures allows comparisons of instructional content emphasized in standards, assessment, and instruction.

Alignment Procedures

The Council of Chief State School Officers (CCSSO) recommended several alignment models for states planning and conducting alignment studies. These include 1) the model developed by Norman Webb (1997), 2) the Surveys of Enacted Curriculum (SEC model), 3) the Achieve model, and 4) the Council for Basic Education (CBE) model (CCSSO, n.d.). The Webb, Achieve, and CBE models examine the alignment between standards and assessments. The SEC model analyzes the alignment between standards, assessments, instruction, or curriculum materials. Two methods, Webb and SEC, have been studied in some detail and will be discussed in the remainder of this chapter.

Content Language

All alignment procedures require a content analysis based on human judgment of academic standards and assessments. Because the nomenclature to describe states' standards is different across the states, subject areas, and grade levels, a common language to describe the levels of specificity within the standards is needed. Most content standards start with the most general statement of the content expectations, subdivided into the more detailed description of the standard creating a pyramid shape as illustrated in Figure 12.1. The top of the pyramid is the most general description of the standard (e.g., mathematics), and the base of the pyramid is a detailed description of a subdomain of that standard (e.g., add two single-digit numbers). Porter and Smithson (2001) refer to the level of specificity as grain size, going from a course grain to a fine grain. In general, most alignment procedures use the most detailed description of the standards (i.e., the bottom of the pyramid) or fine grain size for determining the match between academic content, assessments, and instruction. The problems of selecting the right language and level of specificity for standards and instruction are more complicated than presented in this chapter. Porter and Smithson (2001) and Webb

(1997) review the issues of defining academic content and instruction in more detail (see Figure 12.1).

Webb's Alignment Procedure

Norman Webb provides a systematic procedure for quantifying the degree of overlap or alignment of content standards and assessments. Qualitative expert judgments and quantified coding produce a set of statistics that assesses the degree of alignment. Webb (1997) recommends four criteria for examining alignment between content standards and assessments: 1) categorical concurrence, 2) range-of-knowledge correspondence, 3) balance of representation, and 4) depth-of-knowledge consistency. Webb's criteria provide statistics that describe several dimensions of alignment, such as range of standards covered, pattern of emphasis in standards, and level of difficulty as reflected in state academic content standards.

Categorical concurrence is the consistency of categories for content in the standards and assessments. The criterion of categorical concurrence between standards and assessment is met if the same or consistent categories of content appear in both documents (Webb, 1999). For example, if a content standard or topic is *measurement* (second level down on the pyramid) in mathematics (first level of the pyramid), does the state assessment have items that target measurement? It is possible for an assessment item to align to more than one content standard; for example, if an assessment item requires students to calculate surface area, which is under the content standard of *measurement*, to successfully answer the question the student needs to multiply numbers, which is under the content standard of *operations*. In this case, the item is aligned to both content standards.

To produce an acceptable level of reliability for assessment scores, Webb (1997) recommends at least six items per content standard. In other words, there should be at least six assessment items related to the topic of measurement. Most states have multiple content standards or topics that are defined in their academic standards. If a state included five content standards under mathematics for third graders (e.g., measurement, operations, and so forth), there should be at least six items for each content standard. This does not mean that an assessment would need 30 items to meet the criterion. Fewer items may be needed if assessment items are aligned to more than one content standard.

Although categorical concurrence is the most obvious alignment criterion, additional alignment dimensions are needed to fully capture the complex knowledge and skills that are often emphasized in academic standards. For example, all of the assessment items could be aligned to only a few of the many academic content standards. Examining the range of standards an assessment covers and the balance of assessment items across the standards provides additional evidence about how well the assessment is capturing the breadth of the standards.

The *range-of-knowledge* correspondence criterion examines the alignment of assessment items to the multiple objectives (third level of the pyramid) within the content standards. Range-of-knowledge correspondence is used to judge whether a comparable span of knowledge expected of students based on standards is the same as, or corresponds to, the span of knowledge that students need in order to correctly answer the assessment items. The range-of-knowledge numeric value is the percentage of content standards (second level of the pyramid) with at least 50% of the objectives (third level of the pyramid) having one or more hits. For example, if there were five objectives (e.g., length, area, volume, telling time, and mass) included in the content standard of measurement, a minimum expectation is that at least one assessment item is related to at least three of the objectives. In other words, if there were six assessment items aligned to the measurement content standard, to meet the criterion for range-of-knowledge there should be at least one of the six items aligned to at least three of the five objectives, resulting in 60% of the objectives (i.e., three of five) having one or more hits.

The *balance of representation* criterion is used to indicate the extent to which items are evenly distributed across the content standards and the objectives under the content standards. In our measurement example with five objectives, we would expect items would be evenly distributed across the five objectives. In practice, states may place greater emphasis on specific objectives and content standards. In this case, the assumption of an even distribution would be replaced with the expected proportion, or emphasis, as specified by the state. The formula used to compute the balance of representation index is

$$Balance = 1 - (\sum_{i=1}^{k} \left| \frac{1}{O} - \frac{I_k}{H} \right|)/2$$

where O is the total number of objectives hit (i.e., item has been judged to be aligned) for the content standard, I_k is the number of items hit corresponding to objective k, and H is the total number of items hit for the content standard. The balance index can range from 0 (indicate unbalanced representation) to 1.0 (indicate balance representation) with values from 0.6 to 0.7 considered a weak acceptable balance and values 0.7 or greater considered acceptable.

Depth-of-knowledge (DOK) examines the consistency between the cognitive demands of the standards and cognitive demands of assessments. Important aspects of learning go beyond academic topics and include students' organization of knowledge, problem representations, use of strategies, and self-monitoring skills (Glaser, Linn, & Bohrnstedt, 1997). Completely aligned standards and assessments require an assessment system designed to measure in some way the full range of cognitive complexity within each specified content standard. Webb identified four levels for assessing the DOK of content standards and assessment items. DOK levels are *recall* (Level 1), *skill* or *concept* (Level 2), *strategic thinking* (Level 3), and *extended thinking* (Level 4). To accurately evaluate the DOK level, each DOK level needs to be behaviorally defined, with examples of types of student behaviors that reflect each level. To examine the DOK, each item on the assessment and all academic content standards are rated for DOK. For example, a student may be asked on an assessment to identify which of four squares had the greatest area based on visual inspection. If the state objective for area, which required calculation of the area of a square, had a cognitive level of 2 (skill or concept) and the assessment item was rated 1 (recall), the item falls below the DOK for the standard. Most assessments have items that are below the expected DOK, but there should be items at or above the expected DOK as defined by the state academic standards. According to Webb, an acceptable level for the DOK is 50% or more of the assessment items at or above the state content standard DOK level. A weakly met criterion for DOK level would be between 40% and 50%.

To illustrate how Webb's alignment procedure can be applied, a fictitious example is provided for a mathematics alternate assessment. For simplicity, we will use fewer content standards and objectives than are typically found in most state standards. In our fictitious state there were three content standards for mathematics: 1) number sense, 2) operations, and 3) measurement. The alternate assessment had 30 entries that students completed during the course of their assessment. To study this alternate assessment, three mathematics general curriculum experts and three experts for students with significant cognitive disabilities were trained in the alignment procedures and then asked to independently evaluate the alignment between the mathematics alternate assessment and the state standards in mathematics.

The first alignment statistic we will calculate is the categorical concurrence. For each assessment item, experts identify what objective or objectives were assessed. Webb refers to a match between an assessment item and a standard as a hit. In this example only 20 of the 30 assessment items were aligned to the academic content standards. Of the 20 items that aligned to the standards, 15 of the items aligned to number sense, 10 items aligned to operations, and 5 aligned to measurement. Keep in mind that the sum of the number of standards hit may be greater than the total number of assessment items because items can be aligned to more than one content standard. Two of the three content standards, number sense and operations, had at least six hits, resulting in a percentage categorical concurrence of 66.7%. Ideally we would like to have 100% of all content standards with six or more hits.

Range-of-knowledge correspondence examines the consistency of the breadth of knowledge required in both the standards and the assessment. The range-of-knowledge value is the percentage of content standards with at least 50% of the objectives having one or more hits. In our fictitious example, we have four objectives for each of the three content standards. For example, under the content standard of measurement we might have the objectives of 1) length, 2) area, 3) volume, and 4) telling time. Of the five items that assess measurement, four items were aligned to area and one item was aligned to telling time. In this case, two of the four objectives (50%) had at least one or more hits. If all three of the content standards had hits for at least two of the four objectives, the range-of-knowledge correspondence would be 100%. In other words, three out of the three content standards had at least 50% of the objectives having one or more hits.

The balance of representation examines the distribution of assessment items across the objectives. The calculation of the balance of representation for the measurement content standard assessment is presented in Table 12.1. In this example the assumption is that items should be evenly spread among the objectives. Recall that a balance index score of 0 indicate unbalanced representation and scores close to 1.0 indicate balanced representation, with values greater than 0.7 meeting the suggested cutoff. The balance index for the measurement content standard was equal to 0.45, which suggests that the assessment items are not balanced across the objectives for the content standard. For example, if the remaining two content standards had balance index values greater than 0.7, then 66.7% of the content standards achieved an acceptable level of balance of representation (see Table 12.1).

Depth of knowledge is the percentage of assessment items at or above the DOK for the standards. In our illustrative example, of the 20 items aligned to the

Table 12.1.   Balance-of-representation indices for the measurement content standard

Objective	Expected proportion (E)	Observed proportion N	(O)	|E-O|	Calculation of balance index
Length	0.25	0	0.00	0.25	
Area	0.25	4	0.80	0.55	Σ |E–O| = 1.10
Volume	0.25	0	0.00	0.25	Σ |E–O|)/2 = 0.55
Telling time	0.25	1	0.20	0.05	1–[(Σ |E–O|)/2] = **0.45**

standards, only 5 of the items were at or above the DOK for the hit standard. The DOK for our mathematics alternate assessment would be equal to 25% indicating the DOK for the assessment was lower than that of the standards.

The previous example was based on fictitious data. The alignment of alternate assessments and academic content standards is much more complicated because of the greater number of content standards and objectives. In a study examining the alignment of three states, language arts and mathematics alternate assessments, results indicated that assessment items were aligned to academic content standards, but some academic content standards were receiving less attention than others and consideration needed to be given to ways students could demonstrate higher levels of depth of knowledge (Flowers, Browder, & Ahlgrim-Delzell, in press).

Surveys of Enacted Curriculum Model

The Surveys of Enacted Curriculum (SEC) alignment approach analyzes standards, assessments, and instruction using a common content matrix consisting of two dimensions for categorizing subject content: content topics and cognitive demands (Porter & Smithson, 2001). Using this approach, content matrices for standards, assessments, and instruction are created and the relationships between these matrices are examined. In addition to alignment statistics that can be calculated from the two-dimensional matrix, content maps and graphs can be produced to visually illustrate differences and similarities between standards, assessments, and instruction.

Porter and Smithson (2001) generally recommend six categories for cognitive demand that would vary in description depending on the content area. In this chapter we present all data using only three content areas and three categories for cognitive demand. This limits our examples to only nine cells in a matrix. In practice, the number of cells in a matrix is equal to the number of content areas times the number of cognitive demands categories. Finer grains within the content area can also be examined, but the matrix would become quite large.

To analyze assessments and standards, a panel of content experts conducts a content analysis and codes the assessment and/or standards by topic and cognitive demand. Results from the panel are then placed in a topic by cognitive demand matrix, with values in the cells representing the proportion of the overall content description. An example of an assessment matrix is in Table 12.2. Each cell is the proportion of assessment items coded in each content topic by the cognitive demand. The cell with 0.30 indicates that 30% of the items were coded into

Table 12.2. Content matrix of content topics by cognitive demand for an assessment

Content topics	Cognitive demand		
	1	2	3
Number sense	0.00	0.15	0.10
Operations	0.00	0.30	0.20
Measurement	0.00	0.15	0.10

Note: The cognitive demand categories are 1 (understanding), 2 (skills), and 3 (application).

the content topic area of *operations* and cognitive demand category of *skill*. The remaining cells indicate the proportion of assessment items that align to specific content topic and level of cognitive demand. The same procedure would be used to code academic content standards.

Porter reported that practitioners prefer visual representations of the matrix (Porter, 2002). The information in the matrix could be visually represented using content maps (surface area). A content map of the data from Table 12.2 can be found in Figure 12.2. The darker shades represent higher percentages of items. Most of the assessment items are in the content topic area of operations and at the cognitive demand categories of skills and application (see Table 12.2, Figure 12.2).

Whereas expert judgment of documents is used to collect information for academic standards and assessments, teacher surveys are used to collect data for the content of instruction. Content of instruction is described as the intersection between topics and cognitive demand. Teachers are surveyed on 1) the amount of time devoted to each topic (topics are listed on the survey), and 2) the relative emphasis given to each student expectation (cognitive demand). Using a 4-point scale, the levels of coverage are none/not covered (1), slight coverage/less than one class or lesson (2), moderate coverage (one to five classes/lessons) (3), and substantial coverage (more than five classes/lessons) (4). These basic data are then transformed into proportion of total instructional time spent on each cell in the two-dimensional matrix.

To measure alignment, a cell-by-cell comparison between matrices is made. The results are aggregated to an absolute value. The formula for calculating the alignment index is

$$Alignment = 1 - \frac{\Sigma|X - Y|}{2}$$

where X is the matrix of assessment cell proportions and Y is matrix of standards cell proportions. Table 12.3 demonstrates the calculation of the alignment index. In this example, the alignment between standards and an assessment is being calculated. After subtracting the corresponding cells of the standards and assessment matrix and taking the absolute value, the elements in the new matrix are summed across all the cells. In this example, the sum of the elements is 0.6. This value is divided by 2, and then this value is subtracted from 1, which results in an alignment index of 0.7 (see Table 12.3).

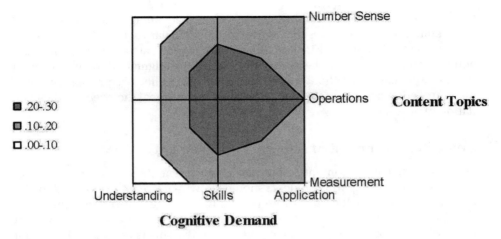

Figure 12.2. Content map of topics by cognitive demand for the example matrix in Table 12.2.

Table 12.3. Demonstration of alignment index

Cognitive demand											
0.2	0.2	0.1		0.2	0.0	0.1		0.0	0.2	0.0
0.1	0.1	0.1	−	0.1	0.2	0.0	=	0.0	0.1	0.1
0.0	0.2	0.0		0.1	0.2	0.1		0.1	0.0	0.1

Topic ↑↓ (left axis labels)

Standards matrix · Assessment matrix · Absolute difference in matrices

Alignment = $1-([0.0+0.2+0.0+0.0+0.1+0.1+0.1+0.0+0.1]/2) = 0.7$

ALIGNMENT OF ALTERNATE ASSESSMENTS TO STATE STANDARDS

Alignment procedures for alternate assessments are more challenging to apply than the traditional general education assessments for several reasons. First, unlike most large-scale assessments, few alternate assessments have standardized assessment items. Some states (29%) provide specific skills that are to be assessed on the alternate assessments, whereas other states (59%) provide optional examples of skills (Cook, Eignor, & Cahalan, 2004). In many states, alternate assessments vary from student to student with teachers selecting the content to include in a portfolio. This teacher-created variation raises the issues of whether each individual alternate assessment is aligned with state standards. A second complication in applying alignment procedures to alternate assessment is that criteria other than student performance are sometimes included. Staff support, participation in general education classes, program quality indicators, and parent satisfaction may be factored into the score (Browder et al., 2005; Thompson & Thurlow, 2001). The result may be an assessment product that requires some gleaning to find the student performance items to be aligned to state standards. The third complication is the option of using alternate achievement standards

(Improving the Academic Achievement of the Disadvantaged, 2003). In setting these standards, some states may narrow the curricular focus (e.g., only assess selected state standards). Finally, the variation in alternate assessment formats across states complicates the goal of demonstrating alignment procedures with national applicability. Although these factors create challenges for applying alignment procedures to alternate assessment, they also reveal the need for the evaluation of alignment.

Research on Alignment of Alternate Assessment

States may articulate content standards, achievement standards, or both. *Content standards* specify what students should know; *achievement standards* delineate how students will demonstrate this knowledge. To determine if there is a match between the general curriculum and alternate assessment, it is important to focus on the state's academic *content* standards. This is especially important now that federal guidelines allow for the use of *alternate achievement standards* for students with significant cognitive disabilities.

Prior to the regulation permitting the use of alternate achievement standards for reporting adequate yearly progress for No Child Left Behind (NCLB) Act of 2001 (PL 107-110) (Improving the Academic Achievement of the Disadvantaged, 2003), states were challenged to determine how to create alternatives to their large-scale assessments. Some states generated extended standards for students with disabilities (Browder et al., 2005; Thompson & Thurlow, 2001). Although they were intended to capture the critical function of the standard so that it could be expressed with alternative forms of achievement, these extended standards ran the risk of losing the academic focus of the original content standard. That is, the extended standard might not be "really reading" or "really math" once translated. This risk was especially high when states generated alternate assessment items first using functional curriculum and then tried to link them back to their state standards. Over time, states began to realize the need to make clear connections between academic content standards and their alternate assessment. In a survey of state special education directors in 2003, Thompson and Thurlow found that only two states continued to conduct alternate assessments that were not connected to the state's general curriculum standards. More resources also emerged in this era to help educators know how to create access to the general curriculum (e.g., Kleinert & Kearns, 2001; Nolet & McLaughlin, 2000; Thompson, Quenemoen, Thurlow, & Ysseldyke, 2001).

Focusing on the early alternate assessments from 42 states, Browder et al. (2004) found that overall the states had developed indicators that reflected priority skills appropriate for students with severe disabilities which were aligned to national math and language arts standards. Examples of performance indicators mathematics experts identified as clearly aligned to national standards were *make simple graphs representing meaningful information and relationships*, and *match number symbols with appropriate amount*. Examples of indicators language arts experts identified as clearly aligned included *identify main characters* and *match picture to word*. In contrast, Browder et al. (2004) found that some states' performance indicators were poorly aligned to national math and language arts standards. These poorly aligned indicators were too broad or too narrow, vague, age inappropriate, or not representative of the academic content.

Examples of poorly aligned math performance indicators included *completes simple puzzles, peg boards, form boards* and *sits upright in a wheelchair.* Examples of poorly aligned language arts performance indicators were *attends to visual stimuli* and *searches for a book that has been misplaced.* In general, some items being proposed to teachers for use in their alternate assessments to demonstrate reading and mathematics achievement were clearly not academic tasks.

In a follow-up study, Browder et al. (2003) conducted a content analysis of the task and context components of the alternate assessment performance indicators of six states that had been nominated by the experts in the previous study as having clear links to academic content, weak links, or a mixture of both. Overall, the predominant curricular philosophy represented in the task components for math and language arts was academics, followed by functional skills, social communication and inclusion, self-determination, and early childhood/developmental skills. The predominant curricular philosophy represented in the context components for math and language arts was functional, followed by academic, social communication and inclusion, and early childhood/developmental skills. These findings indicate that states with mixed or weak links were developing alternate assessment tasks that were based in academics, but to be performed in functional contexts. In contrast, the state alternate assessments that were nominated as being most closely aligned with national standards in reading and mathematics used more academic tasks *and* contexts for their items.

Browder et al. (2004) used a simple method of alignment in which curriculum experts were asked to respond to the face validity of the alternate assessment materials. Two recent research studies applied Webb's (1997) alignment procedure (Flowers et al., in press; Roach, Elliott, & Webb, 2005). Both studies followed Webb's procedures to evaluate the categorical concurrence, depth-of-knowledge consistency, range-of-knowledge correspondence, and balance of representation as described earlier in this chapter. Flowers et al. rated the alternate assessments from three states identified in an earlier study as having exemplary alternate assessments, whereas Roach et al. rated the Wisconsin alternate assessment. Even though both studies found alternate assessments did not meet Webb's established criteria for alignment in language arts and math, both did find a relationship between alternate assessments and general curriculum standards. Additionally, although Flowers et al. found that more alternate assessment items were rated at the bottom of the DOK scale (Level 1, or *recall*), all of the states also contained items that fell at the upper range of the DOK scale (Level 4, or *extended thinking*). Many state general curriculum assessments also fail to meet these criteria (Webb, 1997, 2002; Webb, Horton, & O'Neal, 2002). A question for consideration is whether alternate assessments should be expected to meet these criteria, given that some narrowing of the use of state standards is often necessary in the more time-consuming, individualized formats typical of alternate assessment.

Although more research is needed, the studies by Flowers et al. (in press) and Roach et al. (2005) illustrate how alignment procedures can be applied to alternate assessments. Table 12.4 provides a summary of some of the questions teachers or states may use to consider whether an alternate assessment is aligned to a state's academic content standards. Readers are encouraged to refer to these published studies for more detailed information on how to conduct an alignment study (see Table 12.4).

Table 12.4. Questions to consider in evaluating the alignment of alternate assessment to state's academic content standards

---

1. **What are the state's academic content standards in reading, mathematics, and science? What objectives are listed for each standard?**

A list of these standards is needed to conduct the alignment.

2. **What are the alternate assessment items to be considered?**

Pinpoint all items/entries that reflect student achievement in the academic content area. Omit entries not related to student achievement or not designated as reading, mathematics, or science.

3. **Can each alternate assessment item be matched to an academic content standard?**

This may be simple or complex. A simple method is to check to see if a state standard has been designated for each alternate assessment item. A more complex, but more informative, evaluation is to have a curriculum expert determine whether the entry actually reflects the content standard. This content check is recommended for at least some randomly selected items in the assessment.

4. **How many alternate assessment items are there for each state standard? How many of the objectives are addressed?**

This review focuses on breadth and balance of the alternate assessment. For a more detailed analysis, use the balance index formula given in the chapter.

5. **What is the depth of knowledge reflected in the alternate assessment? Are all items at the level of simple recall? Do some require extended thinking?**

For a more detailed analysis, code each alternate assessment item for its depth of knowledge and compare to depth of knowledge reflected in the state standards. Sometimes alternate assessments can contain "no knowledge" items in which only passive participation is expected. It may be especially useful to scrutinize the assessment items to determine whether any require little or no attention, effort, or thought on the part of the student. It also is important to have higher depth-of-knowledge items to give students the opportunity to perform at higher levels.

ALIGNING INSTRUCTION WITH GENERAL CURRICULUM

English and Steffy (2001) noted that deep curriculum alignment occurs when there is a match between the written, tested, and taught curriculum at the classroom, school, and school-system levels. *Doctrine of no surprises* refers to the practice of instructing students on the standards that will be assessed. This entire book has been created to promote fairness for students with significant cognitive disabilities with regard to access to the general curriculum. Students must be assessed on state standards but, more importantly, they need to receive instruction on this academic content. Students with significant cognitive disabilities need the opportunity to learn the academic content of their assigned grade level.

Besides ensuring that students have the opportunity to learn the curriculum on which they will be assessed, deep curriculum alignment also involves teaching students *more* than the content to be assessed. This means providing students with significant cognitive disabilities the opportunity to learn more than the specific skills to be demonstrated for the alternate assessment. For example, an alternate assessment will only document student achievement on a subset of the reading experiences a student has in a fourth-grade language arts class. Deep curriculum alignment also means students will have the opportunity to meet other educational needs and priorities such as developing social skills with peers, increasing independence in functional routines, and meeting therapy goals such as range of motion.

With the options for curricular focus broadening for students with significant disabilities, it can be confusing to the educational team to know how to set priorities. For example, what should be the content of the IEP? Educators sometimes have confused the IEP with curriculum; that is, IEPs were meant to define every skill the student would be taught in the coming year. The teacher might develop a data sheet for each of these skills to track progress. Although the student might receive some other incidental instruction, implementing the IEP was intended to comprise most of the student's instructional day. If the IEP is confused with curriculum, it becomes an impossible challenge in the current era to define every state standard in academics along with functional goals and other educational needs.

An alternative is to create a standards-based IEP that helps to promote the alignment of instruction with both the general curriculum and other individual educational priorities. Standards-based IEPs are not currently common practice for students with significant cognitive disabilities. There are several barriers to overcome to begin creating standards-based IEPs. First, the team needs to develop a common understanding about the importance of focusing on the general curriculum. In the past, educators have often selected goals based on either a separate, functional curriculum or on an undefined, vague curricular focus with little knowledge of the general curriculum (Browder et al., 2003; Thompson, Thurlow, Esler, & Whetstone, 2001). Sands, Adams, and Stout (1995) found that only 15% of special educators believed that outcomes related to the general education curriculum should be the primary focus of IEPs. The team may need to discuss the rationale for increasing the expectations for the student to learn academic content typically taught to students at this age level. Some of these reasons were provided in Chapter 1; other reasons have been provided throughout this book with examples of what this learning might look like. For example, the illustrations in Chapter 11 may be helpful to teams who need help planning achievement in academic content.

A second barrier is ensuring that the content of the IEP will be relevant to the general education context. Fisher and Frey (2001) followed three students with severe cognitive and physical disabilities who were being provided a fully inclusive educational experience for 3 years. Although the IEPs of these three students did reflect academic outcomes, none of their teachers ever referred to the IEP document. The objectives identified in the IEP also were not consistent with the general education classroom practices, nor were they based on state standards applicable to other students in the class. The general education teacher is a critical member of the IEP team. Although all members of the team should have copies of the academic content standards for the grade level, the general education teacher can help the team understand how these standards are addressed in typical instruction. In the upper grades and in elementary schools that are departmentalized, general education teachers from each grade level will be important to the IEP team.

A third barrier is not understanding how an IEP objective accesses state standards. The team members will quickly find themselves writing a curriculum if they try to have a one-to-one correspondence between each state standard and an IEP goal. Instead, some IEP goals will be broad enough to address multiple

State standard. Students will identify, analyze, and apply knowledge of the structure and elements of fiction and provide evidence from the text to support their understanding.

Seventh-grade standard. Locate and analyze elements of setting, characterization, and plot.

IEP Objective 1. *Camilla will use her AAC to greet peers in seventh-grade language arts class.*

Is this really reading? No. Although this is an important social skill the team decides to use for the IEP, it is not a reading skill. Camilla needs additional language arts objectives that focus on reading for this to be a standards-based IEP.

IEP Objective 2. *Camilla will acquire 20 sight words that relate to activities in her community and home.*

Is this really reading? Yes, it's reading, but it does not link to the specific state standard that other seventh graders will be learning. Again, the IEP team may keep this objective, but more work is needed to access the general curriculum.

IEP Objective 3. *Camilla will select pictures to represent the main ideas, setting, or characters.*

Is this really reading? Yes, it is listening comprehension. Camilla cannot read seventh-grade passages, but she can access age-appropriate literature by listening to stories or story summaries read to her by peers. This task also links to the seventh-grade focus on characterization, plot, and setting. This is a well-aligned objective. Selecting pictures to represent a main idea also can be used to align with standards in other academic content like science.

IEP Objective 4. *Camilla will identify initial consonant and vowel sounds and use this skill in writing words with software that anticipates the spelling of a word from the first letters.*

Is this really reading? Yes, phonics is a key component of reading, but because of Camilla's age she will need emerging phonics skills to write using software that builds on these skills. Although this goal does not align directly with the seventh-grade focus on the elements of fiction (no 1:1 correspondence with a standard), it can broadly access the curriculum (overall alignment) because writing is used in most academic content.

Summary. A standards-based IEP might contain all four types of the IEP objectives shown, including ones that 1) are not academic but promote participation in general education contexts, 2) are academic but with functional applications, 3) align to one specific state standard, and 4) align broadly to multiple state standards for the grade level. To be standards based, some objectives would need to align with specific or multiple standards (3 and 4).

Figure 12.3. An example of how an individualized education program (IEP) team selected objectives that linked to a grade-level state standard for a student with significant cognitive disabilities. (From Courtade-Little, G., & Browder, D.M. [2005]. *Aligning IEPs with academic standards for students with moderate and severe disabilities.* Verona, WI: Attainment Company.)

standards. Others may be more specific to the standard for the grade level. Chapter 6 described how to develop an IEP to include access to the general curriculum. Chapter 11 gave additional examples of how to link to the general curriculum. The example in Figure 12.3, from Courtade-Little and Browder (2005), illustrates how a team selected reading objectives for Camilla while giving consideration to the state standard.

SUMMARY

The alignment of curriculum, assessment, and instruction is critical if students with significant cognitive disabilities are to succeed in their quest for access to the general curriculum. Since the passage of the Education for All Handicapped Children Act of 1975 (PL 94-142), as a field we have come a very long way in securing and maintaining educational rights for students with significant cognitive disabilities and their families. During the ensuing decades, we have worked through several different curricular philosophies (i.e., developmental/early childhood, community inclusion/functional, social inclusion, self-determination, and academic). As Browder et al. (2003) indicated, these curricular philosophies have been either additive or transformative in the effect that they have had on the implementation/application of training strategies. For example, both the developmental/early childhood and functional curricular philosophies were transformative in their effect on how and where students with significant cognitive disabilities were trained, whereas the social inclusion philosophy is seen as additive because students still learned functional tasks, as the setting in which they received their education changed. Our view is that accessing the general curriculum will likely be additive. However, this could change the conceptual framework and approaches that we, as a field, take to the process of curriculum for students with significant cognitive disabilities, as we will need to continue to add more and more material on content components like reading, math, and science.

If we cannot align the instruction that students with significant cognitive disabilities receive with state content standards and appropriate means of alternate assessment, we have not completed the total portrait of a quality education for students with significant disabilities. These students should be assessed on state standards and, more importantly, they need to receive instruction on this academic content (i.e., reading, math, and science). The purpose of this chapter has been to provide a conceptual overview of alignment procedures used in general education and how they can be applied to judge the degree to which there is a match among alternate assessments, general curriculum, and instruction for students with significant cognitive disabilities.

In general, at the most basic level, alignment is the match among written, taught, and tested curriculum. More specifically, it is the agreement, overlap, or intersection among standards, instruction, and assessments. Working from the most overarching area to the most specific, there are subject area standards, content standards, objectives, and performance indicators. In most cases, in the area of severe disabilities, it is the performance indicators, as indicated by our work in the content area of science, that function as the critical element for teaching academic content to these students (Spooner & Browder, 2005). The doctrine of no surprises, as indicated by English and Steffy (2001), also should be in effect for students with significant cognitive disabilities, as there continues to be a match among written, tested, and taught curriculum. Deep curriculum alignment also suggests that students with significant cognitive disabilities will have the opportunity to attain other educational priorities (e.g., developing social skills, increasing independence in functional routines). Potential confusion in setting appropriate educational priorities will need to be addressed with regard to sorting out the application of the IEP objectives (i.e., daily instruction) from the overarching curriculum (i.e., the big picture), and the possibility of moving toward a standards-based IEP despite barriers such as lack of focus on the general curriculum, attention to the general education context, and continued understanding of how IEP objectives access state standards.

REFERENCES

Achieve, Inc. (2001). *Measuring up: A commissioned report on education assessment for Minnesota*. Washington, DC: Author.

Bhola, D.S., Impara, J.C., & Buckendahl, C.W. (2003, Fall). Aligning tests with states' content standards: Methods and issues. *Educational Measurement: Issues and Practice*, 21–29.

Browder, D.M., Ahlgrim-Delzell, L., Flowers, C., Karvonen, M., Spooner, F., & Algozzine, R. (2005). How states define alternate assessments for students with disabilities and recommendations for national policy. *Journal of Disability Policy Studies, 15*, 209–220.

Browder, D.M., Flowers, C., Ahlgrim-Delzell, L., Karvonen, M., Spooner, F., & Algozzine, R. (2004). The alignment of alternate assessment content to academic and functional curricula. *Journal of Special Education, 37*, 211–224.

Browder, D.M., Spooner, F., Ahlgrim-Delzell, L., Flowers, C., Algozzine, B., & Karvonen, M. (2003). A content analysis of the curricular philosophies reflected in states' alternate assessment performance indicators. *Research and Practice for Persons with Severe Disabilities, 28*, 165–181.

Cohen, D.K. (1990). A revolution in one classroom: The case of Mrs. Oublier. *Educational Evaluation and Policy Analysis, 12*, 311–330.

Cook, L., Eignor, D., & Cahalan, C. (2004, June). *Alternate assessments: Key issues and research implications.* Paper presented at the CCSSO Large-Scale Assessment Conference, Boston.

Council of Chief State School Officers. (n.d.). *Alignment Models.* Retrieved April 29, 2005, from http://www.ccsso.org/Projects/alignment_analysis/models/418.cfm

Courtade-Little, G., & Browder, D.M. (2005). *Aligning IEPs with academic standards for students with moderate and severe disabilities.* Verona, WI: Attainment Company.

Education for All Handicapped Children Act of 1975, PL 94-142, 20 U.S.C. §§ 1400 *et seq.*

Elementary and Secondary Education Act of 1965, PL 89-10, 20 U.S.C. §§ 241 *et seq.*

English, F.W., & Steffy, B.E. (2001). *Deep curriculum alignment: Creating a level playing field for all children on high-stakes tests of educational accountability.* Lanham, MD: The Scarecrow Press.

Fisher, D., & Frey, N. (2001). Access to the core curriculum: Critical ingredients for student success. *Remedial and Special Education, 22*(3), 148–157.

Flowers, C., Browder, D.M., & Ahlgrim-Delzell, L. (in press). An analysis of three states' alignment between language arts and mathematics standards and alternate assessment. *Exceptional Children.*

Glaser, R., Linn, R., & Bohrnstedt, G. (1997). *Assessment in transtion: Monitoring the nation's educational progress.* New York: National Academy of Education.

Haertel, E.H (1999). Performance assessment and education reform. *Phi Delta Kappa, 80*(9), 662–666.

Herman, J.L., Webb, N., & Zuniga, S. (2002). *Alignment and college admissions: The match of expectations, assessments, and educator perspectives.* Paper presented at the annual meeting of the American Educational Research Association, New Orleans.

Heubert, J.P., & Hauser, R.M. (Eds.). (1999). *High stakes: Testing for tracking, promotion, and graduation.* Washington, DC: National Academy Press.

Improving the Academic Achievement of the Disadvantaged, 68 Fed. Reg. 68,697 (Dec. 9, 2003) (to be codified at 34 C.F.R. pt. 200).

Improving America's Schools Act of 1994, PL 103-382, 20 U.S.C. §§ 630 *et seq.*

Kleinert, H.L., & Kearns, J.F. (2001). *Alternate assessment: Measuring outcomes and supports for students with disabilities.* Baltimore: Paul H. Brookes Publishing Co.

Linn, R. (2000). Assessments and accountability. *Educational Researcher, 29*(2), 4–16.

No Child Left Behind Act of 2001, PL 107-110, 115 Stat. 1425, 20 U.S.C. §§ 6301 *et seq.*

Nolet, V., & McLaughlin, M.J. (2000). *Accessing the general curriculum.* Thousand Oaks, CA: Corwin Press.

Pelligrino, J., Chudowsky, N., & Glaser, R. (Eds.). (2001). *Knowing what students know: The science and design of educational assessment.* Washington, DC: National Academy Press.

Porter, A.C. (2002). Measuring the content of instruction: Uses in research and practice. *Educational Researcher, 31*(7), 3–14.

Porter, A.C., & Smithson, J.L. (2001). *Defining, developing, and using curriculum indicators* (CPRE Research Report Series RR-048). University of Pennsylvania: Consortium for Policy Research in Education.

Project 2061. (2002). American Association for the Advancement of Science. *Middle grades mathematics textbooks: A benchmarks-based evaluation.* Retrieved July 30, 2004, from http://www.project2061.org/tools/textbook/matheval/default

Roach, A.T., Elliott, S.N., & Webb, N.L. (2005). Alignment of an alternate assessment with state academic standards: Evidence for the content validity of the Wisconsin alternate assessment. *Journal of Special Education, 38*, 218–231.

Sands, D.J., Adams, L., & Stout, D.M. (1995). A statewide exploration of the nature and use of curriculum in special education. *Exceptional Children, 62*, 68–83.

Spooner, F., & Browder, D.M. (2005, February). *Current alignment of national science standards and performance indicators: What this means for students with severe disabilities.* Invited address presented at the annual meeting of the North Carolina Association for Behavior Analysis, Wrightsville Beach, NC.

Thurlow, M.L., Elliott, J.L., & Ysseldyke, J.E. (1998). *Testing students with disabilities: Practical strategies for complying with district and state requirements.* Thousand Oaks, CA: Corwin Press.

Thompson, S.J., Quenemoen, R.F., Thurlow, M.L., & Ysseldyke, J.E. (2001). *Alternate assessments for students with disabilities.* Thousand Oaks, CA: Corwin Press.

Thompson, S.J., & Thurlow, M.L. (2001). *2001 State special education outcomes: A report on state activities at the beginning of a new decade.* Minneapolis, MN: University of Minnesota, National Center on Educational Outcomes. Retrieved September 5, 2001, from http://education.umn.edu/NCEO/OnlinePubs/onlinedefault.html

Thompson, S.J., Thurlow, M., Esler, A., & Whetstone, P.J. (2001). Addressing standards and assessments on the IEP. *Assessment for Effective Intervention, 26*(2), 77–84.

Webb, N.L. (1997). *Research Monograph No. 6: Criteria for alignment of expectations and assessments in mathematics and science education.* Washington, DC: Council of Chief State School Officers.

Webb, N.L. (1999). Alignment of science and mathematics standards and assessments in four states (NISE Research Monograph No. 18). University of Wisconsin–Madison, National Institute for Science Education. Washington, DC: Council of Chief State School Officers.

Webb, N.L. (2002). *Alignment study in language arts, mathematics, science, and social studies of state standards and assessments for four states.* Washington, DC: Council of Chief State School Officers.

Webb, N.L., Horton, M., & O'Neal, S. (2002, April). *An analysis of the alignment between language arts standards and assessments for four states.* Paper presented at the meeting of the American Educational Research Association, New Orleans.

Wehmeyer, M.L., Sands, D.J., Knowlton, H.E., & Kozleski, E.B. (2002). *Teaching students with mental retardation: Providing access to the general curriculum.* Baltimore: Paul H. Brookes Publishing Co.

Index

Page numbers followed by *f* indicate figures; those followed by *t* indicate tables.